KEY CONCEPTS AND THEORY IN SOCIAL WORK

KEY CONCEPTS AND THEORY IN SOCIAL WORK

DAVID HODGSON AND LYNELLE WATTS

First published 2017 by
RED GLOBE PRESS

Red Globe Press in the UK is an imprint of Springer Nature Limited,
registered in England, company number 785998, of 4 Crinan Street,
London N1 9XW.

Red Globe Press® is a registered trademark in the United States,
the United Kingdom, Europe and other countries.

ISBN 978–1–137–48783–4 paperback

This book is printed on paper suitable for recycling and made from fully
managed and sustained forest sources. Logging, pulping and manufacturing
processes are expected to conform to the environmental regulations of the
country of origin.

A catalogue record for this book is available from the British Library.

A catalog record for this book is available from the Library of Congress.

DEDICATION

This book has its origins in countless conversations we have had with each other and with our students over many years of teaching social work. We would like to dedicate the book to the many social work students we have taught, past and present. We agree with sociologist Michael Burawoy that students are 'our first public' (Burawoy, 2014, p. 1608).

CONTENTS

LIST OF TABLES

FOREWORD

Professor Karen Healy

Each age brings new opportunities and challenges. For some, today is a time of opportunity. Advances in public health and medical care have extended the average length and quality of life with the advantages of these developments flowing most strongly to middle to high income people in wealthy countries. Developments in information and communication technologies has connected people to each other and to services and resources in ways never before thought possible. For example, 'tele-health', that is, health services delivered via information and communication technologies, have enabled people to access a range of health and personal care services remotely. In many wealthy countries, more people are completing tertiary education than ever before and these highly educated populations are well equipped for employment opportunities in the new knowledge and service economies.

Despite the promises of our age, many people are left behind. Disadvantaged people continue to bear the disproportionate burden of poor physical and mental health and are more likely to die prematurely than their wealthier counterparts (Wilkinson & Pickett, 2008; see also Gallagher, Jones, McFalls, & Pisa, 2006). Disadvantaged people are also less likely to have access to information and communication technologies through which a host of resources and services are now routinely delivered. Our super-diverse societies continue to be places of oppression for many Indigenous people and for those who are excluded from the educational opportunities needed to participate in the new knowledge and service economies.

What kind of knowledge and skills do social workers need in our changing world? This is a question that our profession has grappled with since its inception and which underpins this book. As a profession that seeks to understand and respond to people in their environment, social workers have always practised with a view to both individual and social change. David Hodgson and Lynelle Watts maintain this dual focus. They note that our profession is united by its commitment to working alongside people who experience exclusion, disadvantage, stigma and marginalisation. We are committed to achieving change through partnership.

This book spans the multiple systems impacting on social work practice. At a local practice level, this book reinforces longstanding principles of social work including the promotion of human dignity, human rights, and social justice. It also extends these principles by encouraging the reader to consider dimensions of human experience often overlooked in social work texts, such as the spiritual aspects of human need. We are encouraged to critically analyse relations of power within our practice environments and to challenge a narrow focus on risk management. We are invited to consider the possibilities for social workers to broaden the focus of our practice towards holistic and respectful partnerships with people who use social work services. This book provides the emerging social worker with a useful framework for negotiating the contemporary challenges of change.

References

Gallagher III, B. J., Jones, B. J., McFalls, J. A., & Pisa, A. M. (2006). Social class and type of schizophrenia. *European Psychiatry, 21*(4), 233–237.

Wilkinson, R. G., & Pickett, K. E. (2008). Income inequality and socioeconomic gradients in mortality. *American Journal of Public Health, 98*(4), 699–704. http://doi.org/10.2105/AJPH.2007.109637

ACKNOWLEDGEMENTS

It is something of a truism that writing a book, in fact writing anything, wouldn't happen without the support of others. This has certainly been the case here. We would like to acknowledge and thank Helen Caunce, Peter Hooper and Louise Summerling from Palgrave. Thanks to Helen for her encouragement in the early stages of the proposal process. We thank Peter Hooper for sending the encouraging and supportive emails as we were writing it and for helping us to work through the final stages. We would like to thank Professor Karen Healy for writing the foreword. For all kinds of support (too various to name) we would like to thank Dr Sharlene Nipperess, Professor Donna Chung, Jacquie Tarrant, Priscilla Vindin, Merle Ann Cochrane, Hovea Wilkes and Jennifer Alamdar. Special thanks to Cheryl Beard and the student central crew at ECU, Sarah, Gemma, Beth, Maddie, and Glenys – an incredible cheer squad – for inviting us to hang out occasionally where the conversation was not about writing and deadlines. Many other colleagues and friends have provided support in so many different ways that it is impossible to include all these contributions except to say we are very grateful.

The book was written in a number of places in addition to our offices. We would like to thank the crew at Café Bean in Bunbury, especially Emma and all the staff there who made us feel so welcome every week. It's a lovely space to write and the coffee is good too. We are grateful also that a few folks offered spaces to use for writing retreats. We owe a huge thanks to Gayle Hall for lending us her house in Collie and to Alan and Mia for the use of their house while they were away in the North of Australia over the winter months.

During the writing process we were greatly helped by a number of people who read various chapters and gave us feedback on the work at different times. For this we thank Andrea Hodgson, Megan Watts, Gayle Hall, Professor Kathy Boxall, and especially Nina Tinning. Nina read almost the entire book and provided critical feedback that gave us important encouragement to keep going. We are also very grateful to Graham Hodgson who cast his proof editing eye over the text and gave it back to us with sticky flags and good advice to follow in the interests of clarity.

We would also like to thank several anonymous reviewers who gave critical and constructive feedback on the book proposal and final manuscript. We have attempted to incorporate their feedback as much as possible and are grateful for their suggestions to improve the text overall.

The section on risk in Chapter 3 and on governmentality in Chapter 4 draws on David Hodgson's PhD research into compulsory education in Western Australia. Chapter 15 on Reflexivity, Reflective Practice and Critical Reflection draws on Lynelle Watts' PhD research into teaching reflective practice. Some of the ideas in Chapter 11, Organisational Contexts, were developed in the course of delivering professional development training to social workers and human service workers on resilience and civility in organisations, and these ideas were presented at the Joint Social Work Education Conference (JSWEC) at Royal Holloway, University of London, 2013. Chapter 13 on professional judgements and decision-making was inspired by our work in the area of social work curriculum mapping.

As with any big project we depend on the support and patience of our families. Our gratitude and thanks go to our family. David would like to thank Andrea, Xavier and Sienna. Lynelle would like to thank Peter, Kate, Beth, Megan and Alicia – it made all the difference and it's finally done.

1

INTRODUCTION

Introduction

Social work is an important role, and one well worth pursuing. It is committed to social justice and human rights, and improving human well-being for individuals, families, communities and societies (International Federation of Social Workers, 2014). Social work is a diverse profession working with different groups and individuals and it operates across many different arrangements for the delivery of welfare and social care. Social work largely grew up within the ambit of the many welfare states of advanced liberal nations and has since spread as a profession across the world. We think the diversity of activities we can call social work is to be celebrated, and given the wonderful variety of ways in which human beings live, work and create communities, we cannot see that it could be any other way. What unites social work across the world, however, is a commitment to the realisation of social justice for all people, and the fact that our work is primarily with people who experience exclusion, disadvantage, stigma and marginalisation.

Our professional commitment to social justice amidst the situation of increasing global change was a theme recently raised by Professor Alastair Christie (Child and Family Research Centre & Christie, 2014) in a keynote presented at the National University of Ireland (NUI) Galway. We agree with him that in the last few years there have been enormous political changes to nation-states, of all political persuasions. In some cases, this has included changes to the relationship between welfare and the State. At the same time, the Global Financial Crisis (GFC) has not resulted in any significant changes to underlying financial systems, but, rather, we have seen the burden of recovery being borne by those least able to do so. Then there are the effects of global warming and the impact of environmental disasters on human and ecological well-being. Increasing levels of violence have been occurring across many places in the world. Consequently, large numbers of people have become displaced as a result of violent conflict and environmental destruction. As we know, these changes often affect those least able to withstand the impact; these are the people with whom social workers practice. Thus, Professor Christie's challenge to his audience, and to us, is to think through what kinds of knowledge and skills social workers will need as they locate themselves as a profession in this changing world. It is for these reasons that social work can be seen as an intellectually and emotionally demanding job.

This book attempts in its own way to take up this challenge by presenting a number of concepts for social work practice and exploring them in depth. The choices of what to include in this book have emerged from years of conversation between ourselves, with students and social workers about the ideas and skills that seem to be recurring themes with social work. For example, power (Chapter 4) seems to be ubiquitous to a social work perspective. Empathy (Chapter 12) seems to be an expectation of good practice. We are both social work educators, and have spent a great deal of time discussing these ideas with students, fellow educators and practitioners. Over time, we have found that these common concepts and ideas are held as crucial to respectful and effective practice. Values such as dignity and worth, human rights, social justice, and the need for hope never stop being central to social work. Notions about risk, the relation between theory and practice, knowledge about poverty and disadvantage and how to work with difference and diversity also seemed to us to be ideas central to social work. Lastly, we think there are particular markers of effective social work practice, somewhat regardless of organisational setting or social work role. These include reflective and reflexive practice, engaging in professional judgement and assessment that is respectful, and being able to negotiate the complexities of organisational life.

We recognise that what is contained in this book is not an exhaustive list. However, we contend that the concepts discussed in the following chapters would be relevant and applicable to any field, role or context of social work. In this respect, some of these ideas will, no doubt, be familiar to many of you already. We have found that many of these ideas have become a kind of disciplinary common-sense in social work, and the ideas presented in this book are typically covered in social work education curricula. Yet, we also find that the meaning of some ideas becomes taken-for-granted, even in many texts and discussions in our discipline. In our teaching roles we have found that it has often been useful to take a rather genealogical approach to exploring these concepts and presenting the theoretical underpinnings and practical implications for students. This can assist in developing a nuanced and critical understanding of concepts that are important to the thinking and practice of social work.

Hence, in presenting these ideas in this book, our approach overall is to engage in a discussion and description of the theoretical underpinnings of each concept. Our goal is to create depth of understanding through a process of explanation and interpretation of the key ideas, as a form of systematic reflection. Each chapter clarifies the definitions of the key concepts being discussed, and reading them and learning them can help with grasping their central meanings and main insights for social work. In this way, the chapters offer an introduction to some key concepts in social work. At the same time, the chapters then go beyond definitions to explore the theory, and, where relevant, the research literature and backgrounds that inform these concepts. This is the approach we have taken in this book. We have started with social work research and literature to create understanding of the topic from a social work disciplinary perspective. We have then extended the discussion by drawing on ideas and literature from other disciplines to deepen and broaden the theoretical perspective of each concept discussed. In doing so, we have drawn on relevant knowledge from philosophy, sociology, psychology, neuroscience, politics, nursing, education, business and anthropology. There are, of course, limitations to the extent to which we can discuss and critique the various concepts and theories included herein. Therefore, the challenge when approaching these concepts and theories is to engage with them critically, to think about their application to practice, and to consider what their limitations may be. There is no theory of everything and no one right way to approach the question of knowledge for, and about practice. It is our hope that exploring these ideas in depth and from different perspectives will contribute to building upon social work's repertoires of inter-pretation (Alvesson & Sköldberg, 2009) and help us engage with the complex problems and situations now facing us all.

Overview of this book

In this section we provide a general overview of this book and explain the topic in each chapter. But first, a note on language. In the world of social work many terms are used to describe the people that social workers work with, such as client, consumer, patient, customer, service user, community member, partici-pant, and so on. All these terms are problematic in some way. In this book, we take our lead from Wilson and Beresford (2000, p. 553) and adopt the term 'service user' throughout, except where it is used in quoted material. Service user is a more encompassing term than some of the others mentioned above. As Wilson and Beresford (2000) explain, service user describes people who, either voluntarily or involuntarily, interact with or use services that social workers and others provide.

As mentioned earlier, each chapter in the book addresses a single topic, usually beginning with the social work literature and expanding from there to draw out the broader theoretical ideas. At the end of each chapter are critical thinking questions, tutorial exercises and suggested readings and web-links. You can read the book from the beginning to end, or alternatively, you may read it according to your interest in the topics. There are significant links between the topics and in some respects we are aware that the boundaries between one topic and another have been maintained primarily for the purposes of focus. In practice, we know that there are many connections and overlapping elements. For example, theory and practice is relevant to nearly all other topics but in that chapter the focus is on the relationship between reasoning, in the form of theoretical thinking and practice, rather than the application of theory to any specific practice fields. Likewise, the topic of risk can be read in relation to assessment, but for ease of presentation we have treated these as distinct topics.

In thinking about how this book is organised, it might be helpful to see that the chapters in this book are grouped loosely in terms of broader *contexts*, certain social work *values*, and some general *skills*. For example, Chapters 2–5 take theory, practice, power, risk, poverty and disadvantage as examples of the broader contexts that influence and shape general orientations towards knowledge and practice. Chapters 6–10 take difference, dignity, respect, social justice, fairness, human rights, spirituality and hope as important social work values. Chapters 11–15 contend that working in organisations, empathy, judgement, decision-making assessment and critical reflection are skills that can be learnt and developed for practice. Let's look at the outline of chapters in more detail.

Chapter 2 is about theory and practice, and as mentioned, we have included a discussion about how to approach theory and we offer a categorisation that organises the main theories important to social work. The purpose of Chapter 2 is not so much to outline the main theories in social work, as there are many texts that do that very well. Instead, the purpose is to engage in a discussion that will help you learn how to think about theory in social work.

Chapter 3 considers the topic of risk and its relationship to social work practice. Risk is such a pervasive idea throughout society and especially in the human services. But it is a problematic concept that needs interrogation. In this chapter we also introduce ideas about resilience, which we think are increasingly important in an uncertain world.

As mentioned earlier, power is relevant to all forms of social work practice. However, it is a tricky concept to grasp and there are many different theories of power. We discuss power in Chapter 4 by exploring structural and post-structural theories of power. It is a complex topic, but understanding it offers social workers a crucial analytical tool for social work practice.

In Chapter 5 we turn our attention to a major focal point of social work: poverty and disadvantage. Inequality, poverty and disadvantage are key drivers of human suffering and poor well-being. Amidst the fall-out of the GFC and rising austerity measures, we think a discussion of poverty and disadvantage is important.

Difference and diversity are examined in Chapter 6 especially with regard to the important contribution feminists have made to our understandings of this aspect of social work practice. The point we make in this chapter is that difference is a normal part of the human condition. However, differences are often the point through which oppression and inequality find expression. Hence, we discuss different theories that can help social workers think critically about difference in ways that can support their thinking within an ethical perspective.

We open Chapter 7 with a discussion about the values of respect and dignity, and a contemporary social theory view about what matters to people. Importantly, the chapter outlines a theory of human social being (Sayer, 2011), that helps social workers discern between universal and particular needs that humans might share, and how respect can be conveyed as part of these commonalities and differences.

Chapter 8 describes social justice from a social work standpoint, but also through the considered philosophy of Iris Marion Young and John Rawls. In this sense, both distributive and critical theories of justice that underpin social work ethical codes are explored. The chapter also explains why social justice matters, not just in terms of moral principle, but as a condition that is elementary to human well-being.

Chapter 9 extends the discussion of political philosophy by concentrating on the topic of human rights, asking the question: can social work be considered a human rights profession? The background to human rights in social work is explained through the lens of philosophy, and we give examples of social work's engagement in human rights practice.

We then pick up the topic of hope and spirituality in Chapter 10. This is a somewhat neglected topic, but we think desperately important for addressing human flourishing and for understanding the meaning of suffering for the people we work with. Both hope and spirituality are attracting increasing interest in social work amidst a context of human suffering, and a search for existential meaning. This is a contested area of social work knowledge, and so the debates and criticisms are outlined and explained.

Chapter 11 positions organisations as a key driver of social work possibilities for action, particularly for advanced liberal states. We hope the chapter provides some ways to navigate this complex aspect of contemporary social work practice. The chapter addresses practice in organisations largely from an empowerment perspective, by drawing on individual attributes and systems thinking in outlining how social workers might contribute to building civil organisational climates.

In the next chapter, 12, we consider empathy from a range of perspectives including anthropology and cognitive neuroscience. We find this topic to be increasingly relevant in light of recent developments in understanding how empathy works. The purpose of empathy is explained; however, some cautions and criticisms of the use of empathy in practice are also offered.

Chapter 13 outlines the topic of professional judgement and decision-making in practice, paying particular attention to what we know about factors that impede or support good judgement. Social workers often have wide latitude to exercise professional judgement and decision-making, and this autonomy is to some extent a marker of the professional role. However, how, and on what basis, social workers make judgements and decisions is an important question, and so this chapter explores the most recent research on human judgement and decision-making.

Chapter 14 picks up this theme of the skills of judgement and decision-making by considering what is meant by assessment in social work, and by outlining different approaches to this important aspect of professional practice. Assessment is such a key part of social work practice, and so the concepts, methods and steps to assessment are outlined. Importantly, the chapter includes a critical thinking perspective, which aims to assist the social worker to be more critically minded when undertaking assessment roles in their practice.

Finally, the book concludes with Chapter 15 on reflective practice and critical reflection, which is now considered a core skill of respectful and effective social work practice. The chapter explores the antecedents to reflection, critical reflection and reflexivity in social work and distinguishes between these concepts. The chapter also offers a model of different kinds of systematic reflection for social work.

Conclusion

It is our hope that the book might provide a mental space in which to engage with ideas, both familiar and strange, in the spirit of learning to consider other perspectives. We hope to contribute to the development of the kind of open-mindedness and depth of understanding that is needed for practice with people from all walks of life. We have also presented many examples aimed at illustrating the ideas being discussed. We hope these contribute to your learning from the experiences of others, but also through how they might resonate, or not, with your own experience. While we are presenting social work theoretical knowledge throughout the book, we have also tried to represent these ideas in ways that do justice to them. In this respect, we have strived to offer an engaged critique in the sense of a thorough evaluation, 'not from everywhere or nowhere, but from within ...' (Jongerden, 2016, p. 102). This is in contrast perhaps to the more usual forms of criticism where the point is to find fault. You will find our own social work values are on display, evident in the choices we have made here. Hence, you may note that overall we are arguing for a pluralist approach to knowledge. Pluralism is the idea that toleration and respect for difference are possible on the basis that there is no single way of being human or expressing this and is considered the predominant status quo in most parts of the world (London School of Economics and Political Science [LSE] & Ramadan, 2016). Pluralism 'provides the basis for the concept of universal human rights' (Grayling, 2002, p. 117), and therefore we ground our review of the theories and concepts in this book within a deep engagement with the values of social justice, respect, dignity and human rights – and the need for people, regardless of their circumstances, to be able to generate hope for the future.

2

THEORY AND PRACTICE

Introduction

Social work utilises numerous theories about people, problems and society, and these ideally inform how social workers practice. Social work has not been immune to various developments in theory and research methodology across the social sciences that have occurred in fields such as sociology, psychology, political science and anthropology. These social sciences are what might be called *informing disciplines* to the profession of social work (Chenoweth & McAuliffe, 2015). Each of these disciplines has different orientations to building theory and they use a variety of methods for conducting social research about people, groups, cultures and societies.

As you can imagine, this introduces a range of complexities when we consider the social work theoretical landscape. Consequently, there are many textbooks that discuss the different theories developed within the discipline of social work (Adams, Dominelli & Payne, 2009a; Healy, 2014; Howe, 2009; Payne, 2014; Trevithick, 2011; Turner, 2011), and other sources that explore the incorporation of theories into the field of social work (Beresford, 2000; Hudson, 1997; Osmond, 2006). In learning about social work theory, you may feel that you are confronted with a vast array of theoretical ideas, concepts and arguments. Further, you will find that many of these theories offer differing, and at times, competing views and explanations for something. This raises important questions for social work practice. How can we know which theories are useful to understanding or explaining the phenomena we might see in practice? And how can theories help us to know what to *do* in practice?

This chapter takes us on a journey through these issues about theory and theorising and how we can understand the role of theory and knowledge for social work practice. We suggest that there is a way to assess the potential of different theories. This process can assist us to understand and incorporate more theorising into our practice, and in doing so, use these explanations to connect social work practice to the uses of imagination, creativity and intuition. We think that this will assist social work practitioners to contribute to efforts of social change for the people they serve.

We begin the chapter with a simple inquiry: What is theorising, what is theory, and how are they different? In this discussion we also outline the relationship between reason and theory in order to answer the question so often asked of us about why there are so many different theories, approaches, perspectives and models in social work. In the next section we offer a framework for categorising the various theories in social work. In this framework we have categorised social work theories into four main *approaches* to social work practice: problem-solving, anti-oppressive, psychological and systems. We have included in the framework the key idea for each theory included in the approach, its historical and disciplinary origins, examples of related theories or research, examples of models for practice associated with the approach, and finally, what kinds of critical reflection (see Chapter 15, on reflective practice and critical reflection) are involved in each theory. We conclude the chapter by suggesting that the key to theory and practice is developing your capacity for reflexivity about theory and theorising in practice. This will help you navigate the relationship between theory and practice.

What is theorising and what is theory?

What is theorising, what is theory, and how are they different? Payne (2014) defines theories as a '... generalized set of ideas that describes and explains our knowledge of the world around us in an organized way' (p. 5). Chafetz (1987, cited in Robbins, Chatterjee & Canda, 2012a) proposes that theories '... consist of a series of relatively abstract and general statements which collectively purport to explain (answer the question of why?) some aspect of the empirical world (the "reality" known to us directly or indirectly through the senses)' (p. 6). As social work has developed within the frame of Western liberal thought, the theories and knowledge utilised by social workers has also been informed by ideas that may be traced back to the Enlightenment and to the scientific methods associated with theory development. Theory development and research practice have played a significant part in the formation of social work's attainment of professional status in its own right (Flexner, 2001). Indeed, social work academics were involved in the creation of research methods for collecting social 'facts' that became central to later sociological projects at the Chicago School of Public Administration (Shaw, 2015) in the United States.

For social work, as for the social sciences generally, theories have been linked to the methods for collecting information and creating hypotheses for testing as well as for generating interpretations of social phenomena. Social work takes this a step forward and its theories have always been inextricably tied to ideas about creating better social conditions for individuals, communities and groups. This is because, as Flexner (2001) states, one distinguishing mark of a profession is that any knowledge generated should be in service to altruistic ends. When we think of *ends* in social work, we are ultimately thinking about how theory, purpose and values can find expression in social work *practice*. This focus on knowledge for practice has resulted in an intimate relationship between theory and practice within the social work discipline. The two aspects are almost always discussed together.

Contexts of theorising and theory

It is important to understand that the terms theory and theorising – although related – are describing different things. Understanding these differences can help you understand what you are looking at when you begin to review the many theories in the social work literature. We can say that in social scientific terms theorising is the *thinking* activity that people engage in to describe social phenomena, and that theory is the *end* product of these activities. What sort of thinking do we mean when we refer to theorising? There are, of course, different kinds of systematic or critical thinking such as 'deduction, induction, generalizing, model-building, analogies, and others' (Swedberg, 2014, p. 2). Thus when we read and understand theories in social work we are actually engaging with the end products of someone else's theorising where they have used these different processes of thinking in a systematic way.

Swedberg (2014) suggests it is helpful to understand the relationship between theorising and theory by considering them as happening in two different contexts. One context is that of *discovery* and the other is that of *justification*. We will use this distinction in the rest of the chapter to discuss theorising and theory. Discovery involves the *activity* of thinking about social phenomena, whereas justification is the *theory* produced from this activity. In the social sciences and in social work we are more readily exposed to theory in the context of justification (for example, a discussion that explains the key elements and concepts of a theory, which might be presented in a textbook). When students are first introduced to learning different social work theories, they are essentially being instructed in theory in terms of a context of justification, or theory as end products. This is because the activity of thinking, and the process the researcher or theorist has engaged in to arrive at a final statement of the social phenomena being thought about (the context of discovery), has been all but erased from the account. Although, sometimes researchers will include fragments of their theorising; however, this is often an outcome of adopting particular kinds of methodologies or methods in research. Feminist and Indigenous scholars often take this approach (Ellis & Rawicki, 2013; Lather, 2006; Richardson, 2001; Rowe, Baldry & Earles, 2015; Smith, 1999) and they will openly write about the context of discovery in their theorising practice. In some respects, these scholars bridge the gap between theory and theorising.

Some of this confusion between theory and theorising has to do with the way theory is presented in journals, textbooks and theory handbooks. Generally speaking, the thinking activity involved in research tends to be condensed into highly codified descriptions of method. An example of this codified process is where you might see in a piece of research a statement like this: 'A thematic analysis is provided, which draws on several client case study vignettes with reference to quantitative data around new connections for clients' (Hall, Boddy, Chenoweth & Davie, 2012, p. 89). This is an accepted academic convention – the point we are making here is that this does not illuminate in much detail the *theorising process* that might have gone into arriving at the themes, for example. As mentioned, in textbooks, and in theory handbooks, the theorising processes all but disappear. This is because theories are often, but not always, presented as certain (White & Stancombe, 2003), and as *finished* products. The point to remember when reading theory is that it is often presented as a justification for something, like an argument, point of view or perspective.

According to Swedberg (2014), the result of this neglect of the *processes* of theorising has seen an emphasis in social science develop that is more interested in teaching methods than in educating future social scientists in the art and science of theorising. To some extent, teaching theory in social work involves encouraging students to grasp the methods, concepts and principles of *existing* theories. Some say this has led to less interesting research into theory development across the social sciences in general (Alvesson & Kärreman, 2011; Alvesson & Sandberg, 2013). Moreover, Swedberg (2014) maintains that much more attention has been given to replicating theory than in teaching the process of discovery, or of *theorising* per se.

Moreover, in recent times, it has become clear that this distinction between discovery and justification is not as sharp in the social sciences as it might have been in the natural sciences (Denzin & Lincoln, 2008; Schwandt, 2000). In other words, learning about theory in social work can help to develop our capacities in theorising and discovery itself. This is particularly so when theory works to introduce new ways of seeing and thinking about phenomena. So, you might find that learning social work theory kick-starts or opens up new ways of seeing the world. This can be very exciting and rewarding. Equally, there has been the development of new qualitative methods of social research, which incorporate the process of theorising within the process of the research. Part of the turn to practice within contemporary theory (Schatzki, Cetina & Savigny, 2001) and its associated research methods has become influential for social work researchers particularly. Social workers are intensely interested in theorising from and in practice (Fook, 2002b; Fook, Ryan & Hawkins, 1997, 2000; Samson, 2014; Sheppard, Newstead, Di Caccavo & Ryan, 2000). Both *theorising* and creating *theory* about social work practice have become especially important in the face of increasing calls for evidence of effectiveness in social care (Gray, Plath & Webb, 2009; Plath, 2009). What is important to remember here, is that theory in social work is intricately connected with practice, what people do, how they approach things, how they view the world, and the concepts, ideas and language they use to communicate in the world of social work.

Thinking critically about theory

When you are reading about the different theories in social work, you will begin to notice that they all make claims of some kind. Many offer an explanation for something. That is, they make claims about why something is the way it is. Specifically, they may make claims about what sorts of conditions or events lead to or cause something else. Or, they may offer explanations of why people and systems behave or operate like they do. Theories, in the form of perspectives, are instructive and directive, in that the bearer of a perspective will *see* the world in a particular manner, and this will shape and inform their practice. Sometimes social workers use the metaphor of the 'lens' (Connolly & Harms, 2012) as a way of thinking about how the perspective shapes what we see or pay attention to. That is, a perspective will act like a lens and focus attention on certain things in certain ways. Perspectives operate to filter and reconstruct reality broadly along the lines set out by the perspective.

Equally, models often serve to give a simplified version of a more complex idea (Chenoweth & McAuliffe, 2015). An example of this is the *ecogram* (McGoldrick & Gerson, 1985). Ecograms are used to illustrate social relationships and resources in a service users' immediate context in pictorial form. Behind the *model* of an ecogram is a set of theories about the importance of social relationships to human flourishing and well-being, and theories about how the interconnections between environment, individuals and institutions can affect individual well-being (Dale, Smith, Norlin & Chess, 2006).

In the next section, we present six points about theory generally, and these are intended to be reference points for thinking about theory. They are useful here but will also serve as good pointers for how to think about the content in subsequent chapters too. These are:

1. Theory contains reasons.
2. Theory contains moral positions.
3. Theory is a form of critical study.
4. Theory is a public good located in a community.
5. Theory in social work is interactive.
6. Theory is linked to a practice context.

In trying to understand and critically evaluate theory, we need to know some-thing about what theory is, and what would be useful sorts of questions to raise and think about. Applying the sorts of insights and questions posed by these six points will not only help you learn about theory generally, but will help you become more critically minded and reflexive in your use and application of theory in practice.

Theories contain reasons

The first point to make is that theories contain reasons, and these are expressed in terms of a kind of rationality. Dennis (2015) has a simple definition of rational-ity that is helpful to our purposes here. He suggests that rationality is the ability to give reasons for the beliefs and values we might hold about the world. Thus, rationality is actually very important to understanding theory, because theories contain beliefs and values about the world. When trying to comprehend social work theory, a good starting point is to try to identify the reasons used to sup-port beliefs and values articulated in the theory. For example, problem-solving theory contends that cognition is important to solving problems: what reasons are offered to support this claim? The strengths perspective places great value on the importance of empowerment and collaboration: what reasons are offered for this?

The ability to reason is a key way in which human beings have long defined their uniqueness (Williams, 2016). Reasons, however, have to come from some-where. The uses of reason and rationality have been a source of debate and contest within the Western philosophical tradition (Foucault & Rabinow, 1984) at least since the Enlightenment period. Since the Enlightenment (mid-1600s to late 1800s) – that period that ushered in the idea that human beings could decide on actions without recourse to God, or other metaphysical laws (Bristow, 2011) – we have seen the use of *reason* reach ascendancy through the Western academic tradition. This is not to preclude forms of reason that may be associ-ated with different cultures, or that have developed since but are not associated with Enlightenment forms of reason. However, one key aspect about the Enlightenment legacy, important to our discussion of theory, is the assumption that what is known (and therefore accords to standards of reason) should be the same for everyone, because it is assumed that the context does not matter to the standards of reason. That is, once reasons are arrived at, they should be persuasive for everyone. This is referred to as *universalism* (for a discussion of Kantian reason, see Williams, 2016).

The idea of universalism has been subjected to extensive discussion and critique, especially in philosophy (Tully, 2008a). For example, it is possible in social theory to see this idea of universalism itself as a *particular* form of reason, and therefore it is not the only form of reason available to us

(Foucault, 1972, 2002). Theories are propositions that contain reasons for or against something, or seek to give an explanatory account of something. If theories are the end products of someone's previous attempts to explain a social condition, an issue, a phenomena, or practice or experience, then what the theorist produces is inherently situated by time, and the moral and political climate from which they emerge (Wilson & Beresford, 2000). This is a particular claim arising from an approach to knowledge that criticises the notion that knowledge can be context independent, in the social sciences at least (see also Bent Flyvbjerg, 2001, for an extended discussion of this issue). Feminist theorists have also extensively argued about this issue (see, for example, Harding & Hintikka, 1983). Hence, theories are situated within a social context and all social contexts include some norms, which may, or may not, be considered universal. Throughout this book we have tried to trace the ideas being presented by situating them within some context. This context might be historical or in relation to other theories or ideas. Therefore, there are social norms about theorising, research and social science inquiry which are associated with certain ethical standards and requirements. These requirements have been formulated within the crucible of higher education institutions and universities and have become standard practices.

When learning theory it is the *reasons* that underpin the theory that need examining. We can think of this as attempts to persuade you that the theory is the best explanation or description or critique of a particular phenomenon. You might ask yourself: What reasons does the theory give to support the claims made? Are these reasons good ones, persuasive? To what extent would these reasons be universally applicable? What are the limitations of these reasons?

Theory contains moral positions

Social work theories are fundamentally concerned with people and so they are not value free. Some of these moral views will be more clearly expressed in some theories than in others. For example, anti-oppressive theory is very clear in its moral standpoints about discrimination, marginalisation, and so on, and this is an important aspect of this theory. Anti-oppressive theoretical approaches include many arguments about how human beings *ought* to be treated. As mentioned, these theoretical approaches are not meant to be neutral, but are deeply connected with the purposeful aims of social work, such as social change or empowerment (Dominelli, 1998).

At the same time, some theories may have the appearance of being neutral or value free, but nestled within the language and concepts of the theory may be particular values and preferences, or political arguments, or extended links to other philosophical and moral frameworks and views about human nature. The moral undertones may not be explicit, but if examined closely, a particular moral position is apparent nonetheless. You will find in many of the chapters in this book that there is an explicit link made between the theory or concept and social work values. For example, problem-solving theory assumes that the ability to solve problems is an important skill that all people need, and that there may be times when the problems in a person's life seem so insurmountable, or a person's cognitive capacity is so overwhelmed, that they will need the help and support of others (Marsh, 2013; Perlman, 1957). If this is the case, does it explain for you why some people who are very distressed or in crisis may find it difficult to think clearly and analytically? What does this suggest about the value of cognitive capacity, and views about human nature? What is required of the student of theory is to detect and critically appraise the moral undertones and implications embedded within theory.

Theory is a form of critical study

As mentioned earlier, the supposed universalism and value-free assumptions of Enlightenment reason has not been without critique. Theory can act as a form of critical study into social and political arrangements, and even operate as a critique of the very idea of rationality itself. By critical study we mean theorising that has pointed out the *limits* of these Enlightenment rationalities and the problems with the practices and institutions that they support and make possible. Various kinds of 'critical study' (Tully, 2008a) have broadened the way in which we can understand public forms and manifestations of reason. For example, critical studies into knowledge and theory have been important as they have called attention to the ways in which freedom and justice can be denied to various members of society through the assumptions of universalism that are embedded within *ideals* and which have become enshrined in Western forms of reason, along with its institutions and assumptions about democratic processes. These forms of critical study have consistently pointed out the inherently social nature of rationality, although this has been hard fought and is still contested in some quarters (Sayer, 2011).

To turn to other examples, there has been critical study about the intersection between democratic institutions and the effects of capitalism (see, for example, Solimano, 2014). Later, there have been studies that have taken up the issues associated with human production and the environment (see, for example, Connelly, 2012). The relations between men and women and the impact of divides between public and private freedoms and equalities (see these examples of feminist argument by Held, 1999; Pateman, 1988; Pateman & Gross, 1986; Weedon, 1999) have launched different social and political movements that have called into question assumptions about the universalism of domestic arrangements for reproduction and care of children, families and vulnerable people. Furthermore, post-colonial and Indigenous scholars have launched a considerable number of critical studies centred on extending justice beyond individual Nation-state borders, and critiques of 'democratic' institutions associated with colonisation (as an example, see Krishna, 2008; in the context of research particularly, see Smith, 1999).

The point we are making is that theories are political because they intersect with processes of understanding, debate, critique and social action and change. Many of the chapters in this book present aspects of these debates in relation to social work practice. Theories are also political because they are forms of knowledge production and dissemination in the sense that publishing and disseminating knowledge in the form of journals, textbooks and other media involves the distribution of information and knowledge for scrutiny and possible debate. Who is able to participate in this exchange of knowledge and criticism remains a matter of inclusion and exclusion (Beresford, 2000; Beresford & Boxall, 2012; Griffiths, 2005). When theories reach the status of publication they also become codified into idealised *versions* of reality. As mentioned, theories are arguments for certain ways of looking at a situation. As we read them, it is easy to forget these are just products of thinking and we can readily fall into the trap of assuming these accounts are describing an objective reality. It is this assumption that introduces a gap between these idealised versions of reality and what actually happens in practice. It helps to recognise theories as the codified forms of someone's thinking about social phenomena or practice situations. It makes them less certain and more open to debate and to being tested in and through practice. Thinking critically about theory and knowledge along these lines means to be sceptical of claims being made, and to identify the limits and effects that might be present in the theory and its expression in practice.

Theory is a public good located in a community

It should be obvious that social work is a community in the sense that it is a *community of practice* (Lave & Wenger, 1991). It shares professional ethics and a set of community norms about standards of practice and reasons for action (Banks, 2006; Banks & Nohr, 2011). This forms a *practical field* in which reasons, processes of theorising, and eventually theories are able to make sense (Schatzki, 2001). Like any community, the reasons for action and the values and beliefs we hold about social work practice are also open to scrutiny for debate, critique and reflection.

As mentioned earlier, theories provide us with sets of reasons or extended arguments for acting one way or another. In entering into the profession of social work, you will be introduced to other social workers, academics, field educators and supervisors – all of whom will provide you with reasons or arguments for acting one way or another. Part of this learning pertains to being socialised into the profession of social work. In most, if not all, cases this socialisation process is guided by social work values, where reasons for and against something are based in notions of what is the right thing to do and the reasons for this, as informed from a social work perspective.

It is along these lines that Pinker and Goldstein (2012) suggest that reason can lead us in directions that are moral, decent and good, but two conditions are required for this to be the case. The first condition is that people exercising reason generally care about their own well-being. That is one of the qualities that must be present in order for *reason* to go to work in the first place. This aspect is obviously present in all of us to some extent; people do tend to care passionately about their own well-being. But the second condition is equally important. The second condition is more complex in that *reasoners* act as members of a community of other *reasoners* who can affect one another's well-being, can exchange messages, and should be able to comprehend each other's reasoning. Hence, in order to enter into a community who have a shared interest in theoretical matters, we *should show regard* to other members of the community. After all, these are the people with whom we are entering into the conduct of reason and debate.

The reason for this focus on regard for others is because reasons (knowledge and theory) are not disembodied ideas that exist 'out there'. They develop, form and are exchanged in a context of others, and they allow people to develop understanding, to exchange ideas, and if necessary, to change their mind about matters important to them. For example, the forms of critical study described previously involved just such a community of *reasoners*. These critical forms of study have been powerful in that they have pointed out how some social practices that we would have seen as natural a century ago are not natural, and therefore our views of some practices and ideas have changed.

In Pinker and Goldstein's (2012) view, this form of regard to ideas involves an ability to empathise. This is not to be confused with agreement. People may disagree, but it means a willingness to attempt to understand reasons from another's point of view. It is not just empathy that is important, but also to the human ability to take reasons that seem logical in one area and apply them to another situation. For example, when men achieved the franchise to vote in democratic countries the reasons for this were seen as sound; therefore, logically, voting ought to be extended to the case of women. In due course, women were eventually able to vote in public elections. Both Pinker and Goldstein (2012) tie this to the fact that people generally do not like contradictions between their beliefs and their practices. As these contradictions are laid bare by the processes of argumentation, critique and reflection, reasonable people feel compelled to change their minds about the reasons they hold for believing one thing or another. This process of communication is an important aspect of how reason has become central to the ideals and practices of democracy too (Williams, 2016). It is through communication across communities that this occurs, and after a time, a practice previously seen as normal and acceptable begins to feel wrong to the majority of people in that community.

Hence, comprehending theory (or reasons for and against) involves trying to empathise with the reasoner, or the proponent of a certain theory; to ask the question, what is this theory/person trying to tell me, what can I learn from this? It does not mean automatic agreement, but it does require attempts at under-standing, or the choice to listen in the first place (Stolz, 2008). Second, it means developing an aptitude to transfer the insights from one domain to another; to ask the question, where else might this apply? In many of the chapters in this book we have tried to demonstrate this in the way we have explained the ideas of others and also incorporated ideas from other disciplines or places too.

Theory in social work is interactive

We have made the case that social work is a community, where theoretical ideas are developed, exchanged, criticised and revised. This demonstrates the inter-activity of social work theory. But there is a second reason to consider the inter-active nature of social work theory and this is because interactivity is tied to the very context and object of theory itself: human beings.

Social science is different to the natural sciences. This difference between the natural and the social concerns the approach taken to studying the *objects* of the social (human) sciences and those of the natural sciences. Social science, and by extension social work, is inevitably concerned with what Hacking (1999) describes as *'interactive kinds'* (pp. 103–109). By interactive kinds, Hacking means that some *kinds* in the universe interact with the labels or explanation we give them. A rock does not have awareness that it is a rock (at least as far as we are able to ascertain with our current knowledge) and so the label we give the rock – 'granite', for example – does not affect how the *granite* views itself and will have no bearing on what it does. People in this respect are different. It matters to people what we call them as people *interact* with these categories and labels (Hacking, 1999). What we say about people in theory has a great impact on how they feel, what they do, and their experience overall. The way people act has an interactive looping effect on the theory too. Thus we would say that people are *interactive* kinds.

The main point to remember is that not only does it make a difference in how we label others, it also makes a difference in how we explain their circum-stances, or their character, for example. It matters to people what theories, or indeed what theorising we do, about them and their experience (Beresford &

Boxall, 2012). For example, early social workers were quite taken with ideas about poverty in ways that ended up ascribing poverty to people's *character* (Chambon, Johnstone & Winckler, 2011). These theories had material effects for who was seen as deserving of assistance and support and who was not. It also meant that certain negative views about people's character were circulated, and in some ways, internalised and adopted by those same people as being truths. Hence, theory interacted with the reality it purported to describe. As a corrective, theories about structures such as class and gender presented competing ideas about the same phenomena (poverty) and fed into social work approaches that reoriented the education of social workers towards empowerment, emphasising the strengths and resilience of service users (Dominelli, 1998; Saleebey, 2009). Hence, thinking critically about theory means to be very mindful of its effects and impacts, and the way that theory interacts with the conditions it seeks to describe and explain.

Theory is linked to a practice context

So far, we have been discussing some fairly big ideas like reason, rationality and interactive kinds. These might seem to be a long way from practice, a long way from the world the social worker operates in. Your job is to help people and make the world a better place, right? Isn't it relatively straightforward? And it seems self-evident that social workers should engage in theorising and create theories about practice so that they can apply these to their work to make things better for individuals, groups and communities. This is true, however the problem is that there are a great many theories out there, and almost as many disputes about the status of these theories.

As discussed earlier, there is not a single approach to theorising or theory within the discipline of social work. Within academic disciplines social work would be considered a 'soft-applied' discipline (Biglan, 1973, cited in Becher, 1994, p. 152). This is because much of our knowledge base is based on theorising producing understandings/interpretations, and these are aimed at a broadly functional purpose, that is professional practice (Becher, 1994, p. 154; for a discussion of theories in the context of professional purpose, see also Healy, 2014). The other complication, also mentioned above, is that social work draws its knowledge from a range of other disciplines, all of which have varying approaches to theory, theorising, knowledge, and the extent to which this can be applied in practice. In this respect learning the theories is itself an exercise in *theorising* as you work through how they might apply in practice.

As there are so many different and changing interpretations of human experience as well as new ways to represent this knowledge within the academy (Albertín Carbó, 2008; Gregor & Smith, 2009; Gwyther & Possamai-Inesedy,

2009), it stands that there are many different and changing theories about such experiences. It is unlikely that social work will ever produce a unified theory of social work practice in light of this diversity. The strength that social work can draw from this breadth of theoretical ideas is the ability to offer relevant and plausible explanations and responses to the ever increasing complexity and diversity that confronts the social worker. This gives the social worker a range of theoretical and social scientific *resources* that can be reflexively incorporated into their practice.

There is a downside however. The sheer breadth can be overwhelming, and, in the busy pace of social work practice, it is tempting and understandable that a social worker might seek to minimise the difficulties presented with so many theoretical choices and instead settle for a few tried and tested favourite theories. Or, a social worker may end up picking bits and pieces of theoretical ideas in a haphazard manner, without really thinking about what these ideas can actually offer their practice, and more importantly, service users. This is a problem as it can lead to an unhelpful eclecticism (Thompson, 1995). This problem leads us to the next section in this chapter, which is how to think about learning and understanding theory in social work.

Making sense of theories for social work

The aim of the chapter is not to discuss in depth theories themselves, as there are other sources that do that very well (Payne, 2014; Turner, 2011). Rather, the aim is to provide a way to think about, learn and critically examine theory in social work. So far in achieving this aim, we have presented six points of reference from which to mount a critical investigation into the development, form and function of theory. This still begs a question about how to consider approaching the study of social work theory. This section gives a brief overview of some of the ways theory in social work is dealt with, before we outline four main ways to categorise social work theories. These are presented in Table 2.1 in the form of a map of social work theory.

As we have mentioned already, we think it is important to avoid seeing theories as correspondent representations of reality, and instead view them as interpretations put forward by others about specific social phenomena. In this way we can see that theories offer ways to give order and meaning to the complicated nature of different practice environments and situations (Howe, 2009). It is in this sense that Howe (2009) explains that social work and social science theories constitute 'ways of knowing' (p. 2) and that theory is an attempt to make sense of the complexity of the world that social workers work in. Social work theories are dealing in the domain of human behaviour, and the social world generally, so they must grapple with the slippery and subjective aspects of human experience.

Classifying theories in social work

There are a great many books that describe in detail the numerous theories available for social work (Connolly & Harms, 2012; Dominelli, 1998; Healy, 2014; Howe, 2009; Nicolson, Bayne & Owen, 2006; Payne, 2014; Turner, 2011). What many of these books also attempt to do is provide a way to group or classify families of theories. O'Connor et al. (2008) broadly classify social work theories as falling into the categories of problem-solving theories, systems theories, strength-based theories, and critical and postmodern theories. Payne (2014) explains that within theories we can also find perspectives, models and frameworks. Payne also contends that theory may be formal (that is, written accounts of theory) and informal (that is, practice wisdom, or theories generated and applied in the context of specific practice situations). We have been using the distinction of theorising and theory to capture Payne's point about informal and formal theory. The use of these different terms for theories adds to the sense that social work theory looks like a smorgasbord (Loewenberg, 1984) from which one can choose whatever one likes depending on the situation. We think that although that is probably what happens in practice, it is good to be able to say where an approach comes from and what it is broadly aimed at understanding about the person-situation-environment.

In order to make sense of the breadth and depth of social work theory we have conducted a review of the main textbooks (Howe, 2009; Payne, 2014; Robbins, Chatterjee & Canda, 2006; Turner, 2011) concerned with theory in social work and categorised them according to four main approaches: Problem solving, anti-oppressive, psychological and systems (see Table 2.1). We chose these categories as they capture theory that has been developed within social work itself (problem solving and psychosocial casework, for example) as well as theories that have originated through informing disciplines such as sociology and psychology (the anti-oppressive and psychological approaches, respectively). In each category there are a number of theoretical perspectives and so we have included these along with a short explanation of the key idea underpinning the theory. We have also included the historical and disciplinary origins, other associated theories and examples of research, and any models for practice that have resulted. In the last column we have included links to the different kinds of critical reflection (see Chapter 15) that might be involved with the various approaches and theories. We tried where possible to use sources that have a direct link to social work authors and theorists, so that overall, the table can assist in the form of a map for locating key sources, authors and materials for further study into social work theory.

Table 2.1 Four approaches to social work theory

Social work approach/ perspective	Key ideas	Historical and disciplinary origins	Theories and/or research base[1]	Models	Critical reflection operations
Problem solving – theories and models that explain, address and utilise the capacities of service users					
Problem-solving casework	First systematically described by Helen Harris Perlman, the approach incorporates four Ps – these are person, problem, place and process. Assumptions are that service users seek help when they are unable to cope with their circumstances or experiencing a crisis, that the agency context is an important factor in the helping process, the relationship between the service user and worker is important, there should be a beginning, middle and end to the period of service with a service user, and lastly, that problems need breaking into component parts to make them more amenable and manageable for action (Shier, 2011).	Philosophy. Psychology. Humanist approaches (Dunlap, 2011).	Dewey's pragmatic theory (Dewey, 1933). Ego psychology (Howe, 2009). Functional theory (Dunlap, 2011).	Problem-solving model (Compton & Galaway, 1994; see also Turner & Jaco, 1996, pp. 510–511).	*Interpretation: An activity of thinking we engage in when we do not already understand a circumstance or practice, or if an already held interpretation is now in some doubt.* In the case of problem solving, interpretation is oriented to understanding the service user's perspective of the problem. *Explanation: Accounting for phenomena in detail including the relationships between them.* In problem solving this may include how each aspect of the problem is impacting on the service user, family, group or community.

[1]Not all possible theories and/or research programs are included here. We have included a sample instead as a starting point for exploring the particular approach.

(Continued)

Table 2.1 (Continued)

Social work approach/ perspective	Key ideas	Historical and disciplinary origins	Theories and/or research base[1]	Models	Critical reflection operations
Task centred practice	Central to this approach is the idea that service users need time-limited and practical help to set goals for transforming their circumstances (Marsh, 2013). Thus, the problem and the goal should be separated and the various tasks are set by the service user in collaboration with the social worker.	Social work research studies (Payne, 2005).	Theoretically tied to observation from original social work practice research (Marsh, 2013). This is a social work practice theory	Brief casework (Reid & Shyne, 1969, cited in Howe, 2009). Task centred model (Marsh & Doel, 2005).	*Interpretation:* This would mean engaging in discussion with the service user, family, group or community about the circumstances presented. *Explanation:* This would mean building a picture with service users about the help required and barriers and resources available to achieving mutually agreed goals.
Crisis theory	Events that upset the equilibrium of people with regard to their environments. Crises are sudden, overwhelm the normal coping mechanisms or practices of the person, family, group or community; generally are time-limited; may produce destructive, socially unacceptable or dangerous behaviours during the time of disequilibrium and people feel especially vulnerable during these periods (Regehr, 2011, pp. 136–137). Crisis models assume that this is also an opportunity for growth and change (Regehr, 2011, p. 137).	Preventative psychiatry (Payne, 2005). Psychology. Community volunteer movement (Regehr, 2011).	Lindemann's observations of the Cocoanut Grove disaster in 1942 (Regehr, 2011).	7-stage model (Regehr, 2011). Crisis model (Payne, 2005). Crisis debriefing (Mitchell & Everly 1993, cited in Regehr, 2011, p. 139).	*Interpretation:* In crisis intervention this would mean suspending worker judgement about the meaning of the crisis event (s) and seeking to understand what this is for the service user. The work would place an emphasis on supporting the service user to recover their own coping strategies. Discussion with people to understand their view of the events that have overwhelmed them is an important form of reflection here.

22

Anti-oppressive – explanations and practice theories about social divisions and their impact for addressing inequality and oppressive power relations

Radical	A social work perspective largely informed by Marxism and communist theory in the 1970s. Social issues experienced by service users are caused by wider economic and societal forces and relations. Different groups experience oppression, inequality and discrimination based on their class position.	Sociology. Philosophy. Marxist theory of class inequality.	Radical practice; anti-racist theory; feminist theory in social work (Turbett, 2014). Radical casework (Fook, 1993).	The web of oppression (Mullaly, 2009, cited in Turbett, 2014, p. 43).	*Critique: Involves comparison between a conception of an **ideal** set of conditions and conditions that may be in operation in the **real**. This* would involve consideration and consciousness of the ways in which wider social forces and structures of oppression might be playing a role in the circumstances of service users.
Critical	A perspective informed by critical social science, this perspective incorporates radical, structural, feminist, anti-oppressive, anti-racist, anti-discriminatory and Marxist social work models and theories (Healy, 2014, p. 185). Society is divided between those who have access to resources and those who do not. People who are excluded by economic and societal forces and relations often	Philosophy. Critical social theory. Sociology. Feminist social theory.	Theory of communicative rationality (Habermas, 1984); Critical theory (Agger, 2006), Paulo Freire's *Pedagogy of the Oppressed* (Freire, 1972); postmodern critical theory (Parton, 2000; Pease & Fook, 1999a); theories about power (Foucault, 1995; Lukes, 1974).	Critical reflection model (Fook & Gardner, 2007). Anti-oppressive practice (Dominelli, 2002a); strengths perspective (Saleebey, 2009); narrative therapy (Madigan, 2013).	*Critique:* Workers from this perspective question the economic and social arrangements surrounding service users. *Deconstruction: Thinking that involves analysing the relation between the sign and signified in language and symbols.* In social work this usually refers to how some person, group or community becomes categorised as 'other' through

(Continued)

Table 2.1 (*Continued*)

Social work approach/ perspective	Key ideas	Historical and disciplinary origins	Theories and/or research base[1]	Models	Critical reflection operations
	accept their exclusion through a process that presents the current order as fair and just, and so people in such circumstances tend to believe the dominant ideas about their circumstances. These dominant ideas suggest that the exclusion occurs due to individual pathology. Thus, different groups experience oppression and discrimination based on their social identities (for example, class, ethnicity, sexuality, gender and so on). Critical approaches assumes socio-economic arrangements are not natural and therefore social work practice should be aimed at challenging the 'constructed nature' of society and consequent power relations that result from these processes (Howe, 2009, p. 130). Social work as a profession should be committed to ending these unequal and diverse forms of oppression.				the use of language and symbols. Workers using this form of critical reflection generally challenge any dominant ways of seeing service user situations including the various categorisations by dominant groups. The dominance of one group is not assumed to be static but changes depending on the context. *Problematisation 2: Thinking aimed at interrogating anything presented as 'natural' for hidden assumptions. Such 'natural' or self-evident truths are assumed to be part of dominant discourses and practices.* Social workers using this form of critical reflection will question the way in which arrangements surrounding service users are accepted as natural and will use forms of critical questioning to unsettle dominant narratives of service user circumstances.

Empowerment	That some people in society experience blocks to their development and exercise of problem-solving capacities due to their experiences of being part of stigmatised collectives (Lee, 1996; Solomon, 1976). The approach includes three aspects: (1) work on the development of a more positive sense of self, (2) building awareness and reflective capacities of service users about the conditions within the environment and (3) 'the cultivation of resources and strategies…for the attainment of personal and collective goals' (Lee, 1996, p. 34).	History, particularly the US civil rights movement. Sociology, particularly critical and radical perspectives. Feminist theory, particularly bell hooks (hooks, 1990, 2003).	Primarily a practice approach, the main theoretical ideas are derived from ecological theory via the use of the life model (Germain & Gitterman, 1980); stigma (Goffman, 1991); multiculturalism and liberation theory via Paulo Freire (1972).	Group work, particularly mutual aid groups (Lee, 1996, pp. 290–350); service user perspectives (Wilson & Beresford, 2000).	*Critique:* Contrasting the notion of what makes a *beloved community* with the actual conditions in the community one lives and works in and using this vision as a guide for action. *Problematisation 2:* Critical questioning is aimed at building awareness for service users of their experiences of being part of various collectives which may be experiencing stigma. Raising awareness of this is a strategy. Workers aim their thinking at interrogating anything presented as 'natural' for hidden assumptions. *Interpretation:* Exploration of how the service user understands their circumstances and membership of oppressed groups, including what capacities and resources are available to them within this membership. This can include workers' reflection on their own membership in different groups. *Explanation:* Reflection here would include paying attention to the relationship between difficult experiences of oppression, powerlessness and inequality and membership in non-dominant groups and identities.

(Continued)

Table 2.1 (Continued)

Social work approach/ perspective	Key ideas	Historical and disciplinary origins	Theories and/or research base[1]	Models	Critical reflection operations
Psychological – explanations and models that consider the psychological and developmental aspects of human behaviour					
Psychodynamic[2]	An early and influential perspective in psychology. The mind has both a conscious and unconscious level and these levels have significant interaction which can affect our behaviour. The task of the social worker is to understand the conscious and unconscious aspects to the situations service users discuss with them – central to this is the relationship with the service user (Nathan, 2013; Ruch, Turney & Ward, 2010).	Psychiatry. Psychology. Medicine.	Attachment theory. Systems theory. Freudian psychoanalytic theory.	Relationship-based model of social work practice (Ruch, 2010a, p. 19).	*Interpretation:* Working with service users to understand and interpret childhood experiences and various defences, coping and unconscious behaviour in the later years. Workers would also engage in building understanding of their own defences, triggers and capacity for containment and building safe relationships with service users.
Humanist perspective	Founded by Abaham Maslow and elaborated by Carl Rogers (Moss, 2015), humanist psychology holds that all humans are 'essentially growth-oriented, forward-moving, and concerned with	Psychiatry. Psychology. Philosophy (humanism, phenomenology, existentialism).	Theory of human motivation (Maslow, 1943); Rogers' nine propositions about personality (Rowe, 2011).	Person-centred (Trevithick, 2011). Maslow's hierarchy of needs (Maslow, 1943); client-centred therapy (Rogers, 2012).	*Interpretation:* In this context this is aimed at understanding the life-world of participants in a process involving a therapeutic relationship, either with families, individuals or groups.

[2]Psychodynamic is a broad term that includes all theories that are based on some aspect of Freudian *psychoanalytic* theory (McLeod, 2007).

	fulfilling their basic potentialities' (Rowe, 2011, p. 62). Thus, the approach seeks to understand the world of the service user, group, family or community in order to support development towards reaching their full potential. The key to this is in the deployment of empathic regard for the service user, family, group or community (Rogers, 2012).		Motivational interviewing (MI) (Teater, 2013a). Solution-focused brief therapy (De Shazer & Berg, 1997; Teater, 2013b).	*Explanation:* In this context a worker would consider the stage of development that a service user or members of a family might be in and whether there is a relationship between that and the current situation.
Developmental theories	This group of theories are concerned with growth, development and decline across the lifespan (Robbins, Chatterjee & Canda, 2012c). There is considerable debate about whether development occurs in stages or as a set of continuous processes (White, Hayes & Livesey, 2013), however, development is increasingly seen as an interactive process between biology and the social milieu into which people are born.	Psychology. Social work. Ethology. Neurosciences.	Various early stage theories including Erikson's[3] epigenetic model of human development (Robbins et al., 2012c, p. 213); Valliant's adaption to life theory (Vaillant, 1977); Levinson's stages of adult development (Robbins et al., 2012c); Attachment theory (Howe, 2013).	Attachment therapy (Milner, Myers & O'Byrne, 2015).

[3] Originally formulated using Freudian concepts, according to Robbins et al. Erikson's theory is now considered as a lifespan theory of psychosocial development and thus we have taken our lead from these authors in including it in this category.

(Continued)

Table 2.1 (*Continued*)

Social work approach/ perspective	Key ideas	Historical and disciplinary origins	Theories and/or research base[1]	Models	Critical reflection operations
Behaviourism	Human behaviour is the result of learning processes, many of which are observable. Three main kinds of learning are important here: operant learning, observational and respondent (Thyer, 2011). Thyer (2011, p. 440) suggests that more complex interpersonal behaviours emerge from these 'fundamental learning mechanisms'. Behaviourism has utilised a research program of experiment to establish the basic premise regarding learning and behaviour.	Neurosciences. Medicine. Experimental psychology.	Experimental research – early examples would be Ivan Pavlov, B F Skinner (Jordan, 2013). Clinical research.	Social learning theory (Thyer, 2011); Motivational Interviewing (MI) (Teater, 2013a).	*Explanation:* A worker might consider and explore any impacts from earlier childhood experiences and how these might explain current situations in terms of learning and motivation for change.
Cognitive	This psychological perspective is concerned with 'how humans perceive, think, and process various forms of situations and then respond to them' (Chatterjee & Brown, 2011, p. 103).	Psychology (Jean Piaget, Lawrence Kohlberg). Anthropology (Malinowski).	Experimental research. Clinical research.	Anger management models (Leadbetter, 2013).	*Interpretation:* Workers would seek to understand the perceptions and thoughts that service users have of the presenting situation.

28

		Sociology (The Chicago School, Talcott Parsons, Berger and Luckman's social construction of reality). Philosophy. Sociobiology (EO Wilson).[4]	Cognitive behavioural therapy (CBT) (Treater, 2013).	*Interpretation:* A worker would engage in discussion aimed at understanding the presenting situation with service users, families, groups or communities. This would be a crucial aspect of understanding the impact of the environment in addition to the intrapersonal factors.
Systems				
Psychosocial casework	Combines systems theory with psychodynamic theories such as Freudian psychoanalytic and ego psychology (Howe, 2009, p. 114). Social casework is aimed at the interaction between individual psychology and the social and external conditions in which people find themselves. The main concept that captures this interplay is the *person-in-situation gestalt* (Woods & Hollis, 2000).	Psychology. Psychodynamic. Sociology, particularly systems theory (Healy, 2014) and the emphasis on roles derived from work by Talcott Parsons and the structural functionalist perspective (Robbins, Chatterjee & Canda, 2012b).	Primarily based on case studies. Bio-psycho-social assessment (Robinson & Kaplan, 2011); Relationship-based social work (Ruch et al., 2010).	

[4]The claims here are drawn primarily from the chapter by Chatterjee and Brown (2011, pp. 105–108).

29

Table 2.1 (*Continued*)

Social work approach/ perspective	Key ideas	Historical and disciplinary origins	Theories and/or research base[1]	Models	Critical reflection operations
	The social worker's attention is aimed at addressing the 'problems arising out of disequilibrium between people and their environments' (Woods & Hollis, 2000, p. 39). *Situation* implies a human situation rather than problems emanating from the natural world.[5]				
Ecological perspective Ecosystems theory	Considers the transactions between people and their environment (Robbins et al., 2012b). The key term associated with this perspective is 'goodness of fit' (Healy, 2014, p. 122). Views people as people as 'purposive and goal seeking' (Robbins et al., 2012b, p. 33).	Anthropology. Sociology (Berger & Luckmann, 1967 cited in Robbins et al., 2012b). Psychology. Gestalt psychology (Robbins et al., 2012b).		Life model (Germain & Gitterman, 1980; Howe, 2009). Ecomaps. Genograms.	*Explanation:* The worker would pay due attention to the interactions between environment and service user, community or group. This means not settling too quickly on causal mechanisms but allowing for two way effects to be explored and understood.

[5]Ecological impacts from climate change are more associated with the ecological model of social work practice.

Conclusion

In this chapter we have considered the difference between theory and theorising and how this is related to the legacy of Enlightenment thinking, particularly by seeing theories as reasons for beliefs or actions. We think that seeing theories as the end-products of other people's efforts to offer explanation or reasons makes them more amenable to reflection, debate and critique. The six key points we have made about theory are intended as reference points from which to develop a critical and reflexive inquiry into learning and understanding theory. In this chapter we have also touched on the abundance of theories available to us in social work, not least due to social works' participation in the social sciences and the professional effort to theorise our own application of theoretical insights to practice. We have offered a way of making sense of this abundant heritage by categorising the main theories into four approaches. This is not the only way in which this heritage could be approached, but it is one that might assist with understanding the history, origin and main ideas that have informed social work theory and practice over the last century.

Critical thinking questions

1. What is the difference between theory and theorising? In your answer, refer to Swedberg's discussion about the contexts of theory and theorising.

2. It is suggested that one way to understand theory is to identify and examine its *reasoning*. What does this mean?

3. It is suggested that theory is interactive, in that the use of theory in practice will affect and shape how people think and act in practice. Explain what this means and give an example of the way that theory interacts with practice.

4. Review the theory classification in Table 2.1. What are the main points of difference between problem-solving and anti-oppressive theories?

5. Many contend that social work utilises a person-in-environment or systems perspective as a theoretical and practice orientation. Choose an area of social work practice, and explain why a systems perspective would be important for this area of practice.

Exercises

Choose any ONE of the theories presented in Table 2.1 (Four approaches to social work theory) and explore this theory in more depth. In your exploration, critically analyse the theory in relation to the following questions: (1) What is the context of discovery of this theory and who was key to its development? (2) What reasons are offered to give the theory its justification? (3) What moral positions are outlined in the theory? (4) What is the practice context(s) that this theory is said to be applicable to?

Further reading

Beresford, P. (2000). Service users' knowledges and social work theory: Conflict or collaboration? *British Journal of Social Work, 30*(4), 489–503. doi:10.1093/bjsw/30.4.489

Healy, K. (2014). *Social work theories in context: Creating frameworks for practice* (2nd ed.). Houndsmills, UK: Palgrave Macmillan.

Howe, D. (2009). *A brief introduction to social work theory.* Basingstoke, UK; New York: Palgrave Macmillan.

Parton, N. (2000). Some thoughts on the relationship between theory and practice in and for social work. *British Journal of Social Work, 30*(4), 449–463. doi:10.1093/bjsw/30.4.449

Payne, M. (2014). *Modern social work theory* (4th ed.). Basingstoke, UK: Palgrave Macmillan.

Links and online resources

A podcast of the presentation by Dr Peter Dennis on the topic of reason and rationality can be accessed here http://blogs.lse.ac.uk/theforum/peter-dennis/

Stanford Encyclopedia of Philosophy is a searchable database on philosophical topics. In this chapter we have utilised a number of the entries on moral reason, rationality, practical judgement and Aristotle. You can access it through this link http://plato.stanford.edu/index.html

The Encyclopedia of Social Work is a joint collaboration between the National Association of Social Work and Oxford University Press. The site contains many links to resources and explanations of key social work terms. There are cultural differences in how some terms in social work can be understood so it's important to keep in mind the site is primarily aimed at a US audience. For access you will need to subscribe for a fee but there are also open access articles available without subscription. It can be accessed at http://socialwork.oxfordre.com/

A blog by Saul McLeod with many handy sections on different theorists in psychology as well as easy to understand explanations of core psychological concepts. This is a UK site and so reflects a UK perspective on psychological ideas. The site can be accessed here www.simplypsychology.org/psychodynamic.html

This is another source for psychological perspectives – an internet resource about mental health started in 1995 by Dr John Grohol and still maintained by him. The site is a good resource for both information and support groups around specific issues in mental health. The site is based in the US. You can access the site via this link http://psychcentral.com/

Steven Pinker and Rebecca Newberger Goldstein: The long reach of reason. www.youtube.com/watch?v=uk7gKixqVNU

3

RISK

Introduction

It seems that as we go about our daily lives we often hear about how risky life has become, how we should be aware of the risks for this or that, and how important it is for people to manage and respond to an increasing number of risks associated with lifestyle, travel, our finances, and our health. The idea of risk has permeated social work too. It is a major organising concept that shapes the way that services operate, and how they assess and respond to human need (Green, 2007). This use of the term 'risk' also presupposes a particular set of assumptions about people, and where responsibility for managing risk sits (Green, 2007). Yet, the definitions of risk, resilience, vulnerability, and so on are plagued by conceptual differences and some confusion (Kaplan, 1999). This chapter draws on social work and other literature to conceptualise risk as a form of knowledge that is used in social work practice and explains the development of the risk management paradigm in social work. At the same time, it critically examines the implications this has for how social workers think, talk and act in relation to their work. The chapter examines different theories of risk to high-light some of the theoretical and practical limitations of risk management that social workers must grasp and think critically about. The goal here is to consider risk as much more than an objectively occurring real thing, but to think about it as a form of constructed knowledge that has implications for the way human services are delivered. As a counterpoint to some of the criticisms discussed about the use of risk theories and tools in social work, the chapter concludes with a brief discussion on resilience and protective factors.

Social work and risky business

What is a risk? What does it mean to say that someone is 'at risk'? Fraser, Rich-man and Galinsky (1999) define risk as 'a probability describing the likelihood of a future event, given a condition or set of conditions' (p. 131). Notice in this definition that there is a future orientation concerned with making some kind of prediction. Some risks may be ill-defined, or very broadly conceptualised (Fraser et al., 1999). It is very difficult conceptually to define what is a risk in clear and

specific terms, and even more difficult to situate that in a model of logical causation where we can predict with reliability and certainty the probability of (a) the
risk occurring and (b) the occurrence of that risk causing or leading to a specific
harm or undesirable consequence (Leshner, 1999). For example, family conflict
may operate as a risk factor with regard to a person's physical or mental health,
but this is not to be confused with it being strictly *causal*. And family conflict is
a very loose term that could be interpreted in numerous ways. So, right away
we have identified something of a problem in that it is quite hard to predict with
reliable accuracy what might occur in a future sense, and what might be the
cause of this occurrence.

Typically, both the predicted event and the conditions that cause or influence it are thought to be *undesirable*, and something to be *avoided* or *changed*.
Hence, it is no surprise as Green (2007) explains that social work frameworks,
services and social policies are increasingly being dominated by the language
and technologies of risk, risk assessment and risk management, given the focus
on trying to change or avoid an undesirable occurrence. At the same time,
however, it should be pointed out that some risks are beneficial, leading to
growth, change and opportunity. Risk-taking can be fun and can bind people
together, so not all risks are inherently bad. Hence, bound up in views about
risks are moral judgements.

Background to the risk paradigm

The historical backdrop to a fixation on risk as a major organising idea for social
work is situated in the context of the Industrial Revolution and its extension into
modernity (Green, 2007). This includes the rise and prominence of science and
the belief that hazards and dangers once thought to be the providence of luck
and chance could now be calculated, predicted and, ultimately, managed (Lupton, 1999). Green (2007) posits that there are three distinct movements that
explain the centrality of risk in social and political thought, including social work.
First, the emergence of globalisation and what writers such as Beck and Giddens
refer to as risk society (Beck, 1992; Giddens, 1990). A risk society denotes a situation where risks have become non-localised, new and more profound (such as
risks associated with the environment, nuclear catastrophe), and reified through
endless media reports about how dangerous and risky everything has become.
In tandem with this hyper-notion of risk is a situation whereby individual people
are increasingly forced to be reflective and actuarial about the choices and decisions they make, partly because one's destiny and fortune or misfortune are
largely deemed a matter of their own responsibility and their own doing. Second, considering the extent that the modern state has been governmentalised,
risk has emerged as a key technology of governmentality. This means that 'the
identification, deployment, and management of risk' (Green, 2007, p. 399) is a

central preoccupation of government and non-governmental actors and author-ities as they seek to use risk management technologies to manage 'risky popula-tions' (Payne, 2011). Third, institutions of government and business have become increasingly risk averse and sensitive to what are called 'institutional risks' (Green, 2007, p. 400), and consequently, they organise much of their efforts in guarding against 'negligence, bureaucratic failure, loss of reputation, and professional error' (Green, 2007, p. 400). These three drivers bring risk technology and theory and practice to prominence in social work.

Implications for social work

Green argues that there are four key consequences of the way that risk domi-nates social work, and none of these are particularly worth celebrating. First, risk becomes the thing that trumps need. This is because assessments of risk are largely future focussed, orientating on what *might be*, whereas assessments of need are usually concerned with the present situation (Green, 2007, p. 401). For service users, focussing on risk means that their future becomes more important than their present, and as Green says, this 'can over-ride today's needs' (Green, 2007, p. 401). Furthermore, risk is largely conceptualised in negative and deficit terms, often overlooking the strengths or benefits associ-ated with some forms of risk-taking and experimentation (Payne, 2011).

Second, risk contributes to changes to the role of the social worker. Practice becomes a technical activity in identifying and managing risk, rather than a therapeutic activity based on care, relationships and empowerment. In this sce-nario, the documents and records of practice have less to do with the details and nuances of people's lives and what they need, and more to do with records of accountability and protection for the social worker and the institutions they inhabit.

Third, risk is posited as an important component of a culture of freedom and individualism, where people are exhorted to become responsible for their own choices, destinies and futures. What this means, however, is that increasingly the onus of responsibility for one's economic and social welfare is passed to the individual rather than being a community or collectively organised system of care and social welfare (McDonald, 2010). Prudentialism, which is the idea that people should act pre-emptively to protect their interests, becomes a cultural norm and social work practice becomes informed by the technologies of 'bio-logical, social, and psychological attributes or deficiencies of the individual' (Green, 2007, p. 405). This leads to the fourth point that risk is intrinsically associated with blame. When things go wrong, as they invariably do, someone is held responsible for failing to identify, respond to, or manage the associated risk. Often this blame falls at the feet of service users. However, professionals are sensitive to this turn of events, too, and will seek to practice in a defensive manner. When things go wrong, trust in public institutions is also diminished. And those who are harmed by the hazards of modern life are held accountable for their own misfortune.

Theories of risk

Risk is not a uniform set of uncontested ideas (Kemshall, 2010), but a collection of theoretical propositions, assumptions, values and technologies. Risk assessment and risk management practice is 'mediated by worker values, ideologies and the routinisation and proceduralisation of work and practice itself' (Kemshall, 2010, p. 1248). What are the key assumptions and explanatory factors associated with risk theory?

Cultural and constructivist theories

Douglas (1986, 1994) anthropological work on risk argues that risk is basically a cultural construct of some kind. This means that what is thought to be a risk is determined by the context that envelopes and produces it. But there is no uniform agreement on what is and what is not a risk, and as such, judgements about risk can be highly contested. Social workers would be familiar with this situation. People will disagree over what is a risk and they will disagree over who might be considered to be 'at-risk', who poses a risk, or what counts as 'risky'. These disagreements can occur among professionals, society as a whole and service users. People who disagree with expert views about risk are often viewed by these same experts as missing the point or being incompetent or ignorant to risks (Douglas, 1994). Health promotion messages often play on this argument, proposing to use expert knowledge to enlighten an uneducated section of the population about dangers and hazards associated with certain lifestyle choices, for example. Yet, disagreement over what is the right thing to do and how people ought to behave, or not behave, could be seen as alternative cultural readings or different responses to risk, that may have merit in their own right (Lupton, 1999). Think for example when you might have ignored a particular health and lifestyle message. Who is to say that your actions are inherently wrong? Actually, someone may very well chastise your actions as reckless because you have not acted rationally in light of expert advice and knowledge. Rational actor theories of risk contend that people should rationally calculate risks based on expert information, and prudentially make decisions to minimise their exposure to risk (Lupton, 1999).

Consequently, policies and services adopting this thinking would emphasise personal choice and responsibility as a condition of receiving services and benefits. This may act to exclude people from services despite their need, and demonise others who are seen to fail to act responsibly (Kemshall, 2010). Stalker (2003), for example, argues that service users' perspectives have largely been ignored in the risk literature, meaning that the reasons why some people take risks, or even actively seek out risk-taking behaviours, are not well understood. Such behaviours may appear to be at odds with professionals' views of what is deemed acceptable risk avoidance conduct, hence the contestation or disagreement, and the blame and chastising. This means that social work may be operating with a conception of what is acceptable risk aversion that is somewhat at odds with that of service users. Therefore, judgements about risk, protection and risk aversion or avoidance will be contested, and possibly misguided.

Realist and objectivist theories

Some of the theory about rationally weighing up risks and acting accordingly to minimise one's exposure to them is driven by what Lupton (1999) refers to as the cognitive science perspective of risk. This perspective is found in the fields of psychology, medicine, engineering, accounting and insurance (Lupton, 1999). Under this view, risks are seen as real objective facts and things that exist in the world that can be identified, quantified and managed. Criticisms of this line of thinking point to the failure in practice of well-resourced institutions to effectively manage the mounting social, political, economic, environmental and security risks that beset governments every day (Beck, 1992, 2003; Douglas, 1986, 1994). If it is possible to quantify risks, how come so many risks and hazards continue to proliferate? Part of this problem is due to the failure to adequately build simple cause and effect models of risk (Beck, 1992; Douglas, 1994) because complex social, economic and environmental problems defy the logic of technical-rational models of risk management. According to Beck, within the complexity of modernity, cause and effect notions of risk cease to be workable or even possible (Beck, 1992) precisely because hazards are non-localised, long term and irreducibly complex (Lupton, 1999).

Governmental theories

Houston (2001) has argued that objectivist approaches to risk identification are flawed and that trying to measure risks with reliability and certainty will fall short of such a promise. Others suggest that risk is a social product, developed, mediated and understood and responded to within the meanings and concepts within a given culture. Under this view, risk is not an objectively occurring thing, but a construction of sorts (Houston, 2001). However, Houston argues that this dichotomy is unhelpful as arguably there are *actually occurring events* and scenarios that are hazardous *and* our subjective and cultural interpretations of these.

Risk can also be thought of as a political problem, which requires political intervention and pre-emption and thus necessitates 'a reorganization of power and authority' (Beck, 1992, p. 34). Risks may be real in terms of clear existing problems, and also unreal in terms of imagined causal outcomes. As Beck explains:

> The centre of risk consciousness lies not in the present, *but in the future.* In the risk society, the past loses the power to determine the present. Its place is taken by the future, thus, something non-existent, inventive, fictive as the 'cause' of current experience and action. We become active today in order to prevent, alleviate or take precautions against the problems and crises of tomorrow and the day after tomorrow – or not to do so. (Beck, 1992, p. 34, original italics)

Although it may be the case that risk is something of invention or construct, and strategies to manage it often falter because models of risk management cannot cope with the complexity they seek to control, programs of risk management and intervention still captivate our attention, and they attract an allocation of resources and political will. Many of these interventions are targeted towards groups of people designated as 'risky' or 'at risk' and this is often seen as unquestionably the right thing to do. A governmental perspective theorises the way that risk becomes a form of knowledge and practice (Lupton, 1999). The existence of risk as a form of knowledge and practice makes possible various subtle and not so subtle governing practices over individuals and populations deemed at risk or risky (Ewald, 1991; Lupton, 1999; Turner, 1997) and these become normalised and thus pass into common-sense.

This means that risk is not just an abstracted theoretical idea, but a practice that has meaningful and material consequences. Dean (1997, 1999 cited in Lupton, 1999) identifies three types of risk strategy: insurantial, epidemiological and case management/clinical. Insurantial risk strategies are concerned to quantify and collectivise potential risks so that they may be insured against capital loss. Epidemiological risk strategies are similar, only that the focus is on disease prevention, rather than compensating for capital loss. Epidemiological strategies target 'lifestyle risk factors', such as diet and exercise, rather than 'contextual risk factors' and this is 'used to exhort individuals to engage in self-regulation' (Lupton, 1999, p. 97). Case management and clinical strategies include 'clinical practice with individuals deemed to be threatening or disruptive in some way to the social order' involving 'qualitative assessment of risk for individuals and groups who are deemed to be "at risk"' (Lupton, 1999, p. 97). Each of these strategies involves steps to seek to control or manage not just individual action and conduct, but the context and environment in which such conduct occurs. Social work plays an important but not unproblematic role in the development and implementation of various risk technologies and practices that have governmental power.

Risk and social service organisation

So far, we have discussed the development and theoretical context of risk in social work, and noted some of the limitations and implications for social work practice. There is a wider context to the permutation of risk into practice that can be analysed at the level of social service organisations. McDonald argues that there has been a large-scale shift in responsibility for managing risks, from governments to not-for-profit or non-government services and agencies. She terms this 'political risk transfer' (McDonald, 2010, p. 214, original italics). The reason for this transfer is that complex and intractable problems that cannot effectively be dealt with or solved by government organisations are transferred to the non-government sector, with little expectation that any meaningful difference or resolution to the problems will take place. She cites work by Siebel in categorising this as 'symbolic problem solving' (McDonald, 2010, p. 214). In this argument, risks are those issues and problems that are complex, intractable and recalcitrant to remedies, despite huge investment and political and community will. The example McDonald develops is child protection, but this could apply equally to a number of persistent social problems. What is important to grasp here is that risk is thought to be something that is *managed*, but not necessarily eliminated. This view accepts that some social problems at least will be enduring.

Likewise, Marston, Moss and Quiggin note a significant trend in the way risk is handled socially and politically over the last 20 years, which has involved the transference of risks 'from the state to the individual, household or charities. This transfer of the burden of risk is what is called the "great risk shift"' (Marston, Moss & Quiggin, 2010, p. vii). Responsibility for managing risks is now less of a collective responsibility, and more of an individual one. The responsibility for managing one's risk fits well with a social and political norm of respecting or at least promoting individual autonomy and self-determination, understood primarily as maximising choice (Mackenzie, 2010). With personal freedom and choice comes individual responsibility, and this is an attractive idea to many. However, this transfer of risk responsibility raises serious moral and political questions, when one begins to critically examine the disproportionate burden of responsibility shouldered by the most disadvantaged and marginalised, and the fact that people have unequal means at their disposal to manage individual risks. For example, someone with a lot of wealth can protect their interests in ways that someone who is very poor cannot. Furthermore, some risks arise in the context of globalisation and overwhelm personal choice and responsibility (think of global economic and environmental crises, for example, and who is most affected by these). If a collective approach to managing risks has given way to an individual one, what does this mean for people who are excluded from the circuits of power, wealth and influence when there are inevitable shocks, be they personal, economic, financial, ecological or relational, for example?

Given the focus on individual choice and responsibility, a consequence is that misfortunes can be thought of as an individual fault or failure. And if misfortune is the result of individual fault or failure, then the person may be regarded as undeserving of compensation or assistance, seen as though they could have (theoretically at least) made better choices to avert or minimise risks associated with their individual action (Moss, 2010). However, individual action is never free or completely autonomous – many of our actions are structured or conditioned by circumstances that are not of our doing or choosing. As Moss states, a deserving/underserving approach to rendering compensation or assistance to misfortune can result in harsh or punitive welfare policy measures that unfairly punish the most vulnerable (Moss, 2010).

Criticisms of the risk perspective in social work

It should be apparent by now that risk theory and practice is not a neutral process, and layered into arguments about what is risk, who is at risk, who is risky, and what should be done are political ideas and social values that inform and shape the specification of problems and the solutions that social workers invariably adopt into their practice (Payne, 2011). The domain of risk work, then, is a site for the analysis and critical reflection upon the key assumptions, ideologies and values that drive theories and practices associated with risk assessment and risk management.

For example, Stanford (2008) argues that 'risk operates as a predominantly morally conservative and repressive social, political and cultural force in contemporary social work' (p. 209). By this, Stanford means that the construct of risk and the ensuing risk management and risk assessment practices contain a moral prudentialism aimed at governing and controlling the conduct of people across multiple social domains, and that this is a key technology of neoliberalism. The problem that Stanford notes is that this neoliberal technology invents or fabricates new categories of risky persons, who are then slated for intervention by state and non-state authorities. Risk work can quickly become an instrument of domination and oppression and it poses a dilemma for social workers who may seek to resist the pernicious influence of neoliberal ideology on social work practice.

An example of the way that moral values find their way into rational technologies is found in research by Roets and colleagues (2015) in their examination of social work student report writing. They found that student responses to a child protection scenario developed a series of normative constructions whereby 'the social work students tend to occupy and maintain a privileged power monopoly towards children and parents, and easily moralise and blame the parents' (p. 205). Roets et al. appeal for social workers using risk technologies to be very aware of the way their power can influence their judgements about risk, but also the fact that even 'benign' risk technologies such as a straightforward risk assessment tool can contain orientating concepts and assumptions that shape and highlight reality in specific ways, while rendering invisible other ways of seeing and considering what is going on (Roets et al., 2015).

Risk assessment tools and their limitations

Risk assessment tools and practices are commonplace in social work. Think of these as various forms of risk technology. They are particularly used to define and predict the likelihood of risks, harms or hazards that may affect service users. They also operate to protect social workers and services from allegations that they have failed in their duty to identify and respond to risks in a reasonable manner. Morley (2009) expresses caution about the use of risk assessment in social work due to their predictive limitations as already noted earlier, but also their potential to act as a discriminatory tool, and their potential to shift blame onto the service user, instead of focussing on the service user's needs and the social conditions that frustrate them.

Likewise, Stevens and Hassett (2012) argue that one of the problems of using structured 'tick box' risk assessment tools is that they empty out the space for professional judgement and they fail to accommodate the complexity that is present within ever changing social systems. Such 'tick box' approaches actually belie what goes on in making a professional judgement, whereby the practitioner may deploy a whole host of knowledge, values and norms towards their judgement (Walklate & Mythen, 2011). Rigid and seemingly objective risk assessment tools give the veneer of being reliable and objective, but this is the very thing that renders them weak and unreliable. A study by Wilkins (2015) concluded that risk assessment tools used too quickly can lead to oversimplified assessments that miss some of the complex nuances important to good practice.

Addressing the critiques of risk work

At this point you might think that risk work and risk assessment in social work is toxic, and given its ubiquitous nature in social work be left wondering what to do. Not all risk-focussed practice is necessarily curtailing and dominating of people's lives, choices, circumstances and action. The point is to think critically about the assumptions and implications of risk in social work and moderate some of the effects noted above by bringing different perspectives to a focus on risk. Recent literature suggests adopting strength and empowerment concepts into risk work. For example, recovery-based approaches in mental health encourage certain steps and benefits associated with taking risks as an approach to developing and exercising strengths and a pathway to recovery (Nolan & Quinn, 2012). According to Greene (2007), a risk and resilience approach combined together adopts a person-in-environment perspective, gives a strengths-based approach (including a focus on positive psychology, health and wellness), and has a prevention focus, using evidence to develop effective preventative interventions.

There is also a place for critical and creative thinking as a counterpoint to the instrumental rationality of risk management (de Ugarte & Martin-Aranaga, 2011). In arguing from a critical realist perspective, Houston (2001) proposes an approach to practice that involves systematic attempts to identify and examine the causal mechanisms that operate in the context or environment, but is qualified with a reflexive engagement in our own pre-existing assumptions and beliefs. The example he uses is child protection, where the social worker is encouraged to systematically identify and examine risks that might pose a causal harm to a child, but at the same time being realistic as to how far they can push the notion of causality, and reflexive in their assumptions that will be filtering their notions of risks, safety, childhood, parenting, and so on (Houston, 2001). Thus, risk assessment can be transacted within an approach to critical reflection, and a focus on strengths.

One way to respond to the criticism that risk is narrowly reductionist is to consider concepts that might give it a more holistic focus. Stevens and Hassett (2012) draw on ideas from complexity theory and social geography to outline a framework to risk assessment that avoids pathologising risk as being located in the individual in ways that are blind to the environment or social context. These ideas include:

- Accept that systems are dynamic and self-organising, meaning that phenomena are best seen as containing *emergent properties*, rather than being strictly causal. This claim suggests that it is very hard, if not impossible, to be able to predict the occurrence of events with consistent reliability. The occurrence of events is seen as indicative rather than predictive.

- Adopt non-linear thinking, which means to think of risks as occurring through a complex network of seemingly disconnected phenomena, and that safe environments can be facilitated in ways that might actually involve positive or adaptive risk taking.

- Conceptualise the intersection of space, time and place, which means an analysis towards risk that incorporates a holistic picture of the context, and in doing so, avoids a narrow and reductionist approach to risk assessment that focuses incorrectly on a select number of variables.

Finally, Payne (2011) suggests that one way to turn the deficit and problematic notions attached to risk discourses is to shift the focus to *security* and *resilience*. By security he means not just physical security associated with safety and the ability to exercise choice and control over one's life, but also ontological security, which means 'being able to maintain in our personal identities a thread of meaning and a stable sense of self-identity' (Payne, 2011, p. 11). This is a more positively and optimistically framed way of considering risk work in social work, because it can act as a counterpoint to the problem-focussed epistemology inherent in risk; this may assist the social worker to identify strengths, and may support a more comprehensive risk assessment (Payne, 2011). Thus, the social worker role should work towards creating secure environments that enable people to flourish and grow, and develop control over their lives and the decisions that affect them.

Resilience and protective factors

Resilience

A concept by Payne (2011), expressed earlier in this chapter is resilience, and this concept has received a good deal of attention in public health, the prevention literature, and child and adolescent development research, for example. Resilience is often discussed in the context of debates about risk, given the way that resilience is thought to moderate or buffer risks. But what does it mean to be resilient?

> To be resilient, one must be exposed to risk and then respond successfully. Resilience is a successful adaptational response to high risk. By definition a person who is not exposed to risk cannot be said to be resilient. By definition resilience is measured by an individual adaptational response. (Fraser et al., 1999, p. 137)

Notions of resilience are typically attached to personal characteristics, such as optimistic outlook and problem-solving skills. Unlike risks, which are usually seen as undesirable, resilience in terms of an outcome factor is thought of in desirable terms (Kaplan, 1999). Importantly, Fraser et al. (1999) state that:

> Although resilience is ipso facto an individual response, it is not an individual trait. It is conditioned on both individual and environmental factors. It should not be viewed as one person's heroic or tenacious efforts to overcome disadvantage. Rather it must be viewed ecologically. (p. 138)

Some conceptual clarity is required here. Resilience can be thought of in terms of an *outcome* and a *cause*. How is this possible? Suppose for example that someone experiences an adverse situation and is unaffected by it, then they may be defined as resilient, and hence resilience is seen as an *outcome* of such adversity. If it seen as a cause, then it is thought that someone may possess the qualities of being resilient and this moderates stressful events and produces (causes) overall coping. In this case, resilience *causes* a desirable measure of coping or benefit in the face of difficulty (Kaplan, 1999).

Numerous environmental factors will condition the way that resilience manifests in an individual's specific responses to risks and adversity. Not everyone is equally resilient, and not everyone's resilience is constant. Think of times when you might have felt resilient and bounced back from adversity, and think of times when you did not, or felt your resilience or coping abilities depleted. Part of this shifting in and out of resilience may be due to the changing context or circumstances. Your resilience may depend on the circumstances you find yourself in.

It is important, then, for social workers to work towards fostering an environment that is conducive to building resilience in people, families and communities (Payne, 2011). This would include:

> individual resources and a variety of family, school, and neighbourhood resources that promote positive outcomes directly (compensatory protective factors) or exert a relatively greater positive effect in the presence of elevated risk (buffering protective factors). Thus, the search for factors that promote resilience must always include family, school, neighbourhood, and other influences that promote successful adaptation in the face of adversity. (Payne, 2011, p. 138)

What sorts of factors may be indicative of resilience? In a review of the literature on resilience, Kaplan (1999) identifies a number of factors positively associated with resilience. These include:

> optimism, empathy, insight, intellectual competence, self-esteem, direction or mission, and determination and perseverance. (p. 48)

And also:

> emotional and management skills, interpersonal and social skills, intrapersonal reflective skills, and life skills and problem-solving ability. (p. 48)

A social network and social support, a sense of coherence and stability, as well as quality of parental care and family support are also important to the development of resilience (Kaplan, 1999). At the same time, some forms of adversity, struggle and hardship can function to build resilience as people learn and refine adaptive coping strategies. So, it is not a straightforward proposition to simply try to protect people from risks and difficulties as though that is the pathway to resilience. As mentioned, some risks and their associated challenges can be formative in positive ways.

Protective factors

Protective factors can mean the absence of risk factors, or 'the presence of ameliorative factors, and, as variables that mitigate the effects of risk factors or strengthen ameliorative effects' (Kaplan, 1999, p. 46). Fraser et al. (1999) say that protective factors, like risk factors, purport to 'predict future outcomes' (p. 134) because they operate to ameliorate risks. By this it means that a protective factor can act as something of an antidote or modifier to risks. It should be pointed out that protective factors are subject to the same conceptual and logical causation limitations as risk factors discussed above (Leshner, 1999). A protective factor is not necessarily a direct opposite to a risk factor, but rather exerts a positive influence. For example, family conflict may present as a risk towards physical and mental health, but good social and community connection can be protective of one's physical and mental health overall, even if the family conflict remains in place. If a social worker can identify protective factors in the domain of the person and environment, then they can practice in ways that support the proliferation of protective factors, and design programs and interventions that increase protective factors overall (Fraser et al., 1999).

Working to support protective factors is important, because as Fraser et al. (1999) state, protective factors may contain compensatory protective effects, which 'directly reduce a problem or disorder' (p. 135). For example, quitting smoking and taking up exercise may have a compensatory effect on one's health. There may also be buffering protective effects, which operate in an interactive manner between person and environment over a sustained period. For example, access to a public library and books for young children may be protective in terms of increasing levels of literacy and engagement in school in later years across a whole community.

Conclusion

Notions of risk occupy a significant place in social work. This focus extends beyond social work to include many domains of social and organisational life – governments, organisations, insurance companies, financial institutions and individuals organise much of their activities and thinking around identifying, predicting and managing risk. It is no wonder that it is thought that we live in a risk society (Beck, 1992). There are, of course, many theories of risk and the ones that are relevant to social work pay special attention to the way the risk becomes a form of cultural knowledge, and how risk can operate as a technology of power for the purposes of social regulation. Writers in social work rightly point out that risk assessment technologies are not fail safe and contain inherent limitations. A focus on risk also has the unfortunate side effect of potentially structuring the thinking and practice of social work along narrow, deficit and problem-focussed channels. This is not to say that there are not real and serious risks that beset many people's lives, only that a focus on risk ought to be a site for critical reflection and analysis, and the social worker can introduce a corrective into their perspective through a holistic and strengths-based approach that seeks to identify and leverage the potential of protective factors and building resilience.

Critical thinking questions

1. Define risk and give an example of a risk from a social work context that conforms to your definition.

2. Why has risk become a dominant idea in social work?

3. What are some of the strengths and weaknesses of the risk paradigm in social work?

4. Identify some of the criticisms of the way risk is adopted in social work, and explain how you would address these in your practice?

5. What are the main conceptual differences between resilience and protective factors? What the strengths and limitations of these concepts?

Exercises

Draw up a list of the sorts of risks that potentially impact your life. Organise this list into groups and themes (e.g. health, lifestyle, financial, physical). Now critically examine your list. What risks on your list do you think are shaped by your social, cultural, political and economic context? That is, what on your list is there due to circumstantial or environmental factors? Describe these factors. Now work out what resilience and protective factors (both personal and contextual) need to be in place to moderate those risks?

Further reading

de Ugarte, L. S. & Martin-Aranaga, I. (2011). Social work and risk society: The need for shared social responsibility. *European Journal of Social Work, 14*(4), 447–462. doi:10.1080/13691457.2010.500478.

Green, D. (2007). Risk and social work practice. *Australian Social Work, 60*(4), 395–409. doi:10.1080/03124070701671131.

Marston, G., Moss, J. & Quiggin, J. (Eds). (2010). *Risk, welfare and work.* Carlton, Victoria: Melbourne University Press.

Payne, M. (2011). Risk, security and resilience work in social work practice. *Revista de Asistenta Sociala, 10*(1), 7.

Stanford, S. (2008). Taking a stand or playing it safe?: Resisting the moral conservatism of risk in social work practice. *European Journal of Social Work, 11*(3), 209–220. doi:10.1080/13691450802075063

Links and online resources

Barskey, A. (n.d.) *Risks of risk management.* The New Social Worker. www.socialworker.com/feature-articles/ethics-articles/risks-of-risk-management/

Social Work Policy Institute (n.d.). *Resiliency.* www.socialworkpolicy.org/research/resiliency.html

Stark, R. (n.d.). *Balancing need, risk and rights – A social work perspective.* International Federation of Social Workers. http://ifsw.org/publications/human-rights/the-centrality-of-human-rights-to-social-work/balancing-need-risk-and-rights-a-social-work-perspective/

Webb, S.A. (2006). *Risk.* Social Work and Society: International Online Journal. www.socwork.net/sws/article/view/166/555

4

POWER

Introduction

Why should social workers care about power? Social work generally sees power as a determining factor in disadvantage and inequality. But power is also relational, networked and discursive. Power has been important to social work practice, so social workers need a good analysis of power that can be understood to be an effect of social arrangements and also interpersonal relations. In this chapter we look at power sociologically, but in two ways. First, we examine how power has been understood and developed in social work in the critical theory tradition, mainly in regard to structural and juridical accounts of power. Then, we draw on the work of philosopher Michel Foucault to explain how power is conceptualised in social work along post-structural lines. We will specifically focus on Foucault's theory of governmentality in this respect. The chapter will facilitate ways to understand how power can be viewed in explanatory terms but also as a form of practice. The purpose of this chapter is to outline a way of conceptualising, interrogating and critiquing the operation of power within social and political systems.

Power and why it matters

Doel and Shardlow make the point that power is something that will continually confront social workers:

> … your impact on the day-to-day experience of many individuals, families and their communities is considerable, and you have regular opportunities to confront injustice and to increase people's sense of power. These opportunities are almost always dilemmas too. How far to confront agency policies which disempower? How to sensitize an individual to their own sense of internalized oppression while not adding to that oppression? How to recognize and use your own power in ways that empower others? This is a lifelong quest. (Doel & Shardlow, 2005, p. 216)

Despite its centrality to social work, power is an elusive and at times difficult concept to grasp. Often, we may directly observe the *effects* of power, rather than the operation of power itself. Think, for example, how is it that some people seem to have great influence over decisions, resources and actions. What kind of power permits these actions? Yet, others may feel as though the course of their lives is completely outside of their control. Why is this so? Some forms of power are overt, operating as a force that constrains, dominates, says 'no' and stops things from happening. We may see examples of this exercised by those who hold positions that are attached to authority. Such people may use those positions to exercise decisions that affect others by constraining their actions, stopping the flow of resources, or administering some form of punishment. A good example might be when welfare benefits are cut or removed, and the recipients of such benefits may have little say or choice or control over such actions and experience disempowerment and harm. Social workers may be implicated in this kind of structural power, perhaps by being part of a system that develops and implements such policies and decisions, or alternatively, by being part of campaigns to challenge, critique and resist such decisions in the course of empowerment and advocacy practices. They may implement empowerment and collaborative practices with service users in this respect, to develop and foster the use of power for specific ends.

Although power is commonly thought of in this constraining and restrictive sense, power can also be thought of as productive and enabling, and can operate in subtle ways by being embodied in knowledge, discourse and disciplinary practice. Power makes things happen, makes things possible, and brings knowledge and action into existence (Foucault, 2003). An example here might be how expert power is used to create new categories of person, new diagnoses and new behavioural terminology that is ascribed to certain people or groups, who are said to exhibit certain behaviours or dispositions. Consider, for example, the concept 'sluggish cognitive tempo' (SCT). This is a fairly recent invention that refers to a collection of 'symptoms' that may include:

> ... sluggish; drowsy; daydreams or gets lost in his or her thoughts; apathetic or unmotivated; stares blankly; underactive; slow moving or lacks energy; difficulty following instructions; absent-minded/forgetful; appears tired, lethargic; and seems to be in a world of his or her own. (Penny, Waschbusch, Klein, Corkum & Eskes, 2009, p. 381)

The location of this concept is parked within the research and theories of ADHD in the domain of psychiatry and psychology. It operates as a form of truth and is increasingly taken up in the context of education, where such a diagnosis may be applied to children who are not performing in school (Watabe, Owens, Evans & Brandt, 2014). Hence, knowledge is related to power too. But how can a concept be a repository for power? Although we can think of SCT as an extension of 'psy' discourses generally, we should also know that it holds a materiality in the form of *practices* as well. The power of this concept lies in its establishment, circulation and application as expert knowledge through journals, conferences, professional training, and so on. It moves beyond conceptual or theoretical knowledge as it will permit interventions from drug therapy to behavioural therapy and its status as professional expertise will establish a normative frame of reference by which certain behaviours are to be judged.

Psychiatric discourses about mental illness and how to treat it have a certain 'logic' to them as these discourses and practices contain rules of formation and patterned regularities (Foucault, 1975; Rose, 1996b). For example, the formation of knowledge about mental illness may be based in the scientific method, and a patterned regularity of knowledge might include a classification of problems as being routinely located within the individual in which drug or talking therapies are routinised and normalised. Its reified and normalised status as disciplinary knowledge (truth) is revealed and created through a complex arrangement of institutions (such as universities, hospitals, research centres), medical and psychiatric knowledge (such as research papers, books, websites and technical language), medical research, therapeutic and assessment and intervention practices, and so on (Dean, 1999). There is no one person at the centre of these arrangements. Hence, power is not simply repressive in its structural form, but enabling, productive and integrated and amplified throughout a network of heterogeneous social and economic arrangements.

It is important to see these different forms of power sketched out above as interacting in complex ways, rather than to see them as oppositional binaries. Power may be vested in certain positions and decision-makers and their structural location, and it may also, at the same time, manifest in forms of knowledge and discourse developed within ordinary mundane practices. Hence, power is relational. Hugman (1991) contends that power can be conceived of in terms of its interpersonal and interactional attributes, and that power exists in social action and social relationships. Therefore, there is no escaping the context and operation of power in practice, and it is for this reason that social workers need a variety of analytical frames to understand, critique, respond to and use power in their practice.

Social work, critical theory and power

Much of social work's theory of power adopts a structural analysis of the ways people are privileged (or not) by class, gender, race, able-bodiedness, sexuality, and religion, for example (Mullaly, 1997). This analysis is central to an anti-oppressive or anti-racist practice and the critical social work tradition. It is argued along these lines that patterns of inequality lead to social divisions and conflict and differential and unequal distribution of resources, power, opportunity, status, and so on (Thompson, 2006, p. 33). Along these lines, power is implicated as a resource people compete for. Accordingly, social inequality is not simply an accident, but is produced and reproduced within the social and political ideas and structures that justify and support inequality as normal and inevitable. Thompson takes a structural view of power, and in this view, contends that power is central in the existence and maintenance of inequality, discrimination and oppression. Writing on social work ethics, McAuliffe (2014) adopts this theory to argue that ethical practice means 'understanding issues of structural power and oppression and the philosophical arguments that are used to support inequality, injustice and the unfair distributions of resources' (p. 24). Likewise, Healy notes the link between power and critical social work as follows:

> In its broadest sense, critical social work is concerned with the analysis and transformation of power relations at every level of social work practice. (Healy, 2014, p. 183)

For Healy, one of the key claims of critical social work and anti-oppressive practice is that 'oppression arises from unequal power across social divisions' (Healy, 2014, p. 192). In this sense, power is something that is unevenly distributed and accessed to the benefit of some groups and individuals at the expense and cost to others. It is apparent, then, that the critical tradition in social work is concerned with an analysis of power, and critical practice involving steps to transform the deleterious effects of repressive power. This forms a good deal of the moral purpose of social work practice overall (Connolly & Harms, 2012; Healy, 2014).

Juridical power

Thinking about power as structural and repressive is to conceptualise it in juridical terms. Juridical power, typically associated with law and legal jurisprudence, was historically exercised by monarchs in the form of absolute rule through force (sometimes violent) over subjects, lands and territories. Juridical power is a power over life and is based in deduction; that is, the wielding of power is to constrain, or take something away – for example, to remove someone's liberty or life (Foucault, 1978).

This juridical notion of power is a fairly common-sense experience of power that many people would recognise. It is generally the case that juridical power operates as a tool for social order and control, and so it is tolerated up to a point. We might not object too much to having certain liberties removed or constrained so long as the exercise of juridical power by ruling entities and systems is fair or just. But it is not always fair or just. Thus, the means for dealing with this has been the creation of a juridical system incorporating checks and balances in the form of formal separations of power. This is why it is important to argue and advocate for legal and political checks and balances to constrain any instance of unfair or unjust use of this kind of power, or to distribute power more fairly (Heywood, 2000). Critical theory contends that quite often the use of power is repressive, and is neither fair nor just because its exercise through institutional, policy or interpersonal methods contributes to the disempowerment, oppression and disadvantage of many. Let's take a look at this theory of power in more detail.

Foucault on juridical power

Philosopher Michel Foucault, whose theories around power have been very influential in the social sciences and social work, considers juridical power to largely entail prohibitions and punishments, or some kind of 'subtraction mechanism' used to appropriate something from someone:

> ... power was exercised mainly as a means of deduction...a subtraction mechanism, a right to appropriate a proportion of the wealth, a tax of products, goods and services, labour and blood, levied on the subjects. Power in this instance was essentially a right of seizure: of things, time, bodies, and ultimately life itself; it culminated in the privilege to seize hold of life in order to suppress it. (Foucault, 1978, p. 136)

This use of power is exercised *over* people – we may experience it as a loss or limitation, and perhaps reasonably describe it using terms such as domination and oppression. If we assume that society is hierarchical, then juridical power is often defined as being 'top-down' because its directionality is administered from official institutions, or governmental institutions, such as laws and the instruments of administering the rule of law. The term 'managerialism' in social work literature sometimes points to a situation of 'top down' juridical abuses of power in institutions. In its extreme form, this kind of juridical power includes violence, as Foucault notes:

> Law cannot help but be armed, and its arm, *par excellence*, is death; to those who transgress it, it replies, at least as a last resort, with absolute menace. The law always refers to the sword. (Foucault, 1978, p. 144, original italics)

It is because of this situation that juridical power is seen as a quantifiable tangible thing, because it operates as a form of subtraction. Power in this sense is seen as a scarce resource that is distributed unevenly, and begs questions such as:

- Who has power, and who does not?

- How can we transfer more power to the powerless, and how can power be shared?

- How can we constrain the worst effects of repressive, structural power – its abuses and misuses?

These kinds of question take a juridical notion of power, and assume that it is a quantifiable force that can be cornered, seized, shared, or redistributed. In summary, juridical power is defined by Foucault (1978) along the following lines:

- *Negative and constraining* – power is used as a force that says no.

- *Applications of rules* – power is translated into law.

- *Prohibition* – power requires renunciation of life's pleasures, which requires the human subject to disappear.

- *Censorship* – silencing, denying and rendering of something invisible.

- *Apparatus* – power is uniformly exercised in a top-down manner.

Structural analysis

This kind of structural power analysis in the juridical sense is important for social work for at least two reasons. First, it provides the social worker with an analysis of the operation of power in juridical terms, meaning that the social worker can identify instances of repressive and constraining power and how this impacts negatively on people. The exercise of this kind of power may be patterned and deeply integrated into the organisation of society – its legal frameworks, business models, rules, policies, economic models, hierarchies and patterns of privilege, and so on (Flyvbjerg, 1998). Together, this refers to social, political, and economic *structures*, which serve as a kind of framework within which a whole host of social practices, routines and habits are transacted and replicated. The social worker can examine decisions, policies, actions and practices that monopolise the use of power, abuse it, or examine patterns and experiences of disempowerment. They ought to include their own actions and positionality in this analysis too, as a form of critical reflection on their implication in the arrangement of structural power.

Second, it provides the social worker a focal point for channelling their energy and strategies to bring about change, which might include various forms of activism, empowerment and advocacy. For example, McAuliffe (2014) links an analysis of power to the practices of empowerment and advocacy, and these are seen as important strategies for seeking after human rights and social justice. Power is a concept that is central to empowerment and advocacy theories generally, which are sometimes incorporated within critical theories (Payne, 2014), because 'empowerment and advocacy are both concerned with a shift of power or emphasis towards meeting the needs and rights of people who would otherwise be marginalised or oppressed' (Leadbetter, 2002, p. 201).

These interventions briefly noted here seek to intervene upon and transform power relations, and are focussed towards the socio-political organisation of society, interpersonal relations, people's individual experiences – experiences that may manifest as instances of oppression, injustice, discrimination, hardship and disadvantage (Connolly & Harms, 2012; Healy, 2014; Mendes, 2009b; Payne, 2014).

Social work, post-structural theory and power

Structural and juridical power discussed above is not the only theory of power incorporated into critical social work theories (Pease & Fook, 1999a). The role of governmental power and knowledge in a post-structural sense is often acknowledged by critical theorists in social work through a consideration of the role of discourse (often referred to as *dominant discourses*) in shaping social thought and material reality (Healy, 2014). There are different variants to the post-structural theme in critical theory, but we focus specifically on what is termed 'governmentality'.

Governmentality

Governmentality was a theoretical concept originally advanced by philosopher Michel Foucault (Dean, 1999; Foucault, 1991, 2007; Foucault, Miller, Burchell & Gordon, 1991; Gordon, 1991). Since Foucault, this idea has been extensively debated and developed further, and you will have no trouble locating further reading on the theory of governmentality in the social sciences and social policy (for example, Dean, 1999; Hook, 2004b; Marston & McDonald, 2006).

This concept represents Foucault's attempt to chart the history of the development of power in modernity that did not rely on juridical or sovereign notions of power only. Without denying the existence of juridical power, Foucault (1978) rejects this restrictive and repressive conceptualisation of power as being too limited to fully comprehend power in the context of modernity and neoliberal societies. This is not to deny juridical power, but to extend the analysis to consider neoliberalism as an ideological, discursive and practical repository for enabling a productive expression of power concerned with *life*, such as power regarding statistics, scores, means and averages, and norms. Consider this statement from Foucault:

> But a power whose task is to take charge of life needs continuous regulatory and corrective mechanisms. It is no longer a matter of bringing death into play in the field of sovereignty, but of distributing the living in the domain of value and utility. Such a power has to qualify, measure, appraise, and hierarchize, rather than display itself in its murderous splendour; it does not have to draw the line that separates the enemies of the sovereign from his obedient subjects; it effects distributions around the norm. … A normalizing society is the historical outcome of a technology of power centred over life. (Foucault, 1978, p. 144)

Notice in this passage the focus on power is that which qualifies, appraises, measures and establishes norms. At first glance we would hardly associate these seemingly benign practices with being oppressive. However, recall the example of SCT earlier in this chapter. Extending the analysis along Foucault's governmental argument means we can pinpoint ways that power is used to elicit conduct, to render things like SCT into existence, to bring forth a raft of normalising and intervening practices for the management of individual conduct. This is not strictly a repressive form of power, but an enabling and productive one. We have used the example of SCT, but consider the way that power can bring all kinds of things into existence that might include a range of subject positions: drug addict, perpetrator, at-risk, mentally ill, criminal, delinquent, victim, at-risk, to name a few.

Governmentality defined

What do theorists of governmentality point to when they outline a conceptual basis of governmental power? According to Rose and Miller, governmentality refers to:

> [t]he proliferation of a whole range of apparatuses pertaining to government and a complex body of knowledges and 'know-how' about government, the means of its exercise and the nature of those over whom it was to be exercised. (Rose & Miller, 1992, p. 174)

Notice how Rose and Miller refer to 'government' in this definition, but this definition is not to be restricted to mean things like political parties, legislation and policy, for that would be to reduce government to its juridical form. Governing is far more complex. Although the following quote by Mitchell Dean is long, we would like you to consider the very broad elements of government and governing described within, as these are important to understanding governmental power. According to Dean, instead of thinking about government in narrowly institutional terms, an understanding of government should be:

> ... approached, rather, as an inventive, strategic, technical and artful set of 'assemblages' fashioned from diverse elements, put together in novel and specific ways, and rationalised in relation to specific governmental objectives and goals. These assemblages comprise a whole host of mundane and humble practices, techniques and forms of practical knowledge which are often overlooked in analyses that concentrate on either political institutions or political thought. These might include: forms of practical know-how, from managerial doctrines of 'total quality management' to recipe books for 'entrepreneurial government'; intellectual tools, such as the flowchart, the map, and the architectural or engineering plan; calculative technologies, from the budget and the statistical table to sophisticated forms of the audit and cost

accounting; modes of evaluating human, natural and financial resources, in terms of entities such as risk, profit, probability and danger; ways of knowing, training and regulating various agents, from those in positions of authority, such as politicians and bureaucrats, to those whose own self-government is thought to pose problems for the exercise of authority, such as the gay community, Aboriginal populations or even the long-term unemployed. (Dean, 1998, p. 8)

This is a very detailed and specific account of government that moves the concept well beyond seeing it as simply the institutional mechanisms of the state. These various practices of government are not fixed as they undergo continual revision and inventiveness. Rose (2000) explains that advanced liberal democracies (as he terms them) are undergoing an explosion in the breadth and depth of governmental controlling and enabling functions that are 'designed in' (p. 325) to things like notions of citizenship, formation of identity, prudentialism, and the methods and circuits of security. Risk management is a good example of this developing rationality and practice (see Chapter 3). So, a theory and practice of risk can be seen as a formation of governmental power.

Conduct of conduct

For governmentality theorists, governing is a *social practice* concerned with the 'conduct of conduct' (Dean, 1998). 'Conduct of conduct' means practices of self-government of one's thought and action, and also the specific ways in which conduct of others is managed, controlled and elicited (Foucault, 2007), even in the name of things like freedom, responsibility and self-determination. 'Conduct of conduct' refers to the practice of guidance *and* the action/behaviour being guided (Dean, 1998, 1999). For example, willingly subjecting oneself to a diet and exercise regime under the tutelage of a trainer is an example of the conduct of conduct. Counselling, therapy, case management, and so on can be considered examples of the conduct of conduct, because they concern the specific regulated and self-guided actions of the social worker *and* service users actions that are produced within a normative rationality of what is considered acceptable, empowering and responsible conduct.

Discipline

It should be apparent that governing and governmental power involves a set of *ordinary* practices that are diffused throughout social relations, institutions, and so on. Rather than being power 'out there', governmental power contains many faces and is situated *internal* to society. It includes things like pastoral care of parents in relation to children, teachers in relation to students, priests in relation to congregations, and so on (Foucault, 2007). As mentioned, this is not to dis-place or ignore the role of juridical power. The principle of sovereignty operates in terms of its juridical functions (Foucault, 2007), and governmental power becomes a conditioning and nuancing mechanism through which the manage-ment of population can be achieved via discipline:

> ... discipline was never more important or more valued than when the attempt was made to manage the population: managing the population does not mean just man-aging the collective mass of phenomena, or managing them at the level of their overall results; managing the population means managing it at depth, in all its fine points and details. (Foucault, 2007, p. 107)

Foucault states that discipline involves managing individuals and populations through intricate interventions that are specified according to developed and coherent accounts of problems and the social and scientific theories that sup-port them. This means that various disciplines such as psychology, health pro-motion, criminal justice and social work may deploy disciplining strategies and interventions at various networked points in the social system. To effectively manage and regulate the conduct of a population means to sharpen and extend sovereign and disciplinary powers using ever increasing sophisticated mecha-nisms and practices, and the circulation of relatively coherent rationalities, dis-courses and systems of thought, upon which governmental power gains legitimacy as common sense (Foucault, 2007). These include theories about human behaviour and social problems, programs of research, service models, intervention tools, case files and records, surveillance and reporting systems, and routine practices such as the home visit, the clinic and the assessment tool. Governing and the exercise of power takes as its object the detailed minutiae of society and its inner workings as sites for the deployment of strategies and tac-tics of power (Dean, 1999, 2006). It is a mistake to assume that these strategies are rooted purely in an economic logic or economic rationality; they are also the necessary means of coming to *know and intervene in* the problems posed by population, and in this sense, the strategies of managing people and their con-duct at the very same time produce knowledge on and about the population and the best methods of managing it (Foucault, 1988).

Dispositif – more than language shaping knowledge

One of the problems in some of the critical social work writing is the reduction of Foucault's use of the term *discourse* to language (Garrity, 2010). This creates the illusion that power in the Foucaultian post-structural discursive sense is about words, narratives, phrases, concepts, meaning and language games (Gar-rity, 2010). It is important to consider discourse in terms of its effects, what it permits, makes possible and the *material* traces it leaves. Discourse does not emanate as a form of meaning from a speaking subject, but rather is constitutive of it. Hence, there is a materiality associated with governmental power, which incites the establishment of *'apparatuses of security'* (Dean, 1999, p. 20, original italics). These apparatuses, sometimes referred to as *dispositif,* include a complex network of 'discourses, institutions, architectural arrangements, policy decisions, laws, administrative measures, scientific statements, philosophic, moral and philanthropic propositions' (Foucault, 1980a, p. 194). These are components of material culture in a regulation society, as Bailey (2013) explains:

> Micro-dispositifs, such as individual prisons, asylums, social enterprises...are thus conceived as material-discursive articulations of power, that is, they are material conduits through which 'invisible' channels of power find traction – they constitute the material expression of power relations. (p. 812)

An apparatus of security forms out of the problems of government and out of the crises and problems facing government (Rabinow & Rose, 2003). These problems may be financial, environmental, security, or health and welfare problems, and in turn, these are dealt with by things such as police, methods of surveillance and intelligence, as well as structures put in place for dealing with health and social welfare (Bailey, 2013; Hook, 2004a) including social work. What transpires are a diverse range of practices that are concerned with 'the regulation of populations and individuals and the psychological, biological, sociological and economic processes that constitute them' (Dean, 1999, p. 210). Hence, as Garrity states:

> It is in this sense that discourse can be thought of as a *practice*; discourse crosses the theory-praxis divide by understanding (discursive) knowledge as a social practice – as doing something. (Garrity, 2010, p. 202, original italics)

Garrity continues:

> Thus discursive formations are groups of statements, and as statements are functions, that is, they do something, discourse can be thought of as a practice. (Garrity, 2010, p. 202)

Knowledge, truth and rationality

It should be clear by now that knowledge, truth and rationality are forms of power. Not all power and regulation are driven by legal and juridical instruments because 'the ends of government cannot be effectively achieved by means of law' (Foucault, 2007, p. 99). Without the rule of law (or indeed, rule by force) power is incited to 'knowledge of things' (Foucault, 2007, p. 100), and knowledge manifests in regimes of truth and practice (Hook, 2004a). Lemke explains:

The concept of governmentality demonstrates Foucault's working hypothesis on the reciprocal constitution of power techniques and forms of knowledge. The semantic linking of governing ('gouvener') and modes of thought ('mentalité') indicates that it is not possible to study the technologies of power without an analysis of the political rationality underpinning them. (Lemke, 2001, p. 191)

These mentalities or political rationalities are the taken-for-granted 'truths' utilised in any strategy of power (Rose & Miller, 1992). Power cannot function without knowledge and truth, and this knowledge must be put into circulation if it is to be effective (Foucault, 2003). How is this knowledge produced? By a range of ongoing practices that inspect, record, communicate, analyse, verify, observe, invent and organise concepts, theorise, and so on. In this way, Foucault couples power with discourses and the production of truth by saying 'there can be no possible exercise of power without a certain economy of discourses of truth which operate and on the basis of this association. We are subjected to the production of truth through power' (Foucault, 1980b, p. 93). Power is circulated through a net or web of relationships and practices and brought into existence through action, and this power constructs what we know about people: 'the individual is an effect of power, and at the same time, or precisely to the extent to which it is that effect, it is the element of its articulation. The individual which power has constituted is at the same time its vehicle' (Foucault, 1980b, p. 98).

Power and resistance

To summarise so far, Foucault (1978, pp. 94–96) advances a number of propositions that conceptualise power in terms of its productive, relational and ever present properties:

- Power is not a possession; it comes into existence by being exercised.
- Power is not merely a structural phenomenon that limits; it has productive capacities too.
- Power operates from below.
- Power is used with specific aims and intent; but the bearers of these aims are often anonymous and non-identifiable.
- Power is relational and exists in tandem with resistance. Resistance is not unified, but plural.

This is a pervasive and heterogeneous notion of power. However, its subtlety and hidden nature is what gives it its potency. Foucault explains:

Let me offer a general and tactical reason that seems self-evident: power is tolerable only on condition that it mask a substantial part of itself. Its success is proportional to its ability to hide its own mechanisms. (1978, p. 86)

In other words, the repressive and visible elements of juridical power are relatively easy to identify and point to. The invisible, masked and productive elements of power are pernicious because their mechanisms are largely rendered invisible. Instead of thinking about power as the occasional overt act of juridical force, for Foucault, power is everywhere and is woven through the fabric of everyday life (Foucault, 1978, p. 93). This is thought to present something of a problem for those who may wish to engage in practices of resistance. How can one resist something that is ever-present, and hard to detect? It is not so much the case that resistances must always be forced into place, for as Foucault states, there is a relationship between power and resistance (O'Farrell, 2005). Power and resistance exist together already in a necessary connection. That is to say, where there is power there is resistance, even though there is considerable variability in the degree to which resistance may be applied. Sometimes resistance is difficult, because governmental power may involve a well-rehearsed and established set of routines and practices that give power a more fixed and rigid formation (Oksala, 2007). As O'Farrell (2005) states, if freedom to resist is 'closed down through violence or slavery, then it is no longer a question of a relationship of power but of its limits' (p. 99).

Analysing and studying power: a post-structural perspective

One way to consider resistance is to begin with a form of analysis, which seeks to unearth or bring to sharper focus, the operations of power in all its multiplicity. What sort of analysis? We could start by looking at powers:

... external face, at the point where it relates directly and immediately to what we might, very provisionally, call its object, its target, its field of application, or, in other words, the places where it implants itself and produces real effects. (Foucault, 2003, p. 28)

Although we might identify power as force that is wielded by a group, or person, over another, we should also attempt to grasp the idea that power is something that 'functions' and 'circulates' through 'networks' (Foucault, 2003, p. 29). As Foucault (2003) states, 'power passes through individuals. It is not applied to them' (p. 29). Following this line, we can analyse power by examining the ways it is expressed in relationships, within networks, and how it manifests as forms of knowledge.

For example, if we accept that disciplinary power is not based simply in legal right, but instead is 'clinical knowledge' (Foucault, 2003, p. 39) such as knowledge of the human psyche, then the analysis might involve unpacking the basis of this clinical knowledge – its vocabularies, formations, practices and rationalities. This can provide insight into how power works to produce certain clinical, pathological and problematic subjectivities, which in turn can be contested, rejected or redefined (Foucault, 2003, p. 46). For example, people can reject the labels given to them; they can refuse to speak when speaking is demanded of them; they can fudge answers on a questionnaire; they can redefine or appropriate concepts and ideas to mean different things; and they can exercise agency and choose to live in ways that challenge or upset the norms that seek to define them. A practice of resistance here might involve '… contesting normalizing power by shaping oneself and one's lifestyle creatively: by exploring opportunities for new ways of being, new fields of experience, pleasures, relationships, modes of living and thinking' (Oksala, 2007, p. 99).

Problematisation

Foucault's analysis encourages an investigation into the application of power towards understanding how knowledge of the human subject is made, how it is drawn into existence, and effectively, how it is *produced* (Oksala, 2007). As mentioned, once we consider the formation of subjectivity as an effect of power, we can start to question seemingly natural categories, labels and various other concepts and terms attributed to people. An example might be to take a label such as NEET (Not in Education Training or Employment), which can be used to classify some groups of young people, and examine it critically. Doing so involves a form of critical questioning and scepticism, to denaturalise and problematise taken-for-granted constructions masquerading as truths (see Chapter 15, critical reflection, this volume). Things are not fixed and determinate; rather, they are subject to rejection, reformation and alteration.

Critically examining and reflecting on this form of power means to identify and examine reasons given for things. Oksala (2007) explains that governmental power requires *reasons* and a coherent rationality to justify its existence and acceptability, and these reasons can always be questioned and problematised. This should take the form of a sustained critique of rationality, as explained by Oksala:

> The political critique that Foucault advocates is thus not reducible to passing judgements. We must question our practices of governing as well as the terms and categories – the evaluative framework – through which political judgements are formulated. (2007, p. 86)

Instead of a critique that involves pointing out what is wrong, this form of criticism means examining the givens, assumptions, truths, concepts and beliefs that often sit unarticulated and uncontested. It means to trace and unmask their effects in governmental power, how they subjugate, categorise, order, regulate and normalise (Foote & Frank, 1999; Oksala, 2007).

Conclusion

This chapter has discussed structural and post-structural theories of power and situated them in the context of critical theory in social work. The intention of this chapter is to distinguish these theoretical orientations, to bring forth the analytical power of both. The ideas presented here are intended to provide some conceptual tools that might aid in the identification, analysis and practices of working with and responding to the complex nature of power.

Much of the critical writing in social work traverses between structural and post-structural perspectives on power. Trying to untangle the different theoretical threads about power in the critical social work literature is challenging (Garrity, 2010). According to McBeath and Webb (2005), there is a conflation of these theoretical orientations, and this conflation is actually a problem because mixing structural and post-structural theoretical accounts together weakens the theoretical power of either position, so we need to be clear about what analysis is being used for what purpose.

McBeath and Webb (2005) state that structural variants of critical theory understate the post-structural Foucaultian contention that there is 'no outside of power'. This means that social workers may be quick to (incorrectly) externalise the locus and effects of power as somehow 'out there'. Rather, power is everywhere, and social workers are implicated in its circulation, effects and exchanges. For example, a term like 'at-risk', at once designated as a signifier to render assistance, can be co-opted as a tool of control, to label and regulate behaviour. So, even the conceptual vocabularies of social work are infused with power that may be deployed in different ways and with different effects (Rojek, Collins & Peacock, 1988).

Furthermore, theories that emphasise a structural and juridical account of power have a tendency to conceptualise power as a totality – a heavy, fixed and largely inflexible force that weighs down on people from above (McBeath & Webb, 2005). Power should be seen as fluid, flexible and comprised of a diverse multitude of strategies and practices. Power comes from below, and power and resistance are present together.

Finally, some of the language used in structural accounts of power actually work against an effective problematisation of power and its effects. McBeath and Webb (2005) argue that some forms of critical theory tend to place the inner workings of power in a 'black box' by using very general and abstract concepts such as bureaucracy, managerialism, oppression and authoritarianism to describe power. This gives a language for criticism, but in effect these are little more than tropes that fail to open up the 'black box' to expose the inner workings of power in all its sophistication, variability, and to identify what Foucault calls the 'micro-physics of power'. Identifying the micro-physics of power will constitute a more nuanced form of critical reflection and analysis for social work.

Critical thinking questions

1. Why is understanding power important for social work theory and practice?

2. What are the main differences between juridical and governmental power?

3. What sorts of everyday examples do you think best illustrate juridical power?

4. What sorts of everyday examples do you think best illustrate governmental power?

5. Foucault states that power is most effective when its mechanisms are hidden. What does this mean, and can you think of an example of power that is pervasive yet its mechanisms remain largely hidden?

Exercises

In your own words, define power. Think of an everyday example that best illustrates your definition. Then, work out what theory of power discussed in this chapter is most applicable to your definition. In what way does your definition and theory of power help you to identify, analyse and critique the operation of power in your example? Using your definition and theory, how might a social worker respond to the operation of power in your example?

Further reading

Dean, M. (1999). *Governmentality: Power and rule in modern society*. London, UK; Thousand Oaks, CA: SAGE.

Garrity, Z. (2010). Discourse analysis, Foucault and social work research: Identifying some methodological complexities. *Journal of Social Work, 10*(2), 193–210. doi:10.1177/1468017310363641

Healy, K. (2014). *Social work theories in context: Creating frameworks for practice* (2nd ed.). Houndmills, Basingstoke, UK; New York, NY: Palgrave Macmillan.

McBeath, G. & Webb, S. (2005). Post-critical social work analytics. In S. Hick, J. Fook & R. Pozzuto (Eds.), *Social work: A critical turn* (pp. 167–186). Toronto, ON: Thompson Educational Publishing, Inc.

Mullaly, R. P. (1997). *Structural social work: Ideology, theory, and practice* (2nd ed.). Toronto, ON; New York, NY: Oxford University Press.

Links and online resources

Allen, A. (2016). *Feminist perspectives on power.* The Stanford Encyclopaedia of Philosophy. Edward N. Zalta (Ed.) http://plato.stanford.edu/archives/fall2016/entries/feminist-power

Kelly, M. (n.d.) *Michel Foucault: Political thought.* Internet Encyclopaedia of Philosophy. www.iep.utm.edu/fouc-pol/

Sørensen, M. K. (2014). *Foucault on power relations.* www.irenees.net/bdf_fiche-notions-242_en.html

5

POVERTY AND DISADVANTAGE

Introduction

It is life that has taught us that an injury to one is an injury to all, and that in the face of these injuries our only weapon is our solidarity.

We are injured when government, on behalf of the rich, steals from the poor. We are injured when unemployment are blamed on the individual instead of fixed by the government. We are injured when instead of a Jobs Plan we're served up a putting-the-boot-into-the-unemployed-plan.

We are injured when universal healthcare is hammered, when public education is attacked, when TAFE is undermined, when universities are deregulated. We are injured when the public sector is dismembered and the common good is wrecked, when people are forced into poverty, compelled to rely on charity when all they long for is justice. We are injured when the maximisation of profits take priority over the rights of workers, including the residualised and discarded, the unpaid, the low-paid, the underemployed and the unemployed.

We have only one enemy. It is called inequality. (John Falzon, quoted in Australian Council of Social Services, 2015, p. 5)
Reproduced with kind permission from The Australian Council of Social Services.

These powerful words by Dr John Falzon, CEO of The Australian Council of Social Services, reminds us that poverty, inequality and disadvantage are structural, moral and political issues, inasmuch as they point to suffering and hardship. Poverty is a problem because it is linked to deprivation and exclusion, and poverty is typically a marker of unacceptable levels of inequality that requires action (Alcock, 2006). Further, entrenched poverty is something that arises out of a deficient social and economic system, because even within wealthy and prosperous nations, poverty may be created and sustained through various social and economic policies and ideologies (Alcock, 2006). Hence, poverty is a moral and political issue. It is a moral issue because it is bound up within judgements about poverty being wrong and something undesirable, and it is political because of the way that the social and economic order in prosperous nations actually creates the conditions for poverty to grow.

Social work has a long tradition of working with poverty and disadvantage in case practice, group work, community development and social activism. In fact, what has historically set social work apart from other helping professions is its focus on addressing both the conditions and consequences of various forms of social, political, economic and other disadvantage. The terms poverty and disadvantage, however commonplace they may be, are not without complications. The chapter will explain what poverty means and give an overview of the extent, scope and theories of poverty. For space reasons we restrict our discussion to poverty in advanced economies and relatively wealthy nations, such as Australia, the United States and the United Kingdom. This should not detract from the very real and serious nature of poverty across the world, particularly in the developing south (Chossudovsky, 2003). The chapter then explains disadvantage and locates the role of social work in responding to poverty and disadvantage.

The meaning of poverty

Saunders (2005) makes an important point that stories of people's lived experiences of poverty add an important but often neglected dimension to much poverty research, the latter of which is typically presented in the form of numbers and statistics. It is very important to listen to people's lived experiences and viewpoints about poverty in order to grasp its meaning and significance (Saunders, 2005). The reason for this is because poverty is dynamic – it changes as people may go in and out of poverty, and people are differentially affected by it across different points in the lifecycle (Alcock, 2006). For example, some people may experience an isolated incidence of poverty, yet others may find that poverty and disadvantage is a life-long experience (McLachlan, Gilfillan & Gordon, 2013).

Accordingly, we begin the chapter by eliciting stories of the experience of poverty. We would like you to exercise your imagination as you seek to try and understand these stories from the perspective of the people telling them.

My name is Isaac. Until 2012, I worked six days a week and had a stable home. However, a vicious, unprovoked attack left me for dead, and after a week in a coma I have lived with severe physical disability. I was initially granted Newstart [unemployment benefits], but that was not enough to pay my rent. I moved into a shed and did maintenance work in exchange for board. However, the property owner wanted more work than I could do and I was kicked out. Unable to find secure accommodation, I put my things into storage, and tried couch-surfing with friends. Although I paid them money for food and expenses, it couldn't last long

▶

and I ended up on the street. In a very short space of time, and through no fault of my own, I had gone from having a job and a home to sleeping on cardboard boxes and washing my face in a creek or at a public tap. Sleeping rough was really hard and exacerbated my injuries. Things were particularly hard when all my belongings were stolen in winter, including my swag and warm clothes. (Quoted in, St Vincent de Paul Society, 2015, p. 9)

Reproduced with kind permission from the St Vincent de Paul Society.

Notice in this example that the catalyst for Isaac's experience was not of his doing. Notice also how Isaac's experience was compounded and exacerbated by a series of events that concentrated together. The following story runs a similar theme.

I am a hard worker and always earned and paid taxes. Occasionally I have had to rely on a Centrelink [social security] payment when work has been inconsistent. My story began when I went from my home in Queensland to Darwin to visit my son and his pregnant and very ill wife. I informed Centrelink of the temporary change of address and that I would only stay for a few weeks. Because I was in Darwin for five and not four weeks, Centrelink put me onto the income management scheme. What happened next was the worst nightmare of my life! The day before I was returning to Queensland, I went to Centrelink and asked for money to be put in my bank account to cover petrol. It took two hours and I was only given half what I needed. I told them I was driving to Queensland alone and wanted emergency money in case of breakdown or other repairs. The response was 'just wave down a Grey Nomad, they will help you'. When I arrived back on the Sunshine Coast I continued to appeal to Centrelink to release me from income management as it was badly hindering my life. I was informed I would remain on it for 13 weeks. I had no choice but to live in a tent in a caravan park, which cost $275 per week. This was a terrible situation and not sustainable. It was very hot, with the temperature around 37 degrees. I couldn't believe my life had become this. Employers looked twice when I said I lived in a caravan park. I couldn't get a rental property when agents saw I was income managed, so it was a catch-22. Being income managed made it appear that I couldn't look after myself and must be so irresponsible that the government had to do it for me. After daily stressful arguments with the income management department and the turn that my life had taken now, my doctor prescribed me anti-depressants. I had begun thinking about suicide as I felt so low, and my car was about to become my home. I was jobless and homeless. (Quoted in, St Vincent de Paul Society, 2015, p. 12)

Reproduced with kind permission from the St Vincent de Paul Society.

In this example the very systems designed to help this person actually conspired to make things worse. Hence, social workers need to be mindful that their actions do not compound the experience of poverty, a point we return to later in this chapter. These examples are important, as they illustrate some of the themes and points we discuss later in this chapter.

The scope and extent of poverty

The earlier section provides some insight into the experience of poverty, but this experience is represented on a mass scale. In the United Kingdom, it is estimated that 'around 13 million people are in poverty' (Cooper & Dumpleton, 2013, p. 4) and 'over 500,000 people are reliant on food aid' (Cooper & Dumpleton, 2013, p. 3). It is reported that 'More than half a million children in the UK are now living in families who are unable to provide a minimally acceptable diet' (Cooper, Purcell & Jackson, 2014, p. 8). Children in particular can bear the brunt of poverty, a situation that they are neither responsible for, nor one they can influence particularly (O'Brien, 2013). Furthermore, the deleterious effects of poverty on children can linger later in life, in terms of health and educational problems, with low socio-economic status being a key social determinant of ill-health. Poverty negatively disrupts the parental role, as the 'non-stop grind of dealing with poverty inhibits them [parents] from finding the time to prevent problems from slowly accumulating' (Saunders, 2005, p. 125).

The scope of poverty in the United Kingdom is reportedly extensive. Data produced by the Poverty and Social Exclusion research project in the United Kingdom reveals the following:

- Over 30 million people (almost half the population) are suffering some degree of financial insecurity.
- Almost 18 million in the United Kingdom today cannot afford adequate housing conditions.
- Roughly 14 million cannot afford one or more essential household goods.
- Almost 12 million people are too poor to engage in common social activities considered necessary by the majority of the population.
- About 5.5 million adults go without essential clothing.
- Around 4 million children and adults are not properly fed by today's standards.
- About 4 million children go without at least two of the things they need.
- Around 2.5 million children live in homes that are damp.
- Around 1.5 million children live in households that cannot afford to heat their home (Gordon et al., 2013, p. 2).

This data is based on a comparison between what the general population consider to be *minimum* living standards compared with what actually exists for many people. In this sense, the report notes that 'the number of people falling below the minimum standards of the day has doubled since 1983' (Gordon et al., 2013, p. 2). This is actually a concern given that the same report noted that –

within the context of a harsh economic climate – the general population has actually *lowered* its perceptions of what they consider to be life's necessities and minimum standards for living in the United Kingdom. For example:

> ... in <u>all</u> previous surveys over the last thirty years, being able to afford to give presents to family and friends once a year (such as on birthdays or at Christmas) was considered to be a necessity by the majority of people. In 2012, the majority of people no longer believe this is a necessity. The minimum expectations of the population have fallen. (Gordon et al., 2013, p. 6, underlined in the original)

And ...

> In the more constrained economic conditions of 2012, the public have adjusted their views of what constitutes a minimum living standard. This reflects the wider mood of austerity and pessimism – in a year when many households both were poorer and felt poorer than a few years before. (Gordon et al., 2013, p. 6)

In many surveys of minimum living standards, top essential items are typically listed as food, clothing, shelter and health care (Australian Council of Social Services, 2014). An inability to access these essential items is a measure of hardship as it describes what people are deprived of within a context that would at the same time define these things to be essential (Australian Council of Social Services, 2014).

Poverty tends to be patterned along particular demographic lines. In Australia, disadvantage and poverty are concentrated among 'people who are locked out of the jobs market, single parents, women and children, people with disabilities, the old, the young, Aboriginal and Torres Strait Island people, and migrants' (Australian Council of Social Services, 2014, p. 5). People who are reliant on social security incomes are most vulnerable, particularly those unemployed or living in a household where the main income earner(s) are unemployed (Australian Council of Social Services, 2014). Data from 2012 reveal that in Australia '2.25 million people (13.9% of all people) were living below the poverty line, after taking in account of their housing costs' and 'one in seven people, including one in six children, lived below the most austere poverty line widely used in international research (50% of median income)' (Australian Council of Social Services, 2014, p. 8).

Income and wealth inequality

Inequality refers to a situation where large amounts of wealth are concentrated in the hands of a few. For example, it is reported that the richest 1% of the world's population owns as much wealth as half the world's population (Sandhu, 2015). The poorest half of the world's people, in contrast, own just 1% of total wealth (Sandhu, 2015). Wealth in Australia is concentrated, with the 'top 10% of wealth holders [owning] ... 45% of all wealth' (Australian Council of Social

Services, 2015, p. 9). However, the level of inequality is worse in the United States and the United Kingdom, when compared to Australia (Australian Council of Social Services, 2015). In 2009 in the United Kingdom, the top 1% owned 13.9% of all income and in the United States, the top 1% owned 19.3% of income (United Nations, 2013, p. 32). While poverty is a problem in its own right, it is inequality that underpins a good deal of the moral outrage about poverty because it is seen as unfair and unjust:

> Inequality is also an issue of social justice. People want to live in societies that are fair, where hard work is rewarded, and where one's socioeconomic position can be improved regardless of one's background. (United Nations, 2013, p. 22)

There is a difference between income inequality and wealth inequality. Income is typically household wages derived from employment, but may also include income from dividends such as shares, or interest, or government benefits. Wealth contributes to future income, and unlike wages or salaries, wealth typically refers to ownership or control of assets that generate further wealth, which may then act as sources of income, or supplements to variances in income levels (Australian Council of Social Services, 2015). Property, businesses, shares and investments are examples of wealth. Some assets are high value sources of wealth (property is a typical example) and some are low value assets that do little to reproduce their own value (cars and home contents are typical examples) (Australian Council of Social Services, 2015).

Like poverty, wealth and income distribution is subject to specific demographic patterns. In Australia, people in the lowest income groups are often 'older people (30% of the lowest income group), sole parents and single person households (33%), people of working age who are not in the labour force (35%), people born in a non-English speaking country (26%), and people in households that rely on Government pensions and allowances (67%), primarily the age pension' (Australian Council of Social Services, 2015, p. 14). People in the higher income brackets '... include[s] people of working age (70%), couples without children (37%), people employed full time (71%), people born in Australia (72%), or to a lesser extent another English speaking country (14%) and those whose primary income source is wages (90%)' (Australian Council of Social Services, 2015, p. 14).

It is immediately apparent that income and inequality distribution are patterned across different sociological and demographic groups. Why is this so?

Theories of poverty

What causes poverty is subject to considerable debate and argument (Alcock, 2006; Saunders, 2005). As Saunders (2005) notes, cause is often confused with a description of poverty itself. For example, low income and poor housing may be describing something about poverty, but these descriptions do not explain what *causes* low income and poor housing (Saunders, 2005). The other problem is the attributions of particular social groups as being a causal factor in themselves. For example, is being a single parent or older person a *causal* factor in poverty? While many people who are single parents or older people may be in poverty, this is not always so, and so the relationship is not always so straight line. Therefore, these are not causal factors in and of themselves.

Despite numerous attempts at conceptual precision, and various instruments used to measure poverty, it is very difficult to reach a consensus on what counts or does not count as poverty (Alcock, 2006). Often it turns on a combination of factors, some objective, and some subjectively related to people's perceptions and experiences. Absolute notions of poverty typically define poverty as a situation in which basic conditions for sustaining life are deficient. Whereas, relative notions of poverty typically define a situation where the conditions for living that would be seen as socially acceptable and customary are deficient or lacking (Alcock, 2006; McLachlan et al., 2013; UNESCO, 2016).

Two main explanatory theories of poverty are offered by Alcock (2006). The first of these can be described as structural theories. These posit that poverty is an outcome of the way societies and economies are organised, and therefore people may experience poverty largely due to external or environmental factors. Examples of these include the nature of the social welfare system, the state of the economy, the conditions of the labour market, the relative cost of living, policy failure, the lottery of birth, and so on (Alcock, 2006; Saunders, 2005). We may also include misfortune here, such as the loss of employment, death of a spouse, or an acquired injury. These may thrust people into poverty through no choice or fault of their own (Saunders, 2005). The examples presented earlier in this chapter illustrate this point. Disasters and conflict are also implicated in poverty, as they may displace people or overwhelm systems and infrastructure supports.

Income relative to living costs is another good example of a structural factor. Unemployment, increase in underemployment, insecure or sporadic contract work, increases in food and fuel costs, falling value in income levels, increasing personal debt, rising housing costs – these may be considered structural factors (Cooper & Dumpleton, 2013, p. 3; Cooper et al., 2014, pp. 9–11). For example, in the United Kingdom 'between 2010 and the end of 2013, energy prices for household gas and electricity rose by 37 per cent' (Cooper et al., 2014, p. 12), and in 2013 in the United Kingdom 'wages only increased by one percent [whereas] annual inflation ... was 2.8 percent in the twelve months to February 2013' (Cooper et al., 2014, p. 13).

Other structural factors concern the changing nature of social welfare systems themselves. Changes in social security that are more restrictive and punitive can lead to a dramatic increase in sanctions or penalties (particularly young people, men and people with disabilities), or delays in payments (Cooper et al., 2014, p. 9), and a reduction in the cash value of social security payments (Cooper et al., 2014, p. 15). When income is insufficient to meet the costs of living, people may be forced to access high risk credit. Consequently, a further problem associated with poverty is a credit trap that many people may become ensconced in. For example, Caplan (2014) discusses two types of predatory lending in the United States that are of particular concern for people with limited financial means or credit opportunities: payday lending, which are low-value short-term loans, and subprime mortgage lending. Such lending practices often carry great risk for the recipient, particularly in relation to excessive fees and interest charges, which may further contribute to the entrenchment of debt and poverty. As noted by Caplan, there is a relationship between poverty and predatory lending because people with limited financial means are often forced to borrow money on the fringes of the credit and loans system in order to simply pay for the necessities of life (Caplan, 2014).

As a final example, we can consider a seemingly innocuous shift in the way food is distributed as a structural factor. There is a trend towards larger supermarkets moving to outer urban areas, and, through the act of dominating the grocery and food market, we begin to witness smaller and local corner stores (fruit and vegetables, butchers, bakers) gradually being subsumed by giant supermarket corporations. The net effect of this means accessing food is harder and more expensive for those with restricted transport. What is accessible is often cheaper food with lower nutritional or diminished nutritional value – calorically dense, high in sugar and fat (Cooper & Dumpleton, 2013, p. 7; Cooper et al., 2014, p. 4).

There are also individual theories that seat the explanatory factor for poverty in the individual and their personal agency. These theories posit that poverty is an outcome of individual choices and actions, and therefore people may experience poverty largely due to the choices, decisions and actions they take throughout their lives. Examples of these include theories of personality, genetics and psychological theories of behaviour. These theories suggest the poverty is the result of psychological or genetic deficiencies. Social work tends to reject these individual theories in favour of more structural theories discussed earlier. This is because many individual theories are primarily ideological and lack evidence, and social work adopts a person-in-environment and social justice perspective. Nevertheless, popular ideologies often circulated by conservative media extenuate the place of individual theories by promulgating the idea that poverty is a result of idleness and a failure of work ethic or character (Alcock, 2006). In fact, people who may be living in poverty can contribute to this view themselves in how they talk about poverty. A study by Shildrick and MacDonald involving interviews with 60 men and women in England found that people in poverty would often adopt and circulate a neoliberal precept that poverty is the 'fault of the individual', even at the same time as they sought to distance themselves from poor 'others' (Shildrick & MacDonald, 2013). This phenomenon makes sense when we consider stigma and shame and their association with poverty, which are discussed later in this chapter.

Overall, individual theories suggest that poverty is a choice, and sometimes this is referred to as behavioural poverty. But as Saunders (2005) asks, why would people *choose* to live in poverty, and why is it that so many people are desperately trying to escape poverty? It hardly sounds like the result of conscious choice? Furthermore, individual theories can lead to many myths about poverty. For example, the view that poverty is due to laziness, which is *not* supported by evidence, as an increasing number of people in Australia and the United Kingdom are working poor (MacInnes, Aldridge, Bushe, Tinson & Born, 2014; Payne, 2009).

Both structural and individual theories can offer something together by considering the way that circumstance and structure may shape or influence individual action. People may make choices and actions that impact their well-being, and outwardly these may look like choices and actions that are free and unfettered. But in fact, our choices are constrained and shaped by a field of experience that extends well beyond individual autonomy. In this sense, the causes of poverty are likely to be a combination of factors rather than single causal factors:

> Events that can in isolation be overcome with relatively little effort, instead combine with others to produce poverty. Many different triggers send people in a downward spiral that ends in poverty: a sick child that overloads a family budget already fully stretched, a work-related accident that involves both extra costs and reduced wages, the loss of affordable housing and the costs involved in relocating, or the 'double whammy' that comes when dual-earner couples suffer job losses when a local business closes its doors. Often, those affected can cope with a single adverse event, it is the combination that overwhelms them. (Saunders, 2005, p. 91)

Given the many uncertainties that plague modern life, what is important from a structural point of view is an overall system that offers a degree of protection across a population. High levels of home ownership, a strong superannuation system, progressive tax system, universal access to public education and a targeted 'social security safety net' are structural protective factors that stave off more widespread inequality and poverty (Australian Council of Social Services, 2015, p. 8). The point to remember here is that these structural factors are important to build upon and *preserve* if we are to make meaningful inroads into halting a widening inequality gap, and decreasing the level and extent of poverty. Hence, thinking about poverty as a structural issue is an important corrective to thinking about it as the 'fault of the individual', or to 'blame the poor for their poverty'.

Disadvantage: what is it and what should be done?

Poverty and disadvantage often co-exist, but they are describing different things. Disadvantage is characterised by problematic structural conditions, vulnerability and stigmatisation. It should be pointed out that disadvantage is not only correlated with poverty, but as discussed in an edited volume on the topic, disadvantage may be associated with ill-health, disability, drug use, sexual orientation and older people (Burke & Parker, 2006). The concept of disadvantage is initially defined by Burke (2006) as '… a factor that permeates the experience of many people who, perhaps not through choice, are vulnerable or stigmatised, or are in other ways incapacitated in their dealings with the situations and experiences of everyday life' (p. 11). Poverty would be a good example here. But here we are discussing poverty not merely in regard to its material forms, but in an interactional sense. Poverty involves an interplay between self and context. The identities that form are negotiated in relation to broader meanings of poverty, and arise as an experience and sense of oneself as 'being poor'. These may be adopted, internalised, or rejected and resisted. The concept evoked to help us understand the interaction of self – as in, one who inhabits or resists the identity of being poor – is stigma:

> The nature of social interaction may define and redefine relationships until one succumbs and adopts an identity that fits in with how one previously treated those who have become one's peers. Self-stigmatisation is an acknowledgement of a sense of failure, when one does not fit in any more. The stigma is a loss of face and a lowered self-esteem. (Burke, 2006, p. 18)

Stigma is a key idea in Burke's framework about disadvantage due to the way that people are treated by others, and ultimately experience themselves in relation to their situation. For example, poverty means more than material deprivation. It carries with it self-perceptions and perceptions of others that may be experienced as painful, shameful, and a form of social exclusion. It may materialise as treatment by others that may include disdain, suspicion, judgement, labelling, blaming and avoidance. The act of seeking assistance – such as seeking a short-term loan or food voucher – may carry with it feelings of shame and failure on behalf of the person needing help.

The reasons that poverty attracts public, and, at times, self-imposed derision, is less to do with the class position people occupy, and more to do with the fact that material and financial deprivation robs people of the capacity to 'live in ways that they, and others, value' (Sayer, 2005, pp. 947–948). For example, in a social and cultural context that normalises consumption and conspicuous displays of wealth, poverty signifies a restricted opportunity for moral regard and worth for those deemed poor. Instead, moral regard and worth is largely bestowed on those who can freely participate in the normativity of consumption (Sayer, 2005).

Relatedly, Sayer (2005) states that shame is 'evoked by failure of an individual or group to live according to their values or commitments, especially concerning their relation to others and goods which others also value' (pp. 953–954). Shame is often experienced as a deeply painful and private emotion, but shame can also be shared among class groups if normative values are strong. For example, consider a situation where wealth and material acquisition are normalised and valorised. This shouldn't be too hard to do given the way that wealth and consumption are on show via numerous media channels. Now consider the same context where poor people are *at the same time* pilloried by media and politicians for being poor. The experience of shame may be amplified individually and according to collective identification and attribution to a specific group (Sayer, 2005). So, shame may manifest in terms of a self-evaluation of moral worth, but also insofar as someone sees and experiences themselves as *belonging to a group* that does not enjoy moral regard and recognition.

Many of the consequences of poverty – such as shame and stigma – are hard to express in the form of a graph or statistic. Shame is a particular consequence of poverty because intertwined in the experience of poverty can be feelings of failure, and the experience of isolation and exclusion (Sayer, 2005). Social workers should be mindful of a welfare support system that intrudes into people's circumstances, making judgements and insinuations about their experiences, which further reinforce a person's loss of dignity and worth (Saunders, 2005).

A framework for thinking about disadvantage

Poverty would certainly be a condition that contributes to vulnerability, stigma and an incapacitation to deal with various life experiences and situations (Burke, 2006). Hence, poverty is traditionally seen as an associative condition of disadvantage (McLachlan et al., 2013). This is distinguished from low income, which may be temporal and therefore not specifically a marker of persistent disadvantage (McLachlan et al., 2013). Disadvantage is typically characterised by the conditions of multiple and intersecting problems that negatively affect a person's overall quality of life and living standards. These are discussed by McLachlan et al. (2013) as including:

1. *Deprivation* – this concerns a situation where someone is considered to be deprived of something that a society would broadly agree to be a something that everyone should have, and that this deprivation is *not of the person's choosing*. This is a measure of disadvantage based on norms, rather than statistical measures like income. Examples of these norms may include basic needs, such as an ability to heat one's home, leisure activities and the ability to purchase basic household commodities. It includes environmental factors, such as adequate housing that is free from pollution, leaks, damp, and so on. Being forced to sell personal belongings to make ends meet would also be an indicator of deprivation (Australian Council of Social Services, 2014).

2. *Capability* – this concept draws on work from Amartya Sen and refers to the capability to exercise one's potential, or function in a way that supports the attainment of well-being. Well-being can be understood to include, for example, financial, employment, health and family, and social well-being.

Disadvantage describes a situation whereby someone's capabilities to attain well-being are compromised due to powerlessness, poor health, marginalisation or exclusion, which when combined, are often associated with poverty (UNESCO, 2016).

3. *Social exclusion and inclusion* – social exclusion was once a term used to describe the long-term unemployed, but more recently it refers to the extent to which someone can participate in social and economic life. Its meaning is very broad and lacks consensus, but generally speaking, social exclusion means being pushed to the fringes of society due to discrimination, poverty, and a lack of ability or opportunity for participation and engagement in decision-making (McLachlan et al., 2013). Inclusion means being able to participate in learning, in work, and to have meaningful social connections. It also means being able to influence decisions and have a voice (The Australian Social Inclusion Board, 2012, cited in McLachlan et al., 2013).

Social work's engagement with poverty and disadvantage

Social work has a long and complex engagement with poverty and disadvantage. According to Dowling (1999), this engagement has three main origins, as follows:

> ... the philosophy and practises of the Charity Organisation Society (COS); the need for an emerging profession to identify with other more powerful professions, in this case, psychiatry, and the administration and bureaucratic development of the casework model. (p. 11)

The COS were instrumental in applying a deserving/undeserving notion of benefit to the poor through a middle-class ideology of charity, the effect of which made moralistic judgements about moral desert that further increased the stigmatisation of poverty (Dowling, 1999). According to Dowling, remnants of this practice can be seen today in the form of food vouchers, distributing clothes and meals. The charity model was subsumed by the influence of psychological theories of counselling and casework that seated the explanatory account of poverty in the individual, and the structuring of social services within welfare states. These were practices that were concerned with income maintenance, which further entrenched a largely individualistic theory and remedial response to poverty (Dowling, 1999).

The welfare state in the form of income security and benefits has been the main instrument for addressing poverty in advanced economies such as the United States, the United Kingdom and Australia. This may include various forms of redistribution that are targeted according to need and circumstance, such as social security payments. Social workers have historically been located in these contexts, particularly in roles that include assessing and case managing people's access to social security and other benefits. O'Brien (2013) states that social work has addressed poverty by ensuring that service users can access and receive the 'benefits they are entitled to' (p. 82), as well as entering into individual advocacy to support service users' access affordable housing or negotiate plans to pay bills and debts. These are actions taken at the level of individuals.

The potential for stigmatising people who access social security, and for granting access to social assistance as an instrument of social control and punishment, is well documented (see for example, Alston, 2010; Martin, 2004; Mendes, 2009b; Tonkens & Verplanke, 2013). Furthermore, there is a long-standing critique of social security as the main policy to combat poverty because it is said to create welfare dependency and lead to poverty and unemployment traps (Alcock, 2006). Problems with the system of regulating and administering social security can mean that errors, omissions and a punitive approach can actually exacerbate people's poverty and disadvantage. Dowling (1999) laments such punitive approaches, stating that 'the agency processes by which clients are evaluated in moral terms and subsequently condemned to inferior treatment must be eradicated' (p. 24) and that 'if social workers are not to contribute to deepening social inequalities, they need to be aware of selection, delivery and rationing systems that can operate against the poor' (p. 25).

Empowerment, education and a structural view of poverty as well as collective responses are offered as an antidote to the problem noted above (Dowling, 1999), and likewise, O'Brien (2013) argues that social work must consider poverty within a framework committed to social justice. At a structural level, O'Brien (2013) argues that social workers should engage in collective action to improve systems, and push for more socially just policies that help lift whole groups and communities out of poverty. This may include more structural responses that are locally organised, such as access to free or low cost health-care, education, public transport, local community and economic development, and so on (Alcock, 2006). Elsewhere, social workers, community workers and activists are looking at creative and non-state approaches to meeting human need and building community and collective solidarity. For example, there is increasing interest in community gardens as a way of creating ecological sustainability, community connectedness and support, and improving local and individual capabilities – all of which can act to moderate and address poverty, including addressing food poverty and poor nutrition (Ferris, Norman & Sempik, 2001; Litt et al., 2011; Schischka, Dalziel & Saunders, 2008).

Other approaches to disadvantage are concerned to improve the way that services are delivered. The Australian Social Inclusion Board report *Breaking Cycles of Disadvantage* (Australian Social Inclusion Board, 2011) outlines three key conclusions that may help address persistent disadvantage:

1. *Addressing the psychological impact of disadvantage* – this links to the points
    made earlier about stigma and shame, because poverty and disadvantage
    can have a lasting negative impact on people's psychological and mental
    well-being. Empathy, respect and dignity (discussed in other chapters in this
    book) provide the conceptual tools for social workers to support and build
    meaningful relationships with service users that don't further deepen their
    disadvantage and cause further harm. In practice, this means a considered
    focus on how people are treated, and 'the benefit of positive strength-based
    approaches, empowering the client through providing opportunities to
    shape the assistance they receive' (Australian Social Inclusion Board, 2011,
    p. 55).

2. *Practical support needs to be flexible, tailored and accessible* – unfortunately
    many services are highly specialised and operate within rigid and largely
    inflexible parameters of service provision. This is a problem in respect to
    addressing persistent disadvantage. Many people have complex and inter-
    secting problems, and splitting the service response into numerous provid-
    ers, appointments and different workers can act to increase mistrust,
    confusion and alienation from services generally (Australian Social Inclusion
    Board, 2011).

3. *Support needs to be provided long-term* – the goal here is to address the short-
    term churn that occurs by only responding to crisis situations through acute
    services. Addressing disadvantage is a long-term prospect, and the social
    work and service response needs to not merely work with the presenting
    concerns of individuals, but to seek to address the *structural conditions that
    generate patterns of disadvantage in the first place*. Continuation of support
    with service users is one approach, but so is investment in transport, services
    and employment generation programs in particularly disadvantaged areas,
    along with an increase in public housing and income support (Australian
    Social Inclusion Board, 2011).

Conclusion

A special issue on poverty published in the journal *International Social Work* in
1992 noted a number of problems related to poverty that would still be familiar
today: failure of market-based economies to deliver economic justice for all; the
neoliberal attack on the welfare state; widening inequality between and within
Nation-states; and a trend in social work to address individual problems through
micro and psychotherapeutic perspectives, thus deepening an unhelpful binary
between individual, case-work responses vs. community and activist practice
(Campfens, 1992). In the same issue, Larochelle and Campfens (1992) argue
that 'the issue of poverty should occupy a much more important place in the

programmes of education and training of social workers than it appears to occupy until now' (p. 117). Two and a half decades later, this need seems more pressing than ever. It is paramount that social work research, education and training understand and grasp the complex nature of poverty, particularly in relation to understanding not only the causes of poverty, but how to respond to it in practice in ways that do not further increase people's disadvantage, stigma and shame (Backwith, 2015).

Critical thinking questions

1. What are the differences between absolute and relative poverty? What are the problems with these terms?

2. Think about your local community. Do you see evidence of poverty? What indicators are you using to make this assessment?

3. What are the main differences of individual and structural theories of poverty? What are the strengths and weaknesses of each?

4. Why might stigma and shame be associated with poverty and disadvantage?

5. How can social workers practise in a way that meaningfully and in a non-stigmatising way addresses poverty and disadvantage?

Exercises

Brainstorm a list of what you think are environmental or structural factors that increase or contribute to poverty. Then, conduct an online search of programs, projects and initiatives that tackle poverty. These can be local to where you live, or from across the globe. Choose one approach to focus on, then critically examine it. To what extent does the initiative address structural factors associated with poverty and disadvantage?

Further reading

Alcock, P. (2006). *Understanding poverty* (3rd ed.). Basingstoke, UK: Palgrave Macmillan.

Cooper, N. & Dumpleton, S. (2013). *Walking the breadline: The scandal of food poverty in 21st century Britain.* Available at http://policy-practice.oxfam.org.uk/publications/walking-the-breadline-the-scandal-of-food-poverty-in-21st-century-britain-292978

Saunders, P. (2005). *The poverty wars: Reconnecting research with reality.* Sydney, NSW: UNSW Press.

Sayer, A. (2005). Class, moral worth and recognition. *Sociology, 39*(5), 947–963.

St Vincent de Paul Society. (2015). *'Sick with worry ...' Stories from the front-line of inequality, 2015.* Available at www.vinnies.org.au/icms_docs/225819_Sick_with_worry_2015_national_report.pdf

Links and online resources

ABC Television 4 Corners (2013). 'On the Brink' www.abc.net.au/4corners/stories/2013/07/01/3791178.htm

Anti Poverty Week Information and Educational Resources www.antipovertyweek.org.au/resources/education-resources

Poverty and Social Exclusion UK www.poverty.ac.uk/

6

DIFFERENCE

Introduction

Grappling with the differences between individuals and groups is an important component in social work efforts to address discrimination and oppression. But how can we understand difference and diversity, and its impact for social work practice? What does it mean to practise social work in ways that are anti-discriminatory? Moreover, how does this relate to the need to demonstrate culturally appropriate practice and sensitivity to the many and varied identities, cultures and conditions affecting people in their everyday lives?

We start from the premise that contemporary society is unequal and there are a range of social divisions that contribute to people experiencing discrimination. The history of contemporary societies, their relative placement within the many forms of colonialism and imperialism from globalisation will be formative with regard to discourses of difference and culture (Connell, 2007). For example, Australia can be seen as having a 'settler majority culture' (Hosken & Goldingay, 2016, p. 53), meaning that some members of society are thus contrasted in relation to the majority as belonging to minorities. How people are positioned in this relation of majority-minority cultures is a complex matter and different in each society. What it means for someone positioned in this way also depends on particular historical, cultural and social arrangements. With this in mind we can see that ethnicity and culture may be just *one kind* of diversity that social workers must grapple with throughout their practice.

When thinking about culture in relation to difference we find it's worth taking a lead from Edward Said (1993) and acknowledging the interplay of culture and imperialism. Said (1993) considers culture in two different ways. First, culture can be seen as 'all those practices, like the arts of description, communication, and representation, that have relative autonomy from the economic, social and political realm and that often exist is aesthetic forms, one of whose principle aims is pleasure' (Said, 1993, p. xii). This includes the 'power to narrate, or to block other narratives from forming or emerging' (Said, 1993, p. xiii). Some of the key ways in which this occurs for people are discussed below in relation to social groups and oppression. The second way Said (1993, p. xiii) discusses culture is to consider it as 'society's reservoir of the best that has been known and thought'. In this sense, culture can be seen as a significant source of identity, which acts as a 'sort of theatre where various political and ideological causes engage one another' (Said, 1993, p. xiii). This is a place where the politics of recognition becomes particularly important, especially for groups aiming to have their rights recognised (Tully, 2008b). Struggles for recognition occur across a range of differences in addition to culture and this is often the result of discrimination and injustice.

This discrimination may be on the basis of people's ethnicity, gender, class, sexual orientation or able-bodiedness; alternatively it can also be about combinations of these differences. Anti-discriminatory (ADP) and anti-oppressive practice (AOP) can be seen as a social work response to the existence of these social divisions (Dalrymple & Burke, 2006; Payne, 2006). The concepts of difference and diversity are the main prism through which social work has tried to develop these responses. According to Lister (2012) and Thompson (1998), it is essential that social work students understand the *theoretical* roots of anti-discriminatory and anti-oppressive practice in order for it to be incorporated into social work practice more broadly. We think, too, that these theoretical roots can serve as important resources for conceptualising social inequality (Habibis & Walter, 2009), for understanding operations of power, as well as for identifying oppressive and marginalising practices.

In light of this, we begin this chapter by presenting ideas about social inequality and oppression. In doing so we will draw on important work by feminist scholars because their work, especially in the second wave of feminism, 'placed a wide range of previously marginalized issues on the political agenda' (Weedon, 1999, p. 1). This work paved the way for many other social movements to raise issues about unequal treatment in society (Tully, 2008a). Since then, a widespread interest has emerged within feminist scholarship to understand the way in which multiple inequalities and/or identities intersect with each other (Walby, Armstrong & Strid, 2012). It is this scholarship that largely informs the AOP movement (Dominelli, 2002a). We see this work as an important set of resources that can be used to consider interlocking and intersecting oppressions (Hulko, 2009) that contribute to discrimination. In a subsequent section of this chapter we shift our focus to consider how the issue of difference has been translated into current codes of ethics within social work. Here it seems the term diversity is used to denote *differences* as a resource and source of strength (Thompson, 2006). This may be seen as a move away from seeing difference in entirely negative terms. Nevertheless, it still remains that the very diversity and differences amongst people are also the source from which oppression and discrimination emerges (Thompson, 2006). It is for this reason we have included a discussion of difference in this book as we see difference as a core concept that permeates all aspects of social work practice. Our chapter closes with an overview of two different anti-oppressive frameworks that might

be utilised to contribute to the creation of non-oppressive relationships in contemporary society.

Social inequality, oppression and difference

Forms of social inequality

We have previously discussed (in Chapter 2, this volume) how social movements in contemporary society have mounted noteworthy challenges to many
of the universalist assumptions underpinning Western reason, especially in the
area of political governance (Tully, 2008a). By social movements we mean those
movements concerned with civil and Indigenous rights, the feminist movement,
and activism aimed at extending recognition of women, disabled people, liberation movements for gay and lesbian people, and of course many workers' rights
movements in addition to environmental rights. Tully (2008a) suggests that
these challenges were important as they have resulted in a substantial widening
of the ways in which public and private institutions engage with various *others*,
struggling for recognition within Western representative Nation-states and
beyond. In this respect, social movements have been a key part of extending
inclusion to previously excluded others in contemporary society (Thompson,
2006). These social movements occur within the theatre discussed above in
relation to culture (Said, 1993).

Iris Marion Young (1990) also points to the impact of these social movements in order to raise questions about the delivery of justice in contemporary
society. Young's book *Justice and the Politics of Difference* (1990) remains a semi-
nal text on social justice (see also Chapter 8, this volume). In it Young argues
that '… justice should begin with the concepts of domination and oppression'
(Young, 1990). Young defines *oppression* as 'the institutional constraint on self-
development' (Young, 1990, p. 37) and she defines *domination* as 'the institutional constraint on self-determination' (Young, 1990, p. 37). In both these
cases, however, institutions are implicated, and Young points to how these
institutions operate to curtail or constrain a person's autonomy and potential.
Oppression is conceptualised in Young's schema as a structural concept, but one
that operates at both macro and micro levels. By this Young means that structural groups are institutionalised as the '… social positions that people occupy
which condition their opportunities and life chances' (Young, 2000, p. 94) and
it is through these institutions that inequalities in society are created.

These ideas have been taken up in social work too. Social worker Neil
Thompson (1998) suggests that oppression and discrimination are outcomes of
different forms of inequality. The kinds of inequality Thompson points to are
shown in Table 6.1.

Table 6.1 Thompson's forms of inequality

Kind of inequality	Explanation
Economic	The 'differential distribution of financial resources and rewards' (Thompson, 1998, p. 10) in society, which result in some people experiencing poverty.
Social	Thompson (1998, p. 10) suggests that the distribution of recognition, privileges and opportunities in society is related to a person's social location. Social location can be considered an emergent property of various social divisions such as gender, class and race.
Political	The capacity to participate and to contribute to the public use of reason via political discourse is unevenly distributed by way of social divisions such as class, gender and race. In this respect some people are more 'heard' than others.
Ethical	This relates to basic values of fairness and respect for human dignity and worth. It should be offensive that some people are unable to participate or reach their potential due to their identification as a member of a group designated as 'other'. Inequality is in this respect a moral issue.
Ideological	This indicates the existence and operation of ideologies and discourses that serve to maintain structures and relations of inequality.
Psychological	The way in which people in society think, feel and act that maintains and extends different forms of inequality and oppression.
	Cognitive: Ways of thinking that are shaped by membership in different groups such as gender, race and class as well as culture and experience. For example, prejudice towards women: 'speech patterns of dominant groups being seen as superior or more prestigious' (Spender, 1990, cited in Thompson, 1998, p. 11).
	Affective: The way emotional responses are shaped by the social milieu that might be traced back to the aforementioned social divisions and culture. For instance, women and men may display different emotional responses to the experience of loss (Thompson, 1998, p. 11). Thus, aspects of affect are socially produced.
	Conative: Refers to the way behaviour is shaped by categorisations based on a person's membership in class, gender and ethnic social groups.

These forms of inequality give rise to various forms of oppression and domination as they shape the way resources, life-chances and power are distributed across society. Moreover, unlike overt expressions of tyranny, many forms of inequality give rise to relations of domination that can operate in a more insidious manner as they are practices that are 'embedded in everyday norms, habits, and symbols, in the assumptions underlying institutional rules and the collective consequences of following those rules' (Young, 1990, p. 41). Oppression and domination can also operate at the level of relations that find expression as social patterns. These patterns can be described as structures of socio-economic status, disadvantage, class and social groups or identities (Nzira & Williams, 2009; Thompson, 2006). Thus, discrimination refers to the vast and deep injustices individuals identified as members of some groups suffer as a consequence of often unconscious assumptions and reactions of well-meaning people in ordinary interactions, media and cultural stereotypes (Dominelli, 2002b). It also occurs through structural features of bureaucratic hierarchies and market mechanisms – all of which find expression in the normal processes of everyday life (Young, 1990, p. 41).

Justice and the five faces of oppression

In calling for justice that takes account of relations of domination, Young (1990) appeals to a *situated* conception of justice, rather than a form of justice that appeals to principles concerned only with universal notions (Healy, 2007). Young (1990) also calls for a conception of justice that can speak about and address the *practices* of oppression and domination that operate through various structures that categorise members of society into *groups*. For Young, a social group (and by extension anyone deemed as part of that group) is oppressed when they are 'subject to one or more of ... five conditions' (Young, 1990, p. 47). These conditions are exploitation, marginalisation, powerlessness, cultural imperialism and violence (Young, 1990, pp. 48–63). Young calls these conditions the five *faces of oppression*. We have set these faces of oppression into Table 6.2 with some examples for illustration.

Social groups and oppression

Individuals may suffer oppression and domination on account of their membership of a social group. Moreover, these operations of oppression prevent members of these groups from the opportunity to flourish and exercise their full capacities. Thus, the concept of group identification is a crucial component in Young's (1990) perspective on oppression and domination. She suggests that a

Table 6.2 Five faces of oppression

Face of oppression	Key aspects	Example
Exploitation	Originally based on Marxist descriptions of capitalism and other arrangements where there is a longstanding practice of labour exchange that results in some people benefiting in an asymmetrical way from the labour of others. Feminists are also able to demonstrate that this occurs for women too, where there has been, at least in part, '… a systematic and unreciprocated transfer of powers from women to men' (Young, 1990, p. 50). This may, for women, extend beyond wage labour and include domestic work as well.	The utilisation of workers from countries without labour protection laws to create products only sold to customers in another country that do have labour protection laws. The operation of different expectations for boys and girls with regard to household work.
Marginalisation	This is the practice by which large categories of people are excluded from participation, whether that is work or in society generally. This can often be through markers of ethnicity or race, but may also include by age, disability, mental health, sexuality and citizenship status (that is, asylum seekers). Advanced welfare states have made provision for addressing some aspects of the deprivation this form of oppression can cause, but in recent years, aspects of the public consensus to provide this support have waned (Esping-Andersen & United Nations Research Institute for Social Development, 1996). Young (1990, p. 53) suggests that this is one of the 'most dangerous forms of oppression … as a whole category of people is expelled from useful participation in social life and thus potentially [they can be] subjected to severe material deprivation and even extermination'.	Asylum seekers who are barred from social assistance and/or working due to their stateless status. Not having access to social welfare benefits due to a policy change that excludes people with certain conditions.
Powerlessness	This kind of oppression describes the way in which people do not have a say in decisions that may affect their lives. This includes relations at work where many people have little or no autonomy in how they approach the tasks before them. Young (1990) suggests that there is a distinction between professional and non-professional workers, which turns on the issue of autonomy and the use of creativity and judgement in people's work.	Working for a call centre where your visits to the bathroom are monitored. Programs that require people to work for social assistance.

Cultural imperialism	This is when one group experiences 'how the dominant meanings of a society render the particular perspective of one's own group invisible at the same time as they stereotype one's group and mark it out as the Other' (Young, 1990, p. 59). This involves an assumption by the dominant group that their view is universally applicable to everyone, everywhere. People who experience this kind of oppression frequently develop a 'double consciousness' (Du Bois, 1969, cited in Young, 1990, p. 60) whereby they experience themselves through the eyes of the dominant group.	An example is when people, who are poor themselves, stigmatise other poor people using dominant arguments about 'scroungers' and 'benefit cheats' (Shildrick & MacDonald, 2013).
Violence	Many groups in society experience high levels of systematic violence on account of their identification with a specific group. Gay men, lesbians, women, people of colour and people with disabilities all experience high levels of violence, often by people holding institutional authority and office (Young, 1990, p. 61).	The high incarceration rate of Aboriginal people in prisons as compared to the non-Aboriginal populations.

High levels of sexual assault experienced by women.

High levels of assault experienced by young black men. |

group is 'a collective of persons differentiated from at least one other group by cultural forms, practices, or way of life' (Young, 1990, p. 41). As mentioned earlier, Young's (1990) approach to differences is primarily structural as it relies on the idea of dominant and subordinate group relations whereby dominant groups *benefit from the oppression* of subordinate groups (Mullaly, 1997). There is an important distinction, too, that Young (2000, cited in Lister, 2003, p. 80) makes between group differences based on structural factors and those that might be based on affiliation or identity differences. The important distinction here is that membership on the basis of structural difference does not rely on substantive *identity markers* of members, but instead, the categorisation occurs through '... practices, special needs or capacities, structures of power or privilege' (Young, 2000, p. 90).

Affiliation and identity differences do intersect with differences based on structural factors; for example, cultural identity deriving from connection with particular territory might intersect with differences centred on race or ethnicity. Social work – through different forms of ADP and AOP – has incorporated a structural view of oppression as discussed above (Dominelli, 2002a; Mullaly, 1997). However, while social work has been moving to address a politics of identity differences (Hicks, 2015; Mattsson, 2014), this move is not without some controversy (Webb, 2009) for those wedded to a more structural position.

Power relations and oppression

Young combines her structural view of oppression with a post-structural analysis of how power operates, especially in her focus on processes of categorisation that occur around membership of social groups and divisions. A post-structural analysis of power takes into account the impact of norms (Allen, 2011) as something that forms a *background* (Hekman, 1999), and it is through this background of norms that categorisation occurs (see Chapter 4 on power, this volume). This background finds expression in the form of the mundane routines and practices of people going about their everyday business, and therefore the processes of categorisation can appear invisible. It can also find expression through instances of deliberate group-to-group or person-to-person oppression, which manifest as deliberate and overt forms of stigmatisation, discrimination and violence.

One example that can illustrate this background and the power relations operating through norms, structures and practices, is the process of administering welfare. All developed nations have welfare systems of various kinds (Garfinkel, Rainwater & Smeeding, 2010). These welfare states are created from the transfer of 'large shares of national income through welfare state programs' (Garfinkel et al., 2010, p. 62). Each country sets up different programs and institutions to enable this distribution and has different health, education and social assistance configurations depending on a range of historical, cultural and political factors. Social work has had a long history of involvement in the delivery of welfare programs (Kessl, 2009). It should be said that the historical, cultural and political factors of each welfare state shape who is able to access these programs (and who is not) and the main way this is done is through recognition of a person's claims of citizenship.

Who is counted as a citizen is a contested issue, according to Ruth Lister (2003). Citizenship itself has the status of being an essentially contested concept (Ruben, 2010), which means that it is contested 'at every level from its very meaning to its political application, [which has] ... implications for the kind of society to which [we might] aspire' (Lister, 2003, p. 3). This means there are competing explanations for the term 'citizen', which are largely irreconcilable. Each explanation has some merit or weight. Originally, the term citizen referred to membership of a community and the relationships between individuals and that state (Lister, 2003, p. 3). This relation includes the powers the state has with regard to its citizens and what rights and responsibilities each individual has in regard to the state. A person's citizenship status therefore has real material effects on their ability to *access resources* but also to how well or easily they might *participate* in society as well. In this way citizenship points to who is included in a community and therefore it carries with it a normative power about who might be counted or included, and on what basis.

Completing and filling out forms to access social welfare is an example of a mundane routine that is commonplace in the transactions of welfare delivery, and form-filling is a somewhat taken-for-granted aspect of participation and citizenship. It is also a practise that most people engage in with the state for welfare purposes. Whether it is for enrolling children at school, accessing health care or applying for assistance such as unemployment benefits, you will be asked a whole raft of questions about your circumstances. These will include aspects such as your address, age, place of birth and citizenship status. It can also include information about your ethnicity, your gender and about your employment, income and financial situation. Answers to these questions will shape perceptions on the 'kind' of person you are. The forms will generally be in the predominant language of the country, although in some cases other languages might be accommodated, and you will need a basic level of literacy in that dominant language to complete these forms. Even the offices where these forms or programs are accessed can be set up in ways that show a set of norms that shape a person's access to participation and resources. For example, talking to a representative of an organisation or institution might require you to access a computer, take a number, and stand in a queue. The office hours might also privilege some members of society over others. Reducing these barriers for service users has required social work to engage in understanding how difference operates against the assumptions of *sameness* built into the background of the welfare institutions we work in.

Summary

In our discussion so far we have established that social inequality exists as a multi-dimensional aspect of society from which relations of discrimination and oppression emerge. We have outlined that individuals in society may have their life-chances affected by their relative position as members of groups considered subordinate to dominant interests. In this, we have summarised a politics of difference based on a *structural* understanding of group-based oppression and domination, whereby people become categorised via their race, class, gender, sexual orientation or able-bodiedness. This categorisation may result in overt forms of abuse, discrimination or violence, or subtly shape people's experience through everyday routines, such as filling in forms. There is a *politics of identity* whereby people can, of course, be identified with more than one group. We can see this in examples of feminist scholars such as Hulko (2009, p. 45), who proposes that her gender classification as a white women is complicated by a simultaneous identification as bisexual and her status of being partnered in a same-sex relationship. These classifications and identifications make her subject to different forms of oppression and relations of domination and privilege (Dominelli, 2002b). These forms of oppression represent an intersection between the structural and identity differences in society and they may be seen as the macro and micro aspects of oppression, domination and discrimination. We turn now to examine the dynamic nature of these forms of oppression as an entrée into the ways in which difference and diversity has been taken up by social work codes of ethics in general.

Interlocking oppressions and intersectionality

Feminist scholarship regarding difference

In feminist scholarship it has been widely acknowledged that early attempts to describe women's oppression did not take into account the experience of Black women (Davis, 2008). By this we mean early feminist scholarship that categorised 'women' as a homogenous group. Hekman (1999) submits that this strategy of erasing differences has its roots right in the beginning of feminist theory with Simone de Beauvoir's *The Second Sex*. There have been a number of shifts in how differences have been theorised in feminist theory since that work, which are now clear:

First, the effort to erase differences between men and women; second, the emphasis on those differences and the valorization of the feminine; third the exploration of the differences among women. (Hekman, 1999, p. 7)

These shifts with regard to differences have created a 'new continent of thought' for feminist theory in Hekman's (1999, p. 7) view. It also explains why it is only relatively recently that feminists began to acknowledge the considerable differences between women at all, and between white women and Black women in particular, especially in the shadow of slavery (hooks, 1981) and colonisation (Moreton-Robinson, 2004). In doing so Black scholars Patricia Hill Collins (1990), bell hooks (1981, 1990) and Indigenous scholars such as Aileen Moreton-Robinson (2004), amongst others, have all called attention to the way in which gender and race intersect. Two different terms have since emerged to describe the macro and micro levels at which gender and race intersect. The first term is *interlocking oppressions,* and according to Patricia Hill Collins (1995, cited in Hulko, 2009, p. 47), this term should be reserved for the 'macro level connections linking systems of oppression.' This is the structural aspect of oppression we have discussed earlier.

The gender-sex system as an example

As mentioned previously, gender is a major structure through which oppression can occur. Seyla Benhabib (1992) describes it as the 'gender-sex' system. Benhabib (1992, p. 152) proposes it as 'the grid through which the self develops an embodied identity, a certain mode of being in one's body and of living the body.' Note here that this system does not only refer to women but encompasses all expressions of gender. This grid is also described as the way in which 'social reality is organized, symbolically divided and lived through experientially' (Benhabib, 1992, p. 152). Thus, people are *produced* as gendered, embodied individuals. Gender-sex grids can change over time and are contingent on social practices, which might widen or narrow the available repertoire for performing gender (Hicks, 2015). Social practices and norms can also be challenged and changed through activist work (Allen, 2011; Butler, 2011).

To illustrate this further, consider the gender-sex grid that a child born in the United Kingdom will experience; it is arguably likely to be different from that of a child born in an African country. The various social prescriptions and normative standards for the child will be different in each context. The whole gender-sex assemblage has since been recognised as a *structure* available for analysis and feminists and Black women scholars have engaged in an extended 'explanatory-diagnostic analysis of women's oppression across history, culture and societies [in order to engage in] articulating an *anticipatory-utopian critique* of the norms and values of our current society and culture' (Benhabib, 1992, p. 152). This explanatory-diagnostic work of feminist scholars conceptualising this gender-sex grid paved the way for other groups, such as lesbian and gay scholars, seeking to extend the normative constraints of the other aspects of the gender-sex system (Rudy, 2000).

Intersectionality

Just as there are structures or assemblages relating to gender-sex, so too there are such grids through which class, race and ethnicity and disability are organised, lived experientially and which shape social reality for people. As we suggested earlier, these systems or assemblages are the macro-level structures that contribute to interlocking oppressions. It is the interaction between these interlocking oppressions that has been described as *intersectionality*. First coined by legal scholar Kimberle Crenshaw (2016), the concept is meant to describe micro-level processes of categorisation by which various others are gendered, classed, racialised and otherwise classified, according to a range of normative standards (Rose, 2013; Young, 1990).

Intersectionality has become the leading way in which feminist scholars have described the interaction between these structures in the last 20 years. Davis (2008) suggests that despite some uncertainty about the theoretical status of intersectionality, it addresses a need that emerged within feminist circles to be able to account for and redress the various exclusions that occurred in the earlier theorising about women. In other words, intersectionality enables an account of both the structures (interlocking oppressions) and their interaction with each other. It also gives a conceptual framework about the *identity* differences between women (Davis, 2008) but without viewing identity as an essential quality (Mehrotra, 2010). Intersectionality theorists readily assume that the structural aspects of oppression exist but instead they place their focus on the politics of identity differences (Mehrotra, 2010). Thus, the concept of intersectionality has been taken up to assist in conceptualising the multiple interactions between different identities and to account for diversity within and between various social groups (Artiles, 2013; Das Nair & Butler, 2012; Gibson, 2015; Hames-Garcia, 2011; Nakhid et al., 2015; Warner & Brown, 2011).

Approaches to categories of intersectional difference

Mehrotra (2010, p. 421) points out that while feminist scholars have used many metaphors to describe intersectionality, it is important to note that '... women's interconnected identities cannot be seen as additive, but, rather, that race, class, and gender combine and interact to create unique and simultaneous experiences'. Mehrotra (2010) outlines a typology, developed by McCall (2005), of the way intersectionality is utilised in research methodologies that illustrates the different positions intersectional theorists can take with regard to identity difference. McCall (2005) describes these positions as the intercategorical; the intracategorical and anticategorical approaches. We will discuss each briefly in turn to illustrate the complexity of intersectional approaches to categories of difference.

Intercategorical approaches on intersectionality broadly entail the adoption of 'existing analytical categories to document relationships of inequality among social groups and changing configurations of inequality along multiple and conflicting dimensions' (McCall, 2005, cited in Meekosha, 2006, p. 162). In social work, this approach is seen in efforts to analyse inequalities between different groups. An example of this approach would be the study undertaken by Alston, Jones and Curtin (2011). In this study, the existing categories of women and disability are used to document understandings of the combinatory effects of the various oppressive relations and discriminatory effects for these women. The main criticism of these kinds of study is that they fail to account for the complexity that exists in the interaction of different identities and the interlocking oppressions. Nevertheless, Mehrotra (2010, p. 423) suggests that this kind of research 'on understanding the significance and degree of social inequality between groups is particularly useful [in social work] … given social work's commitment to social justice and structural understandings of social inequality.' Mehrotra (2010) suggests that the majority of social work research using intersectionality uses this approach.

The next type, the *intracategorical* approach, emerged in the earliest period of intersectional studies (McCall, 2005). This approach has the benefit of focusing attention on a single case or social group within a category. It is thus able to reduce the relative complexity of the issues being studied. Studies of this type tend to be '… narratives [that] take as their subject an individual or an individual's experience and extrapolate illustratively to the broader social location embodied by the individual' (McCall, 2005, p. 1781). In social work, intracategorical approaches can be found in the use of case studies for classroom instruction and in social research that focuses on single cases where service users face multiple overlapping oppressions (Dominelli, 2002a; Mehrotra, 2010). A good example of this research is Phoenix and Bauer (2012) where the narratives of transnational families and their experiences of sibling and parental relationships were used to understand the way gender and migration come together.

Finally, the last approach outlined by McCall is the *anticategorical* one. This is where research is conducted that is:

> … based on a methodology that deconstructs analytical categories. Social life is considered too irreducibly complex – overflowing with multiple and fluid determinations of both subjects and structures – to make fixed categories anything but simplifying

social fictions that produce inequalities in the process of producing differences. (McCall, 2005, p. 1773)

It is most often associated with post-structural feminist approaches that challenge the view that categories of difference are fixed or essential. Mehrotra (2010, p. 424) considers this to be the least deployed approach to intersectional research within social work, primarily because of '... disciplinary and professional commitments to practice, lived lives, and material realities that can be viewed as being in tension with such theoretical frameworks.' A good example of this kind of approach, however, is Hicks' (2005) genealogical research that challenged the hetero-normative discourses of parenting in his research with lesbian and gay carers.

Summary

In summary, this section began with a discussion of the role of feminist theory and the shifts in approaches to difference that have occurred since the second wave of feminist thought with Simone de Beauvoir. We have utilised insights from feminist and Black women scholars to consider interlocking oppressions and the concept of intersectionality as ways of understanding both the macro (structural) and micro (identity) aspects of difference. We closed the section with an outline of the various ways in which scholars approach intersectional categories to illustrate the complexity and importance of using intersectional theory. We turn now to consider the ways in which the social work profession discusses the issue of difference as *diversity*. We do so by examining a number of the codes of ethics from a number of different social work associations. We begin the discussion with the International Federation of Social Work (IFSW) definition of social work.

Diversity as part of defining social work

It is unlikely that you would find disagreement that social workers work with people with a range of different lifestyles, identities, histories and cultures. This is acknowledged in the International Federation of Social Workers (IFSW) (International Federation of Social Workers, 2014) definition of social work:

Social work is a practice-based profession and an academic discipline that promotes social change and development, social cohesion, and the empowerment and liberation of people. Principles of social justice, human rights, collective responsibility and respect for diversities are central to social work. Underpinned by theories of social work, social sciences, humanities and indigenous knowledge, social work engages people and structures to address life challenges and enhance wellbeing.

From this definition we can see that the IFSW considers an acceptance of the diverse ways in which people might live their lives is an important value. Given this link to values, we became interested in how difference and diversity is discussed. We think this offers a picture about the way in which the notion of difference is conceptualised within the social work profession.

Difference and diversity in national codes of ethics

In the Australian Association of Social Workers (2010) Code of Ethics, notions of difference are best encapsulated in the ethical responsibilities of 'respect for human dignity and worth' (5.1.1) and 'culturally competent, safe and sensitive practice' (5.1.2). These sections emphasise the following:

> Respect and acknowledgement of different "beliefs, religious or spiritual world views, values, culture, goals, needs and desires, as well as kinship and communal bonds ..." (Australian Association of Social Workers, 2010, p. 17)

This includes the social worker's awareness of their own beliefs and world views and how these may influence their practise.

It is important to note that the explicit emphasis on knowing one's culture, beliefs and world views forms a basic stance in AOP and ADP. Social workers need a 'working knowledge and understanding of clients' racial and cultural affiliations, identities, values, beliefs and customs ...' (Australian Association of Social Workers, 2010, p. 17). This includes practicing in a manner that is safe and respectful of cultural differences and promoting broader practices and policies that seek to reduce the extent of discrimination, prejudice and ignorance that may result in harmful or inappropriate practice. The same kind of emphasis on respecting customs and beliefs can also be seen in the Singapore Code of Ethics for Professional Social Workers where it states that the social worker must ensure that they create 'an atmosphere that respects all religions and cultures, race, and nationality regardless of political belief, gender, gender orientation, age, marital status, mental and physical disability' (Singapore Association of Social Workers, 2004, p. 3).

The British Association of Social Workers (BASW) Code of Ethics links *respect for diversity* to social justice, suggesting that 'social workers should recognise and respect the diversity of the societies in which they practise, taking into account individual, family, group and community differences' (British Association of

Social Workers, 2012, p. 9). Likewise, the Canadian Association of Social Workers (CASW) Code of Ethics states that 'social workers respect the diversity among individuals in Canadian society and the right of individuals to their unique beliefs consistent with the rights of others' (Canadian Association of Social Workers, 2005, p. 4). This emphasis on respecting culture is also echoed in the Aotearoa New Zealand Association of Social Workers (ANZASW) Code of Ethics, advising against the application of mono-cultural values in practice or mono-cultural practice models and methods. The ANZASW code also sets anti-racist and anti-discriminatory expectations by suggesting that no one should be discriminated against on the grounds of '... age, beliefs, culture, gender, marital, legal or family status, intellectual, psychological and physical abilities, race, religion, sexual orientation, and social or economic status' (Aotearoa New Zealand Association of Social Workers, 2015).

The code that explicitly focuses on oppression, difference and identity is the US National Association of Social Workers (NASW), which states that 'social workers should obtain education about and seek to understand the nature of social diversity and oppression with respect to race, ethnicity, national origin, color, sex, sexual orientation, gender identity or expression, age, marital status, political belief, religion, immigration status, and mental or physical disability' (National Association of Social Workers, 2016). As with the other codes, it states explicitly that social workers should not discriminate along these lines. Furthermore, social workers should act to 'prevent and eliminate domination of, exploitation of, and discrimination against any person, group, or class on the basis of race, ethnicity, national origin, color, sex, sexual orientation, gender identity or expression, age, marital status, political belief, religion, immigration status, or mental or physical disability' (National Association of Social Workers, 2016).

Thus we can see links in these ethical codes between respect, social justice and recognition of difference and diversity. Working with difference has ethical implications because failure to fully appreciate and respond to people's differences may further compound relations of oppression and domination already present. This has been an important area of practice development within social work, resulting in a number of different practice frameworks. In the next section we present a brief overview of just two, which pick up both the structural (macro) and identity (micro) differences discussed earlier in this chapter.

Radical and structural practice frameworks

We will begin with the radical framework as this is one of the oldest developments of frameworks to address inequality. Radical practice has been defined by Iain Ferguson and Rona Woodward (2009, p. 153) as involving four main aspects:

- The use of good practice skills which include communication, critical thinking, flexibility and creativity.

- The use of resistance to any operations that further oppress, stigmatise or contribute to domination of people who access our services.

- Working alongside service users and carers.

- Using collective approaches and contributing to political campaigns that address exclusion and oppressive social practices, processes and policies.

In this respect, for Iain Ferguson and Rona Woodward, radical practice entails a solidarity with the people we work with and resistance to the institutions and structures in society that contribute to interlocking oppressions and intersectional social practices. For Beresford, this means always 'seeing the person as an individual' (Beresford, Adshead & Croft, 2007, p. 105). By this it is meant 'offering a different service according to individual needs and preferences' (Beresford et al., 2007, p. 105). Even though a general principle such as respect may be evenly applied across differences, beneath this the social worker needs to understand and be responsive to the unique experiences, circumstances and needs held by different people. This practice framework addresses both the structural and interpersonal dimensions in social equality.

Structural social work approaches

Structural social work is one of the few practice frameworks that attempts to operationalise Young's (1990) call for justice. For Mullaly (1997, p. 163) social workers using a structural approach should have the following attributes:

- An understanding of the various political and ideological systems that operate in society based on a critical theory tradition that interrogates the limits of liberal, patriarchal, capitalist systems.

- An alternative vision of social relations that are fair, equal and just.

- An understanding of social work as an inherently political activity.

- That social work interventions should always go beyond merely focussing on individual, family or group deficit.

- Use of a social analysis informed by critical theoretical resources.

- That structural social work is more than an approach to practice – "it is a way of life".

This framework works with both structural and identity forms of difference but it emphasises more of the structural than some practice approaches. In this respect, this framework places the emphasis for action within clear lines of work-ing with service users, but always in solidarity. It always keeps in mind that a recognition that the problems of living for many people are created by condi-tions not of their own choosing (Griffiths, 1995).

Conclusion

This chapter has offered a range of social work and interdisciplinary perspectives on the existence of social inequality, which is often expressed in the terms differ-ence and diversity. The chapter has also explained intersectionality as a way of thinking about the politics of identity and utilised the terms *interlocking oppres-sions* and *relations of domination* to point to the structural aspects of social group identification and difference. Both aspects represent important theoretical resources crucial for social workers to understand if they are to practise in anti-discriminatory (Thompson, 2006) and anti-oppressive ways (Dominelli, 2002a). The chapter outlined the various ways in which national social work codes of ethics grapple with difference. The chapter closed with a brief presentation of two frameworks we consider as useful for embedding an approach to practice that can work with both the structural and identity aspects of difference.

Critical thinking questions

1. Define difference and diversity. In what ways are these terms similar? How are they different?

2. Why do social work ethical codes argue that social workers must respect and adequately respond to cultural, social and other differences among people and groups?

3. Referring to the arguments by Iris Young, how do oppression and discrimi-nation operate?

4. What is meant by interlocking oppressions and intersectionality? Give exam-ples of each to illustrate their meaning and application.

5. In what ways do radical and structural social work frameworks help social workers address oppression and discrimination?

Exercises

Refer to Table 6.1 'Thompson's forms of inequality' and Table 6.2 'Five faces of oppression'. In reference to both these tables, extend the summaries presented here by giving specific examples of each of the criterion presented (for example, a specific example for marginalisation (Young) and a specific example for economic inequality (Thompson)). Repeat this process for all criterion in both tables, until you have a list of specific examples for each table. Then, using radical and structural social work frameworks, propose ways that social work might respond to the specific examples you have drawn up. In this way you will have integrated theories of the nature of the problem (for example, Young, Thompson) with a social work response (for example, Ferguson & Woodward, Mullaly).

Further reading

Davis, K. (2008). Intersectionality as buzzword: A sociology of science perspective on what makes a feminist theory successful. *Feminist Theory, 9*(1), 67–85. doi:10.1177/1464700108086364

Dominelli, L. (2002). *Anti-oppressive social work theory and practice.* New York, NY: Palgrave Macmillan.

Gibson, M. (2015). Intersecting deviance: Social work, difference and the legacy of eugenics. *British Journal of Social Work, 45*(1), 313–330. doi:10.1093/bjsw/bct131

Hicks, S. (2015). Social work and gender: An argument for practical accounts. *Qualitative Social Work, 14*(4), 471–487. doi:10.1177/1473325014558665

Thompson, N. (2006). *Anti-discriminatory practice* (4th ed.). Basingstoke, UK; New York, NY: Palgrave Macmillan.

Links and online resources

On Intersectionality – a keynote presentation delivered by Distinguished Professor of Law at UCLA Kimberlé Crenshaw at the Southbank Centre on 14 March 2016 for the Women of the World (WOW) Festival. Professor Crenshaw coined the term *intersectionality* to describe the different ways in which race, gender and other social divisions interact to create discrimination and oppression. The video can be accessed here www.youtube.com/watch?v=-DW4HLgYPlA

From poverty to power – *How active citizens and effective states can change the world.* A conversational blog maintained by Duncan Green, author of "From poverty to power" and advisor to Oxfam GB. This blog can be accessed here http://oxfamblogs.org/fp2p/

London School of Economics (LSE) International Inequalities Institute brings together a wide variety of interdisciplinary scholars to research and develop tools to address inequality. You can access the institute here www.lse.ac.uk/InternationalInequalities/Home.aspx

London School of Economics (LSE) Podcasts. Challenging inequalities debate about inequality between Shami Chakrabarti, Duncan Green, Phumeza Mlungwana, available 25 May 2016. Available here www.lse.ac.uk/newsAndMedia/videoAndAudio/channels/publicLecturesAndEvents/player.aspx?id=3512

7

RESPECT AND DIGNITY

Introduction

Respect is an important aspect of everyday life. It is part of the things most of us learn as children ('respect your elders, teachers, others') and we are expected to demonstrate respect for others in our dealings with people at work, school, on the roads, whilst we are shopping, and in our dealings with public institutions. We expect, too, that we should enjoy recognition and regard from others in turn. Chenoweth and McAuliffe (2015) consider *respect for persons* to be a core value of professional social work practice. Moreover, they consider this value as part of a system of ethics that informs the social work profession. The value of respect is also often placed in the context of human rights and social justice (British Association of Social Workers, 2014; International Federation of Social Workers, 2012; National Association of Social Workers, 2016). We see respect and its fellow term, dignity, as a foundational value for human rights (Chapter 9, this volume) and ideas about social justice and injustice (Chapter 8, this volume). Likewise, Chenoweth and McAuliffe (2015, p. 69) suggest that respect for persons sits alongside other values also important for social work. These are values about respecting difference and diversity; maintaining a belief in the ability of people to make positive change; values about the rights of people to make choices about their circumstances and decisions; the right of people to privacy and confidentiality; valuing the environment; and the rights of people to be able to access services that have integrity.

Respect for persons and associated ideas about dignity underpin these other values because there is an assumption that human beings are moral agents and thus are inherently worthy of moral consideration on that basis. Further, as Maynard and Beckett (2005) suggest, values are not just concepts, they are also guides for action. Thus, respect and dignity are not only important in the many human-to-human transactions that characterise everyday life; they are also crucial to professional social work practice too.

In this chapter our aim is to consider the value of respect and dignity specifically. In the first section we consider respect and dignity by looking at multiple commonplace meanings in everyday life. In a subsequent section we will also consider some foundational ideas about human nature. In our discussion of human nature we demonstrate how respect includes dimensions of autonomy and dependence. This leads to a final discussion of the implications for enacting these values in social work practice. Our emphasis here is on what skills social workers need for recognising and respecting the inherent dignity and worth of all people.

Respect

Respect and obligation

Offering others respect at first may seem largely unproblematic. After all, who could disagree? Who would not want to enjoy the respect of others, and receive it ourselves in turn? Indeed, Dillon (2014) suggests that '... the notion of respect for persons commonly means a kind of respect that all people are owed morally just because they are persons, regardless of social position, individual characteristics or achievements, or moral merit.' Accordingly, it can be seen then that this position is something of a universal position on how we *ought* to treat one another.

What do we mean when we invoke the word 'ought'? Once this term is invoked it '... carries the implication of some sort of obligation to others, a duty to be fulfilled by either an individual or a group of individuals' (Beckett & Maynard, 2005, p. 8). Our sense of how we should treat each other and on what basis can be drawn from a number of different sources. Holmes (1984, cited in Beckett & Maynard, 2005, p. 8) suggests that respect might be self-imposed where 'each individual [has] responsibility for shaping his/her own existence'. Respect, therefore, might be a socially imposed obligation emerging from social arrangements aimed at group cohesion and survival. An example of this is the extensive social obligations Aboriginal people have to one another that emerge from their familial and group memberships (Briskman, 2007). Lastly, sometimes obligations can be considered to be *divinely* imposed. This means that our obligations to others might emanate from beliefs in a deity who has specified the purpose of human existence, and in doing so, has 'laid down rules to enable human beings to fulfil that purpose' (Holmes, 1984 cited in Beckett & Maynard, 2005, p. 8). These different sources of obligations are shaped by culture and experience, thus, resulting in different interpretations and actions about the basis on which people might be owed respect.

The concept of respect also comes with a range of cognitive, affective and behavioural dimensions (Dillon, 2014) that further complicate a straightforward understanding of how respect might be understood. Indeed, Maynard and Beckett (2005) suggest that values generally have five layers for professionals. These are legislative, organisational, professional ethics, personal and societal. Thus how *respect as a value* plays out in practice is shaped by all these different dimensions and layers. For example, in the Australian Social Work Code of Ethics (Australian Association of Social Workers, 2010, p. 12) the following is said about *respect for persons* as a value:

- Respects the inherent dignity, worth and autonomy of every person.

- Respects the human rights of individuals and groups.

- Provides humane service, mindful of fulfilling duty of care, and duty to avoid doing harm to others.

- Fosters individual wellbeing, autonomy, justice and personal/social responsibility, with due consideration for the rights of others.

- Recognises and respects group identity, interdependence, reciprocity and the collective needs of particular communities.

As you can see, this picture of what the profession considers important with regard to respect includes dignity and worth, human rights, autonomy, wellbeing, justice, human interdependence and the interests of groups and communities.

Dignity and respect

Dignity and respect are often discussed together in addition to other terms such as pride, worth and status (Sayer, 2011). In Sayer's view, there is some debate about whether dignity is an intrinsic property of human beings, or is it something that is more conditional and relational? Sayer (2011, p. 193) offers examples of the way people talk about dignity to illustrate this point:

1.   All humans beings are born free and equal in dignity and rights.

2.   I was relieved that my mother was allowed to die with dignity.

3.   Despite all the setbacks I managed to maintain my dignity.

Number 1 implies a property that is intrinsic to human beings, and thus it is considered a non-relational view (Sayer, 2011). Yet, if this was all there was to it we would not feel the need to assert its existence – dignity would exist independently of any circumstance or context. Nevertheless, dignity can be threatened quite easily. Sayer (2011) suggests:

> It [still] depends on the social circumstances in which people live; they may be born equal but their subsequent incorporation into social structures that are often hierarchical and exploitative means that they can become unequal. (p. 193)

The other examples (points 2 and 3) clearly demonstrate the relational and contextual qualities of dignity, and, by extension, respect. Here it is clear we can very easily lose our dignity and that dignity is a 'condition dependent both on how people conduct themselves and how they are treated by others' (Sayer, 2011, p. 193). *How we treat others* can assist in the maintenance of dignity and it can also mean that maintaining this in the face of a lack of recognition and respect from others is difficult. In this way, Sayer (2011, p. 193) suggests that dignity includes elements of 'comportment and conduct within a relationship'. By comportment and conduct, Sayer means not only *what* people say but also *how* they say or convey it (that is, tone of voice, use or avoidance of eye contact). Thus, losing the respect of others is considered to cause suffering as there is a tension between maintaining our individual dignity and our relationships with others. Respect for others and self-respect are thus inherently related (Dillon, 2014; Sayer, 2011). In fact, Dillon (2014) suggests that, like respect from others, there is broad agreement that self-respect too is an important aspect of everyday life.

This relation between the regard of others and our individual selves has been discussed and debated by philosophers, theologians, social theorists and psychologists for some time. Within Western philosophy and social theory generally, the relationship between individuals and their communities (Benhabib, 1992; Griffiths, 1995) has been one that has caused great debate about the extent to which we should view people only as individuals. Asian cultures typically see individuals as part of a social whole '... dignity [and thus respect] is a collective status which individuals are entitled to by virtue of their belonging to a community and assuming certain roles' (Lee, 2008, cited in Sayer, 2011, p. 190). Western culture has long emphasised dignity and respect as they relate to *autonomy* and this is often related back to the capacity to reason (Twomey, 2015). Even so, we would not say that someone with advanced dementia should not be respected or treated with dignity and care if they lack autonomy or reasoning facilities of a certain kind. Indeed, dignity is often discussed in relation to (mis)treatment specifically in areas associated with the right to dignified care, which incorporates recognition of specific kinds of vulnerability (ill-health, disability, age) but which also acknowledges elements of choice and autonomy. This emphasis in the West has led to a problematic conception of the relation between individuals and each other. Feminists have long critiqued the view of the autonomous individual in the recognition that human beings are inherently social and in need of care (Held, 1999; Noddings, 2003). Moreover, it is now recognised that regardless of culture the development of a healthy self-concept occurs through the interactions between human beings (Wiley, 2010). As Taylor (1989, cited in Sayer, 2011, p. 120) asserts 'one cannot be a self on one's own ... the full definition of someone's identity thus usually involves some reference to a defining community.' Ultimately, then, our connections to one another are a crucial aspect of our experiences of giving and receiving respect.

This relational aspect of respect is very evident by the fact that we feel it intensely when people show us disrespect. Further, we do not enjoy witnessing disrespect against others (Miller, 2001). Disrespect can take a number of forms that affect the physical and psychological well-being of people (Honneth, 1992).

Forms of disrespect include direct and indirect violence, exploitation, cultural imperialism (Young, 1990) and all different kinds of personal and collective insult. Disrespect can also include various forms of non-recognition and processes through which people become ostracised and excluded. People may also experience disrespect due to disability, sexual orientation, ethnicity, gender, age, religion or spiritual beliefs, and even their appearance. Sayer (2011) thus points out that dignity exists not just in weighty documents like human rights declarations, codes of ethics and political statements or conventions, but also in the spaces between people. Its conferral, or loss, is therefore felt not just in people's thoughts but also in their bodies. Social workers often encounter the effects of societal disrespect for groups of people where this results in stigma and discrimination, often with long-term debilitating outcomes for individuals and families.

In broad terms, then, the giving and receiving of respect, and the contribution this makes to the dignity of ourselves and others, is an important aspect of everyday life. We notice its absence in our everyday transactions with other people and this can have a significant impact on our own well-being as well as shape the way we approach others in turn. In light of this we can say that there is a relational aspect to respect and dignity in addition to the sense that it has an intrinsic quality on the basis of being human. We can also say that people are interested in their own well-being, and that of others, and are capable of being able to discern when they are receiving due respect and dignity from the society around them (Sayer, 2005). If this is such a commonplace occurrence, why then do we need to consider it so closely? We think the answer rests on these two aspects: the relational and the intrinsic quality of respect and dignity. We think that this twin dimension to respect raises questions about who is owed respect and dignity, and on what basis. We turn to consider this issue next.

Who is owed respect and on what basis?

One of the key debates in ethics with regard to respect concerns how we can understand *human nature*. Dillon (2014) says 'in everyday discourse the word "person" is synonymous with "human being" [but] some philosophical discussions treat it as a technical term whose range of application might be wider than the class of human beings (just as, for legal purposes, business corporations are regarded as persons)'. It appears that while ordinary people have little trouble distinguishing between humans, non-humans and animals (Sayer, 2011), critical questions raised by social scientists, legal scholars and, of course, moral philosophers, mean that we need to treat human nature as a *concept* (Heywood, 2000), and this is a concept that needs some explaining. In early debates there was a hope that we could work out an essential human nature upon which we could all agree. More contemporary notions of human nature admit the possibility of both commonalities and the endless variety in social arrangements, cultural practices, worldviews and beliefs amongst people (London School of Economics and Political Science (LSE) & Ramadan, 2016).

What can we say about human nature and why does it matter?

Descriptions of human nature go a long way back in philosophy and debates about it continue in the present day (Wall, 2005). This is because a large number of political doctrines and social theories are based on a range of implied assumptions about human nature. One example that would be familiar to most people is the debate about whether people are born as a *tabula rasa,* meaning they are born as a clean slate (Mautner, 1997). The alternative to this position is that people are born with innate capacities already available to them, a view associated with Plato (Mautner, 1997). As mentioned above, human nature debates tend to be about trying to account for a range of *essential* characteristics of human beings, those capacities that are innate rather than those gained through culture and experience (Heywood, 2000). The issue here is that as we become more knowledgeable about the intersection of culture and experience with individual characteristics, there have been successive challenges to the notion of a single essential core human nature. What has arisen is a wider sense of the variety of human nature (Sayer, 2011). We think this is a positive thing.

You might be wondering why this should matter. Wall (2005, p. xi) asserts that theories of human nature have very practical consequences because they suggest particular stances on 'the degree to which we are free, the nature of morality, the best type of society, the existence of God, the possibility of life after death, and the existence and nature of gender differences.' Feminist scholars have made many challenges as well to the very idea of an individual essential core human nature on the basis of these practical consequences for women. Feminists were able to point out that the underlying assumptions of these conceptions of human nature utilised male experience as a key measure of essential human characteristics (Benhabib, 1992; Butler, 2011; Griffiths, 1995; Hekman, 1999; Held, 1999). Similar challenges to early ideas about essential human nature as self-interested and driven to power have also been launched in the context of increased globalisation and the on going effects of past and present colonisation (Tully, 2000, 2008a). These challenges present important alternative views about the nature of humans as well as their relation to the earth and each other.

These debates continue and are beyond the scope of this chapter so we do not intend to rehearse them here. Instead what we want to do is present a summary of the various commonalities that might be claimed about human nature as a foundation to understanding the value of dignity and respect. These are drawn from Sayer (2011) who suggests them as starting points for the conditions of respect and recognition. Sayer (2011, p. 106) describes these as 'features of human social being'. We have included examples to illustrate each feature in Table 7.1.

Table 7.1 Features of human social being

Features	Explanation	Example
1. Variation is normal	'human nature encompasses variation as well as commonalities… if we are to avoid earlier conceptions of human nature we have to acknowledge this variation and incorporate it in our conception, not evade it' (Sayer, 2011, p. 108).	Size, shape and different sexualities are all examples of human variation.
2. Human animals and embodiment	We have unique human capacity for reason but we cannot escape our animal *nature* through reason. We also share many animal characteristics as well, including the capacity for flourishing and suffering (Sayer, 2011, p. 109).	Our capacity for reason is inextricably linked to bodily systems not under our conscious control. Many of these systems evolved and similar bodily systems can be found in other species.
3. Human becoming and care	Sayer (2011) suggests that we should consider human nature as one of becoming rather than being because all our capacities exist in *potentia* and depend on environment and experience for their expression. In this respect humans are different than rock or quarks – human capabilities emerge through systems of care and development (Sayer, 2011, p. 110). This means all humans need care and attachments in order for these capabilities to develop. The level and quality of care impacts not only on physical development but also psychological, emotional and intellectual development.	Human infants are born with vocal chords and the brain capacity to learn a language, however, whether the child does so depends on the quality of care the child receives.
4. Neediness, vulnerability, capability and concern	Humans share with non-human animals the capacity to suffer. Humans are vulnerable and also capable of meeting their own needs. We can distinguish between suffering and flourishing, better or worse experience. 'Human flourishing consists of more than the absence of suffering – it has extensive positive content' (Sayer, 2011, p. 114).	Experiencing hunger induces the drive to find food. The drive for pleasure can lead us into playful and creative past-times but for some it can result in addictions and unhealthy obsessions.

5. Reasoning beings	The capacity to reason through language has long been held by philosophers as the ability that distinguishes humans from other beings. We should, however, remember that the mind is not separate from the body but is emergent from it and this also shapes our moral capacity. Emotion and reason are not separate (Haidt, 2001). Human capacity for communication and the creation of meaning are dependent on our upbringing, social practices and the social milieu within which we find ourselves (Sayer, 2011, p. 115).	The human ability to reason and to show concern for themselves and others is acquired through childhood and later participation in the social and cultural practices of the community. Thus, the capacity for reasoning exists as a potential.
6. Fellow feeling	This capacity to understand how another is feeling is a fundamental aspect of human beings; however, it is not infallible – people can make mistakes in understanding. It is a characteristic of human society and while there is variation of it in individuals, it is a crucial aspect of our human social being (Sayer, 2011, p. 118).	We find it easier to empathise with familiar people than with strangers, although it is possible to empathise with strangers with intention (see Chapter 12 about empathy, this volume).
7. Relationality of the self: Going beyond egoism and altruism	Human beings are fundamentally social and 'there is not first an individual who then contingently enters social relations; relations are *constitutive* of the individual and their sense of self' (Winnicott, 1964, cited in Sayer, 2011, p. 119). Therefore, the liberal ideal of the autonomous individual is not particularly accurate with what is known about human development, growth and capacity. Recognition has to occur from subject to subject and with this comes a deeply comparative aspect whereby humans compare themselves to others with whom they have contact. Sayer (2011, p. 122) suggests that 'the comparative orientation is fundamental to morality, being crucial to the feelings of justice and injustice, resentment, envy, pride and shame.' These fundamental relational aspects of human social beings should act as a caution to any theory that suggests humans are inherently or primarily self-interested. Similarly, it should caution advocates of a purist notion of altruism because self-interest and other regarding behaviour need not always be in opposition (O'Neill, 1992, cited in Sayer, 2011, p. 123), Sayer points out that self-interest is not unimportant but that a more differentiated account of it is necessary to illuminate the shades of difference that exist between the poles of altruism and egoism.	The development of the self occurs through 'locating ourselves on a grid of attributes, concepts, comparisons, judgements, and so on that belong to the collective consciousness' (Tallis, 1988, cited in Sayer, 2011, p. 120). Being treated differently, for no apparent reason to others in your social group, can be very painful. Witnessing excellence in others can lead to feelings of elevation (Algoe & Haidt, 2009).

(Continued)

Table 7.1 (*Continued*)

Features	Explanation	Example
8. Attachments and commitments	Human beings are able to form attachments and commitments to other human beings but also to causes, objects, animals, practices and projects (Sayer, 2011, p. 125). Early attachment patterns are crucial to our development and can set us up for later attachments to others (Howe, 2013) Commitments, according to Sayer, are rather different as these take time to develop, involve immersion in activities, practices and relationships to which we become devoted. Over time they come to define our character and identity.	A person may be a staunch union member, a social worker, a drummer, the partner of ..., the mother of ...; and the friend of ...
9. Autonomy and heteronomy	Philosophy and social science, particularly from Western sources, have emphasised individual freedom, choice and autonomy (Sayer, 2011, p. 128). Feminists have pointed out that this model has assumed a particular gendered ideal based on a masculine model that does not take relations of care into account (Griffiths, 1995; Held, 1999). Autonomy is best thought of as '...not as complete independence from others but as self-command and [the] capacity for agency within the context of relationships and responsibilities that afford us some support' (Sayer, 2011, p. 128). Heteronomy has been held up by Kant as other-legislated action, which is action done due to dependence on others – this has therefore been contrasted with autonomy (Mautner, 1997).	Not all dependence is a negative thing – children depend on their parents for the development of a strong sense of self. We gain a sense of ourselves from others and this is important to our well-being and ability to exercise agency and capacity.

10. Virtues, vices, evil and social context	Sayer (2011, p. 129) suggests that 'the kinds of virtues and vices people acquire are strongly influenced by the cultural, social and material character of particular societies.' Moreover, repeated practice entrenches these into dispositions (Bourdieu, 1999). Fortunately we are able to take stock of our vices and virtues by way of our capacity for reflexivity (Archer, 2007). Changing our habits takes awareness, practise and time. The capacity for evil co-exists with the capacity for good and evil is not necessarily the absence of good but can be perpetrated through many different practices such as abuse, torture, systematic genocide and violence.	We might decide to change our habit of being overly cooperative at work and protect our time through being more assertive in saying no to unreasonable requests from colleagues. We might decide to change our eating and exercise habits in order to lose weight and feel more energised. An example of person-to-person evil would be child abuse. An example of systematised evil would be the Holocaust.
11. Well-being: objective and plural but not relative	Human well-being is not *just* subjective. That is, we might have explanations for how we feel that include elements independent of us (Sayer, 2011, p. 135). In other words there are objective conditions that shape our sense of well-being, such as our access to food, water, shelter, education and participation in society and cultural customs. This means that the conditions under which we live can and do affect human well-being and relationships with other human beings. This also means there is variety in arrangements for living that might create either suffering or flourishing and in this respect there are many routes to human well-being. Acknowledging this variety is to take a pluralist view. Sayer (2011, p. 135) points out the pluralism is different to relativism in that relativism assumes that 'what is good is simply relative to one's point of view.' We can also say that there is not one way of achieving well-being and, to a marked degree, individual definitions of it will be in relation to the prevailing customs, cultural and societal attitudes.	Muslim women living in Australia who are targeted for wearing the veil in public. Recipients of public housing being made visible because their house has been built in a neighbourhood with extensive private housing stock but it does not meet the prevailing standard of private housing, (that is, no carport doors, or standard driveways). Aboriginal people being unable to access land necessary to their cultural practices.

Clearly from these commonalities we can derive a number of key points with regard to dignity and respect. One is that human beings are social and that they need care and recognition from other human beings. We can also say that even the enjoyment of autonomy relies on the existence of others (Sayer, 2011). Humans need recognition from each other as subjects (Tully, 2000) and we are capable of both understanding and misunderstanding each other. Humans are capable of reason but this capacity is affected by our emotions and embodiment, and our *relative* opportunities for its development (Chapters 5 and 6, this volume). We can say that humans live in a variety of cultures and settings that offer different mixes of social practices that contribute to either suffering and/or flourishing. Human beings are capable of change because they have a reflexive capability to consider the circumstances in which they find themselves. Moreover, human beings are able to do so with regard to their own and others' actions (Archer, 2000). Despite this reflexive capability, we can say that the ability of individuals to transcend difficult circumstances generally depends on more than individual effort (see Chapter 8 on social justice, this volume). In other words, human beings need *each other*.

Having considered human nature and explained these commonalities, we can return to our discussion of who is owed respect and on what basis and connect this back to social work. Given the human social being outlined above in terms of suffering and flourishing, we draw a clear inference that the basis for *offering respect* and thus dignity is through the way we relate to, and recognise the existence and circumstances of, other human beings. Thus, the primary way we convey respect to others is through communication. In the next section we suggest how this translates into social work practice.

Social work practice and dignity and respect

From our previous discussion it should be fairly clear we are taking a stance towards respect and dignity that includes both universal elements (commonalities amongst human social beings) but one that also acknowledges the emergent expression of variety and difference (the impact of context) that being human entails in plural societies. We agree with Connolly (2013, p. 49) when she suggests that values 'act as moral compasses that help to guide us towards what ought to be the case in practice.' Crucially, social work practice is shaped not only by our own personal values but also organisational, professional and societal values, many of which may be at odds with each other. Nevertheless, we think that a foundation to enabling the expression in practice of *respect for persons* is possible and it rests on the development of a range of individual skills alongside practice skills. We have set them out in the list in the next section.

Skills for respectful practice

- **Verbal and non-verbal communication skills** including being conscious of choosing actively to listen, speaking, sensitivity to miscommunication cues, ability to convey understanding with both speech and through one's body language.

- **Written communications skills** including being able to write clearly, in a non-racist, non-sexist way; development of sensitivity to how case notes and other forms of written communication may shape perceptions of service users.

- **Development of high levels of self-awareness** and self-regulation of emotion and the capacity to be reflexive.

- **Awareness of others** – empathic skills, cultural literacy and toleration.

- **Advocacy skills** – speaking out about injustice and in areas where there is non-recognition of people's dignity; including contesting organisational and societal processes and practices that perpetuate social inequality.

- **Policy skills** – ability to understand and contribute to policy formation and change based on values of respect and social justice.

- **Strategic skills** – the ability to navigate and influence people both within and without your organisation in order to support the needs and aspirations of service users.

- **Organisational skills** – being on time, being organised, time management, knowing how to get things done and following through with tasks on behalf of service users and colleagues.

As you go through the various aspects and activities of learning social work it is good to be aware of how the skills and knowledge you are learning about contribute to your repertoire for enacting respectful practice. Social work students and practitioners with these skills will be well placed to contribute to reducing suffering and supporting the broad aim of human flourishing.

Conclusion

This chapter has discussed commonplace understandings of respect and dignity with a view to illuminating the rather complicated nature of this crucial aspect of professional practice. We have presented respect and dignity as a dance amongst people that involves recognition of their autonomy of choice and capacity but also their vulnerability and dependence on others. This is a difficult and challenging focus but it is nevertheless critical for this value to be meaningful as a driver of respectful practice. As always, we can see also that there is an intersection between who we are as people and the personal and professional values we bring to practice. Ensuring that we are well skilled in communication and practices as outlined above is an important step towards realising *respect for persons*.

Critical thinking questions

1. Why does social work hold respect for persons as an important value?

2. What does it mean to be respectful?

3. Give some examples of disrespect. In your view, what do these examples violate or transgress? What makes them disrespectful?

4. Why are dignity and respect so crucial to human nature and what human beings need from each other?

5. What do social workers need to do in practice to ensure they respect people's dignity and convey respect for persons?

Exercises

Go to the Global Dignity website and review the resources and tools they have on how to run a Dignity Day (www.globaldignity.org/tools/). Run a Dignity Day session with your tutorial or class. You may need to adapt these tools to suit your context.

Further reading

Algoe, S. B. & Haidt, J. (2009). Witnessing excellence in action: The 'other-praising' emotions of elevation, gratitude, and admiration. *The Journal of Positive Psychology*, 4(2), 105–127. doi:10.1080/17439760802650519

Connolly, M. (2013). Values and human rights. In M. Connolly & L. Harms (Eds.), *Social work: Context and practice* (pp. 49–59). South Melbourne, VIC: Oxford University Press.

Held, V. (1999). Liberalism and the ethics of care. In C. Card (Ed.), *On feminist ethics and politics* (pp. 288–309). Lawrence, KS: University Press of Kansas.

Sayer, A. (2011). *Why things matter to people: Social science, values and ethical life*. Cambridge, UK: Cambridge University Press.

Twomey, M. (2015). Why worry about autonomy? *Ethics and Social Welfare*, 1–14. doi: 10.1080/17496535.2015.1024154

Links and online resources

Dignity – Little Things Make A Big Difference is an animation about the dignity and respect by the Northwest Dignity Leeds Network. The animation is aimed at anyone working with others in a caring capacity. You can access it here www.youtube.com/watch?v=ueLqAJRxKpQ

Global Dignity was created in 2006 and is the brainchild of three friends: HRH Crown Prince Haakon (Norway), Professor Pekka Himanen (Finland) and founder of Operation HOPE, John Hope Bryant (United States). They say 'In a world where it seems no-one agrees on anything, a world where politics divides, religion divides, and race and even cultural borders seem to divide, dignity is something that everyone can agree on.' The Global Dignity established yearly Dignity Days and is a non-partisan, non-criticism and autonomous organisation. You can access the website and get involved here: www.globaldignity.org/

Sacks, J. (n.d.). *The dignity of difference – An interview with Jonathon Sacks, former Chief Rabbi of Great Britain.* You can access the podcast here: www.onbeing.org/program/dignity-difference/188

Xavier Le Pichon. (2016). *Xavier Le Pichon – the fragility at the heart of humanity.* In K. Tippett (Ed.), *On Being.* Minnesota, MN: Krista Tippett Public Productions www.onbeing.org/program/xavier-le-pichon-the-fragility-at-the-heart-of-humanity/101

8

SOCIAL JUSTICE AND FAIRNESS

Introduction

Social justice is a core part of the social work profession. Many people enter the social work profession because they have a strong commitment to making things better for people, communities and society, and they bring with them an already formed commitment to social justice (Gardner, 2006). Some organisations profess a commitment to social justice as part of their statement of philosophy or mission (Gardner, 2006) and this commitment can align with service users and community groups who may be pursuing social justice aims too (Chenoweth & McAuliffe, 2015, p. 38).

This chapter explores the concept of social justice and examines its place in the ethics and theory of social work, including the kinds of things that a social justice approach to social work seeks to address. We will explore two main theories of social justice, those of philosophers John Rawls and Iris Marion Young. Each of these theories can contribute an understanding of the principles of fair and just distribution of resources and opportunities, as well as the many aspects of oppression and marginalisation that are at the root of so much injustice. Finally, we draw a comparison between social justice and fairness, and outline an example of how injustice and unfairness can deeply affect people's well-being. The point we make here is that unfairness and injustice account for why people may experience distress and conflict, and negative effects on resilience and health overall (Siegrist, 2005).

Social justice in social work

Ethics

The International Federation of Social Workers (IFSW) states that 'Principles of social justice, human rights, collective responsibility and respect for diversities are central to social work' (IFSW, 2014). This makes it clear that social justice is central to the profession of social work in terms of its mission, theory and practice. Hence, learning what is meant by social justice and how to practise towards it is a key aim of a social work education, and something that should occupy an important place in the practice frameworks and methods used by social workers globally. In fact, social justice is enshrined in various social work ethical codes as a core value. For example, social justice is a core value in the British Association of Social Workers Code of Ethics for Social Work, defined as follows:

> Social workers have a responsibility to promote social justice, in relation to society generally, and in relation to the people with whom they work. (The British Association of Social Workers, 2012, p. 9)

Along these lines, the pursuit of social justice includes: challenging discrimination; recognising diversity; distributing resources; challenging unjust policies and practices; and working in solidarity (British Association of Social Workers, 2012, p. 9). The focus of social justice is concerned with fairness in terms of social resources, but also the way that discrimination and injustice operates through social policies and society generally on the basis of various social markers such as age, gender, race and sexual orientation (British Association of Social Workers, 2012).

Likewise, the Canadian Association of Social Workers Code of Ethics refers to social justice as follows:

> Social workers believe in the obligation of people, individually and collectively, to provide resources, services and opportunities for the overall benefit of humanity and to afford them protection from harm. Social workers promote social fairness and the equitable distribution of resources, and act to reduce barriers and expand choice for all persons, with special regard for those who are marginalized, disadvantaged, vulnerable, and/or have exceptional needs. Social workers oppose prejudice and discrimination against any person or group of persons, on any grounds, and specifically challenge views and actions that stereotype particular persons or groups. (Canadian Association of Social Workers, 2005, p. 5)

The pursuit of social justice in this respect involves upholding rights, advocating for fair access to resources, equality under the law, and 'social development and environmental management in the interests of all people' (Canadian Association of Social Workers, 2005, p. 5). As mentioned in a previous chapter on difference, the Aotearoa New Zealand Association of Social Workers Code of Ethics states that:

> Members advocate social justice and principles of inclusion and choice for all members of society, having particular regard for disadvantaged minorities. They act to prevent and eliminate discrimination against any person or group based on age beliefs, culture, gender, marital, legal or family status, intellectual, psychological and physical abilities, race, religion, sexual orientation, and social or economic status. (Aotearoa New Zealand Association of Social Workers, 2015, pp. 2–3)

According to the Australian Association of Social Workers (AASW):

> The social work profession holds that social justice is a core obligation which societies should be called upon to uphold. Societies should strive to afford protection and provide maximum benefit for all their members. (Australian Association of Social Workers, 2010, p. 13)

For the AASW, social justice practice includes working towards fairness and justice for the most disadvantaged and vulnerable. This takes the form of advocating and changing systems and policies that perpetuate injustice and rights violations. A focus on ecological protection and community participation is also included.

In reviewing these definitions of social justice as articulated by the above ethical codes, a number of similarities are apparent. Although it should be acknowledged that social justice is a contested concept (Heywood, 2000), these definitions in social work ethical codes give social justice in social work a unifying theory and meaning. These include: fairness and equitable distribution of resources; reducing inequality; addressing rights violations; ending prejudice and discrimination; ending marginalisation and disadvantage; and working collectively for the common good. The philosophy of social justice that expresses these aims is discussed later in this chapter.

Social work theory and knowledge

Beyond an ethical standpoint, the commitment to social justice in social work is widely acknowledged as being part of the knowledge base and practice methods of social work (Alston & McKinnon, 2005; Bland, Renouf & Tullgren, 2009; Chenoweth & McAuliffe, 2015; Ife, 2002). For example, social justice – in the distributive sense of fair access to resources – has been a key historical aim of social work (Chenoweth & McAuliffe, 2015, p. 42) and Ife (2012) argues that many social workers would see themselves and their practice as entailing a commitment to social justice. Thus social justice forms a significant part of the values and identities of social workers too.

If you are reading about social justice in social work, you might notice links between advocates of social justice in social work, and the critical theory and radical practice traditions that have developed in social work since the 1970s (Briskman, Pease & Allan, 2009; Mendes, 2009b). Many discussions of social justice in social work are located in this critical theory literature and this development in social work is often traced back to the social reformist work and community organising of social work pioneer Jane Addams (1860–1935) (Mendes, 2009b).

It is along these lines that work towards social justice developed in activist, community-based and grass roots movements for social change, and theory and practice is orientated towards redressing a litany of social injustices and human rights infringements (Briskman, 2014). In this tradition, the role of collectivist and group-based practice is often emphasised over individualist or therapeutic approaches (Lundy, 2004; Shapiro, 2003). In discussing a framework for community development, Ife (2002) develops a number of social justice principles that would be applicable to practice. By way of example, these include:

- *Addressing structural disadvantage* – by 'structural disadvantage' Ife is referring to the accrued disadvantages associated with class, gender and race/ethnicity (see Chapter 6, difference, this volume). These are not unifying categories and people will be differentially placed with such categorical groups. By 'addressing' Ife (2002) means '… affirmative action, positive discrimination, equal opportunity, consciousness raising and education' (p. 206). These are examples of social justice practice.

- *Addressing discourses of disadvantage* – this adapts a Foucaultian notion of discursive power, or the way that discourse is itself a form of power that can categorise, label, construct and invent practices that exert control over people (see Chapter 3, power, this volume). The response here is to think critically about the oppressive potential of knowledge production and application, and how some discourses can work to further entrench disadvantage and injustice.

- *Empowerment* – which means 'providing people with the resources, opportunities, vocabulary, knowledge and skills to increase their capacity to determine their own future, and to participate in and affect the life of their community' (p. 208). If used in the right way, empowerment can be a key plank in a social justice strategy.

- *Need definition* – this includes engaging in and supporting dialogue to the extent that individuals and communities can participate in defining their needs.

- *Human rights* – this means understanding and applying the UN Declaration of Human Rights to the practice of community work, and working to ensure that rights are identified, upheld and defended (see Chapter 9, human rights, this volume).

These are examples of social justice practice principles for community development, but they have transferable applicability to other methods and theories of social work. As mentioned, some of the debate and theory development here is within the context of critical and radical social work approaches. A critical and radical approach to practice is often informed by a diverse array of theoretical and political orientations that may include Marxist, feminist, anti-oppressive, anti-discriminatory and postmodern perspectives (Allan, Pease & Briskman, 2009; Dominelli, 2002a, 2002b; Martin, 2003b). Sometimes the literature uses the term 'macro social work' to refer to things like community development, policy advocacy and social planning (Brueggemann, 2002), as well as social work in international and global contexts, which may also adopt a macro perspective on global issues (Sowers & Rowe, 2007). Others use the term 'radical social work' (Ferguson & Woodward, 2009) and yet others refer to a 'structural social work' approach (Lundy, 2004; Mullaly, 2007). What tends to unite these perspectives is their socio-political perspective on social injustices, the way they take aim at various sources of oppression and domination, and the way they seek social change and transformation through emancipation, consciousness raising, advocacy and social and political action (Allan, 2003). These approaches may also adopt a sustained critique of neoliberal ideology, which many see as being implicated as a root cause of social inequality and social division (Ferguson & Woodward, 2009) and they adopt a social change and social justice purpose to social work, firmly anchored in its methods.

Social justice theories

So far, we have learnt that social justice is key to social work – ethically, theoretically, and in a practical sense regarding purpose, mission and role. Hence, it is important to think about the meaning and theoretical basis of social justice and how this might inform analysis and practice. Yet, in making a claim about the importance of social justice theory, Barry remarks:

> … why produce a theory of social justice? In the poorest countries, people do not need a theory to tell them that there is something wrong with a world in which their children are dying from malnutrition or diseases that could be prevented by relatively inexpensive public health measures. (Barry, 2005, p. 4)

According to Barry, we *need* theories of social justice precisely because people will disagree over what they think the problem is (or is not) and what, if anything, should be done about it, and how it should be done (Barry, 2005; Dominelli, 2004, pp. 70–71). Furthermore, Barry contends that 'we need the right theory of social justice if we are to get the right answers' (p. 4). But what is the right theory? In arguing for social justice, social workers need to be clear about what kind of social justice they mean, and how it should be obtained. For example, according to Ife (2012), justice in the legalistic sense can be conflated with revenge, or alternately, justice can be thought of as being satisfied through the fair application of the rule of law. Given that some laws themselves can be discriminatory and oppressive, this may hardly be a good basis for social justice. So, some conceptual clarification is needed. Furthermore, some medical and other services – despite noble intentions – can themselves be sites of injustice; for example, the instances of poor treatment of mentally ill people in institutional care (Bland et al., 2009).

It should be pointed out that social justice is not just the purview of social workers, and this accounts for the debates and contestation over its meaning. There are different interpretations of what social justice means and arguments between progressive and conservative quarters can often erupt (Dominelli, 2004, p. 70). Some fairly common and somewhat politically conservative arguments tend to follow a conceptualisation of social justice as being equated with rights and entitlements (Nozick, 1974). This is a view of social justice based on merit, contending that 'material rewards should reflect the distribution of ability and effort in society at large' (Heywood, 2000, p. 138). So, along this line social justice is geared towards rewarding effort and ability. This line of thinking occupies a significant place in many public policy discussions, particularly those that promote the idea that success or failure, wealth or poverty, are simply the result of how much effort someone expends, or the level of talent and ability that they have developed and nurtured. The problem with this view is that it is based on a number of errors. First, it assumes that reward and success are based on individual effort and merit, when in fact circumstances that shape one's lives (identities, opportunities, abilities, experiences) are often distinct from individual autonomy, choice and personal freedom to become a certain kind of person. For example, some natural talents that can be leveraged to one's advantage are part of a genetic lottery and have little to do with effort. These might be personality dispositions that happen to thrive in today's competitive cultures. Furthermore, someone may expend considerable effort over a sustained period and receive little. Second, a meritocratic view assumes that the playing field is level, when patently it is not. Some people may benefit from receiving a prestigious education, from a supportive and well networked family, in a context that is safe, stable and endowed with physical and other resources and benefits. The fact that someone may thrive in this situation is not to be confused with the effort they expend to make good of these circumstances that are outside of their choosing. The opposite is also true: poverty, racism, violence and other systemic problems will curtail opportunity and benefits, but that will not stop people being blamed for their problems. If talent plus effort is a flawed basis for deciding who gets what, then what else might we turn to?

John Rawls and social justice

Philosopher John Rawls offers a social justice conception that is based in establishing principles of distribution underpinned by *fairness*, rather than principles of moral desert or meritocracy discussed above. Rawls (1971) equates social justice with egalitarianism and fairness and in this sense it is relevant to a social work pursuit of a just and fair society, with equitable distribution of benefits, burdens and opportunities (see, for example, the Code of Ethics definitions discussed earlier in this chapter). But *what is* fairness, and what are *the methods* by which we can obtain fairness?

Rawls says that justice is the 'first virtue of social institutions' (Rawls, 1971, p. 3). Given that social work operates within a context of mainly public institutions (social welfare, health, social security), and many of the service users social workers deliver services to interact with and are influenced by the conduct of these institutions, then the importance of placing social justice practice as a virtue in social work is immediately apparent. But there is a second reason beyond the domain of practice that social work should be concerned with questions of social justice at the level of social institutions. Social institutions more broadly (government, education, institutions of wealth production and distribution) are part of the distributive mechanisms of wealth, power, opportunity, privilege, and are implicated in the corollary – poverty, disempowerment, disadvantage, and so on. Furthermore, social institutions are discursive insofar as they define needs and problems, and make moral judgements about moral desert. So, questions to do with social justice are really questions on how these social benefits and burdens and their associated discursive properties are produced, and distributed, and the means by which principles of justice in social institutions are sanctioned and operated.

Rawls' (1971) view of justice has been characterised as being liberal left, because Rawls' formula for social justice is about finding a balance between personal liberty or personal freedoms and opportunities and one that is concerned with equality. If we held that justice was just about personal freedoms and liberties only, there is no guarantee that there would be any equality on many of the things considered important, such as freedom of expression and the right to vote. If we focus just on equality for all, that may involve removing personal liberties and freedoms. On the other hand, in order to achieve an equal society in terms of income distribution, then this means that someone who may work hard and earn money is morally obligated to contribute some of their earnings to the benefit of others. And this is somewhat at odds with the prevailing neoliberal ethic of being a rational self-maximiser. Many governments promulgate this idea when they campaign for reducing taxes and cutting public spending. This legitimises the way we become narrowly concerned with our immediate circumstances or those of people close to us, such as friends and family. Yet, social justice requires that we also give due regard to strangers. Rawls tried to find a balance whereby we can retain the just elements of personal liberties and still have social equality or fairness. How do we achieve this fairness and equality? How do we decide on what is fair and equitable?

If we are deciding on issues of justice, it is likely that we will develop principles of justice based on who we are and what we do. For example, a wealthy business owner or shareholder will decide on issues of justice in very different ways to a homeless person, because each would argue for a situation that is favourable to their *specific* interests. In some respects, this is what actually happens in debates about what is just and fair, which is a problem when we consider who has greater access and influence to the key decision-making processes embedded in social institutions (consider for example the differential positions of power between a wealthy business owner and a homeless person in influencing the course and conduct of social institutions and political discourse). So, we end up with distorted conceptions of justice that are favourable to the interests of those most able to influence such conceptions. This explains to some extent why patterns of privilege and disadvantage become entrenched and persist over time.

To correct this problem, Rawls invites us into a thought experiment and asks us to attempt to strip away what we know about ourselves and our own vested interests in order to develop principles of justice unfettered from our own interests, and instead based in an original position, behind a veil of ignorance (Rawls, 1971). Imagine 10 people sitting in a room together. These people are to decide on the rules and principles of a just society, but in doing so, they are deciding on questions of justice in total ignorance of their situation and what benefits they might ultimately derive from such principles of justice. He writes:

> It is assumed, then, that the parties do not know certain kinds of particular facts. First of all, no one knows his place in society, his class position or social status; nor does he know his fortune in the distribution of natural assets and abilities, his intelligence and strength, and the like. Nor, again, does anyone know his conception of the good, the particulars of his rational plan of life, or even special features of his psychology such as his aversion to risk or liability to optimism or pessimism. More than this, I assume that the parties do not know the particulars of their own society. That is, they do not know its economic or political situation, or the level of civilization and culture it has been able to achieve. The persons in the original position have no information as to which generation they belong. (Rawls, 1971, p. 24)

If we are ignorant of our own circumstances and situations, then we are likely to decide on principles of justice that will not *potentially* harm us and therefore we will advocate for principles that are favourable to all – especially as we do not know what position in society we may occupy; once the veil is lifted we may occupy any of a number of social class positions, family backgrounds, possess any number of natural talents or limitations, and so on. Rawls argues that this thought experiment of ignorance is the best way to formulate the rules and principles of society in an objective and unbiased manner. In doing so, Rawls argues that two principles of justice would be chosen in advance by those behind the veil of ignorance, and that these principles would be acceptable to all free and rational agents, and therefore applicable to a theory of social justice.

- *First principle:* '… each person is to have an equal right to the most extensive basic liberty compatible with a liberty similar to others' (Rawls, 1971, p. 60). This means that we may have the right to earn money, spend money, acquire property and enjoy basic freedoms so long as they are equal with others' rights and freedoms to do the same. A social worker following this principle would seek to ensure that basic liberties and opportunities are equally distributed and open to all. These are defined by Rawls as '… political liberty (the right to vote and be eligible for public office) together with freedom of speech and assembly; liberty of conscience and freedom of thought; freedom of the person along with the right to hold (personal) property; and freedom from arbitrary arrest and seizure as defined by the concept of the rule of law' (Rawls, 1971, p. 61). This gives clear direction on the sorts of things that social workers would seek to uphold as they are consistent with Rawls's first principle.

- *Second principle:* '… social and economic inequalities are to be arranged so that they are both (a) reasonably expected to be to everyone's advantage, and (b) attached to positions and offices open to all' (Rawls, 1971, p. 60). This means that there *can* be inequality in a society but it must be advantageous to the least advantaged. This form of inequality may be considered 'socially just inequality'. For example, some people may be taxed at a higher rate than others so long as the benefits go to those who – even if they did not earn the tax through their labour – benefit from it nonetheless in the form of access to public goods and services, for example. This might take the form in publicly funded education, health care, housing and other assistance to those most vulnerable and disadvantaged in other ways. This form of access to various social goods and institutions may, *prima facie*, unequally favour the most disadvantaged, but this is a principle of justice that Rawls contends *would be chosen* by those behind the veil of ignorance. Injustice '… is simply inequalities that are not to the benefit of all' (Rawls, 1971, p. 62). For example, if access to certain positions and offices (think of access to education, jobs, for example) are not open to all, and such restricted access benefits some people to the general exclusion and disadvantage of others, then this is not only unequal, but unjust. So, this form of justice does allow for the generation of wealth and opportunity, and the unequal distribution of wealth is tolerable so long as this inequality is somehow advantageous to all. For example, a position of wealth is obviously advantageous to the holder of such position, but it is only to be tolerated as just and fair if it is part of a system where the mere existence of that position at the same time benefits others, either through a share of the resulting wealth of that position, or because such as position works in a way so as to improve the well-being of the common good, for example. When tax breaks are provided to the most well off and this results in cuts to public goods and services – goods and services that are in the interests of those who are not well off – then we not only have a situation of inequality, but this may now be reasonably defined as unjust as well.

This second principle is known as the *difference principle* and like the first principle it applies at the level of general abstraction to the arrangement and conduct of social institutions and the rules that govern them. Social workers seeking to support the second principle are working towards an arrangement of social institutions where the benefits and rewards of certain positions and offices are open to all, and benefit the common good. Supporting access to the basics such as education is a strategy to ensure that opportunities are open to all. It also means that the benefits accrued from such positions are distributed in ways that are advantageous, so that, for example, someone's talents are put to benefit the most disadvantaged, or wealth is distributed in ways that benefit the least well off.

Rawls's argument is that people in the original position (behind the veil of ignorance) *would* choose these principles as they offer the best chance of a socially just society. Without knowing one's station in life, such principles seek to offer a level of protection for the rational person making a decision about what kind of society they would want to live in once the veil is lifted and both the nature of the society and their particular circumstance within that society are revealed to them. Rawls's argument is that people would want a society that was fair in respect to equal rights and basic compatible liberties, and that they would want a society that tolerated inequality and its associated freedoms so long as that inequality was mutually advantageous. They would not tolerate a principle of inequality that benefited some, but not all, and this form of inequality would ultimately be considered unjust. In the case of the previous example, a wealthy person with access to power and influence would see that it is right and just that the benefits of their position are at the same time used in a manner that is advantageous to someone who is disadvantaged and locked outside of the circuits and networks of power and influence.

Iris Marion Young and social justice

Rawls's theory is a *distributive* theory of justice, and this aligns well with the social justice descriptions and intentions outlined in social work ethical codes. Rawls is criticised mostly for his hypothetical original position and veil of ignorance, that his theory of social justice is located within a Western liberalist paradigm, which has a tendency towards a universalist position (O'Neill, 1986). In reality, we do not decide on questions of justice ignorant of our position and interests. We decide on questions of justice with our own interests at heart, begging questions about who has access and influence over the kind of society we have, and consequently, who benefits and who loses. If we dig below the levels of abstraction offered by Rawls to a more specific analysis of what actually happens in practice we can begin to ascertain some directions that one may take in practical terms to work towards social justice. One way to think about social justice and injustice as a form of everyday practice is to draw from the work of philosopher Iris Marion Young (Young, 1990, 1999, 2000, 2004). Young's works provide a social justice perspective rooted in a 'politics of difference' (1990) and 'deliberative democracy' (2000). Young's (1990) conceptualisation of social justice contrasts somewhat with the Rawlsian version of social justice – that is, Rawls's notion of a fair distribution of social goods and burdens. According to Young, social justice:

> ... must displace talk of justice that regards persons as primarily possessors and consumers of goods to a wider context that also includes action, decisions about action, and provision of the means to develop and exercise capacities. The concept of social justice includes all aspects of institutional rules and relations insofar as they are subject to potential collective decision. The concepts of domination and oppression, rather than the concept of distribution, should be the starting point for a conception of social justice. (1990, p. 16)

For Young, domination and oppression should be the starting point in charting an analysis and practice towards social justice and this makes sense in relation to the critical theory tradition in social work discussed earlier. Like the critical theory tradition in social work, the problem noted by Young is that enduring structural and institutional conditions reproduce and perpetuate *exploitation, marginalisation, powerlessness, cultural imperialism* and *violence* (Young, 1990, pp. 48–63). Young refers to these conditions as the five faces of oppression (see Chapter 6, difference, this volume). Many social workers would be familiar with these as they describe the circumstances and effects in the lives of many service users. Young argues that without seriously attending to these problems, principles of social justice at a level of abstraction offered by Rawls will have little impact.

Young's approach to social justice urges social workers to pay attention to the factors that perpetuate injustice at the level of everyday practices. What sort of practices? There are two examples that we refer to here: democracy and participation; and speech culture. A relationship exists between the two. The former concerns the extent and manner that people can participate in meaningful ways in decisions and actions that affect them. The latter concerns the way that norms associated with public discourse means that some people's voices and views are privileged, listened to and taken seriously, while others are not.

Democracy, participation and speech culture

The kind of democracy that Young argues for, as a necessary condition for social justice, is a form of deliberative democracy. According to Young (2004), deliberative democracy involves 'practical reason' (p. 227) and is 'primarily a discussion of problems, conflicts, and claims of need or interest' (p. 227). This form of democracy is not underpinned purely by 'numerical support' (p. 228) but by 'determining which proposals the collective agrees are supported by the best reasons' (p. 228). Therefore, democratic participation should involve serious attempts at facilitating people who might ordinarily be excluded from public debate and decision-making to contribute to proposals concerning policy, service development and delivery, and the development of wider understanding and appreciation of various social problems – how to think about them and respond to them.

Young (2004) explains that there are 'several normative ideals' (p. 228) that must be in place in order for deliberative democracy to occur. These are inclusion, political equality, reasonableness and publicity (2004, pp. 228–230). Right away we can see the articulation of goals and aspirations for social workers to strive for to attain social justice. *Inclusion* involves developing the capacities for all people to deliberate on proposals that affect them. *Political equality* means that all people should 'have an equal right and effective opportunity to express their interests and concerns' (p. 228), as well as be able 'to respond to and criticize one another's proposals and arguments' (p. 228). Many people are affected by social policy decisions, sometimes quite negatively, but they don't always have the opportunity to be included in the debates and formulations of such policies in an equal manner. *Reasonableness* refers to 'a willingness to listen to others who want to explain to them why their ideas are incorrect or inappropriate' (p. 229).

Quite often, the voices and experiences of the most marginalised are simply ignored, ridiculed or treated with contempt and disdain. Their experiences are sometimes mocked by media commentators and politicians. Alternately, some voices get plenty of air time while others are rendered completely invisible. Social justice practice in response to this is to confront the unreasonableness of a narrowly privileged public discourse, to one that includes a plurality of voices and perspectives, and to try to engineer better opportunities for the most silenced and marginalised members of society to have a voice, and have that voice taken seriously.

Finally, and relatedly, *publicity* involves 'a plurality of different individual and collective experiences, histories, commitments, ideals, interests, and goals that face one another to discuss collective problems under a common set of procedures' (Young, 2004, p. 229). Listening to people, advocating, working with differences, opening up space for dialogue, and even some forms of research can be seen as important social justice practices that try to engage with a plurality of experiences and viewpoints in a public manner. These are Young's ideal normative conditions for constructing the potentials for deliberative forms of democracy. They provide fertile ground for social workers who may seek to practice in ways that support or make possible these kinds of democratic potential.

Rawls's (1971) social justice developed principles for fair and just distribution, whereas for Young the focus is on dominant culture that can become an object of analysis, criticism and change. Young (2000) says that 'speech culture' (p. 39) is a type of culture that privileges certain modes of expression. These privileged expressions include controlled 'dispassionate speech styles' (p. 39) and norms associated with the rules of argumentation and 'correct' expression (pp. 39–45). A context of oppression and injustice can mean more than who gets what, more than who benefits and who loses. It is one in which a form of silencing occurs, where devalued social positions and identities are not included and it is one where decisions in mass society are centred within the privileges of a minority who have access to the means of decision-making and exercise dominantly acceptable public discourse. These conditions will result in a diminished form of democratic potential. It is in this sense that Young foregrounds the links between democracy, inclusion in the broad sense, and social justice.

Fairness, reciprocity and well-being

As discussed, social justice in an ethical and principled sense is important to social work and it has a long history in the development of social work theory and practice. We have also discussed two main approaches to social justice: the distributive approach outlined by Rawls that is based in principles of justice; and the critical approach outlined by Young that is based in a theory of oppression and practices concerned with participation and inclusion. What is at stake here? At a broad macro level, the kinds of injustice discussed by Rawls and Young help to sketch a picture of inequality, violence, discrimination, poverty and various forms of abuse that affect some groups of people in disproportionate ways. These enduring problems stand in stark contrast to deep seated patterns of privilege, including the staggering amounts of accumulated wealth in the hands of some multi-national corporations and their benefactors for example (see Chapter 5, poverty and disadvantage, this volume). But presenting an analysis this way can make things seem very broad and impersonal, and sometimes it is hard to grasp the implications of this in specific ways. We are now going to make a link between social justice theory and *well-being* in a much more personal and specific way. This is an important link that is less often discussed and would be of interest to social work.

It starts with a view about human nature and fairness and we draw on work by Siegrist to make this link. This view can be considered in light of the description of human nature in Chapter 7, this volume, on respect and dignity. According to Siegrist (2005), human beings are hardwired for cooperation and social reciprocity. Cooperation and reciprocity is an evolutionary trait shown to have benefits to group survival and thus it is a trait that is passed down and has now become a part of the human condition (Sayer, 2011). Reciprocity is a form of 'social contract', and so it is understandable that many theories of social justice (including those discussed above) involve some notion of reciprocal exchange expressed in the form of an implicit contract. Examples of contracts include work, interpersonal relationships, trade, sharing, and so on. If you think about your own life, you might be able to identify many situations that involve some degree of reciprocity.

Through such contracts, people engage in various forms of exchange. A good example of this is in regard to paid work. Most people would expect that their efforts at work will involve an exchange of some degree of equivalence, not just in terms of being paid, but in regard to other benefits that go with work, such as recognition, meaning, sense of achievement and competence, feelings of making contribution and social benefits. Not all exchange needs to occur in the sense of being a direct return. Equivalence builds over time and involves a sense that one's efforts and engagement in all sorts of relationships will contribute to an overall sense that one would consider, on balance, to be *fair*. This judgement of fairness will differ from person to person, even though people generally will have views about what is fair and unfair.

Equivalence of exchange that is symmetrical or balanced (and hence thought of as fair) promotes trust, attachment and other conditions that allow people to enter into contracts with each other, even though the outcome of that relationship is uncertain (Siegrist, 2005), and even with strangers. If our exchanges over time are balanced and fair, then norms of reciprocity are created and this is socially beneficial. But, as mentioned, this exchange ought to be symmetrical or balanced overall if it is to be sustainable and functional. However, there are always circumstances where *non-symmetrical* contractual exchange occurs. For example, a person may work considerably hard at work or invest heavily in a relationship for little return. We can probably all think of examples of this.

Now, most people can tolerate non-symmetrical exchange for a while, but if this persists over time, we might start to feel a sense of unfairness creep in and begin to feel aggrieved. Here, we may even label this situation as injustice. We may feel angry. We may seek to actively change the circumstances of this non-symmetrical exchange so that they become fairer. These could be individual actions, or they could take part of wider social movements that occur as forms of activism and a push for social and political change. We are not always successful, however, as there are circumstances that keep non-symmetrical exchange firmly in place. These can be associated with personal and social structural factors of the kinds discussed by Young (1990). Entrenched circumstances may mean that non-symmetrical, unfair and unjust practices will persist over time, and some groups of people will be more exposed to this situation than others. In this case, social justice practice is about *changing those conditions*, not merely focussing on the person with the presenting problem.

We now know that repeated or sustained non-symmetrical social exchange creates psycho-social and neurological stress that is shown to be a significant health risk factor. Siegrist (2005) examines several notable epidemiological studies for evidence showing what happens to people who endure sustained non-symmetrical exchange and violation of the contract of reciprocity; in other words, sustained *unfairness* and *injustice*. According to Siegrist, cumulative or chronic effort–reward imbalance over a long period of time is associated with higher risk, compared with single (baseline) assessment in relation to the following: fatal/non-fatal cardio-vascular disease; angina; type II diabetes; mild to moderate psychiatric disorder (typically depression and anxiety); poor self-rated functioning and health; and alcohol dependence. In fact, the risks for these health problems are twice as high in cases of what Siegrist refers to as 'failed reciprocity' as they are for independent risk factors (Siegrist, 2005). This means that unfairness is not just a moral issue as a matter of principle: repeated instances of non-symmetrical social exchange result in strong perceptions of unfairness and this can manifest as prolonged psycho-social stress and illness. Unfairness and injustice can be thought of as a personal and public health hazard in the form of a social determinant of health (Liamputtong, Fanany & Verrinder, 2012; Marmot & Allen, 2014; Schofield, 2007), because aspects of the brain that deal with 'reward systems' happen to process other physiological functions as well.

In summary, people have evolved with needs for social reciprocity and expectations of fairness and symmetry in social exchanges (Siegrist, 2005). Violations of these needs in specific and often sustained circumstances brought on by social, political, economic and environmental circumstances can manifest as psycho-social stress in the form of distinct physical and psychiatric problems. In short, social injustice and unfairness 'hurts' because it violates something that is fundamental to human beings. Hence, the role of social justice work in social work is central as it is so connected to human well-being more broadly.

Conclusion

It should be clear that social justice is at the heart of social work's mission, ethics, theory and practice. A commitment to social justice is something that is quite often formative in the lives of student social workers and practicing social workers, as many would define their work, their identity and their passion in striving for social justice. Keeping ready access to your relevant social work code of ethics will provide a timely reminder of the centrality of social justice to the ethical commitment social work makes to address inequality, disadvantage, rights abuses, racism, violence, and so on. As discussed, social justice is concerned both with principles of distribution of resources and opportunities, and addressing oppression and domination. According to Rawls, a position of social justice ought to advocate for equality of rights and opportunities, as well as supporting a system that would advantage or benefit the most disadvantaged in society. Furthermore, Young's position on social justice demonstrates the need to work towards greater participatory inclusion, democracy, and tolerance of diversity and difference.

Critical thinking questions

1. What does social justice mean to you?
2. Why is social justice important to the profession of social work generally?
3. List five social work methods or skills that you think would be relevant to working for social justice.
4. Why do social workers need a really good understanding of social justice theory?
5. What are the main differences between Rawls's and Young's theories of social justice?

Exercises

Give three examples of what you think are the top social justice issues that social work should be concerned with. Explain why they are important to you, and explain how the theories outlined by Rawls and Young might assist your work as a social worker in addressing these social justice issues.

Further reading

Allan, J., Pease, B. & Briskman, L. (2009). *Critical social work: Theories and practices for a socially just world.* Crows Nest, NSW: Allen & Unwin.

Ferguson, I. & Woodward, R. (2009). *Radical social work in practice: Making a difference.* Bristol, UK: Policy Press.

Lundy, C. (2004). *Social work and social justice: A structural approach to practice.* Peterborough, ON; Orchard Park, NY: Broadview Press.

Rawls, J. (1971). *A theory of justice.* London, UK: Oxford University Press.

Young, I. M. (1990). *Justice and the politics of difference.* Princeton, NJ; Oxford, UK: Princeton University Press.

Links and online resources

Ahmed, M. (2011). *Social work reform: Promoting rights, justice and economic well-being.* Community Care. www.communitycare.co.uk/2011/03/10/social-work-reform-promo ting-rights-justice-and-economic-well-being/

Australian Human Rights Commission (2007). *Social determinants and the health of Indigenous peoples in Australia – a human rights based approach.* www.humanrights. gov.au/news/speeches/social-determinants-and-health-indigenous-peoples-australia-human-rights-based

Payne, M. (2012). *What's so special about social work and social justice?* The Guardian. www.theguardian.com/social-care-network/2012/jul/10/social-work-social-justice

Reamer, F. G. (2006). *Eye on ethics: Keeping social justice in social work.* Social Work Today. www.socialworktoday.com/news/eoe_0306.shtml

Wenar, L. (2013). *John Rawls. The Stanford Encyclopedia of Philosophy* (Winter 2013 Edition), Edward N. Zalta (Ed.) http://plato.stanford.edu/archives/win2013/entries/ rawls/

9

HUMAN RIGHTS

Introduction

It matters to people how they are treated by others. We established the importance of dignity as a foundation to respectful practice in an earlier chapter (Chapter 7, this volume). In this chapter our intention is to make links between the values of respect and dignity and notions of human rights and social work practice. Thus, we are considering human rights as an expression of certain values about human beings. We do this in line with a point made by Tasioulas (2015), that these rights 'are grounded in the universal interests of their holders, all of whom possess the equal *moral* status of human dignity' (Tasioulas, 2015, p. 70, our emphasis). Connolly and Ward (2007, p. 16) also make a point that there needs to be a moral foundation to human rights, and they consider that 'moral rights are a more extensive category than human rights ... human rights are a subset of moral rights.' While the philosophical foundations to human rights appears less than settled amongst philosophers, for our purposes we will ground our discussion of them in respect to certain moral claims. These are claims 'that human beings make on one another, and in particular on states and institutions and officials, even (or especially) when existing institutional structures fail to protect or secure those claims' (O'Neill, 2015, p. 71). Moreover, even as human rights are grounded in the moral status of human dignity – and this is expressed as a universal good – this does not preclude taking into account contextual elements of culture and variety, which are so characteristic of human social life.

We begin our discussion of human rights with the United Nations Declaration of Human Rights (UDHR) and the political, philosophical and practical issues surrounding its expression globally. The next section will consider contemporary claims that social work is a human rights profession. We conclude the chapter with some recommendations for translating a human rights focus into our social work practice.

Human rights globally

The United Nations preamble to the UDHR can be seen as a beautiful affirmation of the hopes for humanity and recognition of humans as both social beings and as individuals. It is an inspiring document. It is also among the most trans-lated documents in the world (United Nations, 1996a). The preamble uses words like freedom, friendly relations, inherent dignity and worth, social pro-gress, justice and peace. These words sit alongside what seems to us is a clear-eyed acknowledgement that tyranny and oppression exist and must be opposed. Furthermore, the preamble also suggests that the goals of freedom from fear and the enactment of respect for people's dignity and rights will remain unreal-ised where there is continued violence, barbarity and forms of inequality between people, nations, men and women. This declaration was first proclaimed in 1948 (United Nations, 2016) and it should be said it is a remarkable achieve-ment given that it occurred in the shadow of World War II and the aftermath of the Holocaust. Many contemporary thinkers such as Jean Paul Satre, Simone de Beauvoir, Hannah Arendt, Jurgen Habermas, Primo Levi and Viktor Frankl were also shaped by experiences during this period. Many of these thinkers have written about suffering and freedom and the human condition in addition to the nature of evil and compassion in relation to humanity and faith.

While inspirational, the UDHR has also been the focus of intense debate and contestation since it was first proclaimed. These debates about its meaning and what it means for different groups and individuals have led to the establishment of other related conventions such as the International Covenant on Civil and Political Rights in 1966 (ICCPR); the International Covenant on Economic, Social and Cultural Rights (ICESCR), also in 1966, and the important International Convention on the Elimination of All Forms of Racial Discrimination in 1969 (Healy, 2008). In turn, there have also been further declarations about the rights of Aboriginal people (United Nations, 1996b), women (United Nations, 2000); persons with disabilities (United Nations, 1996c) and children (UNICEF, 2016). Tully (2000) suggests that these claims are the outcomes of struggles for recog-nition and in this regard we can see human rights as a field in which people contest their political freedoms in the world, both through the state and also through wider global political forums as well.

Philosopher Onora O'Neill makes the point that a philosophical justification of human rights can be seen as occurring *ex post facto*. This is because it is a document of its time – post-World War II and drafted by states who had a place in the earliest iteration of the United Nations – and 'those that framed the UDHR drew on earlier arguments for conceptions of natural rights and of the rights of man' (O'Neill, 2015, p. 2). To a significant extent, the proliferation of human rights claims has occurred because the earlier conception of human rights has been seen as a cultural product arising from Western Enlightenment conceptions of human beings and assumptions about the existence of certain universal free-doms (Ife, 2012). Thus, it has been seen as not adequately addressing the claims of specific groups such as persons with disabilities or Aboriginal people, for example (Ife, 2012). This means that the UDHR contains a range of ideas about rights, human dignity, social progress and what freedom and peace might entail.

The debates continue about how to conceptualise human rights, about what human rights are, the conditions under which certain rights might be invoked, and what duties are there that a right confers on individuals and others – never mind how we might distinguish between rights that seem to cancel each other out. Think, for example, of the right to free speech versus the right to live free from speech that harms others by being racist or by undermining the dignity of others and their religious beliefs (Veninga, 2015).

Additional to these philosophical and political debates, there are also practical issues. The UDHR preamble and articles point to a number of different mechanisms for achieving human rights for all people. Consequently, we can see that within the UDHR the rule of law has a key place in the protection of human rights if they are under threat from tyranny and oppression. Rather problematically, the UN, then as now, holds no jurisdiction within *states* to ensure that these are actually enacted. In this regard, we can point to many instances where states have perpetrated human rights abuses within their own countries, leading to the establishment of non-state organisations such as Amnesty International (Amnesty International, 2016) or Human Rights Watch (Human Rights Watch, 2016). These groups have the express aim of monitoring human rights globally. Further to the issue of states contravening their adherence to the UDHR, not all states have signed the UDHR. Despite these issues, we can say that recourse to legal remedies remains an important mechanism for upholding human rights (Pruce, 2015), even if it is reliant on states to realise these aspirations for the human rights of various peoples across the world. The UN efforts in this regard have been important in the fight against tyranny, oppression and violence and have lent force to extra-state efforts, in the form of non-governmental organisations such as Amnesty International, to realise human rights (Pruce, 2015).

The UDHR preamble, however, also points to another aspect important to the realisation of human rights and the dignity of all people. That is, it points to the role of norms in the recognition of human rights:

> as a common standard of achievement for all peoples and all nations, to the end that every individual and every organ of society, keeping this Declaration constantly in mind, shall strive by teaching and education to promote respect for these rights and freedoms and by progressive measures, national and international, to secure their universal and effective recognition and observance, both among the peoples of Member States themselves and among the peoples of territories under their jurisdiction. (United Nations, 2016)

Thus, we can see that within philosophical, legal and political respects there is much to contest if we think about different conceptions of freedom and human dignity. In the next section we will consider the claims of social work as a human rights profession.

Social work as a human rights profession

When we consider some social work literature on human rights we can see that much of it takes a juridical approach (Ward & Connolly, 2007; Wronka & Staub-Bernasconi, 2012) (see Chapter 4 on power, this volume) towards human rights, describing various national and international human rights instruments important to particular countries and/or particular struggles. In discussing human rights in social work, it is common to cite the various legislative instruments available for implementing protections of human rights, or for contesting abuses of human rights (Preston-Shoot, Roberts & Vernon, 2001; Wronka & Staub-Bernasconi, 2012). As mentioned earlier, recourse to the law remains important.

Other writers emphasise the values component of human rights (Connolly, 2013; Ward & Connolly, 2007) and others again consider human rights as more of an academic discourse, rather than having much grounding in practice (Harrison & Melville, 2010, p. 153). For these authors, and supported by findings from Nipperess (2013) and Wronka and Staub-Bernasconi (2012), social work education plays an important role in human rights theory and practice, a point we return to later in this chapter.

How are human rights conceptualised in social work?

When explaining what human rights are it has been common in social work to use the work of Wronka (1992, cited in Harrison & Melville, 2010, p. 142) and his typology of 'generations of human rights'. These are summed up by Dr Kim Robinson (n.d., slide 7) and represented in Table 9.1.

Table 9.1 Generations of human rights

First generation	Civil and political rights, such as the right to vote, engage in freedom of speech and enjoy freedom from discrimination. It also means the right to a fair trial free from interference from the state or from other citizens.
Second generation	These rights are economic, social and cultural rights and entail statements that incorporate the right to health, housing, social security and education.
Third generation	These are conceived as rights that are collective in nature and involve the right of groups to development and to enjoy self-determination.

As you may notice, even a cursory inspection globally reveals that the status of some of these claims is barely recognised. Some members of societies may still not enjoy the right to vote. For example, Saudi Arabian women were allowed to vote for the first time only in 2015 and women in the Vatican City are still unable to vote (Zarya, 2015). Likewise, countries have different ways of addressing second and third generation rights for their citizens, demonstrating that human rights are by no means settled in a universal, nor indeed applied in a uniform, way. This demonstrates that not even the so-called developed West, from which human rights are said to have emerged, has complete purchase on the various human rights claims that can be made according to this schema.

Hence, Ife (2012, p. 11) suggests that we should consider human rights as discursive, by which he means that we cannot see these claims as 'fixed or static' and therefore they cannot be completely defined. Furthermore, Ife (2012) situates human rights within a participatory or democratic process, even as he points out the issues with Western conceptions of human rights (mentioned above). In this sense, it is our view that Ife is advocating for a Kantian moral sensibility, because in situating human rights as discursive, Ife thus implies that human rights claims are emergent properties from the public uses of reason and the use of toleration in public life (O'Neill, 1986). In recent times philosopher Jurgen Habermas (1984) has explicated a contemporary version of this with a debt to Kant (Owen, 1999), which is called communicative rationality. This would fit with the basic criteria for human rights that Ife offers, despite the many difficulties we may have in defining human rights. We have included these in Table 9.2 along with the associated philosophical principles each criterion addresses.

Ife (2012, pp. 14–15) concludes with saying that the most frequent justification of these claims is often instruments such as UDHR, and once these are established as claims of human rights, they should take precedence over other rights. In the next part of this chapter we will examine the claim that social work is a human rights profession.

Background to human rights in social work

In 1988, the International Federation of Social Workers (IFSW) declared that social work was and always had been a human rights profession (Healy, 2008; Ife, 2012). This would appear rather uncontroversial; however, social work has not always been seen this way and nor has social work necessarily been viewed as being amongst the forefront of professions concerned with human rights

Table 9.2 Criteria for claims of human rights (quoted from Ife, 2012, p. 14)

Criteria quoted from Ife, 2012, p. 14	Philosophical principles or ideas
Realisation of the claimed right is necessary for a person or group to be able to achieve their full humanity, in common with others.	Inherent dignity and worth (Tasioulas, 2015).
The claimed right is seen *either* (1) as applying to all of humanity, and is something that the person or group claiming the right wishes to apply to all people everywhere, or (2) as applying to people from specific disadvantaged or marginalised groups for whom realisation of that right is essential to their achieving their full human potential.	Kantian principle of moral law – Act according to that maxim that you can at the same time consistently will as universal law (Owen, 1999, p. 23). The difference principle outlined by Rawls where 'diverging from strict equality so long as the inequalities in question would make the least advantaged in society materially better off than they would be under strict equality' (Lamont & Favor, 2016).
There is substantial universal consensus on the legitimacy of the claimed right; it cannot be called a 'human right' unless there is widespread support for it across cultural and other divides.	Kantian principle of moral law – Act according to that maxim that you can at the same time consistently will as universal law (Owen, 1999, p. 23). Arrived at through the public use of reason and toleration (Habermas, 1984; London School of Economics and Political Science (LSE) & Ramadan, 2016; O'Neill, 1986; Tully, 2008a).
It is possible for the claimed right to be effectively realised for all legitimate claimants. This excludes rights to things that are in limited supply, for example the right to housing with a panoramic view, the right to own a TV channel, or the right to 'own' large tracts of land.	Kantian principle of moral law – Act according to that maxim that you can at the same time consistently will as universal law (Owen, 1999, p. 23). Human rights can be viewed as claims of recognition and distribution (Tully, 2000).
The claimed right does not contradict other human rights. This would disallow as [a] human right the right to 'bear' arms, the 'right' to hold other people in slavery, a man's 'right' to beat his wife and children, the 'right to excessive profits resulting in poverty for others'.	Kantian principle of moral law – Act according to that maxim that you can at the same time consistently will as universal law (Owen, 1999, p. 23). Human rights are not understood as divisible – they are seen as universal on the basis of human dignity and worth (Tasioulas, 2015).

(Healy, 2008). Social work has always had a commitment to social justice (Wronka & Staub-Bernasconi, 2012) and human rights may be a route through which social justice can be pursued. Early social work was focussed on documenting poverty (McMahon, 2002; Shaw, 2015); child development (Chambon et al., 2011); the status of women (Martin, 2003a) and individual function within society (Epstein, 1994, 1999). Later, social work became influenced by social movements that focussed on more critical and structural accounts of conditions that contribute to human suffering and/or flourishing (Rojek et al., 1988). There have been debates within the profession about whether human rights can deliver the kinds of broad scale change required for social justice as a goal. These debates have been associated with the radical and critical traditions within social work (Turbett, 2014). It has also been seen as a troubling example of postmodern conceptions of difference that undermine more universal concepts of equality (Webb, 2009). Nevertheless, for Wronka and Staub-Bernasconi (2012), and others (Ife, 2012; Ward & Connolly, 2007), human rights represent an important discourse and sustenance to support social work practice.

One way to settle this question about the relation between human rights and social work is presented by Healy (2008). She asks a range of questions with regard to whether social work can rightly be seen as a human rights profession. In her view, we should look at how conceptions of human rights fit with the mission and values of the profession. We should also consider where we can see the emergence of human rights leaders from within the profession. Lastly, we can ask what has been the presence or absence of social work at critical human rights incidents. We will consider each of these in turn.

Mission and values

What about the missions and values of social work? According to Wronka and Staub-Bernasconi (2012), the IFSW and the International Association of Schools of Social Work (IASSW) created a Joint Commission on Human Rights in Geneva in 2002. These groups have also recently drawn up a global agenda aimed at mobilising social workers, educators and policy practitioners. This global agenda 'stressed looking at the "Dignity and worth of the person"[and] "human rights issues in relation to social, economic, cultural, and political situations"' (Wronka & Staub-Bernasconi, 2012, p. 70). There is a close fit with the various missions and values of social work because *human dignity and worth* is enshrined in numerous codes of ethics (Australian Association of Social Workers, 2010; British Association of Social Workers, 2014; National Association of Social Workers, 2016). Moreover, the IFSW statement outlines the following:

> Social work is based on respect for the inherent worth and dignity of all people, and the rights that follow from this. Social workers should uphold and defend each

person's physical, psychological, emotional and spiritual integrity and well-being. (International Federation of Social Workers, 2012)

In this respect we can see that a human rights discourse fits well within what many see as the core values and mission of social work. Thus we think, along with Healy, that the first criterion is met.

Human rights leadership in social work

In terms of human rights leadership the issue is rather more complex. Healy (2008) makes links between human rights leadership and early social work pioneers such as Jane Addams (United States), Sophonisba Breckinridge (United States), Eglantyne Jebb (United Kingdom), Alice Salomon (Germany) and Bertha Reynolds (United States). Many of these pioneers fought battles on poverty, child health and well-being, women's rights and the needs of families. Moreover, according to Healy, social workers were using the language of human rights well before the advent of the UDHR. In this respect, social work has always been engaged in struggles for peace, for adequate health and welfare, working against poverty and alongside groups struggling for civil and group rights (Healy, 2008). Interestingly though, when scanning some contemporary authors (Ife, 2012; Ward & Connolly, 2007; Wronka & Staub-Bernasconi, 2012) there remains a sense that this link between early pioneers and present-day practice has been forgotten, and that the position of social work as a human rights profession still needs to be argued for as a foundation to present-day practice (Nipperess, 2013). We think this is an echo of the struggle over social and political theory ushered in by the linguistic turn (Deetz, 2003), within which social work became involved in a struggle between universal values and the perceived relativism of adopting postmodern/post-structural thought (Healy, 2005; Ife, 1999; Pease & Fook, 1999b). This battle appears less keen today and human rights ideals now seem increasingly to offer a way to 'orientate workers to the necessary conditions … prerequisites for a life of dignity and a chance at happiness' (Ward & Connolly, 2007, p. 16).

Human rights leaders tend to emerge due to both national and international struggles and sometimes their affiliation to social work may not be known. Healy (2008, p. 740) offers the example of Sybil Francis of Jamaica. Sybil Francis was a member of the IASSW and served as an independent Jamaican delegate to the UN. Francis served on the committee that led to the International Convention on the Elimination of All Forms of Racial Discrimination. As mentioned above, the UDHR lends important weight to activism for human dignity and worth and for social and economic participation across different contexts, because it offers a universal language through which to frame such struggles. In this respect there remains ongoing work for social work as a profession in developing further our understanding and support of human rights struggles (Wronka & Staub-Bernasconi, 2012). Doing so will strengthen the prospects of ongoing social work human rights leadership across a broad array of contexts, struggles and issues.

Social work presence at critical human rights incidents

Lastly, Healy (2008) asks us to think about whether social workers have been present at critical human rights incidents. The answer is yes. Social work – through such organisations like the IFSW and IASSW – played, and continues to play, a major role in contesting human rights violations across the globe. For example, the IFSW and IASSW contested the racist policies of the apartheid regime in South Africa and the campaign for children's rights has led to the establishment of protective children's policy in most countries (Healy, 2008). Jim Ife, a human rights social work activist and author in Australia, was inspired by his work in East Timor during the 1990s and has maintained strong links to human rights activists in that region ever since (Ife, 2001, 2008, 2012). Another example of social work human rights presence at critical incidents is where the Australian Council of Heads of Schools of Social Work (ACHSSW) initiated an inquiry into immigration detention in Australia (Briskman & Goddard, 2007). This inquiry, led by social workers and academics Linda Briskman and Chris Goddard, heard over 200 testimonies and written submissions in 10 locations across Australia. The inquiry was largely run with volunteers and enjoyed only very small donations. According to Briskman, Latham and Goddard (2008, p. 19) submissions were received from 'former detainees, their Australian supporters, ... doctors, nurses, educators, former Department of Immigration officials, ... detention centre employees, migration agents and lawyers'. The inquiry was explicitly framed as a form of human rights activism and linked explicitly to the charter of the ACHSSW, which 'includes addressing national issues in social policy, consistent with the social work quest to work towards social justice and human rights' (Briskman & Goddard, 2007, p. 92). As an example, this can be seen as a very specific struggle that has its roots in many years of debate about the best way to approach the issue of asylum seekers in Australia. It is also one that picks up on historical struggles from colonisation and racist immigration policy (Connell, 2007) in Australia. Nevertheless, these activists were able to place the particularities of this struggle in the context of the universal aspirations of the UDHR.

A further important aspect of this particular example is the process by which the inquiry was held. The point of the inquiry was to provide an avenue for all those involved to tell their stories and, while the Inquiry had no force in terms of changing laws, the simple act of bearing witness (Briskman et al., 2008) and listening (Stolz, 2008) gave dignity to the people who came forward to speak. It is this aspect of inclusion and making room for voices that are not usually heard that is also embodied in family group conferencing (FGC), a method of human rights-informed child and family practice as described by Ward and Connolly (2007, pp. 169–172). Both of these examples point to the kind of presence and leadership that social work can offer to human rights struggles, as so much social work practice involves people struggling for recognition and against the unfair distribution (Tully, 2000) of social goods such as health, wealth, rights to participation and social esteem (Ife, 2012). It is this last area which concerns social workers – how to translate these values and principles into our practice. We turn now to this topic by way of concluding the chapter.

Social work practice and human rights

While some authors (Harrison & Melville, 2010) are somewhat gloomy about the prospects of translating human rights into social work practice, others are more optimistic and hopeful (Calma & Priday, 2011; Nipperess, 2013). All do agree, however, that there is significant work to be done in terms of realising social work's potential in the area of human rights practice. In terms of appealing to the UDHR, Healy (2008) considers the main articles in the UDHR of interest to social workers are those concerned with social and economic rights, specifically article 25:

> Everyone has the right to a standard of living adequate for the health and well-being of himself [sic] and of his family, including food, clothing, housing, and medical care and necessary social services, and the right to security in the event of unemployment, sickness, disability, widowhood, old age or other lack of livelihood in circumstances beyond his control. (United Nations, 2016)

This is because many social workers are often on the frontline of needing to address the distribution of resources in society. This is also one of Healy's theories for the lack of internationally visible leadership of social work in this area: social work has a focus on social and economic rights instead of political and civil rights (Healy, 2008). Social work as a profession often occupies spaces in the interface between the *state* and its people, and in this respect, Ife (2012) contends that social work has an opportunity to enact practices that address human rights. Ife (2012) also acknowledges that social work cannot be seen as being the same in all places and all societies. For example, the kinds of social work practice engaged by social workers within advanced welfare states (Esping-Andersen & United Nations Research Institute for Social Development, 1996) will necessarily be different than social workers working in communities that have little in the way of established redistribution processes for health, education and social assistance. Human rights may provide a common frame for considering human dignity and worth but within an understanding of different contexts as well.

Wronka and Staub-Bernasconi (2012), Calma and Priday (2011) and Nipperess (2013) all provide helpful guides for how social workers might incorporate human rights practice into their work with individuals, families, groups and communities. Below we have included a table of specific inclusions in social work curricula. Many of these address the aspects of human social being discussed in Chapter 7 on dignity and respect. They are presented in Table 9.3.

Table 9.3 Inclusions to address human rights in social work education and practice

Inclusions	Example
Integrate human rights with existing social work theory and considering what additional knowledge, values and skills for professional action are needed (Wronka & Staub-Bernasconi, 2012).	Asking broad epistemological questions: what human rights violations can be identified; how can we explain them; what is the ethical relation between dignity and human rights; can we respect human rights and avoid western colonialism; how do human rights fit with the mission and values of social work; and what methods and skills are needed to implement human rights in the various practice settings social workers occupy?
'Vulnerability' as a main characteristic of social work service users (Wronka & Staub-Bernasconi, 2012).	We would argue that all humans are vulnerable to suffering but that social structures of inequality make social work service users especially vulnerable to human rights violations. For example, asylum seekers and some Aboriginal service users are considered to be especially vulnerable (Briskman & Cemlyn, 2005; Nipperess, 2013).
Emphasis on structural aspects of inequality and thus social, economic and cultural/ collective rights (Calma & Priday, 2011; Nipperess, 2013; Sayer, 2011).	Using a critical social theory lens (Nipperess, 2013). Develop and use empowerment models that incorporate both the structural and personal aspects (Rivest & Moreau, 2014). Using a full range of methods of practice including community development (Ife, 2008), advocacy, policy (Briskman & Cemlyn, 2005), as well as direct practice that incorporate empathy, listening and cultural awareness (see also Nipperess, 2013).

If we were to combine the inclusions listed here with the skills outlined in Chapter 7 for respectful practice, then we think our hopes of realising the potential of human rights for social work service users have a stronger chance of success.

Conclusion

In sum, this chapter has considered the philosophical basis and global status of human rights. We have acknowledged that there are a range of practical, philosophical and political issues that pertain to human rights claims but that these form part of an important on going struggle world-wide for recognition and just distribution of moral regard and social goods such as political power, economic and social resources. We have also discussed whether social work can be seen as a human rights profession and concluded that it can but that there is significant work to be done in fully realising its potential in assisting service users to achieve full recognition of their human rights and dignity.

Critical thinking questions

1. In your own words, define what you think are human rights. What have you included in your definition? What have you excluded, and why?

2. Why do you think social work can be called a human rights profession? Are there instances where you think social work has *not* earned this title?

3. What is the relationship between social work's mission and values, and conceptions of human rights as outlined by the UDHR?

4. Should social workers be involved in critical human rights incidents as activists, observers and in carrying out social work activities? Why or why not?

5. Describe the sorts of characteristics or attributes that you think constitute human rights social work.

Exercises

Research a leader or influential person in social work. Explore their work in relation to human rights. What was the background and context to their work? What is it about their work that would suggest they were working for human rights?

Further reading

Healy, L. M. (2008). Exploring the history of social work as a human rights profession. *International Social Work, 51*(6), 735–748. doi:10.1177/0020872808095247

Ife, J. W. (2012). *Human rights and social work: Towards rights-based practice* (3rd ed.). Port Melbourne, VIC: Cambridge University Press.

Tully, J. (2000). Struggles over recognition and distribution. *Constellations, 7*(4), 469–482. doi:10.1111/1467-8675.00203

Ward, T. & Connolly, M. (2007). *Morals, rights and practice in the human services: Effective and fair decision-making in health, social care and criminal justice.* London, UK: Jessica Kinglsey Publishers.

Wronka, J. & Staub-Bernasconi, S. (2012). Human rights. In T. Hokenstad, K. H. Lyons, N. Hall, N. Huegler & M. Pawar (Eds.), *The SAGE handbook of international social work* (pp. 70–84). London, UK: SAGE Publishing.

Links and online resources

History of Social Work is the work of joint editors Jan Steyaert and Kevin Harris. It offers a timeline of significant people and ideas for the development of social work. http://historyofsocialwork.org/eng/index.php

London School of Economics and Political Science (LSE) & Ramadan, T. (2016). *Equal rights and equal dignity of human beings.* www.youtube.com/watch?v=PjWnWcAZcTA&feature=youtu.be

Social Work History Network – Kings College, London www.kcl.ac.uk/sspp/policy-institute/scwru/swhn/index.aspx

Xavier Le Pichon. (2016). Xavier Le Pichon – the fragility at the heart of humanity. In K. Tippett (Ed.), *On being.* Minnesota, MN: Krista Tippett Public Productions www.onbeing.org/program/xavier-le-pichon-the-fragility-at-the-heart-of-humanity/101

10

SPIRITUALITY AND HOPE

Introduction

This chapter is organised into two main sections. The first discusses spirituality. Rather than focus on religion, our concern in this chapter is to focus on the broader notion of spirituality, which is connected with existential questions of meaning, purpose, and how these relate to well-being, resilience and healing. The background, key concepts, critiques and debates are presented before outlining how spirituality can be incorporated into a social work perspective. The second section discusses hope. The relationship of hope to social work is explained, along with two theories of hope: a cognitive theory of hope, and a critical perspective. Like spirituality, hope is also emerging as a site of social work research and practice, and like spirituality, hope has been considered an essential part of human nature. Hope can be seen as a need, a state, and sometimes a philosophy. In social work, hope is associated with perspectives that emphasise a person's resources and connections to community as a way of thinking about how people are resilient in the face of great difficulties. Both spirituality and hope are important concepts to critically examine in relation to meaningful and purposeful social work practice.

Spirituality

Background and context

Social work has an uneasy relationship with spirituality and religion (Crisp, 2010; Hay, 2012; Holloway & Moss, 2010). This is despite social work's early roots in religious Christian charity movements (Hay, 2012; Holloway & Moss, 2010). However, a push towards more secular and rational approaches towards theory and practice, plus the location of social work in public sector institutions, displaced a more serious engagement with spirituality (Hay, 2012). Until recently, the research in this area has generally been neglected (Holloway, 2007; Larsen, 2011). The problems with a lack of focussed attention and engagement of religion and spirituality in social work education are summed up well by Holden in her reflection of her experience as a social work student:

> ... the topics of religion and spirituality were rarely discussed. One reference I recall being made was the importance of these topics in some people's lives as they grapple with life crises and then attempt to make meaning of the crises. The point being made by the lecturer was not to ignore religion and spirituality in our client's lives. However, there was no further instruction or discussion around how social workers should manage these topics or implement them within an ethical and sensitive framework during practice. The class of social workers, me included, were left with an important point, but with no clear guideline or framework on its implementation. (Holden, 2012, p. 66)

This situation has begun to change, with many researchers and writers in social work exploring and arguing for a deeper engagement with spirituality as part of social work's stated intent and commitment to holistic practice (Canda, 2008; Canda & Furman, 2009; Crisp, 2010; Gale & Dudley, 2013; Hay, 2012; Hodge, 2003; Holloway, 2007; Phillips, 2014). Indeed, Canda and Furman highlight the place of spirituality in social work as follows:

> Spirituality is the heart of helping. It is the heart of empathy and care, the pulse of compassion, the vital flow of practice wisdom, the driving energy of service. (Canda & Furman, 2009, p. 3)

It is clear from this quote from Canda and Furman (2009) the centrality that spirituality has to social work because it is so connected with other important attributes such as empathy, care, compassion, and the purpose of social work generally, which is its mission towards service (Holloway & Moss, 2010). Furthermore, there is good evidence demonstrating the positive health benefits and protective attributes that spirituality can provide individuals and communities (see Gale & Dudley, 2013, pp. 66–67). Spirituality is also considered by Canda to be an important part of being human, and in this respect, many social workers incorporate or add spirituality into traditional bio-psychosocial thinking (Canda, 2008; Hunt, 2014).

To some extent, recent social changes have brought a focus onto the spiritual dimensions of human experience and social work practice. Holloway and Moss (2010) state that the postmodern turn associated with late modernity, and the emergence of economic and environmental crises have forced changes – both in social work and the context in which it practices – leading to a wider acceptance of the importance of spirituality and religion to social work research, education and practice. They say there has been a renewed interest in spirituality specifically as evidenced in conferences, recent research, and amendments to codes of ethics and practice standards in the United States, the United

Kingdom, Australia and New Zealand to incorporate the place of spirituality in professional social work (Holloway & Moss, 2010). Likewise, Payne (2014) notes the influence of religion and spirituality on social work is driven by: the fact that they are important parts of many people's lives; the role that churches play in organised helping; a continuing critique of economic rationalism and commodification; and the importance of social work appropriately responding to ethnic and cultural diversity, including religious and spiritual diversity. Payne (2014) contends that spirituality broadly conceived is universally relevant, but religion is not. This begs questions around the place of religion in social work, at the very least for social work to accept and respond to diverse religious faiths without seeking to impose a particular preference or religious or secular viewpoint.

At the same time, many notions of spirituality are de-coupled from religion and can be seen as broadly non-religious spirituality. There is considerable overlap between many themes in the literature on spirituality and themes in existential philosophy, which is largely humanist and non-religious, but may be considered to have spiritual dimensions (Payne, 2014). Spiritual practice has elements of humanism and existentialism, concerned not with organised rituals and 'worship of a higher being or beings' (Payne, 2014, p. 290), but concerned with matters to do with meaning, purpose, hope, identity, belonging, resilience and well-being (Payne, 2014, pp. 290–291). Although social work has engaged extensively with humanism, despite some notable exceptions (for example, Krill, 2011; Thompson, 1992) social work has largely ignored existentialism (Fraternali, 1998), which has been more richly developed in the counselling literature (Corey, 2009). Payne (2014, p. 274) argues that humanism generally carries favour in regard to its roots in human endeavours towards conscious reasoning and free will, but its more esoteric variants can be attacked on the grounds of 'being vague and idealistic'.

How to locate the place of spirituality and religion into the secular and humanistic frameworks of social work can pose some challenges. Nonetheless, Crisp (2010) suggests to look for areas of convergence and similarity between social work and that which is understood to be spirituality and religion. These include, for example, the fact that much of the early development of social work, and its establishment in formal services, had its origins in religious groups. This is relevant today in respect to the cross cultural nature of social work, which now incorporates insights from many major religions and spiritual traditions into its theorising and practice (Canda & Furman, 2009; Payne, 2014). It also responds to the need for social work to 'engage and work with people from diverse cultural contexts, such that sensitivity to people of different religions and spiritual traditions, is sometimes encompassed in notions of competency for cross-cultural practice' (Crisp, 2010, p. 25).

There is also the matter of social work's longstanding strength in taking a holistic view of the person, insofar as 'it is not possible for social workers to claim to address the whole person and ignore their religion and spirituality' (Crisp, 2010, p. 23). Crisp (2010) notes that many social workers themselves hold religious and/or spiritual beliefs and this is for some social workers the driving force behind their commitment to the aims and values of the social work profession, a point explored in detail by Canda and Furman (2009, pp. 34–44). A survey of social workers in the United States found that religiosity and spirituality played an important part of the majority of respondents' lives, and also their social work practice (Larsen, 2011). Furthermore, respondents in the Larsen study reported that their social work practice also 'influenced their personal and spiritual development' (Larsen, 2011, p. 30). A study of social workers who practise Zen meditation found that that meditation 'helped them to overcome dichotomies in their theoretical and value framework, their direct service to clients, and their work with larger systems' (Brenner & Homonoff, 2004, p. 267) and that the Zen influence in particular aided '*awareness, acceptance* and *responsibility*' (Brenner & Homonoff, 2004, p. 264, italics in original). So there is good evidence that some social workers already incorporate notions of spirituality into their practise.

The place of spirituality in social work education is also gaining interest. Results of an Australian study with social work students and social workers support the inclusion of spirituality into social work education (Hay, 2012). Social work education in Aotearoa New Zealand includes a bicultural approach to spirituality education and understanding as part of a push to 'develop new practice models and teaching methods which take account of Maori cultural and spiritual needs' (Phillips, 2014, p. 74). Research by Edwards (2002) found that social workers in counselling roles equated spirituality with humanism, existential questions and ethical responsibility, and that the respondents in this study lent support for the inclusion of spirituality in social work education more broadly, a finding concerning social work education found elsewhere in the literature (Holden, 2012). Finally, research in the US into social work student views of incorporating spiritual and religious views into practice found that the more religious or spiritual a student was, the more likely they would support the incorporation of religion or spirituality into social work, and the converse was also true as 'those students who did not identify with any particular religious affiliation were more likely to disapprove of such practices' (Stewart & Koeske, 2006, p. 45). Regardless, the authors contend that if 'social workers are not equipped to deal with the religiosity and spirituality of their clients, then it is more likely that such interventions will be utilized inappropriately or ineffectively' (Stewart & Koeske, 2006, p. 47) and that 'there should be a healthy discussion of one's own religious and spiritual belief system and how that may affect working with clients from differing perspectives' (Stewart & Koeske, 2006, p. 48).

Conceptual distinctions

It is important to untangle the differences between religion and spirituality, as conceptually they have different meanings and connotations (Canda & Furman, 2009; Holloway & Moss, 2010), despite some overlapping elements (Crisp, 2010, pp. 4–5). Most writers adopt a broad notion of spirituality that is useful for developing conceptual understanding, bearing in mind that spiritual experiences themselves can be deeply personal and in some cases defy simple explanation (Canda & Furman, 2009). Following an extensive review of the conceptual and research literature into spirituality, Canda and Furman (2009, p. 75, italics in original) arrive at the following definition of spirituality, which is:

A process of human life and development:

- focussing on the search for a sense of meaning, purpose, morality and well-being;

- *in relationship* with oneself, other people, other beings, the universe, and ultimate reality however understood (e.g. in animistic, atheistic, nontheistic, polytheistic, theistic, or other ways);

- orienting around centrally significant priorities; and

- engaging in a sense of transcendence (experienced as deeply profound, sacred or transpersonal).

Spirituality is holistic in the sense that it considers a person in a complete way, taking into account the fullness of the human experience, which is irreducible to any one element, and may or may not involve a religious aspect (Canda & Furman, 2009; Holloway & Moss, 2010; Stewart, 2014). By contrast, religion is defined by Canda and Furman (2009) as follows:

An institutionalized (i.e. systematic and organized) pattern of values, beliefs, symbols, behaviours and experiences that involves:

- spirituality

- a community of adherents

- transmission of traditions over time and

- community support functions … (p. 76)

Research cited by Canda and Furman demonstrates that social workers do make a distinction between religion and spirituality, with religion entailing elements of 'ritual, scripture and prayer' (Canda & Furman, 2009, p. 68) and spirituality referring to 'meaning, personal, purpose, values, belief and ethics'

(Canda & Furman, 2009, p. 67). Hence, spirituality is variously described to include ethics, reflective practice, compassion, and existential questions concerning meaning, purpose, identity and relationships (Hay, 2012).

Critiques and limits

Despite the appeal towards greater incorporation of spirituality in social work, there are some criticisms to be mindful of. Some reasons why spirituality has not been embraced in social work practice in the United Kingdom are canvassed by Holloway (2007). These include the view that spirituality is at odds with evidence-based practice and measurable outcomes, the lack of clear and sanctioned models and frameworks that give direction to spiritual interventions, confusion over what is and is not spirituality, where the line (if any) can be drawn between spirituality and religion, and lack of theoretical development and resources to support a *theory of spirituality* as distinct from, or related to, the underpinnings of the world's major organised religions.

More broadly, Canda (2008) has observed historical examples of how, sometimes, religious imperialism has combined with militaristic and colonising tendencies that result in violence and oppression. Relatedly, spiritual symbolism can be combined with narratives about destiny, moral certainty and dogmatism, which can be put to violent and oppressive ends. The critique of the place of spirituality and religion in social work is summed up very well by Canda and Furman (2009, p. 6) as follows:

> … some people view religion as inherently conservative and oppressive and spirituality as a personal preoccupation that diverts attention from issues of justice. Some are concerned about inappropriate proselytization, confusion between personal and professional boundaries, blurring role distinction between clergy and social workers, inappropriate moralistic judgements, and separation of church and state in governmentally sponsored social welfare.

Likewise, Crisp (2010) notes the longstanding tensions and debates on the appropriateness of spirituality and religion in social work. Partly this is due to the conflation of spirituality with religion, where religion in social work is criticised as follows:

> Concerns about the involvement of religious organisations in social work provision have often been based in fears that vulnerable service users could be readily preyed on by workers driven more by religious zeal than the values of social work. (Crisp, 2010, p. 18)

It seems that this critique is woven into the contemporary social work literature, giving the place of religion and spirituality in social work a less than appealing gloss. A content analysis of 71 leading social work textbooks in the United States found that faith groups were barely discussed in the social work literature at all, and where they were discussed, they were portrayed in a very negative light (Hodge, Baughman & Cummings, 2006). Hodge et al. (2006) conclude that such negative biases must be critically examined and deconstructed if social work is to seriously work towards spiritual competence.

A further criticism is the seeming disjuncture between the amorphous and nebulous aspects of spirituality and the recent push in social work for evidence-based practice, the latter of which relies on the ability to investigate the effectiveness of interventions using rational, quantifiable and evidence-based measures. This, of course, is a matter of considerable debate as to what counts as evidence, and what sorts of things are perhaps beyond rational inquiry; for example, some spiritual experiences seem to defy expression or understanding (Canda & Furman, 2009). Nevertheless, Milner et al. (2015) contend that the lack of theoretical and empirical work in the area of spirituality in social work is a problem. It is a problem because it opens up spaces for atheoretical experimentation and a disorganised approach to spiritual eclecticism that can at times merge with neoliberal ethics of consumerism and new ageism – the latter suggesting falsely that structural and systemic problems can be remedied with personally styled practices associated with self-development and responsibilism.

Other criticisms concern the very manner that spirituality is conceptualised in social work. As mentioned earlier, spirituality may or may not include a religious component and attempts are made in the literature to distinguish these concepts. However, Wong and Vinsky (2009) are critical of this bifurcation between religion and spirituality in the literature, which they term the '"spiritual-but-not-religious" discourse in social work' (p. 1343). While not advocating that these concepts ought to be collapsed together, they do issue a caution insofar as neat conceptual separations do not always accurately reflect the different interpretations and experiences that people bring to their understanding of the intersectionality of belief, faith and culture, which may be rendered marginal by individualistic binary conceptualisations of spirituality *contra* religion (Wong & Vinsky, 2009).

Other critiques of the spirituality concept are concerned that spirituality may be framed too inwardly, narrowly concerning matters of interiority and personal reflection with the self (Ferreira, 2010). As a counterpoint, Ferreira (2010) argues for a more outward-looking orientation of spirituality to involve the incorporation of eco-spirituality into social work, which, like deep ecology, concerns a 'manifestation of the spiritual interconnection between human beings and the environment' (Ferreira, 2010, p. 6). An eco-spiritual perspective rejects the dominant ideologies associated with modernity, individualism and consumerism that have separated humans from nature and caused widespread social and ecological destruction and crisis. Eco-spirituality is a form of radical activist practice at a personal and political level, rejecting Cartesian dualism, focussing instead of holism and integration between humans, non-human animals and the environment (Ferreira, 2010).

Finally, Hodge (2003) argues that there is a lack of Evangelical perspectives and voices in the development of the emerging social work spirituality scholarship, and this may unhelpfully distort social work's orientation towards spirituality in non-theistic ways. According to Hodge, a narrow but largely dominant non-theistic view is not only a problem in regard to the development of a spirituality epistemology and theory, but it violates other social work principles aimed at inclusion and respecting spiritual diversity and experience (Hodge, 2003).

These are just a sample of the criticisms of spirituality in social work, but it is clear that this is a complex and contested area of practice, even at the same time as spirituality is gaining significant purchase and interest in social work in recent times (Canda, 2008). How to practise ethically in this area is a question concerning spiritual sensitivity, which really concerns grounding such approaches strongly in social work's mission, ethics and social justice.

Spiritually sensitive practice

Spirituality in social work is considered to be an aspect of culturally sensitive practice and should be strongly grounded in principles of social justice (Gale & Dudley, 2013). To achieve this requires working towards a respectful engagement with the spiritual world views of service users at the same time as demonstrating reflective self-awareness of one's own spiritual world views (Gale & Dudley, 2013). Incorporating a spiritual dimension into social work practice would mean working in a way that supports ethical practice in relation to rights and anti-discrimination. These intentions are reflected in various social work ethical codes. For example, the British Association of Social Workers Code of Ethics for Social Work states:

> Social workers should respect, uphold and defend each person's physical, psychological, emotional and spiritual integrity and well-being. (The British Association of Social Workers, 2012, p. 8)

Likewise, the Australian Association of Social Workers Code of Ethics states:

> Social workers will recognise, acknowledge and remain sensitive to and respectful of the religious and spiritual world views of individuals, groups, communities and social networks, and the operations and missions of faith and spiritually-based organisations. (Australian Association of Social Workers, 2010, p. 18)

Crisp (2010) notes that '... there is widespread agreement within social work that social workers should never impose their religious beliefs on service users' (p. 19). Furthermore, according to Nelson-Becker, Nakashima and Canda:

> ... spiritually sensitive practice requires a strengths-based approach that includes listening to the profound and diverse questions clients express and demonstrating openness to hear all expressions of grief, longing, confusion, and joy that emanate from human experience. Spiritually sensitive practice involves the ability to recognize and respond to these expressions with clients, but it does not impose a viewpoint that is contrary to the perspective of the client. (Nelson-Becker, Nakashima & Canda, 2006, p. 797)

The core attributes expressed in the above definition are listening, a focus on strengths, refraining from judgement or imposition of values, and empathy. These are basic social work skills and could apply across all social work settings, regardless of spiritual focus or not. Canda and Furman (2009) contend that many of the criticisms of spirituality in social work can be resolved with some thought and reflection on the ways that religion and spirituality can benefit or align with social work practice more broadly. Furthermore, social workers should be alert to, and mindful of, the problems of spiritual practice so that 'social workers can be prepared to prevent, ameliorate, or overcome unhealthy, discriminatory, or oppressive impacts' (Canda & Furman, 2009, p. 6).

Canda and Furman (2009) discuss the ethical principles of social work as outlined by the NASW Code of Ethics and then articulate that in the context of what they call 'spiritually sensitive social work'. Crisp (2010) also argues that there are several components of spirituality that are universally relevant to being human, and therefore articulate well into the concerns and considerations of social work generally. We have summarised the key points from Canda and Furman (2009) and Crisp (2010) into Table 10.1 to outline an ethical and social work framework for spiritually sensitive practice. In this sense, the place of spirituality is articulated into a social work ethical frame instead of merely displacing it. These ideas from Crisp (2010) and Canda and Furman (2009) provide a useful set of ethical principles to guide practice that responds to some of the criticisms noted earlier in this chapter.

So far, we have discussed the concepts, debates and applications of spirituality in social work. We turn now to explore hope. Hope may be related to spirituality, but it is conceptually different and most of the research into hope is located in psychology and philosophy. Nevertheless, hope is distinctly relevant to social work, and research into hope and social work is emerging.

Table 10.1 Principles of spiritually sensitive practice

Canda and Furman (2009)		Crisp (2010)	
Purpose and mission of social work	'Spiritually sensitive social workers rise above personal interest to service and benefit others' (Canda & Furman, 2009, p. 53).	Transcendence	Awareness or experience that goes beyond oneself to include others, the environment, and broader experiences to include moments of questioning and making meaning out of the pleasures, struggles and difficulties life presents us with. Canda (2008) refers to this as being a liminal social worker: '...a liminal person is betwixt and between. She or he is comfortable and confident when shifting and transcending contexts' (p. 36). This requires an ability to work comfortably within shifting contexts and amidst diversity – personal, cultural, geographical and spiritual.
Pursuit of social justice	'Spiritually sensitive social workers pursue positive social change and social justice, particularly with and on behalf of vulnerable and oppressed individuals and groups of people, including targets of negative spiritual discrimination' (Canda & Furman, 2009, p. 53).	Connectedness	Connectedness with other people, but also the drive and experience of connecting with a community, ideals, our feelings and beliefs, or the sense that one's experiences in life are shared by others to some extent.
Valuing human relationships	'Spiritually sensitive social workers understand that healthy relationships between and among people and other beings are important for growth' (Canda & Furman, 2009, p. 54).	Identity	Establishing a sense of identity is important to well-being and this answers questions such as 'who am I and where do I come from, where do I belong?' Identity is also formative in a context of others insofar as we may relate to other people with shared views, interests and connections that enable us to be affirmed and validated in a meaningful way.
Integrity	'Spiritually sensitive social workers remain aware of the profession's values and ethics and practice in a manner consistent with them' (Canda & Furman, 2009, p. 55).	Meaning	All of us at various points in our lives will seek meaning, sometimes in the context of struggles and difficulties, and sometimes simply as a process of figuring out what gives life purpose, direction and energy (Buchbinder, 2007).
Competence	'Spiritually sensitive social workers continually strive to increase their professional wisdom, knowledge, and skills for effective practice' (Canda & Furman, 2009, p. 55).	Transformation	This is a process of change, growth and development (Canda, 2008). Ideally, such transformations should be positive and of some benefit to oneself and others, even though this is hard to evaluate. Crisp (2010) gives examples of transformative moments, which at first might be thought to be positive, but later turn out to have deleterious effects, and vice versa. But change is invariably part of being human, even insofar as the world around us changes.

Hope, optimism and positive emotions

'To live is to suffer, to survive is to find some meaning in the suffering' wrote philosopher Frederick Nietzsche. Karl Marx also wrote, *'The human being as an objective, sensuous being is therefore a suffering being, and because he (sic) experiences this suffering, he (sic) is also a passionate being'*. Both Marx and Nietzsche were critical of organised religion in the Christian tradition, but they, like other philosophers, understood that to be human is to engage in struggle for meaning, recognition and a better life. As Sayer (2011, p. 112) says 'to avoid suffering we need to replenish and reproduce ourselves continually'. For Marx this replenishment and reproduction was a utopian vision of revolution; for Nietzsche, this was the will to power. However, human beings do not only experience suffering in their lives – they also experience *hope* in theistic and non-theistic forms. Hope that things will get better, that they can set and achieve goals, and that they can realise themselves, their values and their purpose.

Social work has organised its activities at the pivotal intersection of much human suffering, and so it is no secret that the work that social workers do can invariably involve having to confront the harsh reality of terrible injustices, the consequences of abuse, suffering, deprivation and maltreatment. The context of social work itself can be a site for heightened emotions and grief (Chan et al., 2016), and some organisations exist in a state of chaos, uncertainty and ongoing difficulty (Collins, 2007). This context can be a source of immense satisfaction, meaning and purpose, but also a site for higher than usual occupational burn-out and turnover (McCarter, 2007). Therefore, it is entirely understandable that service users and social workers may at times experience and share a sense of hopelessness. This is actually a problem given that hopelessness is shown to have a detrimental effect on physical and mental wellbeing. Hopelessness can lead to decreased cognitive functioning and lower performance, and can spread from social worker to service user and vice versa (McCarter, 2007). How can the social worker remain hopeful? Can and should they build hope with service users? Collins provides a detailed answer to these questions:

> Hope is an essential quality in social work. It helps maintain faith and belief in the future – the potential for transformation and change in societies, communities, organisations, families, individual clients and social workers themselves. It encourages vision, movement, working towards development of, and improvement in, the political context, agency services, self-competencies and capabilities. It can help to maintain resistance and persistence in the face of difficulties, by adopting an active, positive orientation that looks forward to progress and growth. Hope is important for clients in helping to look beyond possible feelings of despair and hopelessness and in maintaining commitment to change. (Collins, 2015, p. 209)

Clearly, hope is an important concept for social work practice. Hope is pragmatic and humanistic and underscores the belief that the world can and will improve through human intervention (Koopman, 2006). Hope has personal benefits too. Hope and a positive outlook on life have been positively associated with mental health recovery (Houghton, 2007; Matsuoka, 2015) and are factors in adjustment to serious acquired disability (Dorsett, 2010). By contrast, hopelessness is associated with poorer mental health, such as depression (Houghton, 2007).

Positive emotions and optimism

Positive emotions are a subset of hope and it is suggested they can support hopefulness and are psychologically beneficial. If sustained over time, positive emotions become habitual and support resilience, insofar as positive emotions are indicated in 'flexibility, more creative open thoughts and solutions. They are active ingredients in coping and thriving – in spite of adversity' (Collins, 2007, p. 260). According to Collins (2007), there are three important conditions that underpin positive emotions. These are (1) *positive reappraisal*, which is an effortful cognitive strategy to reframe difficulties in a more positive light, (2) *goal directed problem-solving*, which involves cognitive rational steps in identifying solutions to problems and implementing strategies to reach goals, (3) *finding meaning*, which is an existential approach to locate meaning, purpose and commitment in terms of one's efforts and self-identity; for example, to see the work that one does in social work as meaningful and important.

Positive emotions are also associated with optimism. Optimists tend to view the world in favourable terms, or are adept at cognitively reframing difficulties and disappointments more positively (Collins, 2007). This optimistic outlook may be dispositional (a global view that good things outweigh bad things) and explanatory (a view that when bad things happen they are due to external factors, which can be changed and modified) (Collins, 2007).

In summary, hope is an important concept for social work, and underpinning a hopeful outlook generally are positive emotions and optimism. These resources are not always readily accessible, and so researchers have turned their attention to how hope can be understood and developed.

Hope theory

Hope research has its origins in medical research, religion, political science and philosophy (McCarter, 2007). More recently it has been taken up as a distinct area of research in the areas of psychology, health psychology and social work (Houghton, 2007; McCarter, 2007), and disability (Dorsett, 2010). Hope is hitherto conceptualised in the literature as a multi-dimensional concept, that may include 'a subjective experience, a capacity, a need, a state, a change-agent, a source of reformation, a resource for life, and a perceived sense of possibility' (Houghton, 2007, p. 2). This makes the concept of hope a difficult proposition to grasp as an orientation for social work practice, even at the same time it is acknowledged that there are substantial benefits for the social worker and service user alike to develop realistic hopeful outlooks.

The benefit to social work lies in the fact that hope can be taught and nurtured with practice, and hope can be learnt (Rogers, 2013). This is also an idea that has been taken up by positive psychology; for example, in learned optimism (Seligman, 1992). Hope typically includes:

1. a future orientation;

2. a view that this future is or will be better than the present;

3. a cognitive and affective appraisal of the present/future distinction; and

4. a belief that the future state will manifest in due course (Dorsett, 2010).

Hope may be particular (that is, in relation to a specific issue/object) or generalised (that is, a non-specific general outlook on life) (Dorsett, 2010). *Trait hope theory* is assumed to be a naturally occurring personal disposition whereby some exhibit a hopeful outlook on life generally regardless of the circumstance, whereas *state hope theory* is circumstantial, situational and may alter with context (McCarter, 2007). State hope may be temporal and tied to specific goals.

An influential model of hope is the Snyder (2002) model, which is largely cognitive in nature (Dorsett, 2010) and situational. This model has some application to social work practice, given that the core conditions of the model can be subject to intentional learning and practice. There are three interrelated elements to this model:

1. *Goals* – something someone wants to achieve, accomplish, see happen, or desire (Dorsett, 2010; McCarter, 2007). Conscious intent and seeking after goals and purpose is an existential condition shared by human beings, and so hope is linked to existential meaning and purpose (Fraternali, 1998). Goals are also familiar territory in problem-solving theories of social work practice (Compton, Galaway & Cournoyer, 2006).

2. *Pathways* – a belief in at least one practical means to attain goals. Pathway thinking refers to the ability to conceive of multiple pathways to a goal or to revise and develop new pathways once previous pathways have failed (Dorsett, 2010; McCarter, 2007). As above, establishing pathway thinking towards goal attainment and the identification and completion of tasks is

congruent with problem-solving theory and task-centred practice in social work (Compton et al., 2006; Fortune & Reid, 2011).

3. *Agency* – belief in the capacity to achieve a goal (Dorsett, 2010), sometimes referred to as willpower, motivation, and the ability to generate pathways to goals (McCarter, 2007). Agency also concerns moving from a state of existential bad faith (blaming others, for lack of agency) to a position of authenticity underscored by empowerment (Fraternali, 1998). The link to social work here is the emphasis on autonomy, self-determination and empowerment.

Snyder's (2002) hope theory emphasises cognitive strategies; however, emotions are still a conditioning force in the experience of hope or hopelessness. Positive or negative emotions that arise in the context of this model of hope are thought to be manifestations of perceptions of success or failure in relation to goal attainment, and self-perceptions about establishing pathways and one's sense of agency (Dorsett, 2010). For example, an inability to identify alternate viable pathways towards goal attainment may lead to negative emotions and a loss of hope.

It seems something of a cruel paradox that what is needed to achieve hope is cognitive and internal resources concerned with agency and self-belief, yet when people are most overloaded, exhausted, burnt out and disillusioned, they are denied the very things they need the most to attain hope. This may well be exacerbated in people who are socially isolated, marginalised, oppressed and stigmatised, underscoring the importance of human connection in building hope. Hence, 'critical hope', discussed below, provides a theoretical rationale for supporting the development of hope not merely in a cognitive way, but drawing on social, critical and activist traditions.

Critical hope theory

The previous section emphasised the place of hope as a series of cognitive and goal seeking abilities that can be fostered and developed. These are valuable attributes that can be fostered in practice. However, hope is also said to arise in a context of others, and therefore is not merely a psychological trait or characteristic, or a cognitive skill as discussed above, but may be bolstered with professional and social support (Houghton, 2007). Hope is therefore collective and interactional. Hope (or hopelessness) can flower as an interaction between social worker and service user, or between social worker and their work context. Context and circumstance can interfere with hopefulness. For example, some research demonstrates that stigma and medicalised and psychologically reductionist and deterministic accounts of mental illness can undermine hope towards mental illness recovery (Houghton, 2007). Hence, the social worker's attitudes towards others, their practice, and towards hope generally will influence the interaction of hope in a context of others.

Hope has been a crucial ingredient in activist practice, social movements, and work towards social justice (Freire, 2004; hooks, 2003; Rogers, 2013). As noted by Rogers (2013), the research into hope in the context of activist practice is less developed than in the domains of psychology discussed above. Nevertheless, in following Paulo Freire, Rogers uses the term 'critical hope' to refer to 'an understanding of the material reality of oppression and the alternative reality that can be achieved through struggle' (Rogers, 2013, p. 219). This conceptualisation of hope is a mix of critical theory and realism and moves beyond naïve and fuzzy concepts of hope as wishful thinking – or 'useless hope' as referred to by Rogers (2013) – to a deeply practical and grounded form of political, personal and social activism aimed at realising social justice and emancipation: it is pragmatic, realist and focussed on working towards the attainment of tangible concrete goals (Rogers, 2013). Longing for something to happen without action, or complaining without sincerity is a form of bad faith – a disempowering surrendering of agency that leaves everything as it is whilst disingenuously promising the fulfilment of change (Rogers, 2013). How can critical hope be developed in a practical and tangible form?

In a compelling essay originally delivered as a speech, social work academic Dorothy Van Soest critically examines the context of US society and its deep economic recession with widening inequality, the fall-out, cost and consequences of war, and the failure and mistrust of democracy and the institutions of government (Van Soest, 2012). In this rather bleak picture, there is much to feel hopeless about. However, there is much to feel optimistic and hopeful about too, especially when we are reminded of the activist history of social work and our professional commitments to social justice. Van Soest concludes her essay with 10 suggestions for building hope in regard to social justice work, framed as what she refers to as a 'peace consciousness' (Van Soest, 2012, p. 103). We conclude this section by summarising the 10 points from Van Soest, with illustrative examples, each of which are future-oriented, goal-seeking strategies towards building critical hope (see Table 10.2).

Conclusion

It appears that spirituality in social work occupies increasing interest in research, education and social work practice. The criticisms mentioned in this chapter are important to understand and think carefully about. However, the literature on

Table 10.2 Strategies towards critical hope

Principle from Van Soest	Illustration, example
Use your imagination	Imagine the world you want to live in, how things should be. Hold on to that view. Work towards it.
Be a critical, analytical thinker with a heart	Ask questions, be sceptical of claims, seek knowledge, critically examine arguments, motives, interests – who benefits, who loses?
Know that no action is too small, that every action counts	This is expressed in the Paul Kelly and Kev Carmody song, 'From Little Things, Big Things Grow', which famously tells the story of Aboriginal land rights activism in Australia.
Don't let those who have power intimidate you	Reject the voices or messages that seek to undermine your will. Live, think, speak and act independently.
Pair a deep-seated sense of social justice with pragmatism	Take an ethical or idealised vision and enact that through practical, strategic attempts at building relationships, partnerships and solving problems.
Reframe issues to reach more people effectively	Work out what is important to people and frame your practice and your social justice aspirations in ways that they can comprehend and align with. Hope transpires in solidarity with others and through conscientisation (Rogers, 2013).
Never give up	Persistence is key, and if necessary, play the long game.
Know when to step back	Don't let anger cloud your judgement; suspend your righteousness, embrace humility.
Hold our leaders accountable	Reject simplistic explanations from our leaders for why things can't improve or can't be done, especially when it comes to the trouncing of public services, education, health, welfare. Expect better, demand more. In Rogers' (2013) terms, connect the personal to the political.
Believe that, in the long run, justice will win out	Adopt the view that good things do happen, things are not fixed or determinate, change is possible. In Rogers' (2013) terms, critical hope involves 'an understanding of the need for social, political, and economic change, coupled with a belief that change *is* possible' (p. 231, italics in original).

spiritually sensitive practice and spiritual assessment provides some helpful direction towards an ethical incorporation of spirituality in social work. The key point is that the incorporation of a spiritual perspective in practice should be grounded in social work purpose and ethics and should, like all forms of practice, be in the interests and well-being of the service user. Likewise, hope can be developed as a resource that may aid in problem solving and goal setting, and can support an outlook that is broadly positive and optimistic. As shown in this chapter, hope is humanistic and pragmatic, and as a concept to inform practice, can be leveraged to support agency and action towards social justice.

Critical thinking questions

1. What is the difference between religion and spirituality?

2. What are three criticisms or cautions about using spirituality in social work practice?

3. Why is it important to integrate spirituality into a social work ethical framework?

4. What are the three key conditions of Snyder's hope theory? Give an example of each where you have applied a cognitive approach to realising hope.

5. Define positive reappraisal and optimism. How could these concepts be used to support social work practice?

Exercises

1. Think about your interest in social work, what do you hope for? How would you go about realising this goal?

2. Do you consider yourself a spiritual person? How would you address the spiritual needs of service users?

Further reading

Canda, E. R. (2008). Spiritual connections in social work: Boundary violations and transcendence. *Journal of Religion & Spirituality in Social Work: Social Thought, 27*(1), 25–40. doi:10.1080/15426430802113749

Canda, E. R. & Furman, L. D. (2009). *Spiritual diversity in social work practice: The heart of helping*. New York, NY: Oxford University Press.

Crisp, B. R. (2010). *Spirituality and social work*. Farnham, UK: Ashgate Publishing Group.

Holloway, M. & Moss, B. (2010). *Spirituality and social work*. Basingstoke, UK: Palgrave Macmillan.

McCarter, A. K. (2007). The impact of hopelessness and hope on the social work profession. *Journal of Human Behavior in the Social Environment, 15*(4), 107–123. doi:10.1300/J137v15n04_07

Links and online resources

On Being with Krista Tippett, is part of a Civil Conversations project and a US public broadcast that is non-denominational but interested in conversations about spirituality and faith. You can access it here www.onbeing.org/

Society for Spirituality and Social Work http://societyforspiritualityandsocialwork.com/

11

ORGANISATIONAL CONTEXTS

Introduction

Social work practice generally occurs within organisations. These organisations range from small non-government agencies to large statutory bodies that may employ hundreds and even thousands of people. Organisational structures can vary. The day-to-day practices and procedures of workers within these organisations also vary enormously. What these organisations have in common is their focus on the delivery of social care. Social work as a profession has developed wide ranging analyses of the way in which organisations and bureaucracies impact on and shape practice (Gardner, 2006; Hughes & Wearing, 2007; Ife, 1997; McDonald et al., 2011). Social workers often state that their work with service users sometimes feels like it is the easier part of the job. What is it about working in organisations that contributes to the negative experiences of workers? What kinds of skills and knowledge does it take to work well in teams, collaborate on projects, network effectively for service users and thrive in your work as a social worker?

In this chapter we begin with the social work literature on human service organisations (HSOs). We will be taking an empowerment approach to the issue of working in organisations. Rivest and Moreau (2014) suggest that an empowerment approach should encompass both structural and individual aspects and incorporate attention to the context in which the problem occurs. Our aim here is to develop your critical consciousness of the array of factors involved in this aspect of social work practice. In this respect, then, we will be examining organisational practice by considering its place within wider contexts of welfare and service delivery. As mentioned earlier, we find that social work has a well-developed literature on the place of organisations within the wider delivery of welfare in contemporary liberal states. We will draw heavily on this in our discussion here. We will then consider organisations themselves through a *systems* perspective. Here we will also incorporate the interdisciplinary literature about organisational climates and culture (Schneider, Ehrhart & Macey, 2013; Six, 2007), as well as what might assist with building civil practices (Bruhn, 2009; Roberts, Scherer & Bowyer, 2011) within the workplace.

In a subsequent section we will then turn our attention to *individual factors* that might contribute to worker well-being in these contexts. Building understanding of both individual and systemic factors can make the difference between just surviving, and thriving in your workplace. We also canvass some of the research on burn-out (Arman, Hammarqvist & Rehnsfeldt, 2011; Ericson-Lidman & Strandberg, 2007; Maslach, Schaufeli & Leiter, 2001). We find in our work with practitioners, students and other educators that the idea of burn-out often causes concern. This is especially the case for new social workers. We close the chapter with some strategies we have built through our practice, drawn from the rich inheritance of social work practice wisdom and combined with interdisciplinary ideas. These strategies are designed to support the development of personal and professional resilience (Grant & Kinman, 2011). First, we begin with what the profession of social work has to say about the context of HSOs within contemporary society.

The context of social work practice and human service organisations

There has been a long history and recognition within social work of the important role organisations play in the delivery of social care services (Compton & Galaway, 1994; Perlman, 1957). For Compton and Galaway this turns on the issue that social work is one of a number of professions which are involved in delivery of *social welfare.* Social welfare is '... an organized set of norms and institutions which put into effect our collective responsibility to care for each other' (Compton & Galaway, 1994, p. 13). Organisations are central to the way in which society delivers this care. Even so, it seems that until relatively recently, little attention had been paid to this arena as a specific and important opportunity for the development of skills and knowledge. Indeed, Jones and May (1992) spend considerable space in an early chapter of their classic Australian text, *Working in human service organisations – A critical introduction,* outlining the case for why social workers need to develop skills in organisational practice and analysis. The authors outline six main propositions and their associated implications for organisational practice:

1. *Location:* The location of social work practice is primarily within organisations. This is still the case in the contemporary environment, although fragmentation of the sector, forecast by Jones and May in 1992, has increased in scale and complexity (Connell, Fawcett & Meagher, 2009).

2. *Nature of the occupation:* Social care work is an organisational and professional occupation, which means that professional standing is often negotiated within organisational contexts. This can create tension between workers, not least from participation in the many different kinds of teams that social workers find themselves in (Ozanne & Rose, 2013).

3. *Purposes #1:* Social work professional purpose, which, according to the International Federation of Social Workers (2014, n.p.), '... engages [with] people and structures to address life challenges and enhance wellbeing'. This requires workers to engage in negotiations within organisations about many care and control tensions. These tensions include the shape and nature of direct practice, policy, and who has access to services and assistance.

4. *Purposes #2:* Social work also aims to contribute to social change and the delivery of effective human services and social policy. Knowing how to influence and advocate both within your organisation and outside is an important skill for social workers (Epstein, 1999; Greenslade, McAuliffe & Chenoweth, 2014).

5. *Consumers:* The key way in which citizens engage with the 'state' is through organisations. A social worker's practice should include advocating for organisational processes that promote just practices and embed values of equity and participation (Burke, 2013; Dominelli, 2002a).

6. *Personal needs of workers:* Organisational life can be stressful, with competing demands and tensions. Social workers need a range of theoretical and practical knowledge and skills to be able to operate effectively without undermining their own well-being.

It is the last aspect that this chapter will primarily focus on, that is, the practice and theoretical resources that might be useful for the personal and professional needs of workers. Fortunately, since Jones and May (1992) published their text, there has been an increasing range of literature that provides detailed theoretical and practical accounts of HSOs and the requirements for practicing in them (Gardner, 2006; Hasenfeld & Abbott, 1992; Hughes & Wearing, 2007; McDonald, Craik, Hawkins & Williams, 2011; Ozanne & Rose, 2013). Let's first examine some more of the context that impacts on HSOs.

It is clear that there are some distinct challenges faced by the social work profession including those responsible for leading the development and practice of services (Coulshed, Mullender, Jones & Thompson, 2006). It seems that some of these challenges have always been the case for social work. For example, Compton and Galaway (1994, p. 195) discuss social work as an *interstitial profession.* Here, Compton and Galway mean that the profession of social work is authorised by the state to deliver services and interventions, but social work also advocates for those people who access services, back to the state. This places social work in a Janus-faced position (Epstein, 1999) where '... social work occupies an insecure, yet uniquely insightful, location at the nexus of social inclusion and exclusion, looking ... in both directions at once' (Hyslop, 2012, p. 407).

This was a reasonably tenable position for the profession while there was broad agreement about the need and benefits of welfare within Western liberal states. Since the 1970s, there has been a significant erosion of this agreement across the same liberal states, leading to what some authors consider a whole-sale change to welfare state arrangements (Esping-Andersen & United Nations Research Institute for Social Development, 1996; Jamrozik, 2005; Morrow, Hankivsky & Varcoe, 2004). This change essentially reassembled the 'social' (Kessl, 2009) away from the universal forms of welfare and collective care responsibilities and norms described above by Compton and Galaway (1994). Instead, welfare provision shifted to a focus on personal and individual *obligation* and placed greater emphasis on individual responsibility, which further highlighted welfare as the management of risk (Murphy, 2010, see also Chapter 3 this volume). This change was particularly felt by social work, because as Kessl (2009, p. 308, emphasis original) suggests, it:

> … highlighted the contrast between the social work profession and the established professions like medicine or law: professional social workers had only a *specific autonomy* because they were much more strongly tied to the organisations that employed them. And welfarist social work was also more directly tied to the specific context of each client (e.g. family structures or institutional arrangements like schools or the job market).

Since the earliest occurrences of changes to welfare provisions, we have seen an ongoing program of change across welfare states in all countries (Baines, 2006; Esping-Andersen & United Nations Research Institute for Social Development, 1996). These changes also move at different speeds and contribute to different effects for workers on the frontline (Baines, 2010; Brenner, Peck & Theodore, 2010). We have also seen significant reductions in social service budgets (of all kinds) (McDonald & Chenoweth, 2009; Wallace & Pease, 2011) as well as increasing levels of contracting to non-government entities that operate at some distance from the state (Gray, Dean, Agllias, Howard & Schubert, 2015). This is in relation to continuing neoliberal programs of change and extensive austerity measures (Miller & Hokenstad, 2014; Pentaraki, 2013), especially after the 2008 Global Financial Crisis (GFC). As a result, we are witnessing the emergence of new types of social service arrangements, organisations, social problems and challenges that social workers must understand and respond to.

This means that social workers need the skills to adapt and be inventive in terms of how they deal with these new systems, policies, processes and expectations. This aspect is not always easy (Carey, 2009; Jones, 2001). In light of this, professional and personal resilience is needed more than ever because social workers must deal with the idea that change is perennial and the future remains uncertain. These pressures on social work leaders, managers and workers call for the development of resources that will assist with understanding, adapting and responding to this situation in creative and productive ways.

The kinds of pressure that need to be considered are issues like the uncertainty of job tenure, continued existence of high caseloads, increasing emphasis on judging risk and organisational chaos. Some pressures come from the environment in the form of policies and practices, changes in funding arrangements and the need to engage in collaboration across a complex sector. Other pressures arise from the behaviour of colleagues and managers occupying teams and organisational units. These factors can impact on people through a range of different kinds of workplace behaviour, some positive and some not so positive. For example, there is evidence to suggest that organisational chaos is directly related to all forms of workplace incivility, with the only exception being sexual harassment (Roscigno, Hodson & Lopez, 2009). Moreover, low staff morale and burn-out are also features of practice environments characterised by high levels of uncertainty and change (Kisamore, Jawahar, Liguori, Stone & Mharapara, 2010). This is why the context of state-based and organisational conditions pose not only strategic, professional and operational challenges, but interpersonal and relational ones too. At the same time, social workers must still find ways to leverage opportunities and develop new practice responses and approaches.

The social work literature does not just report on these problems, it also has developed a way to *think* about them. In a general sense, the context of practice of social work in the domain of the welfare state is seen to be an unhappy mix of inherent tensions, contradictions and competing interests (Gardner, 2006). In examining some of the literature on social work in organisations, we find that conflict of some nature is the frame through which organisational contexts are examined (Ife, 1997; Jones & May, 1992). Human service organisations are seen to be conflicted places where contradictory values regarding the principles of the organisation, its structure and culture (Hasenfeld, 1992) and political and value differences between managers and practitioners are often emphasised (O'Connor et al., 2008). This is because HSOs are essentially a set of moral activities, drawing on and recreating social values in their practices (Hasenfeld, 1992). HSOs constantly define and redefine the technological basis of their work, where technology can be seen as both the intellectual and practice basis of social work (Hasenfeld, 1992). However, these technologies are based on institutional sanctioning – debates over the values and merits of these also exist in HSOs – in the same way they exist in the social and political domain of practice (Gardner, 2006; Hasenfeld, 1992).

Furthermore, large-scale social and political changes, and changes to the policy and state context of social work (Adams, Dominelli & Payne, 2009b) bring about wholesale changes to the nature of social work itself (Cree, 2002). Human service organisations are often thought to be in a state of perpetual crisis 'often attributed to fiscal uncertainties' (Hasenfeld, 1992, p. 10). Even where there is stability in funding, what tends to affect the organisation is the 'symbolic process of constantly having to justify the budget and shore up the

organizational legitimacy, while satisfying contending ideologies, that gener-
ates the aura of a crisis' (Hasenfeld, 1992, pp. 10–11). These changes can often
manifest in stress, interpersonal conflict, racism and burn-out among practitioners (Thompson, Stradling, Murphy & O'Neill, 1996). Such day-to-day concerns
play out among tensions and dilemmas over funding, roles, the increasing
nature of managerialism, the need to effectively work in teams, and trying to
deal with the pervasive influence of the risk paradigm on practice – all of this sits
on the shoulders of the social worker (Chenoweth & McAuliffe, 2012; O'Connor
et al., 2008).

The points raised here are important and may well be a fairly realist account
of the context of practice, but they are far from optimistic. For example,
O'Connor, Wilson and Setterlund (2003) open their introductory text on social
work cautioning the newly graduated student of social work that they may
experience practice as a 'burden to bear' that 'for most of us there is little joy in
carrying such a load' (O'Connor, Wilson & Setterlund, 2003, p. 1). Other writers
on social work in organisations offer similar counsel (Ozanne & Rose, 2013).

If this is the way that problems in the context of organisations are thought
about, what tools and concepts can social workers and social work leaders and
managers draw on to frame their analysis and practice? We agree with Jones
and May (1992) who stress that social workers are 'part of and not detached
from the organisational and policy processes and structures they seek to influence' and that '[S]haping organisational and policy processes is integral to the
achievement of desired outcomes for consumers' (Jones & May, 1992, p. 23).
Chenoweth and McAuliffe (2012) likewise make the case that social workers
should aspire and seek to occupy leadership and management roles and positions, but they make a distinction between management (as a form of technical
administration) and leadership (as a practice of guiding visions and supporting
others). We see that both roles can be undertaken in tandem and they are not
always mutually exclusive or even necessarily in opposition. Now that we have
considered the context of organisations within the welfare state and wider
changes associated with neoliberalism, we would like to turn our attention to
organisations themselves. Here we intend to use a systems approach to understanding organisations towards a positive framing.

Everything is connected – a systems conception of organisations

We think a good place to start to build your understanding is to apply some
systems thinking to the problem of organisations. This means being able to map
and visualise your organisation as a whole system, with many interacting parts.
This allows for a conception of the organisation as many subsystems with
boundaries that may be more or less permeable (Dale et al., 2006). We can

visualise the different teams or groups within organisations as these subsystems. These subsystems interact with each other within and across the boundaries and around key tasks. Individuals are important conduits for action within these subsystems. As Archer (2010) states, it is human beings that create action within organisations and it is the reflexivity of human beings through which organisations demonstrate their engagement with social conditions.

The key message of systems thinking is that *everything is connected* (Robbins et al., 2006). That means change in one part of the system affects other parts of the system. Systems approaches also allow us to make connections between HSOs and their environments. Taking this view also includes a recognition that organisations are changeable, capable of adaptation, decline and, of course, renewal. We certainly are not the first to suggest systems thinking is a useful tool for visualising organisations. An influential text that introduced systems thinking to social work is by Pincus and Minahan (1973, cited in Leonard, 1975, p. 52). This view works in such a way that it focuses attention on interaction within multiple and interlocking parts of a system. Likewise, Gardner (2006, p. 97) suggests that systems thinking 'helps workers and managers see why change in large organisations is often slow; it is not enough to change the practices of one part of the organisation if other parts remain the same.' This brings us to the issue of change and equilibrium.

It is thought that within systems there are forces that push change and those that resist change, both of which are mechanisms for achieving homeostasis. Homeostasis simply means *stability* within the internal conditions of the system (Dale et al., 2006). The theory suggests that if the human service organisation undergoes a great deal of change then homeostasis is difficult to achieve. Organisations, in these conditions, will work to adapt in order to maintain differing levels of stability (Robbins et al., 2012b). There are two assumptions about systems, homeostasis, equilibrium and changes that need challenging. The first is that the pace of change will be the same across the whole system. Generally, this is not the case. Not all parts of the organisation work at the same speed. The second assumption is that there is an ideal state the system will return to once equilibrium is achieved. In reality, organisations, and the people who work in them, learn and adapt to the changes and therefore there is no ideal state to which we might return.

Organisations as a river system: slow and fast variables

We would like to adopt the analogy suggested by Ramo (2009) in thinking of an organisation as a river system. The parts of the river system go through cycles at different speeds. The fish, insect and birdlife move at a different speed of change than that of the granite bedrock over which the river runs. If something bad happened to the water, this would have a devastating effect for the bird and fish life, but eventually the river would flush out and life would return. It may be different, but it will return nevertheless. If, however, something happens to the bedrock, this would be more catastrophic for the entire system. In following this metaphor, Ramo (2009) suggests that all systems are made up of fast and slow variables, aspects of the organisation that change quickly and those that change slowly. Too often, however, we pay attention to the aspects of organisational practice that are the fast variables. We spend less of our attention and effort on the slow ones. The problem is the slow variables are like the bedrock of the river. Without them nothing functions very well. Worse, they are so important and integral to our system that they are sometimes invisible. That is until they no longer work. Slow variables in human systems are our sense of ourselves, our participation in families, and communities, our health. These are all aspects of our lives that for the most part generally change slowly, because relationships usually take time to build (Collins, 2007; Ramo, 2009).

In organisational terms, slow variables might be your relationships with co-workers and other agencies. Another slow variable would be the mission or purpose of the work being undertaken by the organisation. The professional purpose or mission that individuals bring to their work through their aspiration to help others is also a kind of slow variable. Fast variables in human service organisational practice would be daily email, changes to administrative practices and processes, some aspects of working with service users, and in some organisations even the managers and management practices could be seen as changing at faster rates than our slower variables. We tend to pay more attention to, and give more energy to, fast variables, when really it is the slow variables in organisations we should nurture and protect.

The reason for this is that all organisations (systems) experience shocks. Shocks are events that upset the equilibrium of the organisation and its various subsystems. These are very hard to plan for or even predict. Restructuring, loss of funding for programs, and associated retrenchments or redundancies are often the kind of shocks that organisations face. Teams lose key people, are reshaped, reformed, or worse, sometimes decimated. As these shocks cannot always be predicted by organisations, and the workers inside them, we have to develop processes and practices that ensure they can withstand shocks when they do occur. Paying more attention to the slower variables is a form of resilience building for when you need it. Relationships with others is an example of an organisational slow variable so we would like to turn our attention to why relationships form a key part of the health of an organisation.

Organisational climate and culture

Relationships are the key to *civil* organisational climates and cultures. Schneider, Ehrhart and Macey (2013) can help us understand organisational climate and cultures. They begin their paper by tracing the differences between organisational climate and culture with a view to bringing together these two related but distinct aspects of organisational theory. Studies of climate originated within the discipline of psychology and were concerned with measuring relationships between climate and delivery of services, ethics and justice. Organisational culture research originated within social anthropology. Organisational culture is more concerned with the symbols, meanings and practices that characterise organisational culture. Thus the two constructs have different emphases. Organisational culture, according to Schneider et al. (2013, p. 362), may be defined as:

> the shared basic assumptions, values, and beliefs that characterize a setting and are taught to newcomers as the proper way to think and feel, communicated by the myths and stories people tell about how the organization came to be the way it is as it solved problems associated with external adaptation and internal integration.

The emphasis in the social work literature tends to be on culture (Agbényiga, 2011; Coulshed, Mullender, Jones & Thompson, 2006; Gardner, 2006; McDonald et al., 2011). Jones and May (1992, p. 229) are a good example when they suggest that 'organisations are themselves culture-producing phenomena'. Cultures of organisations have a significant effect on the well-being of workers within them. Further, as organisations are made up of subsystems there can be many different cultures operating within any organisation. This adds layers of complexity to the navigation required of workers as they move around their organisations. In addition to the systemic aspect, many HSOs have a range of professional groups, all with their own disciplinary cultures which can '... involve clashes between different sub-cultures' (Jones & May, 1992, p. 230). Subcultures can be operating at different speeds and with different practices, norms and meanings to the wider organisational culture and operations. Cultures are necessarily complex and difficult to change (Thompson et al., 1996).

Organisational climate can be defined as the 'shared perceptions of and the meaning attached to the policies, practices, and procedures employees experience and the behaviours they observe getting rewarded and that are supported and expected' (Schneider et al., 2013, p. 362). This construct, as mentioned earlier, arose out of psychology. It is this construct we wish to discuss in relation to workplace incivility because we think workplace civility is a key way in which organisational culture and climate might be influenced by workers and managers alike.

Workplace incivility

Roberts, Scherer and Bowyer (2011, p. 449) define incivility as '... a mild, yet prevalent, form of interpersonal deviance that violates norms in the workplace, thereby creating a work environment characterized by rudeness and disrespect.' Generally behaviours of incivility are mild, deviant and ambiguous. For example:

- *Mild* – uncivil behaviours are typically low level that might also be called annoyances or hassles. These include ignoring people, being rude or abrupt on the phone or in emails, not cleaning up after making a mess, talking negatively about other employees, and so on.

- *Deviant* – these are behaviours that violate existing workplace norms, or cultures. Most workplace norms are generally about cooperation and facilitating productive relationships to get the work done. Behaviour that works against this norm may be considered deviant in this concept.

- *Ambiguous* – it is not always clear what can be easily classified as uncivil behaviour, nor is it clear that the behaviours are intentional or targeting anyone in particular. This makes it hard to create formal rules and sanctions for workplace incivility (Roberts et al., 2011).

Studies (Doshy & Wang, 2014; Estes & Wang, 2008; Smith, Andrusyszyn & Spence Laschinger, 2010; Taylor, Bedeian & Kluemper, 2012) have shown that workplace incivility results in loss of productivity, higher staff turnover, increased absences, lower job commitment, decreased performance and a reduction in positive organisational behaviours overall. It has been established empirically that job stress (Roberts et al., 2011, p. 450), which '... refers to this discomfort a person experiences as a result of his or her work situation', can lead to negative emotional and behavioural responses. Behavioural responses often include 'counterproductive work behaviours' (CWBs), defined by Penney and Spector (2005, p. 777) as 'behavior by employees that harms an organization or its members and includes acts such as theft, sabotage, verbal abuse, withholding of effort, lying, refusing to cooperate, and physical assault.' These behaviours are sometimes seen as attempts to reduce the work stress but are often not helpful at reducing it.

The main message from this research on workplace incivility is that there are significant links between stress in workplaces and incivility, which in turn creates a vicious cycle of counter-productive workplace behaviours. This is most likely what workers are describing when they say working in organisations is more challenging than their work with service users. Given the wider context of uncertainty and the changing nature of the work described earlier, it is not surprising perhaps that social work and human service professionals were amongst the first groups to be studied for symptoms of burn-out (Maslach, Schaufeli & Leiter, 2001).

Burn-out

Burn-out is defined as a response to chronic work stress experienced by professions whose work is '… characterised by constant, systematic and intense attention paid to people in need of care' (Sánchez-Moreno, de La Fuente Roldán, Gallardo-Peralta & Barrón López de Roda, 2015, p. 2369). Generally, burn-out involves three components: emotional exhaustion, depersonalisation, and a reduction in personal agency or accomplishment (Maslach et al., 2001). In the study by Sánchez-Moreno et al. (2015), it was found that informal social support, defined as support provided by family and friends, was an important factor in the prevention and recovery from burn-out. This is in addition to other studies that point to the importance of co-workers, managers and organisational cultures in supporting people with burn-out, and/or preventing burn-out in the first place (Gkorezis, Kalampouka & Petridou, 2013; Hamama, 2012). This indicates the importance of paying attention to our formal and informal relationships, the slow variables in our lives, we discussed earlier. Positive supportive relationships with others, both inside and outside workplaces, are therefore very important for good mental health and professional and personal well-being. Moreover, these relationships support workers to maintain core values of civility and respect towards themselves, service users and colleagues.

In this section we have considered systems thinking as a way of conceptualising organisational life. Using the analogy of organisational life as a river system we have suggested that the bedrock of organisational civility is with the relationships between people within this ecosystem; an ecosystem that often has many subcultures and boundaries. Positive relationships with co-workers and informal support through family and friends are important mediators in the prevention of burn-out (Ericson-Lidman & Strandberg, 2007; Gustafsson, Norberg & Strandberg, 2008). These supports are also crucial to recovery from burn-out as well (Ekstedt & Fagerberg, 2005). Not only that, we have suggested that in a wider environment of uncertainty and unpredictability, positive relationships between colleagues, family and friends are important sources of resilience for withstanding the continuing forces of change across the sector. We turn our attention in the next section to the individual factors that can assist with maintaining these relationships and contribute to building more positive and supportive organisational climates at all levels.

Individual factors that support thriving in HSOs

Psychological capital – or, the HERO within

In recent decades, psychological research in some areas has shifted its focus away from documenting pathology, towards understanding the more positive human traits that contribute to human flourishing (Seligman & Csikszentmiha-lyi, 2000). It is from this psychological domain that we draw on new research into an important construct called *psychological capital,* or *PsyCap* for short. PsyCap has been described as containing four main resources that individuals can draw on to support themselves. These are: hope; efficacy; resilience; and optimism (Luthans, Avey, Avolio, Norman & Combs, 2006):

- *Hope* is considered to be a positive motivational state based on successful goal directed energy and planning to meet such goals (Avey, Wernsing & Luthans, 2008, p. 53). Hope aids people to solve problems and find alternate routes to meet their goals (see Chapter 10 on spirituality and hope, this volume).

- *Efficacy* is the conviction in one's ability to (a) generate multiple pathways to realise a goal; (b) take actions towards the goal; and (c) be successful in goal attainment. Efficacy is strongly related to performance overall and has been linked with tenacity and courage.

- *Resilience* is the extent to which a person is able to bounce back from adver-sity and demonstrate a positive response to change, thus often thriving even in very challenging situations (see Chapter 3 on risk, this volume).

- *Optimism* is when people *expect* that good things will happen, whereas pes-simistic people *expect* that bad things will happen. This is based on an appraisal of the likely result of a given course of action. Optimists tend to make 'internal, stable, and global attributions for success and external, unstable and specific attributions for failures' (Avey et al., 2008, p. 54). This means that when failure happens, optimists judge that it is not a result of an internal factor peculiar to them, but the result of external, unstable and spe-cific factors. This means that people will keep trying because they judge that a second attempt would not particularly result in the same failure because the cause of the failure is unstable and specific, or a unique occurrence (that is, not part of a predictable pattern or structure).

Youssef-Morgan and Luthans (2015, p. 180) call these '... the HERO within'. Other studies (Luthans, Norman, Avolio & Avey, 2008; Roberts et al., 2011) showed that employees with high levels of PsyCap can:

- Produce increased commitment among others.

- Reduce negative workplace behaviours.

- Decrease the levels of counter-productive work behaviours (CWBs).

- Reduce deviant behaviours amongst staff groups.

The research by Roberts et al. (2011) indicated that PsyCap was a better predic-tor of these benefits than demographic characteristics, personality traits, and even organisational fit.

One of the ways in which social work addresses these constructs of PsyCap is through discussions of self-care practices (Carson, King & Papatraianou, 2011; Grant & Kinman, 2011; Ingram, 2013; Moore, Bledsoe, Perry & Robinson, 2011). Social work also uses professional supervision as a way of building formal professional support (Davys & Beddoe, 2010). The use of reflective practices with others (Watts, 2015b) and through the use of journaling (Hickson, 2013) are also methods through which people build hope, efficacy, resilience and optimism in social work practice.

However, social workers and others in human service organisations should not need to bear the full costs or responsibility for ensuring people are able to work productively, safely and with purpose. Work on creating humane and civil organisational structures needs to occur at the societal and community level as well. Further, people in management and leadership positions certainly have a significant role and impact on organisational behaviour (Avey, Palanski & Walumbwa, 2011; Laschinger, Wong, Cummings & Grau, 2014; Toth, 2012). We do think, however, that workers at all levels can contribute significantly to the organisational climate and culture of their own organisations. Workers can do so by attending to aspects of both the wider system and their own well-being. Below we list some practical strategies that we have tested through our own participation in various organisations as well as through our engagement with the social work and interdisciplinary literature, as we mentioned earlier. We distilled these strategies into some pithy taglines to remind ourselves to attend to the role we play in the culture and climates around us.

Strategies for navigating organisational systems and ourselves

Respect at all times

Even in times of stress, disagreement and even duress, it is important to remain civil and respectful in our dealings with others. As mentioned, workplace incivility is a major impediment to positive change and productivity (Roberts et al., 2011; Roberts, Scherer & Bowyer, 2011). People respond better when interpersonal interactions are done out of respect for others' dignity and humanity.

Empathy for everyone

Empathy is crucial to building relationships (see Chapter 12). All people, no matter their station, have concerns and worries and appreciate it when other people can empathise with them. We should demonstrate empathy and regard for others both horizontally and vertically in an organisation, even for those who do us wrong or cause us harm. People respond better and are generally more supportive and agreeable when interpersonal interactions are conducted with common feeling. We should not reserve our unconditional positive regard just for service users, colleagues are important too.

What's the norm here?

Organisations and sub-groups (teams) tend to develop their own patterns of behaviour, values, beliefs, stories and myths. These create a 'frame' that people become part of and resonate with. The main resonation frames are *hedonist*, *gain* and *normative* (Six, 2007). *Hedonists* are likely to swing with whatever makes them feel better straight way. People who resonate in a *gain* frame look after their own interests first, most of the time. Those in the *normative* frame tend to rise above their own self-interest and look out for a higher purpose. If most of the team resonate in the same frame, regardless of whether this is a good thing overall, those in the team will feel comfortable. Sometimes, people do not resonate with the frame that is dominant and this will cause a disturbance, a friction. A sub-group can develop its own resonation and frame that might be quite different from other parts of the system. This might be protective in an organisation where hedonism or self-interest reigns. The point is to build team and sub-group norms by demonstrating the kinds of behaviour you would want others to adopt, and remind people of what these are. This helps to contribute to team goals that go beyond immediate payoffs or individual self-interest as this will encourage more altruistic and collegial atmospheres.

What game am I in? Building virtuous circles

Axelrod (1984) suggests that most successful strategy with others is *generous tit-for-tat*. This strategy allows for cooperation to develop in groups and stops cheats from prospering (Singer, 1993). It is a form of prisoner's dilemma (Axelrod, 1984) and it depends on the existence of multiple rounds, which makes it a good organisational strategy. This means that each interaction or encounter with another presents an opportunity for cooperation or defection. The choice in each encounter is whether you cooperate or not (in prisoner's dilemma terms we use the word *defect*). If you always defect, in the end no one will want to work with you; if you always cooperate, even in the face of defection by others, you run the risk of becoming exploited. The *generous tit-for-tat* strategy suggests we should start with a generous and cooperative stance towards others, and then do whatever they do. If they cooperate then we reciprocate with cooperation, if they defect, then we reciprocate and don't play again. The only time this may not hold is if there is a higher purpose to cooperation as opposed to defection. This is a judgement you can make based on your participation in the many organisational games going on. The key is to pay mindful attention to what others do (see our point about resonation earlier). The other important thing is to ensure you are someone who keeps their word and is trustworthy – that way people are more likely to want to cooperate with you in the first place.

Conclusion

In this chapter we have introduced an empowerment approach to analysing organisational context. We began with a tour of the context of both professional social work and the delivery of welfare in contemporary welfare states. We then focussed on systems thinking for drilling down into the actualities of organisational life. Here we introduced the idea that systems and subsystems operate at different speeds and what we often pay attention to are the fast variables when in fact what needs our attention are the foundational relationships, the slow variables that take time and careful tending to build and maintain. This attention is key to building sustainable, civil environments that can withstand the constant change and unpredictability that characterises human service practice. Our hope is that by offering some positive strategies that workers can address for themselves, we will all benefit from a shift from surviving to thriving in our aspiration to make difference with the people we serve.

Critical thinking questions

1. What do you think about the distinction between workplace incivility and bullying? Do you have experience of workplace incivility? What does it look like? What are its effects?

2. It is said that higher levels of psychological capital can reduce the incidence of workplace incivility. How might people go about building psychological capital amongst their staff, colleagues and workplaces?

3. What is organisational climate and what is organisational culture? In what ways are these concepts different, and in what ways are they similar?

4. How would you recognise someone in your workplace who was experiencing some form of interpersonal distress? This is really about how well you know your colleagues. How would you recognise it in yourself?

5. How might you carefully challenge or support someone to reframe their thinking and action around situations that cause distress, and adopt more adaptive and resilient approaches to dealing with workplace difficulties?

Exercises

This exercise will get you thinking about your work, study and family as an interconnected system. Take a large piece of paper and some coloured markers. Draw your workplace and other systems (family, personal and so on) in the form of an eco-map. Importantly, try to work out or include in your drawing the 'fast variables' and the 'slow variables' that are operating in your system. Work out where the tipping points or soft points are. When stress or shocks are placed on your system, what impacts or effects do you notice? How would you apply ideas about psychological capital, respect and empathy to increase resiliency in your system? In what ways could these ideas be transferred as practice skills to working in human service organisations?

Further reading

Collins, S. (2007). Social workers, resilience, positive emotions and optimism. *Practice, 19*(4), 255–269. doi: 10.1080/09503150701728186

Connell, R., Fawcett, B. & Meagher, G. (2009). Neoliberalism, new public management and the human service professions: Introduction to the special Issue. *Journal of Sociology, 45*(4), 331–338. doi: 10.1177/1440783309346472

Gkorezis, P., Kalampouka, P. & Petridou, E. (2013). The mediating role of belongingness in the relationship between workplace incivility and thriving. *International Journal of Employment Studies, 21*(2), 63–78.

Gray, M., Dean, M., Agllias, K., Howard, A. & Schubert, L. (2015). Perspectives on neoliberalism for human service professionals. *Social Service Review, 89*(2), 368–392. doi: 10.1086/681644

Six, F. (2007). Building interpersonal trust within organizations: A relational signalling perspective. *Journal of Management and Governance, 11*(3), 285–309. doi: 10.1007/s10997-007-9030-9

Links and online resources

McGregor, K. (2001). *Social Work Reform Board: The contexts and organisations capability.* Community Care. www.communitycare.co.uk/2011/06/10/social-work-reform-board-the-contexts-and-organisations-capability/

Pink, D. (2009). *The puzzle of motivation.* www.ted.com/talks/dan_pink_on_motivation?language=en

Sliter, M. (2013). *What is workplace incivility, why should we care, and what should we do?* HRZONE. www.hrzone.com/perform/people/what-is-workplace-incivility-why-should-we-care-and-what-should-we-do

Venkatesh (n.d.). Organisational climate: Meaning, characteristics and factors. www.yourarticlelibrary.com/organization/organisational-climate-meaning-characteristics-and-factors/53226/

12

EMPATHY

Introduction

The ability to experience and demonstrate empathy is said to be key to effective social work practice (Engelberg & Limbach-Reich, 2015; Gerdes, Segal, Jackson & Mullins, 2011; Grant, 2014; King, 2011). If asked, most social workers and social work students would consider themselves to be naturally empathic. Furthermore, most people would assume that empathy is morally virtuous. When asked what empathy means, many would answer by saying that it means seeing things from another's perspective, feeling what another feels, or attempting to understand another person's situation and experience, and that empathy is a good thing and therefore desirable. This would be a fairly reasonable answer. But it is more com-plicated than that. Many questions can be raised about the forms and functions of empathy. Can someone empathise without feeling anything, and can the other person tell? What role does imagination play in empathy? In what ways are empathy, sympathy and compassion the same, and how are they different? Can empathy be taught and learnt? How would a social worker develop empathy and why is this important for action and for guiding social work practice? Are there limits to empathy?

One of the problems associated with the empathy literature is that there is little agreement on what empathy actually is, or what it means (Bernhardt & Singer, 2012; Duan & Hill, 1996; Stueber, 2012). However, there are some common notions and these can serve to provide a conceptual basis of empa-thy that is useful to social work. In order to develop conceptual clarity, we begin the chapter by exploring the literature on empathy from neuroscience, social neuroscience and psychology (Bernhardt & Singer, 2012; Walter, 2012). Due to the way that empathy has been examined and researched in these disciplines, much work has already been invested in developing and testing theoretical constructs of empathy, and these, too, can provide a useful starting point for our discussion. It is from there that we articulate empathy within a social work disciplinary perspective specifically. One of the issues we found in reviewing the literature is that there are recognised limitations and problems associated with empathy, and these will be noted. Despite these criticisms, it is clear that the place of empathy in social work education, research and practice is considered of primary importance. Although some have argued that empathy is not reducible to a skill (Myers, 2000), we surveyed some of the literature on teaching and learning empathy to extract some of the interrelated background skills and teaching strategies that support the attainment and expression of empathy in practice. These can provide a good basis for ongoing learning, practice and reflection towards thinking critically about empathy in practice.

Defining empathy and its related terminology

The concept of empathy has a long history, particularly in the early development of psychology, psychoanalysis and counselling (Duan & Hill, 1996). Gerdes and Segal (2011) note that empathy research more recently is informed by primatology, ethology, neuroscience, developmental psychology and social-cognitive neuroscience. Hence it is no wonder that it is widely recognised that the meaning of empathy eludes universal definition (Bernhardt & Singer, 2012, p. 2). This problem is partly due to different theories of empathy, each of which contain different assumptions about empathy. For example, it is sometimes considered to be a personality trait, or a highly specific cognitive state that is context dependent, or a staged process whereby different levels of empathy may develop and deepen over time (Duan & Hill, 1996). Sometimes empathy is mixed up unhelpfully with sympathy (Gair, 2008). In social work, many see that empathy should be focussed on the service user, whereas others contend that empathy should be broadened and extended to include an analysis and critique of the historical, cultural, economic and social context that impacts people's lives (Jessup & Rogerson, 1999). However, is the latter really empathy, or is it a person-in-environment social analysis? These different theoretical traditions mean that different definitions of empathy have proliferated, making it hard to empirically measure and validate empathy, and this may explain why, for a while at least, little empirical research was conducted into empathy (Duan & Hill, 1996).

Despite these theoretical and conceptual confusions, we need a starting point if we are to have an intelligible discussion about what we mean by empathy. In a straightforward sense it is said that empathy 'occurs when an observer perceives or imagines someone else's (i.e., the target's) affect and this triggers a response such that the observer partially feels what the target is feeling' (Singer & Lamm, 2009, p. 82). A good conceptualisation of empathy in social work – adapted from Decety and Jackson's review of the empathy definitions in the social sciences – is offered by Gerdes et al. (2011):

> (1) the capacity for an automatic or unconscious affective response to others that may include sharing others' emotional states; (2) a cognitive capacity to take the

perspective of another; (3) the ability to regulate one's own emotions; and (4) a level
of self/other-awareness that allows some temporary identification between self and
other, but also ultimately avoids confusion between self and other. (p. 112)

In a very similar way, Singer and Lamm, writing in the context of neuroscience,
say that empathy involves the following elements:

(1) an affective state (2) which is isomorphic to another person's affective state, (3)
which was elicited by observing or imagining another person's affective state, and
(4) when we know that the other person's affective state is the source of our own
affective state. (Singer & Lamm, 2009, p. 82)

A few points can be summarised from these definitions. Empathy involves
an *affect*, which may include emotions, moods or feelings, and that this
affect is isomorphic, which refers to something being identical or of similar
form, shape or structure (Merriam-Webster, 2015). It involves taking on or
experiencing a similar affective state of another person(s) through observa-
tion, automatic or cognitive processes. There is a degree of regulation on
the part of the observer such that they are self-aware of the location and
origin of their affective state, and such that they maintain a clear distinction
or boundary between the affective state of the other person(s) and
themselves.

In the empathy literature there are some related concepts, such as *mimicry, emotional contagion, sympathy* and *compassion* that are important to
define because they are considered to be distinct from empathy itself, but
may be part of the empathic experience overall (Singer & Lamm, 2009).
Singer and Lamm define mimicry as the 'tendency to automatically synchro-
nize affective expressions, vocalizations, postures, and movements with
those of another person' (Singer & Lamm, 2009, p. 83). Mimicry is a good
example of responding to another person's affective state through observa-
ble behaviours. For example, if someone is very worried and they are discussing their worry with another person, often that other person will
demonstrate a look of worry and concern on their face too. This is actually
quite important in terms of congruency. For example, if someone was very
worried and they were met with a smiling face it would feel uncomfortable
for the worried person and they probably wouldn't be feeling much empathy from the listener. At the same time, someone could be mirroring another
person's affective state through mimicry, but not actually be sharing the
affective state. Hence, although contributing to empathy, mimicry on its
own is not empathy per se.

Emotional contagion denotes the tendency to 'catch' other people's emotions (Singer & Lamm, 2009, p. 83). For example, imagine a group of children
aged 2–3 playing and one hurts themselves and starts crying uncontrollably.

Sometimes other children may start crying too, even though they are not hurt. But in this case the child who was crying first is quickly forgotten about by the other children, as they become solely focussed on themselves. This is a normal experience concerning an automatic empathic response, but it is not strictly empathy in the more developed form as it does not contain a more nuanced appreciation of 'self-awareness and self/other distinction' (Singer & Lamm, 2009). When emotional contagion occurs, people generally are unable to accurately distinguish the source of the emotional state they experience, and in the process may lose sight of the emotional state of others (Bernhardt & Singer, 2012).

It is important to note that empathy involves an isomorphic feeling state with another, whereas in compassion and sympathy, these associated feelings do not necessarily align with the affective state of the other. Singer and Lamm give the example as follows:

> Empathizing with a person feeling sad will result in a feeling of sadness in the self, whereas sympathising with, or being empathically concerned, or feeling compassion for a sad person will result in either pity or compassionate love for the person, but not sadness. (Singer & Lamm, 2009, p. 84)

> ... empathy denotes that the observer's emotions reflect affective sharing ('feeling with' the other person) while compassion, sympathy, empathic concern denote that the observer's emotions are inherently other oriented ('feeling for' the other person). (Singer & Lamm, 2009, p. 84)

Bernhardt and Singer (2012) explain how 'advances in neuroscience have provided important new insights into the brain basis of empathy' (Bernhardt & Singer, 2012, p. 2). Studies of the brain show good evidence for how empathy operates in response to pain in others, but also with other feeling states such as disgust, and social situations that involve matters such as reward and exclusion (Bernhardt & Singer, 2012). For example, one may feel a sense of joy and pride witnessing someone receive a reward, or a sense of shame and embarrassment while observing someone being excluded. The discovery of a mirror neuron system demonstrates a neurological basis to empathy. Observing the experiences in others can trigger a similar neurological response in the observer, like mirroring (Gerdes & Segal, 2011). For example, let's say you are watching an advertisement on television where someone is devouring a delicious chocolate coated ice-cream. Certain neurons in your brain will be activated in ways that mirror the experience of eating the chocolate ice-cream and you can develop a degree of empathic identification with the experience of eating chocolate ice-cream. The same may occur through observing people experiencing disgust, anger or fear, for example. This demonstrates the working hypothesis of the physiological basis of empathy, and in common parlance may be expressed as 'I feel your pain' (Gerdes & Segal, 2011, p. 144). The feeling may not be identical, but there is a physiological basis to it, and in some instances actual pain or discomfort is possible.

Bottom-up and top-down theories of empathy

Following these advancements in the empathy research, a distinction has been made between what is called bottom-up and top-down empathy (Gerdes, 2011; Singer & Lamm, 2009). Both bottom-up and top-down empathic processing are intertwined producing meta-cognition, from which automatic empathic responses are combined with deliberative cognitive appraisals or judgements.

Bottom-up empathic processing is automatic, unconscious and spontaneous. For example, if you witness someone getting a paper cut, you might spontaneously wince and grimace in reaction. This reaction may seem automatic and beyond your control. Emotional contagion and mimicry are also examples of bottom-up processing; they occur without effortful conscious work, but they can be constrained with effort. For example, you might witness someone accidently getting a paper cut but you constrain and regulate your response, even though you might experience an internal reaction to this.

Top-down empathic processing is effortful and deliberative, involving 'contextual appraisal [and] cognitive processes' (Singer & Lamm, 2009, p. 88). This has several implications. First, the empathiser actually has to 'pay attention' to and observe the emotions of others, because 'the way we attend to the emotions of others substantially modulates our empathic responses to them' (Singer & Lamm, 2009, p. 89). The upshot is that if we ignore the emotional content of others this will decrease our empathic responses. This requires a good deal of imagination, but imagination of a certain kind. It is the case that imagination skills are important to place oneself in the experience of another, but if we do so imagining *ourselves* in that experience we will undoubtedly end up in a self-regarding egoist situation. In which case, we may find this uncomfortable and seek to remove ourselves from that experience, or we may lose sight of the self-other distinction that is important to empathy. Whereas, if we imagine what it might be like *for the other person* we will result in a higher level of 'other-oriented (altruistic) motivation' (Singer & Lamm, 2009, p. 90) to act in the other person's interests. The point is that the moral and practical purpose of empathy in social work should be that it is put to service in the interests of the service user, and it is for this reason that empathy is located in social work as a practical and morally virtuous endeavour.

Empathy in social work

So far we have looked at the research and conceptual foundations of empathy. Empathy has an important place in the teaching and practice of social work. According to King (2011), empathy in social work largely has its roots in the humanistic psychology and person-centred approach of Carl Rogers. Many writers on empathy in social work contend that empathy is a key ingredient in effective social work practice (Engelberg & Limbach-Reich, 2015; Gair, 2016; Gerdes & Segal, 2011; Gerdes et al., 2011; Grant, 2014). However, Gerdes et al. (2011) contends that the place of empathy in social work is assumed rather than carefully explicated and it is not explored in sufficient detail in the social work literature, nor is it adequately addressed in social work curricula or practice standards. Where empathy is discussed in the social work literature it is often in the context of interpersonal skills and communication (Chenoweth & McAuliffe, 2012). This makes sense because according to Oatley (2009), 'emotions are communications to ourselves and others' (Oatley, 2009, p. 206) and therefore emotions comprise forms of knowledge that can be communicated and shared. So, in order to effectively respond to emotion in practice (our own and others) we must at the same time be adept communicators and self-aware and reflective.

The many benefits that empathy can have for social work are evident. Empathy is considered by Singer and Lamm to be closely linked to pro-social behaviour (Singer & Lamm, 2009) and others demonstrate the way that helping behaviour is supported by positive empathy (Telle & Pfister, 2016). Gerdes and Segal (2011) cite research demonstrating strong correlations between practitioner empathy and service user outcomes, and conversely, a lack of empathy is strongly correlated with violence, bullying and aggression (Gerdes & Segal, 2011). Furthermore, empathy is key to building relationships of all kinds. Research by Myers (2000) explains that service users who experience empathic listening in therapeutic counselling reported improved outcomes and relationships with their therapist. A study by Engelberg and Limbach-Reich (2015) found that empathy greatly supported effective case management practices and outcomes, and they conclude that empathy is essential to social work.

So it is clear that empathy in social work is important to effective practice and good outcomes for service users. The articulation of the concept of empathy in social work tends to concern the affective, cognitive and behavioural or action orientated dimensions. This reflects social work's primary role of translating thinking and feeling into action of some kind. Three dimensions of empathy in social work have been outlined in King (2011), and these are similar to those proposed by Gerdes et al. (2011). Table 12.1 presents two concepts of empathy as articulated in social work. These conceptions follow the lines of affect, cognition and action.

Table 12.1 Concepts of empathy and practice implications for social work

King (2011)	Gerdes et al. (2011)
Affective dimension – 'The affective dimension of empathy in social work is an interactive process of emotional connection and concern for others. It involves emotions defined by how a person feels in the context of an interpersonal helping experience' (King, 2011, p. 687). Examples include demonstrating an ethic of care and moral regard for others that is responsive to the emotional aspects of the helping relationship (King, 2011).	*Affective response* – 'encompasses the involuntary physical and emotional reactions (MNS) that are triggered by our exposure to external events' (Gerdes et al., 2011, p. 116). Examples of these affective and involuntary responses may include mirroring, mimicry and conditioning (Gerdes et al., 2011). Intensive experiential and reflective learning may support neural pathway development towards affective responses (Gerdes et al., 2011).
Cognitive dimension – 'The cognitive dimension of empathy involves IS [interpersonal sensitivity], intellectual flexibility, and openness to understanding the experiences and taking the perspectives of another' (King, 2011, p. 669). Interpersonal sensitivity involves careful emotional perception, an ability to appreciate the content of the emotional experience within the wider social structural context, and an exploration of the thoughts and cognitive appraisals of the service user's concerns. Perspective taking requires an ability to accurately perceive another's point of view – in this case, the point of view of the service user as it is shaped by emotional and environmental contextual factors (King, 2011).	*Cognitive processing* – 'voluntary mental thought that strives to interpret the physiological sensations as well as the thoughts that mirroring triggers' (Gerdes et al., 2011, p. 116). The practices here are more familiar to much social work, and include things such as role-taking, emotional regulation, judgement and perspective taking. Use of boundaries, mindfulness and role plays can support empathic cognitive processing (Gerdes et al., 2011).
Behavioural dimension – '…behavioural manifestations of empathy involve interpersonal motivations and actions. These are other-directed and outwardly observable expressions of empathy, and they demonstrate functional aspects of the concept and its concrete applications' (King, 2011, p. 690). According to King, the practice concepts that support this dimension are altruism and the therapeutic relationship. Altruism concerns clearly guided ethical rationales and actions to render assistance to those in need. The therapeutic relationship is a central component of being 'accepting, nonjudgmental, supportive and empathetic' (King, 2011, p. 691).	*Conscious decision-making* – 'part of social work's well-established tradition of taking action' (Gerdes et al., 2011). The behaviour and conscious response side of empathy translates into action, and may include an expanding circle of altruism and social empathy, and the promulgation of moral principles. Moreover, behavioural decision-making may translate into social work actions, such as advocacy, organising and social action (Gerdes et al., 2011).

Critiques and limits to empathy

While there are many benefits and virtues associated with empathy and its place in social work, there are some criticisms and limitations that need to be noted. There are many factors that may operate to strictly limit the extent to which empathy may occur, and some ethical matters to consider too.

First, someone who has little understanding of their own emotions will find it difficult to empathise with others' affective states. This underscores the importance of self-awareness, because '... understanding your own feeling states may be a prerequisite to engage in vicarious simulation for a better understanding of other people's feeling states' (Bernhardt & Singer, 2012, p. 14). The implications for social work are that social workers should develop and demonstrate reflective capabilities and a vocabulary for describing and understanding their own and others' affective states. In fact, this reflective ability on empathy can act as a protective barrier to burn-out and personal distress (Ekman & Halpern, 2015).

Second, empathy is differentiated when observers (for example, social workers) assign different traits and characteristics to others (for example, service users). Examples of this include appraisals of fairness and unfairness. If someone judges that a person is behaving unfairly, this will reduce quite significantly the extent that they will experience empathy with that person. The reason this happens is quite possibly a 'neurobiological mechanism that helps reinforce punishment of defectors in social situations' (Bernhardt & Singer, 2012, p. 14). In a similar way, perceptions of in-groups and out-groups will also moderate empathy. Empathy is more likely to occur in interactions between people who share similar in-group characteristics and relationships. Feelings of revenge (more likely amongst men according to Singer & Lamm, 2009, p. 91) and *schadenfreude* will curtail empathy (Bernhardt & Singer, 2012) because 'the social evaluation of the suffering person may modulate the balance of the two systems [bottom-up and top-down], which in turn motivate either egoistic or altruistic behaviour' (Bernhardt & Singer, 2012, p. 14).

Conversely, elevated empathy is more likely to occur as a consequence of an identification of loved ones or compatriots when compared to strangers, and any initial empathic response for strangers will undergo a higher degree of appraisal and regulation, as compared to empathy for loved ones, which is more automatic and has less top-down filtering and demands less effortful response (Bernhardt & Singer, 2012). For example, Gair (2013) conducted a teaching and learning research inquiry into the extent to which social work students could empathise with a variety of real life vignettes. She found that students struggled to empathise with situations that they had not had at least some experiential or identified connection with, and had to exert more conceptual effort in engaging in an empathic response towards difference.

Third, context and circumstance will shape the nature and extent of empathy. People are more likely to empathise with pleasant emotions than with some unpleasant emotions, except for sadness, which is more readily amenable to empathic sharing than other unpleasant emotions (Duan, 2000). People may be more motivated to empathise if empathy is culturally rewarded (Duan, 2000), suggesting that the motivation to enter into intentional cognitive top-down empathy may be reduced in cultures or situations where empathy is not socially rewarded or encouraged, or where empathising with certain groups or situations is actively discouraged.

Fourth, empathy can lead to over-identification with another person's suffering, which can break down the self-other distinction that is critical to effective empathy (Ekman & Halpern, 2015). A problem here is that in losing a distinction between self-other the social worker may (through empathic over-identification) be projecting their needs onto the service user (Rohr, 2012, p. 454). Furthermore, this situation is indicated in emotional exhaustion and burn-out, sometimes referred to as compassion fatigue (Ekman & Halpern, 2015). In response, Ekman and Halpern (2015) argue for emotional training interventions to support workers who work in emotionally demanding jobs. This makes sense, because as Bernhardt and Singer (2012) note, various studies – including longitudinal studies into the plasticity of empathic development – have concluded that empathy is a malleable attribute and is responsive to training and intervention, a point also noted by Gerdes and Segal (2011).

Finally, anthropological research into the concept of empathy further demonstrates some cautions concerning the ethics of empathy (Bubandt & Willerslev, 2015). In practically all the literature in social work, including counselling and the helping professions generally, the default theory of empathy is that it is associated with moral virtue, altruism, compassion and is something to be encouraged. As discussed above, there are good reasons to take this view. However, despite this conceptualisation, not all empathy is altruistic and morally virtuous. Empathy itself contains no *a priori* moral code and the idea that it is a universal good is dubious. For example, in some cultural contexts there are no direct words that translate for empathy, and furthermore, the idea that someone would *want* to take up another person's perspective so as to see through their eyes and access their thoughts and feelings would be inappropriate and resisted (see, for example, Bubandt & Willerslev, 2015, pp. 12–13).

Although empathy may frequently take the form of altruism and morally virtuous behaviour, this is not its only *form*. A darker form of empathy known as 'tactical empathy' is described by Bubandt and Willerslev (2015, p. 6). Tactical empathy delivers insight into an 'Other', and can produce forms of mimesis (a kind of imitation or copying) that may be leveraged as a tool for strategic forms of deception, exploitation and violence. Like morally virtuous empathy, tactical empathy occurs in many human interactions, demonstrating its sociality – deception for example, like cooperation, may have an evolutionary basis towards adaptive survival, and hence empathy is a facility to aid the function of both cooperation and deception.

The helping professions, folk psychology and liberal humanist philosophy have enabled the 'implicit moral economy invested in the concept of empathy' (Bubandt & Willerslev, 2015, p. 10) to proliferate: the morality of empathy is layered into its meaning and attributes, rather than existing prior to them. The idea of morality as the *raison d'être* of empathy can be traced to the liberalism of Adam Smith and David Hume (Bubandt & Willerslev, 2015, p. 10). Of course, much empathy can be seen as morally virtuous, and social work has tied empathy to social justice, an important value. But the extensive focus on this particular form of empathy has meant that there is a distinct gap in the theory and research of other *forms* of empathy, such as tactical empathy and its link to deception and exploitation. The point to recall is that empathy is not always automatically a morally virtuous action. It may be, but it may also not be. This critique demonstrates the importance of intentionally connecting the *purpose* of empathy in social work practice, to social work ethics and values, and social justice, and to guard against the use of empathy for morally dubious purposes.

Learning empathy: the skills dimension

A suggestion mentioned earlier in this chapter is that although empathy is not reducible to a skill, it can be learned and developed. Hence, there are some background skills that the social worker can engage in to increase their level of the experience and intentionality of empathy. The purpose of entering into this intentionality should always be underscored by social work ethics. We have surveyed some of the social work literature concerned with teaching empathy and distilled some key practices and skills that may support the attainment of empathy. These are presented in Table 12.2.

Table 12.2 Skills associated with learning, developing and demonstrating empathy

Techniques and skills[1]	Goal or purpose	Description and rationale
Affective sharing/perception and action coupling (Gerdes & Segal, 2011).	To increase perceptual abilities and powers of observation.	Empathy is more than a cognitive or affective activity. Over theorising or analysing may blunt the important role perception plays in facilitating non-judgemental observations, which are important to 'truly see the client's actions, gestures, facial expressions, and other behaviours, and truly hear the words, tone of voice, and content of the client's experience' (Gerdes & Segal, 2011, p. 145).
Self-other awareness (Gerdes & Segal, 2011; Turnage, Hong, Stevenson & Edwards, 2012).	To maintain boundaries and reduce the risk of over-identification, enmeshment and burn-out and to develop a strong sense of self-awareness.	Pushing affective sharing too far can lead to the social worker taking on service users' feelings and experiences as though they are their own, which can lead to burn-out (Gerdes & Segal, 2011), particularly in contexts that lack the resources to make effective change (Ekman & Halpern, 2015). As stated by Gerdes and Segal, 'Self-awareness allows us to disentangle our own feelings from the feelings of others, prevents empathic overarousal (sic) in emotion sharing, and allows us to make cognitive inferences about the mental state or perspective of others' (Gerdes & Segal, 2011, p. 145).
Mental flexibility and self-emotional regulation (Gerdes & Segal, 2011).	To develop an ability to switch perspectives from self to service user and back again, and to develop an aptitude for 'conscious, intentional effort to control one's thoughts, emotion, or behaviours' (Gerdes & Segal, 2011, p. 146).	This means being able to turn on, or tune in to, another's perspectives and affective state, but also to be able to, where appropriate, adopt a more detached standpoint in order to maintain a degree of objectivity, self-regulation and moderate against burn-out (Gerdes & Segal, 2011).
Experiential learning (Grant, 2014), psychodrama, Gestalt techniques, role-playing and imitative play (Gerdes et al., 2011, p. 121), body awareness (McNaughton, 2016).	To activate mirror neurons, facilitate insight into others' experiences/perspective sharing, increase emotional exploration and understanding, develop mental flexibility and increase self-other awareness.	The sorts of techniques described here have long been part of social work education pedagogy, and their role in supporting the development of empathy is indicated. Experiential learning can include the use of vignettes, service user perspectives and engagement in teaching and structured role play (Grant, 2014).

[1]Includes reference to key sources in social work education.

(Continued)

Table 12.2 (Continued)

Techniques and skills[1]	Goal or purpose	Description and rationale
Mindfulness (Gerdes et al., 2011; Grant, 2014).	To improve cognitive skills and abilities, reflective ability, resilience, increase self-awareness and perceptual abilities and the powers of observation.	The benefits of mindfulness have been widely promulgated, and these benefits are thought to support the development of empathy (Grant, 2014). This is particularly insofar as mindfulness supports increased self-awareness, emotional regulation, concentration, perceptual abilities and tolerance for unpleasant emotions (Gerdes et al., 2011).
Engage with art, film, fictional and non-fictional literature, biographies, and so on (Gerdes et al., 2011; Grant, 2014; Turner, 2013).	To activate mirror neurons, broaden emotional repertoire, increase reflectivity, facilitate insight into other's experiences/ perspective sharing, develop skills in learning from others, develop mental flexibility and increase self-other awareness.	Music, film and literature have long been recognised for the power to invoke affective responses, insights into self and others, and widening and introducing new perspectives. As stated by Gerdes et al., 'each of us can probably recall a movie or book that touched our lives deeply and created a way to understand social conditions different from ourselves' (2011, p. 123). Watching a film, for example, will often produce a range of affective responses. A study by Turner (2013) involved social work students reading 'a work of fiction or a biographical work in which the main character lived a life that was markedly different from their own' (p. 858). Results showed that this method provided a way for students to increase their abilities to develop insights into others' experiences, where those experiences are outside of their frame of reference and experience.
Conscious decision-making (Gerdes et al., 2011).	To intentionally combine intuitive and bottom-up forms of empathy with social work knowledge, values and skills. Bottom-up and top-down empathy are combined forms of intuition and reasoning.	According to Gerdes et al. (2011), although empathy is an important ingredient in tolerance and civic engagement, on its own it is not enough. For empathy to be truly effective it must integrate with other social work knowledge, values and skills and translate into action 'towards economic and social justice' (p. 123). This requires the conscious and intentional use of theory, values and skills toward the aims and purposes of social work.

Learn from others, build trust, deep listening (Gair, 2008; Gair, 2012, 2013).	To increase one's knowledge and understanding of people, situations, circumstances outside of the realm of one's experience or frame of reference.	The cultivation of empathy concerns an ability to learn from other's experiences, particularly the ability to learn through listening and exchange of ideas. According to Gair, empathy is a two-way process, whereby empathy is developed in a context of trust and mutual understanding between social worker and service user. Advanced interpersonal skills, especially those that pertain to listening and observation, may facilitate this learning and trust building that supports empathy.
Critical reflection (Gair, 2011; Gair, 2016).	To critically examine the influence of race, class, gender, and so on, on one's positioning and empathic ability towards others, and to increase confidence in ability to engage across difference.	Research by Gair (2011; 2016) contends that critical reflection is an important step in building empathy, as this will facilitate engagement and understanding across difference, as well as self-awareness and understanding. The kind of reflection Gair refers to is a critical theory form of critical reflection (see Chapter 15, reflexivity, reflective practice and critical reflection, this volume), which, in this instance, includes a form of reflection aimed at unpacking the influence of differentially positioned identities, subjectivities and social histories on the social worker's ability (or lack thereof) to confidently engage with and empathise across differences.

Conclusion

Empathy has a long history in the helping professions including social work, and it is clear it is a valuable attribute worthy of research, teaching and development for the theory and practice of social work. There has been an emerging interest in the research of empathy in the areas of cognitive neuroscience and anthropology that can add much to how the discipline of social work conceptualises and applies empathy into practice. Empathy involves feeling with another person, and the purpose of this is to elevate understanding, insight and engagement. It is a quality that can be learned and developed, particularly through experiential and reflective methods. The criticisms of empathy highlighted in this chapter demonstrate the centrality of good supportive and supervisory spaces for social workers to understand and unpack any empathic or shared affective states that may arise in the course of their practice. This is an important step towards addressing burn-out that is a factor in work with an elevated emotional dimension, like much social work practice. Finally, we contend that the purpose of empathy in social work should always be underscored by a commitment to social work ethics and social justice.

Critical thinking questions

1. What is empathy? Give some examples to illustrate your definition.
2. What are the benefits that empathy may offer the helping relationship?
3. What are the differences between top-down and bottom-up empathy?
4. List three criticisms or limitations to empathy.
5. If you wanted to increase your empathic abilities, what sorts of things could you do?

Exercises

A point made in this chapter is that in order to empathise one must exhibit self-awareness and emotional understanding. This ability is also an attribute of emotional intelligence (EI). Using a search engine of your choice, search using the phrase 'emotional intelligence test'. You will find a list of results of different websites that allow you to take a short online test on emotional intelligence. Some will ask you a series of questions, some ask you to identify emotions in photographs of people, and so on. Choose three websites and complete three tests. It doesn't matter which ones you choose, but the point of this exercise is for you to notice and pay close attention to the sorts of questions the EI tests ask of you. What do these questions suggest about EI, and how does this help you understand the role of self-awareness and emotional understanding in relation to empathy?

Further reading

Bernhardt, B. C. & Singer, T. (2012). The neural basis of empathy. *Annual Review of Neuroscience, 35*(1), 1–23. doi:10.1146/annurev-neuro-062111-150536

Gair, S. (2016). Pondering the colour of empathy: Social work students' reasoning on activism, empathy and racism. *British Journal of Social Work*, 1–9. doi:10.1093/bjsw/bcw007

Gerdes, K. E. & Segal, E. (2011). Importance of empathy for social work practice: Integrating new science. *Social Work, 56*(2), 141–148.

Gerdes, K. E., Segal, E. A., Jackson, K. F. & Mullins, J. L. (2011). Teaching empathy: A framework rooted in social cognitive neuroscience and social justice. *Journal of Social Work Education, 47*(1), 109–131. doi:10.5175/JSWE.2011.200900085

King, S. H. (2011). The structure of empathy in social work practice. *Journal of Human Behavior in the Social Environment, 21*(6), 679–695. doi:10.1080/10911359.2011.583516

Links and online resources

Goleman, D. (2013). *Daniel Goleman explains emotional intelligence.* www.youtube.com/watch?v=ZsdqBC1tHTA

Krznaric, R. (2012). *RSA ANIMATE: The power of outrospection.* www.youtube.com/watch?v=BG46IwVfSu8&feature=player_embedded

Lackay, S. (*Breaking boundaries with empathy: How the therapeutic alliance can defy client/worker differences* n.d.). The New Social Worker. www.socialworker.com/feature-articles/practice/Breaking_Boundaries_With_Empathy%3A_How_the_Therapeutic_Alliance_Can_Defy_Client-Worker_Differences/

National Association of Social Workers (2005). *NASW Practice Snapshot: Mincing words: Empathy and sympathy.* www.naswdc.org/practice/behavioral_health/0605snapshot.asp

13

PROFESSIONAL JUDGEMENT AND DECISION-MAKING

Introduction

All people form judgements – they can't help it. It is part of the way the human brain works (in/out, like/not like, and so on). The important point for social workers is to know when a judgement is being made, how, and what its content is. To do this involves skills in problem definition and clarification, planning, strategic thinking, an ability to work with ill-structured problems, metacognition, statistical and abstract reasoning, developing and using heuristics, and skills in comparing and contrasting (Billing, 2007). Of particular importance is the ability to develop an aptitude for working with novel or perplexing situations of increasing challenge and complexity (King & Kitchener, 2004). Judgement is deliberation on various alternatives, whereas decision-making is more about the actions taken as a result of these deliberations.

Social workers are required to make a whole range of judgements and their judgements and actions are (and should be) open to scrutiny. Within the complexity and uncertainty of practice, social workers need to be able to suspend their initial gut reactions and moments of judgement in order to be able understand the factors that are influencing their judgement. This is not an easy thing to do generally, or in professional practice for that matter. As we discuss in this chapter, the content and basis on which judgements are made and decisions taken have been the subject of intense debate about the use of evidence in practice. Moreover, we know that judgement is affected by emotion in various ways (Oatley, 2010).

In this chapter we consider decision-making and judgement but we do so in the context of the professional social work role. The chapter will illustrate the implications of different kinds of reasoning, and the effect of emotion on judgement and decision-making. This chapter begins with a definition of terms with regard to judgement and decision-making, taking our lead from Taylor (2010). We do so in order to set the scene for a survey of the current thinking in social work about decision-making and professional judgement, looking in particular at the debate about the use of evidence and knowledge for making judgements. This is to emphasise the point above about understanding the basis of decisions and judgements. In a subsequent section, we discuss what is known about processes of judgement and decision-making from the perspectives of the cognitive sciences and psychology. We conclude the chapter with a discussion of how these interdisciplinary ideas might inform the demands of social work practice with a particular consideration of the moral and emotional dimensions of social care.

Social work and decision-making: what's at stake?

Social work as a profession occupies a terrain situated between private and public domains of social life. This means social workers are intimately involved in making judgements and decisions about the lives and conduct of the people they come into contact with through their work. According to Banks (1995, p. 87), this '... puts decision-making at the heart of social work as a core professional activity.' The basis for past decisions, actions and sometimes non-actions have often been the subject of a number of public inquiries in recent times (Australian Institute of Family Studies, 2014; Hopkins, 2007; Department of Premier Cabinet South Australia, 2008; Laming, 2012; Badman, 2009). As Carolyn Taylor and Sue White (2006) suggest, 'social workers clearly need to be able to make sound judgements and decisions that [can] bear the weight of retrospective and external scrutiny' (p. 937). There has also been a substantial push to address the uncertainties and contingent nature of social work practice. This usually involves calls for improvements to assessment processes and tools. Given these conditions of uncertainty, social work is often characterised as a moral enterprise, and as such, professional judgement in social work inevitably involves the use of moral or ethical reasoning. Thus, we agree that social work should be seen as a practical-moral activity (Jordan & Parton, 2004; Taylor & White, 2001), rather than a technical process. In light of this, the '... range of rationalities upon which social workers depend in making their judgements requires rigorous analysis' (Taylor & White, 2001, p. 37).

Judgement and decision-making defined

Taylor (2010) suggests that although decision-making and judgement are often utilised interchangeably, they can and should be distinguished. The Oxford English Dictionary offers a number of definitions for the term judgement, stating that judgement can include:

> 6. The pronouncing of a deliberate opinion on a person or thing, or the opinion pronounced; criticism, censure. 7.a. The formation of an opinion or notion concerning something by exercising the mind upon it; an opinion, estimate. 8.a. The faculty of judging; ability to form opinion; that function of the mind whereby it arrives at a notion of anything; the critical faculty; discernment. (Simpson & Weiner, 1989, p. 294)

What characterises these definitions is the *use of thought* to arrive at a conclusion about something. For Taylor (2010), judgement is the assessment of alternatives in the context of a professional role. Professional judgement therefore utilises a range of different sources of *knowledge* including '… statutes, case-law, policy, theory, research, standards, principles, protocols, procedures, values and experience' (Taylor, 2010, p. 10). Milner et al. (2015) suggest, too, that judgement '… is about what is good enough and what is not, what is dangerous and what is reasonably safe, what is of a reasonable standard and what is not' (p. 2).

Decision-making is more about the outcomes of deliberative processes and in this sense is tied closely to action. For Taylor (2010) decision-making is the result of engaging in processes of judgement where '… the selection of a course of action as a result of a deliberate process by one or more people' (p. 10) is made. For Milner et al. (2015), decision-making is about action and also, sometimes, *inaction*. In light of these definitions, in this chapter we will use judgement to refer to the ability to engage in an *assessment process about alternatives* and decision-making to refer to the *courses of action* that result from such deliberations.

The use of evidence in judgement and decision-making

According to Taylor and White (2006, p. 939), there are questions to be asked about the way social workers enact these deliberative processes. For example, Taylor and White (2006) cite various child death inquiries that found retrospectively that social workers tend to '… rush to judgement and stick with that view of a case regardless of any contra-indicators' (p. 939). So, while Taylor above suggests that judgements incorporate a range of knowledge sources, what these are and how they are applied or utilised in practice remains an open question. Further, this uncertainty about the way in which judgements are formulated begs a question about the kinds of knowledge and information social workers utilise to engage in deliberation about alternatives, and for deciding on various courses of action.

The kinds, sources and extent that social workers use knowledge to make judgements and enact decisions for action have been the source of considerable research (D'Cruz, 2012; Fook et al., 2000; Hudson, 1997; Sheppard, 1995, 1998; Sheppard et al., 2000) and debate (Taylor & White, 2006; White, 2009; White & Stancombe, 2003). There has been, and continues to be, substantial pressure for social workers to be able to account for their decisions and judgements and to be transparent about the basis for both. This has coalesced into a debate between those who would argue that practice decisions should be based on 'the conscientious, explicit and judicious use of current best evidence … [for] the care of individual patients' (Sackett, 1996, cited in van de Luitgaarden, 2009, p. 246), and those who raise issues with the proposal for a *specific kind of rationality* towards social care practice (Plath, 2009; Webb, 2001; White, 2009). This has become known as the evidence-based practice (EBP) debate.

Evidence-based practice (EBP)

Evidence-based practice emerged in the professions of medicine (Plath, 2006) and became established as part of health policy in the United Kingdom and the United States (Webb, 2001; White & Stancombe, 2003). It has also been adopted in other countries such as Australia and New Zealand (Mullen, 2004). Part of the debate is whether this approach is appropriate for settings beyond medicine and health, such as social care and welfare practice. Nevertheless, in the United Kingdom EBP has found its way into social work through a noteworthy investment in the late 1990s in the Centre for Evidence-based Social Services (Webb, 2001). In Australia, EBP was also part of the movement to create outcomes and standards in health and mental health (Mullen, 2004). There are still debates about the basic premises of EBP today (Petersén & Olsson, 2014), its adoption (Gray, Joy, Plath & Webb, 2015) and how to effectively implement it in practice (Plath, 2014).

According to Plath (2006), evidence-based practice has three core concepts. These are intervention, evidence and effectiveness. First, *intervention* concerns the proposition that decisions should be based on clearly delineated presenting problems. For example, the social worker should be able to account for the nature, extent and form of the problem that is seen to warrant a particular kind of intervention. Accordingly, there should be a logical congruency between the defined problem and proposed solution. Second, the concept of *effectiveness* is used to ask the question: *what works?* The social worker is tasked with justifying the state of knowledge and understanding concerning the effectiveness of the proposed intervention. Third, *evidence* is important and it should be of particular kinds. Here, Plath (2006, p. 62) contends that the term evidence implies '... authority, legitimacy and [the] statement of fact'.

Criticisms of evidence-based practice in social work

Evidence-based practice as an approach to intervention is sometimes considered less amenable to social work practice than in other disciplines where there is a controlled or stable understanding of problems and proposed interventions. This is because in the context of social work, presenting problems are not always what they seem to be; there may be multiple and conflicting 'stories' and information to be sorted through. Further, theory can sometimes provide '... a supple lubricant which can appear to both rationalize and inject caring into decisions which may be driven by quite different imperatives' (Taylor & White, 2006, p. 941). There is considerable evidence, too, that judgements in social work practice are often arrived at through the very processes of assessment (Milner et al., 2015) and case formulation (Keddell, 2011; White & Stancombe, 2003) undertaken as a core social work activity.

Hence, the issue of effectiveness in social work suffers from the difficulty of both context and perspective. As Plath (2006) suggests, judgements about the effectiveness of an intervention may be different from the perspective of the person delivering the intervention and the service user who has been on the receiving end. For much social care practice, there are multiple paths that might be considered to work effectively and thus the different standpoints become an important factor in judging the effectiveness of decisions taken or not taken. Lastly, while all these core concepts have been subjected to extended critique it is perhaps the issue of what counts as evidence that has attracted the most debate. This is not least because it is related to wider debates within the philosophy of science about what *counts as knowledge* generally. Social work has not been immune to the debates about knowledge in the social sciences and philosophy.

What is evidence?

For EBP, evidence has come to mean knowledge that is derived from '... the accumulation of research conducted by experts according to strict scientific criteria' (Harrison, 1999 cited in White & Stancombe, 2003, p. 25). The kind of rationality underpinning this concept is a *scientific-bureaucratic* one where '... it promises a secure knowledge base ... [and] ... rational foundations for clinical decisions ... [and which can be] ... codified and manualized through the use of protocol, guidelines, and computer models' (White & Stancombe, 2003, p. 25). The other important aspect to EBP is the use of an evidence hierarchy where randomised control trials (RCTs) occupy the top as most reliable and where case studies and professional judgements are rated as less rigorous (Petersén & Olsson, 2014). This hierarchy has been extensively critiqued due to its emphasis on certain kinds of social research that emphasise universal knowledge at the expense of more local context-dependent approaches to knowledge that use case study or practice wisdom (Flyvbjerg, 2001; Plath, 2009; Webb, 2001).

Overall, the problem for social work is that EBP does not translate as well into social work practice as it does for medicine, for example, because as mentioned earlier, practice decisions are often taken as part of an emergent process (Plath, 2006; White & Stancombe, 2003). Such processes are inevitably tied to the context in which case formulation is occurring and thus '... the stronger the demands of scientific evidence, the less flexibility for practical relevance' (Petersén & Olsson, 2014). Indeed, Petersén and Olsson (2014) suggest that the only way to address the need of practitioners for manoeuvrability is to create a '... broader understanding of evidence in terms of different knowledge views [to] increase the room for practical relevance ...' (p. 3). This means taking an inclusive stance towards all the different *kinds* of evidence needed for practice and using these in ways that are closer to a practical rationality than a scientific or technical-rational approach. This inclusive stance towards knowledge echoes Taylor's (2010) point above outlining the many different sources of knowledge that social workers incorporate into their various judgements and decision-making.

Given these criticisms of the EBP premises as applied to social care contexts, important work has been undertaken to address the criticism that social work judgement is not sufficiently informed by research *in addition* to other kinds of knowledge. This includes research that outlines how social workers use personal and professional knowledge (Anscombe, 2009; Wendt, Schiller, Cheers, Francis & Lonne, 2012); practice wisdom (Chu & Tsui, 2008; O'Sullivan, 2005) and enact judgement in ways that include developing these forms of practical rationality, which take into account context, professional goals and aims. This kind of practical rationality is also known as *phronesis* (Petersén & Olsson, 2014; Taylor & White, 2006).

Phronesis and practical judgement

Phronesis needs to be placed within the context of Aristotle's knowledge triad (Petersén & Olsson, 2014) where it sits beside *episteme* and *techne* (Flyvbjerg, 2001). In contrast to *episteme* – which is considered to refer to context-independent knowledge and often associated with the scientific method within Aristotle's triad – *phronesis* is applied knowledge used in specific practical situations. It involves practical judgement. With this kind of practical judgement, the emphasis is on knowledge that is context-dependent and therefore involves sensitivity to the specific context within which the judgement is being made. Practical judgement, or a sensitivity to context, is a skill that is acquired by the social worker that involves engagement in practice over time. This engagement over time facilitates the discernment required to judge between alternatives (Vokey & Kerr, 2011). By discernment, we mean this to be the '... ability to arrive intuitively at a sound ... judgement in the face of complexity in a way that can incorporate, without being limited to, analytical or deliberative forms of human cognition' (Vokey & Kerr, 2011, p. 66). This is an important aspect of social work practice often discussed as practice wisdom (Chu & Tsui, 2008; Samson, 2014). The development of this capacity often begins for social workers in their field placements as students and, therefore, this aspect of a social work education is considered by some to be crucial to the education of social workers overall (Larrison & Korr, 2013). Supervision, mentoring and critical reflection are processes that may enable the acquisition of *phronesis* (practical judgement). Should social workers seek to develop practical and intuitive judgement, then it is important to understand this capacity in relation to human cognition and intuition, which we turn to in the following sections.

Cognition and judgement

Given the limitations and critiques of EBP, we have made the case above that social work can be seen as a *practical-moral* activity, which involves making judgements and decisions, in collaboration with services users and others, and that this involves choices between different alternatives. These deliberations are important to the core activities of decision-making that lie at the heart of social work practice. In this section we look at types of reasoning, bias and heuristics, and the impact of emotion on judgement.

Types of reasoning

It has long been observed that there are distinctive forms of reasoning, not just within cognitive psychology, but also within philosophy (Evans, 2011). There have been major developments in our understanding of how human cognition works and something of a consensus has emerged that human beings have two main types of cognition at their disposal. One kind of thinking is fast and intuitive; the other tends to be slow and deliberate. For example, sometimes we may reach a decision, or a judgement or an opinion, on something very quickly, without much effort or deliberation. Other times we may not have a quick response, but instead will need to spend time thinking something through before arriving at a conclusion. This notion of two kinds of cognitive reasoning process has come to be known as a *dual-processing* account of cognition (Evans, 2008). These two types have different characteristics (Evans & Stanovich, 2013). Both types can be seen as forms of cognition, an aspect to bear in mind, but they differ in a number of important respects. Table 13.1, adapted from Evans and Stanovich (2013, p. 22), presents some of these different characteristics.

Table 13.1 Type 1 and Type 2 processing

Intuitive – Type 1 processing	Reflective – Type 2 processing
Autonomous – does not require resources from memory to work.	Effortful – uses resources from working memory.
Characterised by a fast response to situations (capacity is high).	Takes longer as it relies on deliberation (capacity is limited).
Thinking is highly contextualised.	Thinking occurs at more abstract levels.
Decisions rely on experience and practice.	Decisions are supported by the ability to mentally simulate events and consequences.
Not related to cognitive ability or intelligence (few continuous individual differences) (Stanovich, 2011).	Correlated with cognitive ability (Stanovich, 2011) due to the need for capacity to engage in mental simulations to generate alternatives for action.
Based on associative thinking.	Generally appeals to rules/principles.

There remain important debates about the exact relation between the two kinds of cognitive process outlined in Table 13.1 (Evans, 2008; Evans, 2011; Evans & Stanovich, 2013). For example, it is still an open question as to whether some reflective thinking processes become habits of mind and thus end up as part of the intuitive type one processing (Evans, 2008).These debates are somewhat beyond our discussion here. What Table 13.1 does is illustrate the work of many different cognitive scientists on the *existence* of different cognitive processes. For our purposes we will use the terms *type one* (intuitive, fast) and *type two* (reflective, slow) processing in the following discussion.

Dual process thinking

It is generally thought that type one processing probably evolved in humans earlier and that this form of thinking largely works autonomously. Type one (intuitive) does not require conscious effort to engage (Evans, 2011). Type one processing does not appear to require access to the resources of working memory (Evans, 2008). Thus it is characterised by responses that are fast and do not seem to carry any conscious deliberation between alternatives. In contrast, type two (reflective) processes are associated with thinking that is slow and deliberate, effortful to engage in, and does require access to working memory (Evans, 2008). Type two processes also rely on the ability to hypothesise through a process of decoupling real events in order to carry out simulations in the mind of the various alternatives available for the situation. In general, this happens in a serial fashion and the process, compared to type one processing, is slow and is consequently more of a drain on the cognitive resources of individuals (Stanovich & Toplak, 2012). Evans (2008, p. 259) suggests that many theorists consider '[type] 2 [*sic*] ... to be associated with language, reflective consciousness, and *higher-order control* and with the capacity to think hypothetically about future and counterfactual possibilities.' In sum, some judgements and decisions in social work often occur quickly, intuitively, and without much effort. Some judgements and decisions are slower, more reflective and require more cognitive effort.

Bias and heuristics

In terms of researching reasoning in judgement and decision-making, there have been three main programs of research within this area of psychology. These are, in the areas of (1) biases and heuristics, (2) decision-making in the context of risk, and (3) how social judgement occurs where there are '... multiple cues in the environment' (Evans, 2008, p. 266).

The existence and operation of biases and heuristics within reasoning processes has been extensively studied by Kahneman and Tversky (1972, cited in

Taylor, 2012, p. 266), amongst others. This is particularly important for social workers to understand because much social work practice involves dealing with large amounts of complex and often incomplete information. Distinguishing between large amounts of information is a difficult task and so to deal with this, human beings have developed cognitive processes that act like shortcuts. These are called heuristics (or, rules of thumb). Social workers may use these heuristics to deal with the complexities of their practice. Generally, these processes are helpful because judgements and interpretations arrive fast and the methods of producing knowledge and understanding do not require huge resources in terms of working memory and cognitive processes. Working with heuristics, or shortcuts, helps social workers to cope with complexity quickly amidst high workloads. When our heuristics fail to render a correct judgement, then this is called a cognitive bias.

There are some common heuristics and there are common cognitive biases as well. Two common heuristics are that of *representativeness* and *anchoring*. The *representative heuristic* is where one makes a judgement based on the '... [the use of] readily available data, or how easily an example can be bought to mind' (Taylor, 2012, p. 552). An example might be a judgement not to name your child Mike because you think that all boys named Mike are trouble-makers based on your experience of a boy you knew named Mike who was continually in trouble with the teacher when you were at school. In practice, social workers need to guard against the inappropriate use of representative heuristics if it is actually an incorrect attribution of one case to another.

The *anchoring* heuristic is where decisions are made based on the first information received (Taylor, 2012). This can be seen in practice where subsequent judgements about service users are shaped by the *initial* intake or referral information. The anchoring bias is a particular issue in social work according to Taylor and White (2006) as '... there are no reliable diagnostic tests to confirm or disconfirm [any] anchor hypotheses' (p. 939). Therefore, the social worker may be inclined to form their judgement based on the *first available information*, and fail to revise or amend that judgement in light of new or disconfirming information that arrives later.

Evans (2008) suggests that heuristics and shortcuts can cue *default judgements*, which are fast and typically associated with type one processes. A corrective to this problem would involve a situation where '... high-effort deliberative reasoning may be applied, which can inhibit the biased response and replace it with one based on reflective reasoning' (p. 266). Therefore, it is possible to intervene in the use of heuristics (and work against making errors) by using the slower, more deliberative reasoning systems at our cognitive disposal. This is particularly important. For example, in social work assessment practices, cognitive bias can really impact in a negative way due to the fact that a great deal of practice seems to involve '... judging the moral adequacy and worthiness of service users [which is] ... a key element in social work assessments' (Taylor & White, 2006, p. 942).

The upshot is that deliberative, reflective cognitive reasoning processes associated with type two processing can assist in the quality and calibre of social work judgements and subsequent decision-making.

Emotion and judgement and decision-making

Our discussion of human cognition, reasoning and judgement has so far not really considered the role of emotion in shaping judgement and by extension decision-making. In the last 10 years there has been a noteworthy movement to incorporate and account for the role of emotion in reasoning and in decision-making within psychology and neuroscience (Lerner, Li, Valdesolo & Kassam, 2015). There is a considerable consensus building that emotion, judgement and decision-making go hand in hand and, moreover, '… many psychological scientists now assume that emotions are … the dominant driver of most meaningful decisions in life' (Lerner et al., 2015, p. 801). Lerner et al. (2015) conducted a survey of 35 years of research that specifically looks at emotion in the context of judgement and decision-making. Lerner and her colleagues (2015) identify eight different themes from this substantial program of experimental research. These are:

1. *Integral emotions*, which are elicited from the situation at hand where a judgement is called for (Lerner et al., 2015, p. 802).

2. The influence of *incidental emotions* on decision-making, which are emotions that 'carry over from one situation to the next, affecting decisions that should, from a normative perspective, be unrelated to that emotion' (Lerner et al., 2015, p. 803).

3. What is known about *emotional valence* for making decisions, where valence refers to the 'the positive versus negative value of affect' (Lerner et al., 2015, p. 803).

4. How emotions shape decisions through *content of thought*.

5. Emotional impact on the *depth of thought*.

6. The contribution of emotions to *goal activation*.

7. Emotions and *interpersonal factors*.

8. What factors moderate or ameliorate any unwanted effects of emotion in decision-making (Lerner et al., 2015).

Clearly, emotions play a considerable role in influencing the form and function of judgements and decision-making. This research is primarily experimental and so it is not specifically applied to social work practice at this stage. Nevertheless, given the important influence emotion has on social work practice, there are some noteworthy aspects for thinking about the role of emotion for professional judgement and thus decisions for intervention in social work practice contexts. The main points to take away from this research about the effects of emotion on judgement and decision-making are:

1. There is a documented effect that occurs between *integral* emotions and the judgement at hand. For example, if the social worker is feeling anxious, they are more likely to choose safer options than if they were feeling happy. Equally, anger or sadness can orient people to different assessments of the choices available to them (Lerner et al., 2015).

2. Emotions carry over between situations. If a social worker experiences an event that makes them angry, this anger can elicit a motive to blame individuals in other situations even though the targets have nothing to do with the source of the anger from a different situation (Ask & Pina, 2011). This means that emotions can be transplanted from an unrelated event or context to influence a judgement or decision elsewhere.

3. There is new research (Yip & Côté, 2013) that looks at moderating factors for the situation described in point 2. This research suggests that those with high levels of emotional intelligence are more able to identify *where* the incidental emotions have come from and can work to moderate their carryover into the new situation (Yip & Côté, 2013). This is an area being explored by social workers (Keinemans, 2014) and examined in the context of emotional intelligence in social work generally (Morrison, 2007).

4. Emotions contain 'action tendencies' (Frijda, 1986, cited in Lerner et al., 2015, p. 805), which coordinate and motivate judgements and decisions. These tendencies save on cognitive processing, which is more effortful. A well-known example is that anger elicits a *fight* tendency whereas fear triggers a *flight* response. The key point is that emotions can act as a short-cut substitution for type two processing and reasoning. Interestingly, positive emotions such as *gratitude* and *pride* tend to elicit more helpful and prosocial behaviour and perseverance with completing tasks respectively (Lerner et al., 2015).

5. The link between thought (cognition) and emotion is still regarded as important as it is a mechanism for appraising situations and is therefore crucial to judgement and decision-making. This is known as the *appraisal tendency* framework proposed by Lerner and Keltner (2000, cited in Lerner & Keltner, 2001). An appraisal tendency is where 'emotions activate a cognitive and motivational disposition to appraise future events according to appraisal dimensions that triggered the emotion (emotion – cognition)' (Lerner et al., 2015, p. 807). The link is two way where emotion triggers cognitive

processes but cognition can also affect emotion through appraisal and reappraisal (Oatley, 2010). The point is that it is redundant for the social worker to try to remove emotions from cognitive or rational judgement processes; rather it is better to become aware of how, when, and to what effect emotions are influencing cognitive processes.

6. There are implications for judging risk associated with appraisal tendencies discussed in point 5 above. According to Lerner and Keltner (2001) fear and anger elicit different appraisals of risk. Anger appears to generally elicit a lower estimation of risk than when people experience fear. So for example, if someone is in a state of anger they may under-estimate the degree of risk, whereas if they are in a state of fear they may over-estimate it. Indeed '... these emotion-related processes guide subsequent behaviour and cognition in goal-directed ways, even in response to objects or events that are unrelated to the original cause of the emotion' (Lerner & Keltner, 2001, p. 146). This means that emotions can be misaligned to the judgement or decision made.

7. Emotion influences information processing, including the depth of thought in which people engage when attempting to make decisions (Lerner et al., 2015). The implications of this is that emotion can affect the extent to which people engage in more type two processing in order to make judgements or decisions.

8. Emotions are social and thus have an interpersonal influence (Lerner et al., 2015; Niedenthal & Brauer, 2012). Emotions help us to understand other people's emotions, their beliefs and intentions. Emotions allow us to engage in communications that have a social cost-benefit component. An example of this is that it has been found that gratitude can trigger generosity in others (Lerner et al., 2015) and witnessing generosity can trigger the desire to act altruistically in others too (Algoe & Haidt, 2009). Thus emotions evoke complementary, reciprocal and shared emotions with others (Algoe, Haidt & Gable, 2008; Lerner et al., 2015). For example, the ability to empathise can be affected by perceptions of fairness or group membership (Bernhardt & Singer, 2012). However, more research is required on how this works with regard to groups and group decision-making (Lerner et al., 2015).

Given the ubiquitous role that emotions play in cognitive judgement and decision-making processes, it is worth considering the sorts of steps people take to intentionally utilise the emotional component in a deliberative manner. There are a number of approaches used by people to moderate the effects of emotion on decision-making and judgement. The main ones that have been researched are time delay, suppression and reappraisal.

1. Time delay is the simplest strategy but is hard to implement in some circumstances due to the *action tendency* associated with some strong emotions. Nevertheless, studies have demonstrated that eventually people do return to a baseline emotional state after some time has passed (Wilson & Gilbert 2005, cited in Lerner et al., 2015). This may involve *post hoc* reflective or reappraisal strategies, where a judgement or decision is re-examined in light of a different emotional state. It could also include peer or supervisory processes as part of reflecting on the judgement and its antecedent emotion component.

2. Suppression of the emotion is another strategy that has been well documented, however this has been shown to be somewhat counterproductive as it can rebound and sometimes intensify the very emotion being suppressed (Wenzlaff & Wegner, 2000). Suppression of emotion in practice may have deleterious effects over time. There is a link to a form of emotional labour described as 'surface acting ... [whereby] employees modify their [emotional] displays without shaping their inner feelings' (Grandey, 2003, p. 87). This form of emotional labour and surface acting has been linked to the emotional exhaustion that characterises burn-out in the human services (Maslach et al., 2001). Again, a supportive work culture, good staff development and sustained supervisory and debriefing practices can support processes to address and intervene in emotional suppression.

3. Reappraisal is considered to be a strategy that is superior to time delay and suppression. This strategy is where one engages in reframing the stressful events through self-talk and talk with others and it has added benefits as '... it mitigates physiological and neurological responses [to stressful events]' (Jamieson, Nock & Mendes 2012, cited in Lerner et al., 2015, p. 812). Grandey (2003, p. 87) refers to 'deep acting', which is the ability of employees to bring their emotions into line with the situation. Although this is characterised as a form of emotional labour, it is likely that the mechanism of reappraisal is at work. Supervision and reflection on practice strategies can aid in reappraisal strategies.

It is possible to see that emotion is a substantial element in judgement and decision-making in everyday life, and there is an important relationship between cognition and emotion. As much of this research is still emerging and is primarily experimental not much of it has yet found its way into applied disciplines such as social work, although there is evidence of some interest starting to emerge. The main issue is how to account for emotion in social work (Morrison, 2007) and the insights around the need for emotional intelligence in working with service users (Collins, 2007).

Conclusion

We began our discussion with the important place that judgement and decision-making have in the conduct of social work practice. We agree with the idea that social work practice is a practical-moral activity and therefore requires attention to the ways in which social workers think and act morally. We also outlined the idea that various kinds of evidence should inform judgements in professional contexts. What kind of evidence, and how this should be taken into account within social work practice, remains contentious. There is, however, agreement that social workers should be able to account for their decisions. Indeed social workers have had their decisions, actions and inactions scrutinised by various inquiries, which is partly what has precipitated these keen debates about knowledge use in judgement and decision-making. With these important debates in mind, we have sought to present understandings of what is possible within the architecture of human cognition, the place of reasoning and emotion in forming judgements. Doing so demonstrates that it is important to recognise both limits and possibilities of these human capacities, and to use this knowledge to inform how we think about learning, teaching and practicing social work. This means that social workers should engage in effortful, reflective deliberations on their immediate, intuitive judgements, which is a crucial part of engaging in professional practice. We also know this is effortful and requires support in terms of workplace culture (see Chapter 11 on organisational contexts, this volume) and practices like professional supervision (see Chapter 15 on reflective practice, this volume). These aspects are important if we, as social workers, want to ensure our practice decisions are able to work effectively and sensitively with vulnerable individuals, groups, families and communities.

Critical thinking questions

1. What is evidence-based practice (EBP)?

2. Why is it considered important to social work and what are the criticisms and limitations of EBP?

3. What are heuristics and how are heuristics used in social work decision-making?

4. In what ways does emotion impact on decision-making? What are the implications for social work?

5. What is the relationship between intuition and judgement, and in what ways does culture and social context shape intuitions?

Exercises

It is sometimes said that social workers rely on intuition when forming judge-ments and making decisions in practice. This can occur in the absence of reliable information and when the outcome is uncertain or carries ethical implications. Furthermore, intuitive judgement can be used in lieu of structured decision-making tools. There are strengths and weaknesses associated with the use of intuition in social work practice decision-making. Discuss and debate the place or otherwise of intuition in decision-making and judgement in social work.

Further reading

Algoe, S. B. & Haidt, J. (2009). Witnessing excellence in action: The 'other-praising' emotions of elevation, gratitude, and admiration. *The Journal of Positive Psychology, 4*(2), 105–127. doi:10.1080/17439760802650519

Evans, J. & Stanovich, K. E. (2013). Dual-process theories of higher cognition: Advancing the debate. *Perspectives on Psychological Science, 8*(3), 223–241. doi:10.1177/1745691612460685

Keddell, E. (2011). Reasoning processes in child protection decision-making: Negotiating moral minefields and risky relationships. *British Journal of Social Work, 41*(7), 1251–1270. doi:10.1093/bjsw/bcr012

Lerner, J., Li, Y., Valdesolo, P. & Kassam, K. S. (2015). Emotion and decision-making. *Annual Review of Psychology, 66*, 799–823. doi:10.2246/annurev-psych-010213-115043

Morrison, T. (2007). Emotional intelligence, emotion and social work: Context, characteristics, complications and contribution. *British Journal of Social Work, 37*(2), 245–263. doi:10.1093/bjsw/bcl016

Links and online resources

Dietrich, C. (2010). Decision-making: Factors that influence decision-making, heuristics used, and decision outcomes. Inquiries Journal. www.inquiriesjournal.com/articles/180/2/decision-making-factors-that-influence-decision-making-heuristics-used-and-decision-outcomes

Lee, S. & Lebowitz, S. (2015). 20 cognitive biases that screw up your decisions. Business Insider. www.businessinsider.com/cognitive-biases-that-affect-decisions-2015-8?IR=T

Reamer, F. G. (2002). Eye on ethics: Making difficult decisions. Social Work Today. www.socialworktoday.com/news/eoe_101402.shtml

Social Work Policy Institute (n.d.). Evidenced-based practice. www.socialworkpolicy.org/research/evidence-based-practice-2.html

Surface, D. (2009). Understanding evidence-based practice in behavioral health. Social Work Today. www.socialworktoday.com/archive/072009p22.shtml

14
ASSESSMENT

Introduction

Social workers engage in assessment in every role in which they work. From policy advocacy through to working with families and children, social workers have to be able to do the complex work of assessment. Assessment has many functions. It assists in engagement and way of working with and for service users and systems, helps to identify problems, forms the foundation for planning interventions and actions and, lastly, assessment is a way of making sense of information and situations. Therefore, it is fair to say that assessment is a generic skill in social work (Crisp, Anderson, Orme & Lister, 2006) and it involves lots of other skills too: interpersonal skills; interviewing techniques; and data collection and analysis. Good assessments involve classifying and organising phenomena and ideas, creating hypotheses and theory building. Thus, assessments mean working with multiple perspectives and are used for decision-making and planning. This chapter defines the meaning and stages of assessment before exploring the way that theory is used in assessments. Here, we particularly focus on strength-based assessment and risk assessments. The importance of hypothesising and critical thinking are explained, demonstrating the centrality of the social worker's thinking and judgement in the course of doing assessments.

Assessment and its many forms

An immediate problem with learning about assessment is coming to grips with a bewildering array of different assessment tools, approaches, methodologies and models. These include, but are not limited to, genograms and eco-maps (McGoldrick, Gerson & Petry, 2008; McGoldrick, Gerson & Shellenberger, 1999; Pope & Lee, 2015; Poulin, 2000; Yanca & Johnson, 2008), mental status examination (Poulin, 2000), sociograms (Poulin, 2000), bio-psychosocial assessments (James & Gilliland, 2005; Poulin, 2000), person/family/group in environment assessments (Poulin, 2000), risk assessments (Morley, 2009; O'Connor et al., 2008; Waugh, 2011), carers' assessments (Watts & Hodgson, 2015), transactional family assessments (Yanca & Johnson, 2008), needs and community profile assessments (O'Connor et al., 2008), not to mention a vast array of diagnostic and assessment tools within the DSM-V used in psychology and psychiatry (Ruffolo, Perron & Voshel, 2016). Different fields of practice will utilise different tools and approaches. Some organisations have their own assessment tools that they require their employees to use. Invariably, social work students and social workers will encounter different assessment frameworks and tools and they need to learn and understand how they work and how to think critically about them. One way to do this is to raise a number of critical questions: What is it that the assessment framework and tool purports to do? What are its central concepts and assumptions? What does it focus on, what does it exclude? What are its strengths and limitations? Whose interests are being served by the endorsement and adoption of a particular assessment approach or tool?

Defining assessment

As mentioned, assessment is a core skill that is applicable in all fields of social work practice and in all kinds of roles. As stated by Weber and Giles (2011, p. 166):

> Whatever the practice context, assessment of the situation by the practitioner is the foundation of decision-making and planning for future action.

Let's look more closely at what assessment means. A good definition of assessment is offered by Coulshed and Orme (1998, p. 21) as follows:

> Assessment is an ongoing process, in which the client participates, the purpose of which is to understand people in relation to their environment; it is the basis for planning what needs to be done to maintain, improve or bring about change in the person, the environment or both.

A few points are worth highlighting from this definition. First, they say that assessment is an *ongoing process*. Our social world and our experiences in it are in a constant state of change and flux. This means it is impossible to conduct just one assessment on the assumption that the circumstances and information that informed that assessment are fixed and settled, when they are not. New information, different perspectives, and even a change of mind will mean that the foundations of an assessment are subject to change, review and revision. In practice, this means that the social worker will need to re-assess and perhaps revise or extend and deepen their assessment over time.

Second, it is stated that the *client (service user) participates* in the assessment. This is something that should be facilitated as part of an ethic towards collaborative, strength-based and anti-oppressive practice. But there are some practical reasons why the service user should participate in assessment, foremost being that the service user may have a greater depth of insight and understanding of the situation at hand than the social worker, and this can be leveraged to support a more accurate and relevant assessment. It is also empowering for the service user to participate in the assessments made about a situation because these assessments will ultimately form the basis of any future or current interventions, plans, goals, and so on, that will affect them. This kind of collaboration and sharing of information and perspectives is akin to an exchange model of assessment, in which 'people are regarded as experts in their own lives. The emphasis is on exchange of information, listening to the client's construction of their difficulties and striving for mutual understanding of what is being experienced' (O'Connor et al., 2008, p. 115). The exchange model as described here can be contrasted with other models that put the social worker in a more expert role – a role with a predetermined notion of what is important to their assessment, such as in assessment processes that emphasise rigid tick-box approaches to assessment that are done *to* the service user, not with them (O'Connor et al., 2008).

Third, assessment should be a *purposeful means of developing understanding* about the service user and their interaction with their environment (O'Connor et al., 2008). For O'Connor et al., this understanding is intentionally connected to social work's mission, which involves 'reducing tensions between people and their social arrangements, working towards more equitable relationships and increasing people's power and control over their lives' (O'Connor et al., 2008, p. 113). Right away we can notice the ethical and political nature of assessment. Practically speaking, using assessment to arrive at understanding for change means that it is a process of building knowledge, hypotheses, and generating theories that may be unique to the service user. This does not mean that the assessment is narrowly individualising, but rather, that the assessment avoids stereotyping people into specific patterns or types, and is instead tailored to the specific circumstances of the service user and their interaction with their environment (Gambrill, 1997).

Finally, assessment is the *basis for planning*. That is to say, assessment is the foundation that supports decisions about how to think about something and 'what to do'. The quality of an intervention, a course of action, or a series of decisions or steps that may impact on the service user really depends on the thoroughness, rigour and appropriateness of the assessment that is built and created in partnership between social worker and service user (Gambrill, 1997).

Stages of assessment

Many writers on social work assessment consider that there are different stages or sequences to the assessment process overall (Milner et al., 2015; Milner & O'Byrne, 2002; O'Connor et al., 2008; Weber & Giles, 2011). They present the stages of assessment in a chronological order. The order of these stages has a general logic to it, but in practice, the social worker may move back and forth between these stages as they go back to gather more information and re-assess the situation. Including the service user in these stages is important to a collaborative assessment process. The assessment process described by O'Connor et al. (2008) is similar to that of Milner et al. (2015) and we refer to both in the section below. An abridged version of Milner and O'Byrne's (2002) stages of assessment can also be found in Weber and Giles (2011):

1. *Identify desired outcomes in a general sense* (O'Connor et al., 2008). Milner et al. (2015) refer to this as 'preparation'. Even in the initial stages of doing assessment, a sense of what needs to happen, how things could be different, or better, or what someone might hope or wish for can be canvassed and discussed. This can start the process of orienting towards key concerns and build a sense early on of the possibilities and potentials.

2. *Gather information* (O'Connor et al., 2008). Milner et al. (2015) refer to this as 'data collection'. Here, the social worker collects and organises data and information from a variety of sources using a variety of methods. Initially, these methods and sources might be in interviews, observations, documents from existing files or reports or referral notes, conversations with other stakeholders, or by using formal assessment tools and processes. Looking broadly for sources of information is important to a well-rounded assessment, and so these sources may also include: social and public policy; other people; the physical environment; tasks and activities (behaviours and actions taken); biophysical factors such as health and mental health; thought patterns (their form and function); feelings and moods; cultural differences; and the developmental and life stage of the service user (Gambrill, 1997, pp. 221–224). Clearly, this list provides many avenues to explore, many sources of potential information, resources, and clues to help support an assessment. The overall aim of assessment in social work is to take the idea of being holistic in orientation seriously, and 'to devise responses to individual problems and situations that take into account the wider contexts in which people live their lives' (Moss, 2012, p. 42).

3. *Analyse information* (O'Connor et al., 2008). Milner et al. (2015) refer to this as 'analysing the data'. Data on its own is nothing unless it is analysed and organised in a meaningful way. For O'Connor et al. (2008), this means analysing the way that parts relate to each other or the whole. It will mean analysing how some parts evident within the data may be important in explaining their influence on the existence and maintenance of the problem, or how some parts can be used to resolve or change some aspect of the situation, and so on. At this level, the analysis involves looking for

possible causal links, building explanatory and predictive hypotheses from the data, and utilising theory to guide the organisation and analysis of information. Later in this chapter we discuss theory in assessment and hypothesis building, which would be applicable in this stage of data analysis.

4. *Critically apply knowledge and theory to the analysis* (O'Connor et al., 2008). Milner et al. (2015) refer to this as analysing the data and it involves similar actions as described in point 3. The critical application of theory to the assessment analysis involves a good deal of reflection and examination of the social worker's thinking. What do I know? Where do I know this from? What might be missing from my analysis? What else do I need to find out? How am I thinking about this and what other perspectives might be helpful; are there other points of view that should be considered and weighed up? Later in this chapter we discuss critical thinking skills, which would be applicable at all stages of the assessment, but particularly at this stage.

5. *Negotiate outcomes* (O'Connor et al., 2008). Milner et al. (2015) refer to this as 'utilising the analysis'. Once an assessment has been developed and shared, and discussed and negotiated with the service user, some sense of what might happen and what outcomes are posited can be established. Again, this is a process of negotiation between the social worker and service user, and formed within the constraints and opportunities of available resources, and organisation role and mandate. Other factors – practical, ethical and preferential – will influence the course of the negotiation, and so the social worker needs very good communication skills to convey and reach agreement on the form and function of the assessment. Negotiated outcomes are tied to the purposeful nature of assessment, insofar as assessment can be the basis for planning and intervening. A skilled social worker will be able to exercise negotiation and high level communication skills in the formulation of an assessment.

Theory in assessment

As mentioned earlier, theoretical thinking is a key aspect of developing a comprehensive and purposeful assessment. Here, we are talking about the development of a perspective and the establishment of knowledge about the person-situation-context that concerns the assessment. Many writers on assessment will note that assessment should be grounded in a theoretical orientation (for example, Cournoyer, 2014; Milner et al., 2015; Ruffolo et al., 2016). Cournoyer explains that assessment brings together the social worker's professional knowledge in collaboration with 'the client's firsthand experience' (Cournoyer, 2014, p. 338). In combination, this shared knowledge can be developed to provide an explanation of what's going on, and some ideas about what needs to happen in the course of developing a plan for action (Cournoyer, 2014). Importantly, how one thinks about a phenomenon will profoundly bring to light a picture of that phenomena in particular ways. In doing so, a certain version of reality is constructed within the assessment.

What do we mean by a certain version of reality? Try this simple experiment: The next time you are travelling by road, remember to look out for and notice only red cars. You may be surprised at how many you see, whereas on any other day red cars would barely register in your consciousness. But if by focussing on red cars means that suddenly it seems as though red cars are everywhere, that does not mean that there *are* more red cars than there are on any other given day – it just *seems* that way. Assessment is similar: what you choose to pay attention to, and how you choose to think about it, will highlight certain things in certain ways, and these perceptual choices are shaped by your training, role and professional location. For example, if we focus our assessments on problems, limitations, risks, deficits, then arguably the information we collect, and how it is organised and interpreted, will reflect this. Likewise, if we focus our assessments on strengths, assets, resilience and opportunities, we may get a different picture. It is for this reason that many argue that social work assessments should avoid from the outset being too problem-focussed as this may end up pathologising the situation in deficit terms (Anglem & Maidment, 2009; Saleebey, 2009). A strengths and systems focus can counter a narrowly forensic view that may take hold of the assessment. At the same time, we should not pretend that problems do not exist. Some balance is needed, and the social worker should strive for building a comprehensive, holistic and collaborative approach to assessment.

Work by Milner, Myers and O'Byrne (2015) provides a comprehensive discussion of theory and assessment. Their work also covers assessment practice in the context of children's services, adult services, and they include a focus on spiritual assessments too. We restrict the section below to some common theoretical perspectives in social work as discussed by Milner et al. (2015), and these theories can also be found in detailed discussion in many social work theory texts (for example, Healy, 2014; Howe, 2009; Payne, 2014). These are summarised in Table 14.1 in order to demonstrate the way that theory can be incorporated into assessment processes. The point to remember is that theory will support an orientation towards what information is collected, how it is analysed and communicated, what assumptions are contained in the assessment, and the implications for how a situation is thought about and responded to.

Table 14.1 Theory in assessment

Theory	Brief description	Application in assessment	Criticism and response
Anti-oppressive practice	Concerns a focus on access to and use of power, an analysis of structural disadvantage and oppression along lines of class, gender, race and ethnicity, age, able-bodiedness and sexual orientation (Agger, 2006). Assessment here would factor in these wider structural, cultural and personal factors (Thompson, 2006) and their role in creating and sustaining power inequalities and abuses of power and how these harm, paternalise, disempower, blame and castigate people for their problems.	Fundamentally, assessment here should be collaborative, transparent, open to perspective sharing, respectful, based in clear and accountable reasoning, and incorporate the role of social structural factors into the assessment data generation, analysis and proposed course of action (Milner et al., 2015).	A criticism of this approach concerns the contested nature of concepts like equality and rights, and the way that concepts like empowerment can be trivialised as superficial tropes without any substance (Milner et al., 2015). The social worker needs to take empowerment seriously and be clear about their position around matters to do with rights and social justice.
Systems approach	Concerns a focus on micro, meso and macro systems and ecological contexts of people's lives, such as family, community, neighbourhood, physical environment, economic and socio-cultural contexts, and the way that these systems interact, change and influence the course and experience of people's lives (Robbins et al., 2012b).	Assessment adopts a person-in-environment perspective by collating data that is broadly holistic, and examining the interactions and influences between the different systemic elements (Milner et al., 2015). Instances of stressors as well as assets and resources within the system can be identified and prioritised for action. As above, service user 'participation in the process is seen as essential, as is their collaboration in the prioritizing of what issues need immediate action, what can be set aside for now and what can be ignored' (Milner et al., 2015, p. 82). This will allow the social worker and service user to develop a plan that tackles the issues in context, and in a way that prioritises where resources and energy should be best directed.	A criticism of this approach is that despite developing a systemic perspective, it lacks a deeper critical engagement with oppression and social injustice (Milner et al., 2015). The social worker can counter this by bringing an anti-oppressive frame to a systems analysis.

(Continued)

Table 14.1 *(Continued)*

Theory	Brief description	Application in assessment	Criticism and response
Psychodynamic approaches	Concerns a focus on the psychological functioning of the person, particularly in regard to how this transacts within interpersonal relationships and the influence of past experiences on things like anxiety, ego, emotion, sense of self and general coping (Nathan, 2013). Attachment theory falls into this theoretical grouping due to the way that problems with child/caregiver attachment that manifest during a child's early developmental years are thought to give rise to personal and interpersonal dysfunction in later years (Milner et al., 2015).	In psychotherapeutic practice, the assessment identifies the person's capability to think psychologically about their situation, their ego strength and the extent to which this relates inner thoughts to an external reality, the person's affect or emotional feeling state and disposition, and their ability to control frustrations and impulses (Caparrotta & Ghaffari, 2004). In the context of an assessment concerning attachment, the assessment will focus on the functioning or otherwise of relationships (especially between child and caregiver/parent), any historical or contextual factors that may have influenced present relationships and attachments, and, following Bowlby, an assessment of the 'kind' of attachments that may be observed (Howe, 1995).	The main criticism of psychodynamic approaches is that the theory can drag the assessment foci into the past, exploring historical events, and inner emotional experiences, and so on (Milner et al., 2015). This may shift the focus away from important information to do with present and relevant co-existing material concerns, such as poverty. Furthermore, psychodynamic theories can overplay the importance of emotional reflection, which may not always be appropriate (Milner et al., 2015).
Behavioural approaches	Concerns a focus on the way certain behaviours and responses are the result of conditioning and social learning (Thyer, 2011). Problematic behaviours, attitudes, beliefs and thought patterns are said to be products of antecedent experiences that are built up over time. The theory states that these can be unlearned or changed through interventions such as Cognitive Behavioural Therapy (CBT) and other behavioural modification approaches (Milner et al., 2015).	Assessment processes are concerned to create a baseline of the behaviours that warrant changing, and an analysis of the conditions that might be contributing towards or sustaining such behaviours. The assessment can then proceed to establish new sets of behaviours, conditions and practices that might bring about a change in the learned and conditioned response (Milner et al., 2015).	The main criticism of this approach is that it is psychologically reductionist, thereby ignoring the social, cultural, political and economic context within which many problems manifest and are rooted (Milner et al., 2015).

Task-centred approach	Concerns a focus on the relationship between emotions and beliefs and how this may support or interfere with solving problems, or performing a range of tasks associated with problem solving (Marsh, 2013). The assessment involves a collaborative effort between the social worker and service user 'puzzling out together what to do' (Milner et al., 2015, p. 142).	The assessment seeks to locate and identify how problems might be interlinked, maintained and caused, thought about and experienced, and what obstacles are in place that prevent the problem being addressed. The assessment can include: exploring these problems (experienced as wants); classifying them; setting goals; and agreeing on what tasks should be completed in order to reach these goals; implementing and then reviewing the tasks (Milner et al., 2015).	Milner et al. (2015) argue that there are many benefits to the task centred approach, but care needs to be exercised by the social worker that they don't end up dominating the definition of what constitutes a problem, and taking over the main role of completing tasks, which may disempower the service user.
Strengths-based approach	Rather than a focus on problems (and to some extent deficits and pathologies) a strengths approach focuses the assessment on resilience, solutions, growth, strength, capacity and potential (Saleebey, 2009). This is a departure from an approach that focuses on the past, or locates the source of the problem as being rooted in the individual to such an extent that the individual becomes blamed for their situation. Instead, a strengths approach 'means everything you do is predicated on helping discover and develop people's strengths and resources to help them achieve their goals, realize their dreams, and become independent of welfare services so that they and their families have better futures' (Milner et al., 2015, p. 166).	A strengths approach to assessment means listening, using empathy, and taking people's concerns, needs and hopes and aspirations seriously (Milner et al., 2015). It includes a questioning technique that assists the person to explore these in the context of developing capacity, resilience and locating resources and assets that can be put to work to resolve the problem. The problem is conceptualised as being distinct in some ways from the person (that is, the problem is the problem, the person is not the problem) (Saleebey, 2009).	Criticisms of this approach point to the potential for a strengths approach to gloss over serious problems, or to over-simplify things offering only short-term solutions at the expense of a deeper engagement with things like power, oppression and structural inequality (Milner et al., 2015).

(Continued)

Table 14.1 (*Continued*)

Theory	Brief description	Application in assessment	Criticism and response
Spiritual assessment	Stewart defines spiritual assessment as 'the process of gathering and synthesizing spiritual and religious information into a specific framework that provides the basis for, and gives direction to, subsequent practice decisions' (Stewart, 2014, p. 65). Milner et al. (2015) state that the 'most important element of spiritual social work practice is that assessment is unfettered by judgement; people are not labelled with diagnoses or categories' (p. 248).	The practice of spiritual assessment might take the form of including in the assessment process some questions or discussions around religious and spiritual beliefs and activities (Crisp, 2010). Such discussions can be useful to form a more comprehensive assessment (Nelson-Becker et al., 2006). If deemed appropriate, the assessment may involve activities that assist the service user to connect with their spiritual or religious beliefs in an effort to provide support for resolving an issue or concern, or to refer to specific religious or non-religious groups or services that may further assist the service user. Examples of spiritual assessment tools and methods can be found in Hunt (2014) and Stewart (2014).	Nelson-Becker et al. (2006) make a distinction between implicit and explicit interest and activities. If the service user does not express an interest in religion or spirituality then the focus is constrained to implicit activities that may concern strengths or existential approaches or techniques such as meditation and relaxation. If the service user has an expressed interest in the place of spirituality in the professional relationship and intervention then this opens up scope to discuss, with service user approval, specific activities, interventions and conversations that have an overt spiritual or religious dimension (Nelson-Becker et al., 2006). This is an ethical consideration on behalf of the social worker to be clear about the purpose of their practice, so that 'there is no motive aside from the welfare of the client' (Nelson-Becker et al., 2006, p. 805).

Strength-based assessment

Two commonly discussed approaches to assessment are strength-based approaches and risk assessments, and we discuss both in the section here to give an illustration to the importance of drawing on strength-based perspectives even in the context of risk assessments.

Recent writing in social work assessments underscores the importance of strength-based perspectives in the assessment process. Anglem and Maidment (2009) clearly situate their discussion of assessment within a strengths perspective. Kirst-Ashman (2007) notes the distinction between what she refers to as 'traditional' and strength-based assessments. In traditional assessments, the focus is on identifying and examining problems. In doing so, the source or location of these problems is seen to be rooted in the service user. A strengths perspective offers an alternative view.

Identifying problems may still be a necessary and important part of the assessment, but a strengths assessment should be empowering and bring balance by assessing for strengths, opportunities, potentials and resources (Kirst-Ashman, 2007). By this it is meant that assessment ought to be a collaborative endeavour between social worker and service user, and must take into account the 'socio-economic context from which current problems arise' (Kirst-Ashman, 2007, p. 134). In Saleebey's words, this means to avoid 'context stripping' (2009, p. 5), or being careful not to screen out important aspects of the environment that contribute to or sustain the problem.

Overall, a strengths approach to assessment seeks to avoid pathologising or problematising some aspect of the service user and their experience in narrow and reductionist ways, and is very mindful of the use of language that may unhelpfully construct deficit assessments (Gambrill, 1997). For example, an assessment framed as a 'diagnosis' can lead to a host of negative outcomes for the service user, such as labels that emphasise weaknesses and negative stereotypes that are thought to be owned by the service user. The diagnosis as label may become attributed to an inherent or essentialist view of the service user's being and identity. Some labels may work to over-generalise problems, resulting in stock-standard interventions that are applied to service users as though they all share the same characteristics and problems, when in fact they may not (Poulin, 2000).

Risk assessments

Risk assessments are a particular kind of assessment concerned primarily with the identification and management of risks. Specifically, risk assessments are concerned with gathering information and making judgements about consequences (good, bad, catastrophic) and likelihoods (predictions and probabilities) (Carson & Bain, 2008). As noted in Chapter 3, the place of risk is increasingly dominating the context of social work, and there are numerous criticisms of the risk management paradigm in social work.

In citing Stevenson and Parsloe (1993), the kinds of risks that may focus the attention of the social worker are described by Doel and Shardlow (2005) as being (i) physical, (ii) social, (iii) financial and (iv) emotional. The sorts of questions that the social worker may consider in making a risk assessment are listed in Doel and Shardlow (2005, p. 198) and these are discussed below. So, in simple terms, the social worker may seek to assess for (a) consequences and likelihoods, in relation to (b) physical, social, financial and emotional domains, and (c) for each of these domains, raise the following questions (Doel & Shardlow, 2005, p. 198):

1. *What is the nature of the risk?* The social worker needs to work out if there is a risk that warrants attention at all, what the source of the risk is, and what it means. Life is full of risk and not everything is worth paying attention to, but some things certainly are. The social worker needs to define and conceptualise the risk, to give it meaning and clarity.

2. *Is there a risk to a minor or vulnerable person?* People are differentially positioned in relation to the risks and hazards of life. Some people have resources and capabilities to detect and manage risks, others are more vulnerable and exposed. An assessment along these lines will alter the meaning and significance of risk based on the degree of vulnerability of the person and their level of exposure.

3. *Is this a subjective or objective definition of risk?* This is really a question concerning the basis and foundation for the assessment of risk. As noted in Chapter 3, there are many criticisms of objective accounts of risk. But the social worker could explore the extent to which an assessment of risk is shared or consensual, and the areas of disagreement and contestation.

4. *What protective measures can people take themselves against the risk?* As mentioned in Chapter 3, thinking about strengths, resilience and protective factors can provide some fruitful lines of inquiry into sources of support and avenues to address perceived risks and harms. Thinking about protective measures can also moderate the tendency for risk assessments to become reductive and victim-blaming.

5. *Are there risks if you do intervene, and how are these weighed against non-intervention?* Clearly, intervening itself may carry risks and the very actions of the social worker or service user can elevate the degree of risk. For example, in the context of a domestic violence situation Morley (2009) explains 'that the risk of violence increases when the perpetrator knows the woman has disclosed his actions to others, or if she decides to leave him, and at or shortly after separation' (p. 157).

The elements of risk assessment outlined previously are combined and summarised in Table 14.2.

Table 14.2 Model of risk assessment

Type of risk	In relation to	Questions to explore
Physical		What is the nature of the risk?
Social		Is there a risk to a minor or vulnerable person?
Financial	Consequences	
Emotional		Is this a subjective or objective definition of risk?
	Likelihoods	What protective measures can people take themselves against the risk?
		Are there risks if you do intervene, and how are these weighed against non-intervention?

An assessment of risk requires a professional judgement and this is used to inform 'decisions about what actions are required to address the identified risks' (Waugh, 2011, p. 103). According to Waugh, there are three main models to risk assessment:

1. *Actuarial models* – these are typically tick-box type assessments that are based on a systematic appraisal of similar cases and situations (see also Doel & Shardlow, 2005, p. 197). These sorts of tools will often seek to quantify the likelihood of certain specified risks. For example, there are risk profiling tools used in corrections that predict the likelihood of (re)offending behaviour (Trotter, 2015). Some suicide assessment tools will seek to appraise certain behaviours and actions to arrive at a quantifiable assessment of suicide risk (see, for example, at www.psychology.org.au/ATAPS/resources/).

2. *Consensus models* – these are approaches that are based on general theories and research evidence, which might be applicable to certain situations, groups or individuals. For example, the view that child maltreatment may co-occur with family and domestic violence (Shlonsky & Friend, 2007), suggesting that the latter is a risk factor for the former. The issue here is the degree to which a consensus exists, as some theories and the evidence base around some claims may be contested. For example, the idea that young people who drop out of school early are consequently at risk of unemployment or under-employment and by extension are at further risk other social and economic disadvantages (Saddler, Tyler, Maldonado, Cleveland & Thompson, 2011). While there is some evidence to support this (Saddler et al., 2011), it does not mean that the risk of early school leaving is deterministic and total – there are exceptions. Therefore, the social worker should be cautious of slippery slope fallacies. These are propositional arguments that contend that a particular risk is an undesirable outcome deterministically predicted by a series of conditional causal links expressed in a chain of

reasoning. In some cases, the causal logic may hold, but in others, the chain of reasoning does not hold and the purported risk at the end of the sequence of events is unfounded or doubtful.

3. *Professional judgement models* – these are models that rely heavily on practitioner judgement, and may be supported by their knowledge of theories and ethics. In this approach, the skills required of the practitioner are similar to other assessment approaches and include gathering information such as: information about the person, the context or environment; perceived harms or threats; and systems and resources that may moderate or ameliorate these harms or threats. Risk assessment using professional judgement also includes skills in analysis and making sense of that information. This requires: being clear about what constitutes a risk or harm; a judgement about its severity, and likelihood of occurrence; the degree of vulnerability of the person(s) who may be exposed to the harm; and the degree of capacity and level of resources available to offer avoidance or protection (Waugh, 2011). The social worker must also be able to develop a plan that outlines what actions should be taken to manage or intervene in the assessed risk.

Like other forms of assessment, one of the problems with risk assessment concerns questions over who decides what is and what is not a risk (Carson & Bain, 2008). As mentioned in Chapter 3, disagreements tend to occur between professional and lay perceptions over what is and is not a risk and risky, and who is or is not at risk, and so on. The assessor's values – both personal and professional – will influence the assessment of risk (Carson & Bain, 2008) and these may be at odds with the service user's view. Focussing forensically on risk may limit the extent that the values of social justice and empowerment are factored in, meaning the risk assessment process may drift away from the mission and purpose of social work.

One way to address the problems outlined above is argued by Morley (2009), who contends that risk assessments should be based in an anti-oppressive and strengths approach. This is mostly applicable when using a professional judgement or clinical model of risk assessment, which allows for a greater degree of collaboration and negotiation between social worker and service user over the identification, meaning and assessment of risks. It allows for an approach with a focus on social justice and structural factors, which acts as a counter-point to overly reductionist and deficit approaches to risk assessment. The social worker is still tasked with exercising professional judgement and expertise, and can call on the assistance of structured decision-making and risk assessment tools, but with some thought and skill can incorporate these into an anti-oppressive and strengths approach (Morley, 2009). This would involve very good communication skills, sharing perspectives and assumptions, and negotiating different understandings and interpretations of risk. It also includes steps to facilitate service user input in the risk assessment process, assessing for strengths and resources and capacities inasmuch as sources of harm and danger. It also involves clearly connecting the analysis of risk to a wider context of systems and environmental factors and conditions that are implicated in the manifestations of risk (Morley, 2009).

Hypothesis building

It should be clear so far that assessments support thinking about what is going on and what should be done in practice. Cournoyer (2014) explains that social workers will invariably hold explanations for '"why" problems occur and "what to do" to resolve them' (p. 319), and a good assessment can provide the information and evidence to inform such views. Importantly, Cournoyer (2014) notes that service users will also have theories and hypotheses about these matters, and this exemplifies the importance of reaching a shared and collaborative understanding and assessment of the situation and what ought to be done. Here we discuss the role of hypothesis building as a way of giving structure and direction to an assessment process that may facilitate explanation and understanding, as well as plans for action.

What is a hypothesis?

> 'Hypothesis' refers to propositions made about the case, or an aspect of it, against which subsequent assessments or investigations could be made. They provide, in other words, points of reference for the collection of empirical data which would serve to confirm or falsify the hypothesis developed (and which might, in turn, through processes of critical appraisal, help to generate further hypotheses). (Sheppard, Newstead, Di Caccavo & Ryan, 2000, pp. 474–475)

Cournoyer makes a distinction between *explanatory hypotheses*, which are 'ideas used to explain or understand the reasons that a problem exists and the factors that contribute to its persistence' (Cournoyer, 2014, p. 319) and *change-oriented hypotheses*, which 'are predictions about how resolutions of problems or achievement of goals could or should occur' (Cournoyer, 2014, p. 320). Like assessments generally, hypotheses are not etched in stone and may be revised and refined over time as new information comes to hand. Hypotheses should form a component of the communication between social worker and service user, and communicating the thinking about what's going on and what should be done and why is a skill that the social worker should seek to develop (Cournoyer, 2014).

The ability to generate and critically examine hypotheses is central to reflexivity and good practice overall. Developing good hypotheses is a skill that can be taught, developed and learned (Sheppard et al., 2000). Sheppard et al. (2000) make a distinction between what they call 'partial case hypotheses', 'whole case hypotheses' and 'speculative hypotheses'.

1. *Partial case hypotheses*, like their namesake, give explanation and understanding to a particular element of the situation or case presented to the social worker (Sheppard et al., 2000). Partial case hypotheses are explanatory and involve making sense or explaining some aspect concerned with what's going on. The social worker may collect information or specific details to try and make sense of or explain some aspect of the phenomena or concern facing them and the service user. These may manifest as spontaneous explanations that arrive quickly within the context of information as it comes to hand (Sheppard et al., 2000).

2. *Whole case hypotheses* are of a more general nature that provide 'a proposition, or propositions, which covered the whole case' (Sheppard et al., 2000, p. 477). More than one whole case hypothesis can be developed, and these are not so much spontaneous; rather, they are the product of a more systematic process of data collection and post hoc reflection on what's going on with the case.

3. *Speculative hypotheses* are future-orientated, based on causal inferences that can be made about possible consequences or the results of specific interventions and actions that the social worker and service users may take (Sheppard et al., 2000). They are often conceptualised as 'if … then' statements, that purport to make some kind of prediction about a course of future events.

In a practice sense, Sheppard et al. (2000) suggest that an ideal reflexive process of hypothesis building and critical thinking may entail the following steps:

- The social workers are given information through, for example, a referral, which they scrutinise.

- The information is subject to critical appraisal, with a development of emergent implicit hypotheses.

- From this appraisal explicit or implicit hypotheses are developed, the latter in the form of questions.

- Social workers conduct speculative appraisal, formulating possible alternatives of what they will find.

- They evolve 'if … then' statements about possible practice actions. (Sheppard et al., 2000, p. 481)

Generating, examining and sharing hypotheses can form an important aspect of the assessment process overall. However, the social worker should think critically about the kinds of conclusions reached in the assessment, the robustness of the data and evidence collected, the assumptions that underpin judgements made, and the plausibility or otherwise of hypotheses generated from an assessment process.

Critical thinking and assessment

Critical thinking is an important skill in social work generally, but we argue that it has particular significance in the processes and products of assessments. In writing about social work skills, Cournoyer notes the centrality of critical thinking to practice generally, and dealing with information of a complex nature specifically:

> Social workers must possess an extraordinary breadth and depth of knowledge, have access to even more, and be able to understand and analyze a massive amount of emerging information to provide effective, up-to-date services to people facing difficult challenges. The intellectual demands faced by social workers in contemporary practice are daunting. (Cournoyer, 2014, p. 55)

The reason for this demand in forming a good assessment concerns the sheer complexity of practice, the volume of information that must be gathered, sorted, and made sense of, and the fact that a lack of good critical thinking 'represents a genuine risk of harm to our clients, our colleagues and ourselves' (Cournoyer, 2014, p. 58).

Moore's (2013) study into critical thinking in higher education provides a useful framework for considering the application of critical thinking in the context of social work assessment. It is useful because it picks up some of the understandings about assessment in social work generally, and expresses them as a skill that is expected of students in higher education. This means that the skill of critical thinking that can be developed in the context of a social work education generally and can be applied in social work practice in the context of assessment specifically. Moore (2013) concedes that there is no universally accepted notion of critical thinking, but following the philosopher Wittgenstein, Moore (2013) seeks to examine the *doing* of critical thinking, rather than its semantic meaning. Drawing on interview data from academics in different disciplines, he arrives at the following seven definitions of critical thinking in action, and we refer to these here by making links to the practice of social work assessment:

1. *Critical thinking as judgement* – this means to decide, reach a verdict, make a moral or epistemological proclamation about something (good/bad, valid/invalid, right/wrong, true/false) (Moore, 2013). Writing on social work knowledge, Sheppard refers to this as *critical appraisal*, which concerns 'initial judgements about the nature and quality of ... information' (Sheppard, 1998, p. 471). Assessments are based on information (data, knowledge, theories, values) and thinking critically here means to think about the nature and quality of the information being used to form and substantiate an assessment.

2. *Critical thinking as a sceptical and provisional view of knowledge* – this means to exercise a degree of caution or scepticism about claims made, to question claims to truth, to unpack or examine assumptions more closely, to resist jumping too quickly to conclusions or taking things on face value, to challenge dogma or accepted wisdom, and 'to apply the same critical view towards … [ones] own ideas, beliefs and assumptions' (Moore, 2013, p. 512). An assessment can be thought of as a provisional view of knowledge, and therefore subject to critical scrutiny and debate.

3. *Critical thinking as simple originality* – rather than being critical of existing knowledge, this notion of critical thinking means to engage in the production of knowledge, to develop novel interpretations or original thinking, to arrive at a conclusion or interpretation of something, to make a case, and to make connections between seemingly disconnected phenomena (Moore, 2013). Clearly, an assessment can be thought of as knowledge production, and it will contain elements of originality that are particular to the service user, situation or case at hand.

4. *Critical thinking as a careful and sensitive view of the text* – this means spending time and effort to patiently sort through a range of ideas and concepts and materials so as to develop deep understanding (Moore, 2013). It means getting beneath the surface of appearances to appreciate something in its wider context and infer from this the subtleties, subtexts and implications that may be non-obvious, but important nonetheless. This form of critical thinking in assessment involves a degree of empathy, a deeper engagement with the situation that reserves or suspends judgement – at least for a while – in ways that allow understanding to fully develop.

5. *Critical thinking as rationality* – this means to consider something (for example, an argument, point of view, conclusion reached) in terms of the *reasons* that underpin them, and in particular, to try to assess the best reasons for accepting something, and conversely, to be critical of propositions that lack solid reasons to support them (Moore, 2013). An assessment may well contain an argument or point of view about something, and it may be presented in the form of a conclusion. Think critically about the reasons given that are said to support or justify the conclusion/assessment.

6. *Critical thinking as the adopting of an ethical and activist stance* – this means to tie thinking to action, and to recognise that knowledge is not neutral – it has a material consequence, is political, and may have distinct ethical implications (Moore, 2013). In a context of assessment, the role of the critical thinker is to subvert those forms of knowledge that perpetuate violence, oppression, discrimination, marginalisation, inequality, and so on.

7. *Critical thinking as self-reflexivity* – this means to turn the examination onto oneself, one's mode of thinking, assumptions and values – to be self-aware, and reflective (Moore, 2013). Rather than considering assessment as an objective knowledge product, reflexivity concerns knowledge as a *process*, particularly at the level of hypothesis building and testing (Sheppard et al., 2000). For Sheppard (1998), the reflexive social worker is '… (i) an active thinker, one able to assess, respond and initiate action, and (ii) as a social actor, one who actually participates in the situation with which they are concerned in the conduct of their practice' (p. 767). Reflexivity in social work means being distinctly aware of, and responsive to, the social, practical and intellectual interplay of practice – the way that knowledge, context and the social worker's own conduct and role interact with service users, with other knowledge and with context. This is a form of self-awareness, particularly of the 'assumptions underlying the ways they 'make sense' of practice situations; and who is able to do so in relation to the nature and purposes of their practice' (Sheppard, 1998, p. 767).

Conclusion

This chapter has presented assessment as a generic and transferable skill in social work that is applicable to all areas of practice and all roles that the social worker may undertake. Within an assessment task, there are numerous sub-sets of skills that must be learnt, practiced and developed. These include the ability to generate and analyse information, to think theoretically and analytically about that information, to apply critical thinking skills to the process of assessment, and to work in collaboration with service users in ways that build a holistic, comprehensive and participatory assessment process. Assessment forms the foundations of planning and intervention, and so the social worker is beholden to ensure that assessments are robust, well thought through, ethical and defensible. As mentioned in this chapter, there are numerous assessment tools, frameworks, models and theories, and the task of the social worker and student social worker concerned with career long learning is to practice developing their understanding and skills in the art of making good assessments.

Critical thinking questions

1. Define assessment and explain its importance to social work.

2. Name and describe the five stages of assessment.

3. Why are some writers critical of assessments that focus on problems in an individual way?

4. What are the differences between whole case, partial case and speculative hypotheses?

5. Give three examples of critical thinking and explain why they are important for doing assessments.

Exercises

In thinking critically about assessments, you might like to consider your own experience as a student, especially while on field placement. In the context of field placement education, assessment involves evaluation of the student's performance. This may involve students undertaking a self-assessment, but others such as supervisors and practice teachers may contribute to this assessment. Students may be invited to make assessments of the quality of their supervision and their placement experience (Cleak & Wilson, 2013). Think about your own experience of being assessed: Was the process empowering, fair, did it help you improve your practise? What lessons might you take from being assessed as a student into your social work practice?

Further reading

Crisp, B. R., Anderson, M. R., Orme, J. & Lister, P. G. (2006). What can we learn about social work assessment from the textbooks? *Journal of Social Work, 6*(3), 337–359. doi:10.1177/1468017306071180

Milner, J., Myers, S. & O'Byrne, P. (2015). *Assessment in social work* (4th ed.). London, UK: Palgrave Macmillan.

Sheppard, M., Newstead, S. Di Caccavo, A. & Ryan, K. (2000). Reflexivity and the development of process knowledge in social work: A classification and empirical study. *British Journal of Social Work, 30*(4), 465–488.

Waugh, F. (2011). Risk assessment: Working within a legal framework. In A. O'Hara & R. Pockett (Eds.), *Skills for human service practice: Working with individuals, groups and communities* (2nd ed., pp. 102–120). South Melbourne, VIC: Oxford University Press.

Weber, Z. & Giles, R. (2011). Conducting assessment: Some general guidelines. In A. O'Hara & R. Pockett (Eds.), *Skills for human service practice: Working with individuals, groups and communities* (2nd ed., pp. 166–184). South Melbourne, VIC: Oxford University Press.

Links and online resources

Australian Psychological Society – Assessment Tools and Resources. www.psychology.org.au/ATAPS/resources/

Australian Government – Australian Institute of Family Studies. Risk assessment in child protection (Price-Robertson & Bromfield, 2011). https://aifs.gov.au/cfca/publications/risk-assessment-child-protection

Social Care Institute for Excellence – Assessment in social work: A guide for learning and teaching. www.scie.org.uk/publications/guides/guide18/index.asp

15

REFLEXIVITY, REFLECTIVE PRACTICE AND CRITICAL REFLECTION

Introduction

Reflecting on and in practice is one of those ideas that is widely used and accepted in social work (D'Cruz, Gillingham & Melendez, 2007; Gould & Taylor, 1996; Gursansky, Quinn & Le Sueur, 2010; Kessl, 2009; Milner, 2009; Ruch, 2007). Many say that reflecting is not enough – that in fact one must not just reflect but do so *critically* (Fook & Askeland, 2007; Fook & Gardner, 2007; Thompson & Thompson, 2008; White, Fook & Gardner, 2006). But what does it mean to be critical? What does it mean to reflect? And how do these two things relate to each other? Being critical means to break something down into component parts and understand the relationship between the parts. This is sometimes also referred to as critical thinking. In social work, *critical* is often code for a variety of theoretically received ideas associated with the radical and critical theory traditions in social work. Therefore, when social work students are asked to critically reflect, they may be expected to import a particular theoretical basis of criticism to their reflection on something.

Hence, there are a number of terms and meanings reserved for reflection and reflective practice and this sometimes results in confusion (D'Cruz, Gillingham & Melendez, 2007). Moreover, there are some authors who consider that reflective practice is different from critical reflection (Connolly & Harms, 2012; Fook, 2002a; Morley, 2011). These authors contend that critical reflection goes further than reflective practice as it is seen as incorporating knowledge of both individual and structural factors that impact on practice (Fook & Askeland, 2007; Fook & Gardner, 2007; Morley, 2004; Morley, 2011; Ruch, 2009; White, Fook & Gardner, 2006). Sometimes the terms reflection, reflectivity and reflexivity are used interchangeably, whereas others (Fook & Askeland, 2006; Thompson & Thompson, 2008; see also Rolfe, Freshwater & Jasper, 2001) make a distinction between reflection and reflexivity and suggest that the terms should not be used interchangeably. For example, these authors reserve the term *reflection* to denote *thoughtful self-awareness* and being *reflexive* to describe a practitioner's '... ability to recognize their own influence – and the influence of [their] own social and cultural contexts on research, the type of knowledge [being] created and the way in which [it is] created' (Fook & Askeland, 2006, p. 45). From this we can say that *reflectivity* or *reflection* is the process by which social workers are able to tune into the activities of practice in a thoughtful way. Social workers do this by bringing self-awareness to their work, so that they can respond to what is going on with themselves and the people they are working with. Reflexivity is this self-awareness combined with understanding wider social and cultural factors that might impact on practice. Social work combines all these aims into one term: 'critical reflection'.

In this chapter, we outline how some of this confusion about these terms has arisen, and trace their development and place in social work. The aim of this chapter is to examine the different meanings that exist within social work about the terms reflection and reflexivity and how these relate to engagement in *reflective practice* and *critical reflection*. We begin the chapter by making a distinction between reflection and the capability of *reflexivity* and how this capability is central to the development of reflective practice and critical reflection. In the next section, we outline the emergence of different reflective practice models that utilise the reflexive capabilities of social workers for the goals and ends of professional social work practice. We then describe the different forms of critical reflection and outline how these might be utilised for the purposes of understanding contemporary conditions of social care practice. Finally, the chapter concludes with examples of the types of practice issues that are addressed by different kinds of critical reflection.

Background to reflective practice in social work

As is evident from our discussion in previous chapters, social work is a profession that utilises knowledge from related but distinct disciplines such as sociology, psychology, philosophy, political science and anthropology (Chenoweth & McAuliffe, 2015). Each of these disciplines considers reflection and/or reflexivity through the perspective of their own disciplinary knowledge base. In this way, we can trace these understandings through these different informing disciplines and how they have been adopted and adapted to the purposes of social work.

Reflection

Reflection is a process used to understand novel or unusual things, or to come to examine our own place in relation to these novel or unusual phenomena. Given that much social work practice is non-routine in the sense of dealing with diversity and different situations, it is understandable that the capability to reflect is a requisite for good practice. The capability to reflect on the problems of living was described by philosopher John Dewey in the 1930s (Haggis, 2009). For Dewey (1910), reflection is a response to events that are surprising or troubling. This has been described as a 'felt difficulty' (Gibbons & Gray, 2004, p. 22). Generally, such surprising or troubling events interrupt the routine flow of everyday life. This kind of thinking is referred to as *reflection* and thus in this conception reflection and habitual action are often contrasted with each other (Archer, 2010; Bourdieu, 1999; Fook et al., 2000; Hickson, 2013). The idea of 'felt difficulty' can be seen in the adoption of critical incident analysis in some of the current reflective practice models.

Dewey was interested in the capacity for reflection as part of his work on how people think and approach problem-solving. Dewey's work was subsequently taken up by a range of educational and practice theorists such as Donald Schon (1983, 1987), Jack Mezirow (1998) and David Boud and Sue Knights (Boud & Knights, 1996). The most influential of them all is Donald Schon, who formulated a reflective practice approach. It is from his work that Thompson and Thompson (2008) derive their definition, where reflection is seen as a way of bringing awareness to the flow of practice. Schon's work was also adopted and adapted to social work through the development of other social work specific reflective practice models (Fook, 1999; Redmond, 2004; Ruch, 2000).

Dewey's work was also influential within psychology and led to the development of understanding about educational instruction and practices aimed at increasing critical thinking about knowledge generally (Baxter Magolda, 2004; Hofer, 2002; Kitchener, 1986; Perry, 1970). In philosophy, reflection as a form of thinking about public and social conditions may be traced back to Immanuel Kant's influential essays on the use of reason and enlightenment (Owen, 1999; Tully, 2008a). This kind of Kantian philosophical reflection is different from those outlined by Schon and Dewey, and indeed differs from some authors in social work (Fook, 1999; Thompson & Thompson, 2008).

Another form of reflection developed in social work is that of *parallel process* – this form is discussed by Kadushin (1985, pp. 204–206) for the purposes of educative supervision. Parallel process reflection is informed largely by psychodymanic theories and has been incorporated into contemporary social work reflective practice models such as that by Ruch (see Table 15.1). Lastly, we can also see Schon's work in the Integration of Theory and Practice (ITP) Loop model outlined by Bogo and Vayda (1989, cited in Boisen & Syers, 2004, p. 208) – this model is based on work from David Kolb's (1984) learning cycle which owes a considerable debt to Schon and by extension Dewey. These discipline specific forms of reflection – such as those in social work – are highly developed *operations of thought* that have distinct approaches to considering different kinds of problem that emerge within a disciplinary context. We can call these systematic forms of reflection. These forms of systematic *reflection* are discussed later in this chapter. Some reflective practice models have since combined Schon's work with forms of systematic critical reflection such as critique and deconstruction. This explains why the model is often called a *critical reflection* model (Fook & Gardner, 2007).

Reflexivity

The term reflexivity is more likely to be used within the discipline of sociology, rather than that of reflection, which is located in social work, for example. This is because sociology is concerned with descriptions of society and the individual in a sociological context, and sociology is a discipline which is primarily attempting to produce knowledge about social phenomena. In contrast, while social work utilises a great deal of sociological knowledge, social work tends to use the term reflective practice or critical reflection as a *method for practice*.

In sociology, reflexivity and its relation to human agency is contested (Archer, 2003). It has, nevertheless, come to be seen as a necessary development for individuals as societies shift from traditional ways of living to a situation characterised by rapid social and technological change in the context of globalisation (Giddens, 1993). Certainly, some theorists in sociology have taken the notion of reflexivity and applied it to the way various organisations and institutions of society have begun to respond to massive environmental, social, technological and political change (Beck, 1992; Beck, Lash & Giddens, 1994). There is some disagreement with this position, especially by sociologist, Margaret Archer. Archer (2010) suggests that as organisations and institutions are made up of individuals, and as the activities within these are undertaken by human beings, reflexivity can only be enacted by human beings. This means we should see the operation of reflexivity as a human action. Moreover, Archer does not see reflexivity as a 'special' quality of modern society; rather she considers it to be a core attribute of being human, and hence Archer contends that reflexivity is a capability all people possess, even those from more traditional societies (Archer, 2000). However, the need for reflexivity becomes sharper for people when there is rapid social change and traditional ways of approaching the problems of living no longer work as well as they once did. Hence, social workers may be considered reflexive in the sense that they are part of the condition of social change themselves and because they work in institutions and organisations confronting the sharp end of rapid change.

Seeing reflexivity as a core attribute of human beings can be seen as 'an Enlightenment conception of *self-reflection* as a uniquely human cognitive capacity that enables progressive understanding of the human predicament' (Lynch, 2000, p. 34; emphasis added). Thinking of reflexivity in this way fits with the broad value base of social work and it also links clearly to the conception outlined by Fook and Askeland (2006), where reflexivity is about understanding our own cultural and social influences. Dunk-West (2013) discusses this as an important aspect of reflexive engagement necessary for the development of a social work identity. In light of this, we recommend the adoption of Archer's definition of reflexivity as '[T]he mental capacity that all normal people possess to consider themselves in relation to their social contexts; and their social contexts in relation to themselves' (Johnson, 2011, May 12). Reflexivity, in this sense, also incorporates the ability to reflect as outlined by Dewey and Schon earlier. In the next section we examine how this capability works in professional practice by discussing the emergence of various models of reflective practice in social work.

The emergence of reflective practice and critical reflection in social work

Given the impetus for reflection on novel or perplexing situations, as a method for self-knowledge, and as an aid to critical thinking and problem solving, and for a reflexive disposition in a context of rapid social change, it is no surprise that extensive work has gone into developing models for reflective practice in social work and elsewhere. Models and ways of teaching to engage people's reflexivity emerged in education circles in the late 1980s and 1990s (Brookfield, 1993; Cowan, 1998; Mezirow, 1990; Schon, 1983; Taylor, 1996). These models were largely taken up in social work in the latter part of the 1990s (Fook, 1996, 1999; Gould & Taylor, 1996; Yelloly & Henkel, 1995) and reached a fair degree of acceptance within social work as an important approach to field education (Cleak & Wilson, 2013; Tsang, 2013) and for teaching social work across the 2000s (Bellefeuille, 2006; Brookfield, 2009; Clare, 2007; Humphrey, 2009; Ruch, 2000, 2002; Watts, 2015b; Watts & Hodgson, 2013). These models can be seen as a professional response (McDonald, 2006; Morley & Dunstan, 2012) for addressing the use of knowledge, accountability and decision-making within a welfare sector that was being dismantled through the impact of neoliberal practices (Bay, 2011; Burchell, 1996; Connell et al., 2009; Gray, Dean et al., 2015; McDonald, 2006; Rose, 1996a). By neoliberal practices we mean the incorporation of market forces and managerial processes into the welfare sector. These forces changed the way social care was being delivered across many advanced liberal democracies (Baines, 2006; Greenslade et al., 2014; Hyslop, 2012) and reflective practice and critical reflection were posited as a way of understanding and responding to these forces and changes, because in many ways, these changes are part of the context of rapid social change themselves.

All reflective practice models incorporate processes for returning to an experience and for thinking about how that experience is shaped by various factors in the context. Generally, they also include some emphasis on the personal factors of the person reflecting. Table 15.1 sets out a number of models of reflective practice. These models have been chosen as exemplars; there are other models of reflective practice in social work, education and nursing that could be utilised just as well. For each model presented, we have included a description of its key aspects, and any steps or stages involved in the model. We also include information about its application to social work practice, learning or supervision.

Table 15.1 Models of reflective practice

	Description	Steps or stages (if any)	Application
Schon's model: The reflective practitioner	Rejects positivist approaches to the application of theory to practice. The model is aimed at developing knowledge from practice through the use of reflexivity. Assumes there is a gap between what we say we do (espoused theory) and what we actually do (theory-in-use). The model incorporates discussion with experienced mentors as important to undertaking reflective processes. The model utilises the idea that there is a realm of knowing that is tacit and that reflection may assist workers with accessing this dimension of knowing.	Two main kinds of reflection are presented: *Reflection-in-action* is said to occur as the action is unfolding in relation to novel, surprising or troubling occurrences outside of the routine habitual aspects of practice that have been acquired through experience. *Reflection-on-action* which is undertaken *post hoc* to the action and often involves discussion with others to facilitate the reflective process.	Widely utilised within field education, amongst practitioners and educators in social work. Underpins a number of other models developed within social work.
Fook and Gardner's (2007) *Critical reflection model*	Incorporates the same rejection of positivism in Schon's model. Utilises a critical incident technique developed in psychology and small group work. The process is usually undertaken in small groups but has been adapted to supervision within a dyad arrangement and in research (Morley, 2011). Has adopted the notion of a gap between espoused theory and the behaviour in use for practitioners.	Uses small small groups of no more than 12 participants. Incorporates the use of a critical incident usually written prior to attending the workshop. Group participants take turns discussing their critical incidents. Participants engage in reflective dialogue designed to uncover the following: Assumptions;	Practitioners, field education, group supervision. Has been utilised within classrooms teaching social work (Morley, 2008).

(Continued)

233

Table 15.1 (*Continued*)

	Description	Steps or stages (if any)	Application
	This model focuses on understanding power relations in practice. Utilises a focus on deconstructing language as a way to uncovering this gap and for locating hidden assumptions and power relations. The model is primarily sociological in that its focus is on the external social and organisational conditions which impact on the practitioner and service user.	Power relations; Language practices; Values, beliefs and attitudes; Own personal experience and/or biographical aspects that might impact on the interpretation of events described in the critical incident, and new forms of practice for the future.	
Ruch's *relationship model* (2005)	Rejects the positivist approach to practice. Combines *relationship based social work ideas*, which include: Psychodynamic ideas that can be traced back to psycho-social casework of Hollis (1964) including transference, counter-transference, containment and defence mechanisms and ideas about anxiety and its antecedents in attachment relationships (Ruch, 2010b). Incorporates the processes of *reflection-in-action* and *reflection-on-action* from Schon's model (Ruch, 2005).	Does not utilise a stepped process, however, the following principles for developing relationship based practice are offered by Adrian Ward (2010, p. 185): 'Placing a premium on working with the experience and process of the helping relationship; Attending to the emotional as well as the cognitive elements in practice; Maximising the opportunities for helpful communication; The need for reflection at a deep level; Focussing on the self of the social worker; And [an] emphasis on personal qualities and values.'	Widely utilised in child and family social work but has applications to all fields of social work practice (Ruch, 2005).

234

Thompson and Thompson Reflective practitioner (2008)	This model uses three dimensions to think about reflection. These are the: Cognitive; Affective; Values dimensions (Thompson & Thompson, 2008). Also incorporates the Schon (1983) and the Fook and Gardner (2007) models. In particular, the cognitive dimension is informed by ideas of *critical thinking* using processes of hypothesis testing, examination of assumptions, weighing evidence, evaluating arguments (Thompson & Thompson, 2008, p. 27). There is a second sense in which *criticality* is addressed: understanding the wider socio-political aspects of knowledge and practice (p. 28). This aspect is addressed in the values dimension. Affective dimensions include the development and use of empathy; emotional intelligence including regulation of one's own affect and understanding the affect; feelings and moods of others; and managing anxiety (Thompson & Thompson, 2008, pp. 39–46).	The authors outline a range of techniques or strategies to address the different dimensions mentioned above.	Students, practitioners and educators in health and social care.

235

The models in Table 15.1 have all been developed under different conditions, and as such, are aimed at different aspects of professional practice. Schon's model, for example, was developed in the context of professional education, but it has been widely adopted in many different professional fields. The foundation of Jan Fook's model may be traced back to her work in radical casework (Fook, 1993), which she later extended and adapted for use in practice research (Fook, 1996, 1999). This work formed the basis for the development of the Fook and Gardner model of critical reflection (2007) developed for use with practitioners, particularly. The Fook and Gardner model has since been utilised in classroom settings with both postgraduate and undergraduate students in social work. Ruch's (2005) model has been developed in the context of advocating for a particular approach to reflection that incorporates the use of psychodynamic principles, and its focus is aimed at developing this within students and practitioners. Thompson and Thompson (2008) have created a model of reflective practice that bridges a range of social care settings and can be used by health, welfare and social care practitioners. The Thompson and Thompson model utilises perspectives from Fook and Schon and incorporates theoretical ideas drawn from anti-oppressive practice as well (Thompson, 2006).

All of the models in Table 15.1 have applications to social work education and practice. Having a diversity of approaches to how we approach practice is a substantial strength of social work because we work with a diverse set of circumstances, service user groups and individuals, and there is no single approach that may work with all of these contexts. Hence, it is important to adopt reflective models in particular ways for particular purposes. We turn now to consider the different kinds of systematic *critical reflection* that are also available for different kinds of problem in practice. Each kind of reflection has been characterised as a form of *critical* reflection (Tully, 1989) and so the section begins with a discussion of what we mean by the term *critical*.

Critical reflection: forms of systematic reflection

What does it mean to be *critical* in the context of being reflexive or engaging in reflective practice? In social work the concept *critical* can be traced to various informing bodies of knowledge that have become influential within the discipline over time. What happens is that over time concepts like 'critical' can become *containers* for a range of ideas, which then acquire a specific meaning with a discipline or profession. Thus, for many social work authors, the term *critical* is a short-hand way to denote a theoretical and practice response to forms of inequality and oppression in society (Fook & Askeland, 2006; Morley, 2004; Thompson, 2006; Thompson & Thompson, 2008). It also includes a way of thinking that involves being sceptical towards knowledge claims that may be presented as natural or self-evident. Such natural ideas are often discussed as *dominant* ideas about people or groups in society. An example of a dominant idea that has been challenged is that poverty is an outcome of laziness. This idea has been challenged by social theorists who have been able to point out how economic systems that support capital at the expense of workers' interests create poverty for some groups in society (see Chapter 5, this volume, on poverty and disadvantage).

Even by accepting the notion that there might be dominant or subordinate *ideas* can be seen as taking a *critical* stance. Thus to be *critical* is to refuse to take things for granted and to use your analytical skills to uncover hidden and damaging assumptions circulating within forms of knowledge. The purpose of doing so is to uncover these dominant ideas and practices with a view to creating changes in society for the better. This notion is tied to another related concept, that of *emancipation* (Cemlyn, 2008; Dominelli, 1998; Rivest & Moreau, 2014; Saleebey, 2009; Turbett, 2014). This form of being *critical* is a particular kind of systematic reflection (Tully, 1989), which is to perform an analysis aimed at interrogating the gap between the ideal (for example, conditions in society free of inequality and oppression) and the real (for example, what is actually existing in current arrangements that may include inequality and oppression).

These ways of approaching knowledge and the existence of inequality and oppression can be traced back to early forms of radical, structural and feminist social work (Bailey & Brake, 1975; Leonard, 1975; Rojek et al., 1988). Later, these ideas were explicitly traced to forms of critical theory that were adopted through various social movements and associated theories (Agger, 1991; Leonard, 1975; Leonard, 1997). When forms of reflexivity are combined with the term *critical* in social work it has become a signal for a particular kind of critical reflection that incorporates aspects of *critical theory*.

Not all forms of critical reflection share this theoretical pedigree. Since Immanuel Kant (1724–1804) described different orientations to thinking (Owen, 1999), philosophers have discussed different ways of thinking about contemporary conditions, which they themselves term *critical reflection*. This is because Immanuel Kant is widely considered to be fundamental to the emergence of Enlightenment thinking with his extended treatment of the uses of reason and thinking in *A Critique of Pure Reason* (Kant & Meiklejohn, 1934; Owen, 1999). It is from Kant that the word *critical* has come to denote the possibilities of *different* kinds of thinking on the present (Foucault & Rabinow, 1984). Moreover, since Kant many philosophers and historians (Allen, 2011; Derrida, 1966; Foucault, 1972, 2001; Foucault & Rabinow, 1984; Habermas, 1984, 1989; Hacking, 2002; Koopman, 2013; Tully, 2008a) have developed a range of critical reflection forms, which we now consider as *systematic operations of thought* about the conditions and limits of the present (Tully, 2008a). One of these forms is similar to how social work utilises the concept of critical, that is, *critique*. Yet, there are other forms and these are outlined in Table 15.2. It should be said that this list is not exhaustive (Tully, 1989). Instead, we have

Table 15.2 Kinds of systematic reflection based on Kantian enlightenment traditions

Kind of critical reflection	Main operation of thought	Aim	Example
Critique	Comparison between an end (the ideal) and the present condition (the real).	Change and understanding the current limit in the context of already prescribed ideal or ends (Owen, 1999).	An example would be the 1851 slogan *From each according to his ability, to each according to his needs!* (The British Library, n. d.)
Interpretation	An activity of thinking we engage in when we do not already understand a circumstance or practice, or if an already held interpretation is now in some doubt.	To build new understanding of things we do not already understand through our immediate practice (Wittgenstein 1981, cited in Tully, 1989, p. 196).	Attempting to understand service user behaviour in order to make an assessment. May use existing theories or models as forms of interpretation offered by others.
Explanation	Accounting for phenomena in detail including relationships between them.	Building theory and models for the purposes of communicating ideas about society and individuals and the relations between them.	Systems theory is a form of explanation for how phenomena connect to each other and mutually condition and affect each other.
Problematisation 1 – a form of critique	Thinking aimed at interrogating anything presented as 'natural' for its hidden assumptions.	Creation of new consciousness by uncovering the ways in which societies create *false consciousness* in people. False consciousness is a method by which people accept inequality and forms of oppression as natural and inevitable.	Asking what being a citizen means if you cannot participate in society because you are unemployed and/or a single woman with children and/or a person with a disability?
Problematisation 2 – a post-structural form	Thinking that questions conceptualisations of specific issues with a view to understanding the conditions (practices, processes and phenomena) that make them possible in the present.	To create the space to think differently about these issues and to be able to trace how they became possible in a given present.	Asking how we ended up with Conduct Disorder as a category in the Diagnostic Statistical Manual-V (DSM-V). Further, asking how it is that the DSM-V emerged as a definitive descriptor of forms of behaviour and mental life?

Genealogy	Thinking that traces the way issues are 'questioned, analysed, classified and regulated' (Deacon, 2000, cited in Bacchi, 2012, p. 1) by attention to specific conditions and contingent events.	Aimed at presenting a form of critique that does not specify a preferred end or outcome, but rather presents a range of alternative possibilities.	Tracing the way that some groups of young people become classified as at-risk, risky, or disengaged from education and employment, and what the effects of this classification have for practice, for the deployment of power and interventions with young people, and for their identities.
Archaeology	Thinking that considers discursive and non-discursive practices without viewing these as originating within human consciousness. This kind of reflection relies on a process of setting aside forms of critique (see above); for example, setting aside a critique that relies on a conception of the good (ideal) and/or which rely on reflection as a form of human interpretation.	Enables a consideration of how ideas and practices emerge as contingent and not as linear developments from historical events.	Consider how the term *critical* emerged as a way to consider inequality and oppression within social work.
Deconstruction	Thinking that involves analysing the relation between the sign and signified in language and symbols.	Illuminates the unstable and contingent relations between concepts and allows for discovery of hidden and/or unconscious absences and relations between signs. This kind of reflection is also aimed at reversing the relation between authors of signs and consumers of signs/texts.	Asking what the relation is between the following pairs: White/black Male/female Hetero/homosexual Rational/emotional Normal/abnormal Functional/dysfunctional

chosen a list of critical reflection forms that are likely to be of use in a social work reflection toolkit. In addition to describing some of the more useful forms of critical reflection, Table 15.2 also outlines the operation of thought required, the aim of each kind of reflection, and it offers an example of where it might be applied to problems or issues within social work.

These forms of critical reflection require some practice as some of them involve quite distinct and focussed operations of thinking. For example, archaeology is difficult to achieve if one is simultaneously holding a predetermined critique, as the operation of archaeological thought depends on achieving a level of scepticism concerning *all* claims about the ideal. Thus, a social worker would generally deploy such thinking in very specific circumstances. Equally, holding a view that is sceptical of any, or all, ideals would limit social workers in being able to choose from different alternatives for action. This is because in this view all claims for any ideal situation could be considered equal. Thus, social workers need to know what each and all these forms of critical reflection do, and where and with what kinds of issues, problems or situations in practice they might be useful for.

This is where reflective practice models can really be useful as these often embed different forms of critical reflection as described in Table 15.2. For example, Schon's (1983) model is broadly *interpretative* and aimed at building understanding in practice. Fook and Gardner's (2007) model utilises a combination of *critique, interpretation, problematisation-2* and *deconstruction* applied to practice situations in order to generate practice theorising. Ruch's model entails *interpretation, explanation* and possibly *critique* to enable practitioner engagement and containment of anxiety in working with difficult practice situations. Thompson and Thompson's model can be seen as combining *interpretation, explanation* and *critique*.

Conclusion

In this chapter, we have considered the different conceptions of reflection, reflexivity and critical reflection. Reflexivity is a capability all people possess to consider their circumstances and their own influence on such circumstances. This capability has become important in recent years in social work and other professions concerned with understanding social and public conditions amidst rapid change. Reflective practice models have been important ways in which social workers have codified and created means to engage social work students and practitioners in using their reflexive capabilities for professional ends. We have also outlined that the term critical reflection can be traced back to Enlightenment thinking – including Immanuel Kant – and that since then, many forms of critical reflection have become available to think about the social and political conditions in which social work operates. These require practice so that social workers are able to engage in different kinds of systematic thought about the problems of living and working in contemporary conditions.

Critical thinking questions

1. What is meant by reflection and what is meant by reflexivity? What are the differences between these two terms?
2. Why is reflective practice said to be so important to social work?
3. Define critical reflection? What sort of reflection is emphasised in critical reflection? What does this kind of reflection focus on, and why?
4. Refer to Table 15.2: what are the main differences between 'critique' and 'problematisation' with regard to reflection?
5. How might social workers practice in ways that increase their powers of reflection?

Exercises

Conduct a literature review of the reflective practice in social work. Summarise the main themes of the review and work out what kind(s) of reflection are being conceptualised in the literature you have selected. Use Table 15.2 to help you work out the different kinds of systematic reflection being discussed in the literature. What have you learned about reflective practice in social work from this exercise?

Further reading

Allen, A. (2011). Foucault and the politics of our selves. *History of the Human Sciences, 24*(4), 43–59. doi:10.1177/0952695111411623

Archer, M. S. (2000). *Being human: The problem of agency.* Retrieved from http://ezproxy.ecu.edu.au/login?url=http://site.ebrary.com/lib/ecu/Top?id=10065232

Fook, J., & Gardner, F. (2007). *Practising critical reflection: A resource handbook.* Maidenhead, UK: Open University Press.

Kitchener, K. S. (1986). The reflective judgement model: Characteristics, evidence and measurement. In R. A. Mines & K. S. Kitchener (Eds.), *Adult cognitive development: Methods and models* (pp. 76–91). New York, NY: Praeger Pyblishers.

Ruch, G. (2005). Relationship-based practice and reflective practice: Holistic approaches to contemporary child care social work. *Child & Family Social Work, 10*(2), 111–123. doi: 10.1111/j.1365-2206.2005.00359.x

Links and online resources

Professor Jan Fook discusses critical reflection in social work – the video can be accessed here www.youtube.com/watch?v=fOo5qgbDqV4

Professor Margaret Archer on Reflexivity – Podcast can be accessed here www.youtube.com/watch?v=bMpJ5wnuB64

REFERENCES

Adams, R., Dominelli, L., & Payne, M. (2009a). *Critical practice in social work* (2nd ed.). Basingstoke, UK; New York, NY: Palgrave Macmillan.

Adams, R., Dominelli, L., & Payne, M. (2009b). Introduction. In R. Adams, L. Dominelli & M. Payne (Eds.), *Social work: Themes, issues and critical debates* (3rd ed., pp. xvii–xx). Basingstoke, UK; New York, NY: Palgrave Macmillan.

Agbényiga, D. L. (2011). Organizational culture-performance link in the human services setting. *Administration in Social Work, 35*(5), 532–547. doi: 10.1080/03643107.2011. 614536.

Agger, B. (1991). Critical theory, poststructuralism, postmodernism: Their sociological relevance. *Annual Review of Sociology, 17*, 105–131. doi:10.2307/2083337.

Agger, B. (2006). *Critical social theories: An introduction* (2nd ed.). Boulder, CO: Paradigm Publishers.

Albertín Carbó, P. (2008). Reflexive practice as ethics and political position: Analysis in an ethnographic study of heroin use. *Qualitative Social Work, 7*(4), 466–483. doi: 10.1177/1473325008097141.

Alcock, P. (2006). *Understanding poverty* (3rd ed.). Basingstoke, UK: Palgrave Macmillan.

Algoe, S. B., & Haidt, J. (2009). Witnessing excellence in action: The 'other-praising' emotions of elevation, gratitude, and admiration. *The Journal of Positive Psychology, 4*(2), 105–127. doi: 10.1080/17439760802650519.

Algoe, S. B., Haidt, J., & Gable, S. L. (2008). Beyond reciprocity: Gratitude and relationships in everyday life. *Emotion, 8*(3), 425–429. doi: 10.1037/1528-3542.8.3.425.

Allan, J. (2003). Practicing critical social work. In J. Allan, B. Pease & L. Briskman (Eds.), *Critical social work: An introduction to theories and practices* (pp. 52–71). Crows Nest, NSW: Allen & Unwin.

Allan, J., Pease, B., & Briskman, L. (2009). *Critical social work: Theories and practices for a socially just world.* Crows Nest, NSW: Allen & Unwin.

Allen, A. (2011). Foucault and the politics of our selves. *History of the Human Sciences, 24*(4), 43–59. doi: 10.1177/0952695111411623.

Alston, M. (2010). *Australia's rural welfare policy: Overlooked and demoralised* (Vol. 15, pp. 199–217). Emerald Group Publishing Limited. doi: 10.1108/S1057-1922(2010)00000 15012.

Alston, M., & McKinnon, J. (2005). Context of contemporary social work practice. In M. Alston & J. McKinnon (Eds.), *Social work: Fields of practice* (2nd ed., pp. xvii, 325). South Melbourne, VIC; New York, NY: Oxford University Press.

Alston, M., Jones, J., & Curtin, M. (2011). Women and traumatic brain injury: "It's not visible damage". *Australian Social Work, 65*(1), 39–53. doi: 10.1080/0312407X.2011. 594898.

Alvesson, M., & Kärreman, D. (2011). *Qualitative research and theory development: Mystery as method.* Retrieved November 14, 2016, from http://ezproxy.ecu.edu.au/login?url=http://srmo.sagepub.com/view/qualitative-research-and-theory-development/SAGE.xml.

Alvesson, M., & Sandberg, J. (2013). *Constructing research questions: Doing interesting research.* London, UK: SAGE.

Alvesson, M., & Sköldberg, K. (2009). *Reflexive methodology: New vistas for qualitative research* (2nd ed.). London, UK: SAGE.

Amnesty International. (2016). *Home page.* Retrieved July 22, 2016, from www.amnesty.org/en/.

Anglem, J., & Maidment, J. (2009). Introduction to collaborative assessment. In J. Maidment & R. Egan (Eds.), *Practice skills in social work and welfare: More than just common sense* (2nd ed., pp. 133–147). Crows Nest, NSW: Allen & Unwin.

Anscombe, B. (2009). *Consilience in social work: Reflections on thinking, doing and being.* (Doctoral dissertation), Charles Sturt University, Wagga Wagga, NSW.

Aotearoa New Zealand Association of Social Workers. (2015). *Chapter 3. The code of ethics of ANZASW.* Retrieved May 19, 2015, from http://anzasw.org.nz/documents/0000/0000/0664/Chapter_3_Code_of_Ethics_Summary.pdf.

Archer, M. S. (2000). *Being human: The problem of agency.* Retrieved November 14, 2016, from http://ezproxy.ecu.edu.au/login?url=http://site.ebrary.com/lib/ecu/Top?id=10065232.

Archer, M. S. (2007). *Making our way through the world: Human reflexivity and social mobility.* Cambridge, UK: Cambridge University Press.

Archer, M. S. (2010). Routine, reflexivity, and realism. *Sociological Theory, 28*(3), 272–303, 354.

Arman, M., Hammarqvist, A.-S., & Rehnsfeldt, A. (2011). Burnout as an existential deficiency – lived experiences of burnout sufferers. *Scandinavian Journal of Caring Sciences, 25*(2), 294-302. doi: 10.1111/j.1471-6712.2010.00825.x.

Artiles, A. J. (2013). Untangling the racialization of disabilities: An intersectionality critique across disability models. *Du Bois Review, 10*(2), 329. doi: 10.1017/S1742058X13000271.

Ask, K., & Pina, A. (2011). On being angry and punitive: How anger alters perception of criminal intent. *Social Psychological and Personality Science, 2*(5), 494–499. doi: 10.1177/1948550611398415.

Australian Association of Social Workers. (2010). *Code of ethics.* Retrieved November 10, 2013, from www.aasw.asn.au/document/item/1201.

Australian Council of Social Services. (2014). *Poverty in Australia 2014.* Retrieved May 5, 2016, from www.acoss.org.au/images/uploads/ACOSS_Poverty_in_Australia_2014.pdf.

Australian Council of Social Services. (2015). *Inequality in Australia: A nation divided.* Retrieved May 5, 2016, from http://acoss.wpengine.com/wp-content/uploads/2015/06/Inequality_in_Australia_FINAL.pdf.

Australian Institute of Family Studies. (2014). *Child deaths from abuse and neglect.* Retrieved August 22, 2016, from https://aifs.gov.au/cfca/publications/child-deaths-abuse-and-neglect.

Australian Social Inclusion Board. (2011). *Breaking cycles of disadvantage.* Canberra, ACT: Australian Government.

Avey, J., Palanski, M., & Walumbwa, F. (2011). When leadership goes unnoticed: The moderating role of follower self-esteem on the relationship between ethical leadership and follower behavior. *Journal of Business Ethics, 98*(4), 573–582. doi: 10.1007/s10551-010-0610-2.

Avey, J. B., Wernsing, T. S., & Luthans, F. (2008). Can positive employees help positive organizational change? Impact of psychological capital and emotions on relevant attitudes and behaviours. *The Journal of Applied Behavioral Science, 44*(1), 48–70.

Axelrod, R. M. (1984). *The evolution of cooperation.* New York, NY: Basic Books.

Bacchi, C. (2012). Why study problematizations? Making politics visible. *Open Journal of Political Science, 2*, 1–8. doi: 10.4236/ojps.2012.21001.

Backwith, D. (2015). *Social workers must work with service users to tackle brutal poverty of austerity.* Retrieved May 5, 2016, from www.theguardian.com/social-care-network/social-life-blog/2015/may/06/social-work-poverty-austerity-welfare.

Badman, G. (2009). *Baby Peter serious case review: Statement from Chairman Graham Badman.* Retrieved August 24, 2016, from www.haringeylscb.org/baby-peter-serious-case-review-statement-chairman-graham-badman.

Bailey, P. L. J. (2013). The policy dispositif: Historical formation and method. *Journal of Education Policy, 28*(6), 807–827. doi: 10.1080/02680939.2013.782512.

Bailey, R., & Brake, M. (1975). *Radical social work.* London, UK: Edward Arnold.

Baines, D. (2006). 'If you could change one thing': Social service workers and restructuring. *Australian Social Work, 59*(1), 20–34. doi: 10.1080/03124070500449754.

Baines, D. (2010). 'If we don't get back to where we were before': Working in the restructured non-profit social services. *British Journal of Social Work, 40*(3), 928–945. doi: 10.1093/bjsw/bcn176.

Banks, S. (1995). *Ethics and values in social work.* Basingstoke, UK: Palgrave Macmillan.

Banks, S. (2006). *Ethics and values in social work* (3rd ed.). Basingstoke, UK; New York, NY: Palgrave Macmillan.

Banks, S., & Nohr, K. (2011). *Practising social work ethics around the world: Cases and commentaries.* Retrieved November 14, 2016, from www.ECU.eblib.com.au/patron/FullRecord.aspx?p=735283.

Barry, B. (2005). *Why social justice matters.* Malden, MA; Oxford, UK: Blackwell Publishers; Polity Press.

Baxter Magolda, M. B. (2004). Evolution of a constructivist conceptualization of epistemological reflection. *Educational Psychologist, 39*(1), 31–42. doi: 10.1207/s15326985ep3901_4.

Bay, U. (2011). Unpacking neoliberal technologies of government in Australian higher education social work departments. *Journal of Social Work, 11*(2), 222–236. doi: 10.1177/1468017310386696.

Becher, T. (1994). The significance of disciplinary differences. *Studies in Higher Education, 19*(2), 151–161. doi: 10.1080/03075079412331382007.

Beck, U. (1992). *Risk society: Towards a new modernity.* London, UK: SAGE.

Beck, U. (2003). The silence of words: On terror and war. *Security Dialogue, 34*(3), 255–267. doi: 10.1177/09670106030343002.

Beck, U., Lash, S., & Giddens, A. (1994). *Reflexive modernization: Politics, tradition and aesthetics in the modern social order.* Cambridge, UK: Polity Press.

Beckett, C., & Maynard, A. (2005). *Values & ethics in social work: An introduction.* London, UK: SAGE.

Bellefeuille, G. L. (2006). Rethinking reflective practice education in social work education: A blended constructivist and objectivist instructional design strategy for a web-based child welfare practice course. *Journal of Social Work Education, 42*(1), 85–103.

Benhabib, S. (1992). *Situating the self: Gender, community and postmodernism in contemporary ethics.* Cambridge, UK: Polity Press.

Beresford, P. (2000). Service users' knowledges and social work theory: Conflict or collaboration? *British Journal of Social Work, 30*(4), 489–503. doi: 10.1093/bjsw/30.4.489.

Beresford, P., Adshead, L., & Croft, S. (2007). *Palliative care, social work, and service users making life possible.* Retrieved November 14, 2016, from http://ezproxy.ecu.edu.au/login?url=http://site.ebrary.com/lib/ecu/Top?id=10182452.

Beresford, P., & Boxall, K. (2012). Service users, social work education and knowledge for social work practice. *Social Work Education, 31*(2), 155–167. doi: 10.1080/02615479.2012.644944.

Bernhardt, B. C., & Singer, T. (2012). The neural basis of empathy. *Annual Review of Neuroscience, 35*(1), 1–23. doi: 10.1146/annurev-neuro-062111-150536.

Billing, D. (2007). Teaching for transfer of core/key skills in higher education: Cognitive skills. *Higher Education, 53*(4), 483-516. doi: http://dx.doi.org/10.1007/s10734-005-5628-5.

Bland, R., Renouf, N., & Tullgren, A. (2009). *Social work practice in mental health: An introduction.* Crows Nest, NSW: Allen & Unwin.

Boisen, L., & Syers, M. (2004). The integrative case analysis model for linking theory and practice. *Journal of Social Work Education, 40*(2), 205–217. doi: 10.1080/10437797.2004.10778490.

Boud, D., & Knights, S. (1996). Course design for reflective practice: Research, theory and practice. In N. Gould & I. Taylor (Eds.), *Reflective learning for social work* (pp. 23–46). Aldershot, UK: Ashgate.

Bourdieu, P. (1999). Structures, habitus, practices. In A. Elliot (Ed.), *The Blackwell reader in contemporary social theory* (pp. 107–118). Oxford, UK: Blackwell Publishers.

Brenner, M. J., & Homonoff, E. (2004). Zen and clinical social work: A spiritual approach to practice. *Families in Society, 85*(2), 261–269. doi: 10.1606/1044-3894.315.

Brenner, N., Peck, J., & Theodore, N. I. K. (2010). Variegated neoliberalization: Geographies, modalities, pathways. *Global Networks, 10*(2), 182–222. doi: 10.1111/j.1471-0374.2009.00277.x.

Briskman, L. (2007). *Social work with indigenous communities.* Annandale, NSW: Federation Press.

Briskman, L. (2014). Reflections of an activist social worker: Challenging human rights violations. In C. Noble, H. Strauss & B. Littlechild (Eds.), *Global social work: Crossing borders, blurring boundaries* (pp. 301–310). Sydney, NSW: Sydney University Press.

Briskman, L., & Cemlyn, S. (2005). Reclaiming humanity for asylum-seekers: A social work response. *International Social Work, 48*(6), 714–724. doi: 10.1177/0020872805056989.

Briskman, L., & Goddard, C. (2007). Not in my name: The people's inquiry into immigration detention. In D. Lusher & N. Haslam (Eds.), *Yearning to breathe free* (pp. 90–99). Sydney, NSW: The Federation Press.

Briskman, L., Latham, S., & Goddard, C. (2008). *Human rights overboard: Seeking asylum in Australia.* Melbourne, VIC: Scribe Publishers.

Briskman, L., Pease, B., & Allan, J. (2009). Introducing critical theories for social work in a neoliberal context. In J. Allan, L. Briskman & B. Pease (Eds.), *Critical social work: Theories and practices for a just world* (pp. 3–14). Crows Nest, NSW: Allen & Unwin.

Bristow, W. (2011). Enlightenment. In E. N. Zalta (Ed.), *The Stanford Encyclopedia of Philosophy* (Vol. Summer 2011 Edition). Retrieved November 14, 2016, from http://plato.stanford.edu/entries/enlightenment/.

British Association of Social Workers. (2014). *Code of ethics.* Retrieved June 16, 2016, from www.basw.co.uk/codeofethics/.

Brookfield, S. (1993). Through the lens of learning: How the visceral experience of learning reframes teaching. In D. Boud, R. Cohen & D. Walker (Eds.), *Using experience for learning* (pp. 21–32). Buckingham, UK: Open University Press.

Brookfield, S. (2009). The concept of critical reflection: Promises and contradictions. *European Journal of Social Work, 12*(3), 293–304. doi: 10.1080/13691450902945215.

Brueggemann, W. G. (2002). *The practice of macro social work.* Belmont, CA: Brooks/Cole, Thomson Learning.

Bruhn, J. (2009). The functionality of gray area ethics in organizations. *Journal of Business Ethics, 89*(2), 205–214. doi: 10.1007/s10551-008-9994-7.

Bubandt, N., & Willerslev, R. (2015). The dark side of empathy: Mimesis, deception, and the magic of alterity. *Comparative Studies in Society and History, 57*(1), 5–34.

Buchbinder, E. (2007). Being a social worker as an existential commitment: From vulnerability to meaningful purpose. *The Humanistic Psychologist, 35*(2), 161–174. doi: 10.1080/08873260701273894.

Burawoy, M. (2014). Public sociologies: Contradictions, dilemmas, and possibilities. *Social Forces, 82*(4), 1603–1618.

Burchell, G. (1996). Liberal government and techniques of the self. In A. Barry, T. Osborne & N. Rose (Eds.), *Foucault and political reason: Liberalism, neoliberalism and the rationalities of government* (pp. 19–36). London, UK: UCL Press Limited.

Burke, B. (2013). Anti-oppressive practice. In M. Davies (Ed.), *The Blackwell companion to social work* (pp. 414–416). Chichester, UK: John Wiley and Sons.

Burke, P. (2006). Disadvantage and stigma: A theoretical framework for associated conditions. In J. Parker & P. Burke (Eds.), *Social work and disadvantage* (pp. 11–26). London, UK: Jessica Kingsley Publishers.

Burke, P., & Parker, J. (2006). Introduction. In J. Parker & P. Burke (Eds.), *Social work and disadvantage* (pp. 7–10). London, UK: Jessica Kingsley Publishers.

Butler, J. (2011). *Bodies that matter: On the discursive limits of "sex".* Routledge classics. Retrieved November 14, 2016, from www.ecu.eblib.com/patron/FullRecord.aspx?p=683946.

Calma, T., & Priday, E. (2011). Putting Indigenous human rights into social work practice. *Australian Social Work, 64*(2), 147–155. doi: 10.1080/0312407X.2011.575920.

Campfens, H. (1992). Special issue: The new reality of poverty and social work interventions: Introduction. *International Social Work, 35*(2), 99–104.

Canadian Association of Social Workers. (2005). *Code of ethics.* Retrieved May 19, 2015, from http://casw-acts.ca/sites/default/files/attachements/CASW_Code%20of%20Ethics.pdf.

Canda, E. R. (2008). Spiritual connections in social work: Boundary violations and transcendence. *Journal of Religion & Spirituality in Social Work: Social Thought, 27*(1), 25–40. doi: 10.1080/15426430802113749.

Canda, E. R., & Furman, L. D. (2009). *Spiritual diversity in social work practice: The heart of helping.* New York, NY: Oxford University Press.

Caparrotta, L., & Ghaffari, K. (2004). *The function of assessment within psychological therapies.* London, UK: Karnac Books.

Caplan, M. (2014). Predatory lending. In M. J. Austin (Ed.), *Social justice and social work: Rediscovering a core value of the profession* (pp. 209–220). Thousand Oaks, CA: SAGE.

Carey, M. (2009). 'It's a bit like being a robot or working in a factory': Does Braverman help explain the experiences of state social workers in Britain since 1971? *Organization, 16*(4), 505–527. doi: 10.1177/1350508409104506.

Carson, D., & Bain, A. (2008). *Professional risk and working with people: Decision-making in health, social care and criminal justice.* London, UK; Philadelphia, PA: Jessica Kingsley Publishers.

Carson, E., King, S., & Papatraianou, L. H. (2011). Resilience among social workers: The role of informal learning in the workplace. *Practice, 23*(5), 267–278. doi: 10.1080/09503153.2011.581361.

Cemlyn, S. (2008). Human rights practice: Possibilities and pitfalls for developing emancipatory social work. *Ethics and Social Welfare, 2*(3), 222–242. doi: 10.1080/17496530802481714.

Chambon, A., Johnstone, M., & Winckler, J. (2011). The material presence of early social work: The practice of the archive. *British Journal of Social Work, 41*(4), 625–644. doi: 10.1093/bjsw/bcq139.

Chan, W. C. H., Fong, A., Wong, K. L. Y., Tse, D. M. W., Lau, K. S., & Chan, L. N. (2016). Impact of death work on self: Existential and emotional challenges and coping of palliative care professionals. *Health & Social Work, 41*(1), 33–41. doi: 10.1093/hsw/hlv077.

Chatterjee, P., & Brown, S. (2011). Cognitive theory and social work treatment. In F. J. Turner (Ed.), *Social work treatment: Interlocking theoretical approaches* (pp. 77–102). Upper Saddle River, NJ: Allyn & Bacon.

Chenoweth, L., & McAuliffe, D. (2012). *The road to social work & human service practice* (3rd ed.). South Melbourne, VIC: Cengage Learning Australia.

Chenoweth, L., & McAuliffe, D. (2015). *The road to social work & human service practice* (4th ed.). South Melbourne, VIC: Cengage Learning Australia.

Child and Family Research Centre, & Christie, A. (2014). *Keynote by Professor Alastair Christie.* Paper presented at the Human Rights and Social Justice in Social Work, Galway, Ireland. Retrieved November 14, 2016, from www.youtube.com/watch?v=WUSK6J_hoaY.

Chossudovsky, M. (2003). *The globalization of poverty and the new world order* (2nd ed.). Pincourt, QC: Global Research.

Chu, W. C. K., & Tsui, M.-s. (2008). The nature of practice wisdom in social work revisited. *International Social Work, 51*(1), 47–54. doi: 10.1177/0020872807083915.

Clare, B. (2007). Promoting deep learning: A teaching, learning and assessment endeavour. *Social Work Education, 26*(5), 433–446. doi: 10.1080/02615470601118571.

Cleak, H., & Wilson, J. (2013). *Making the most of field placement* (3rd ed.). South Melbourne, VIC, Australia: Cengage Learning Australia.

Collins, P. H. (1990). *Black feminist thought: Knowledge, consciousness and the politics of empowerment*. New York, NY: Routledge.

Collins, S. (2007). Social workers, resilience, positive emotions and optimism. *Practice, 19*(4), 255–269. doi: 10.1080/09503150701728186.

Collins, S. (2015). Hope and helping in social work. *Practice, 27*(3), 197–213. doi: 10.1080/09503153.2015.1014335.

Compton, B. R., & Galaway, B. (1994). *Social work processes* (5th ed.). Pacific Grove, CA: Brooks/Cole.

Compton, B. R., Galaway, B., & Cournoyer, B. R. (2006). *Social work processes* (7th ed.). Belmont, CA: Thomson, Brooks/Cole.

Connell, R. (2007). *Southern theory*. Crows Nest, NSW: Allen & Unwin.

Connell, R., Fawcett, B., & Meagher, G. (2009). Neoliberalism, new public management and the human service professions: Introduction to the special Issue. *Journal of Sociology, 45*(4), 331–338. doi: 10.1177/1440783309346472.

Connelly, J. (2012). *Politics and the environment: From theory to practice*. Retrieved November 14, 2016, from www.ecu.eblib.com/patron/FullRecord.aspx?p=956894.

Connolly, M. (2013). Values and human rights. In M. Connolly & L. Harms (Eds.), *Social work: Context and practice* (pp. 49–59). South Melbourne, VIC: Oxford University Press.

Connolly, M., & Harms, L. (2012). *Social work: From theory to practice*. Cambridge, UK; Port Melbourne, VIC: Cambridge University Press.

Connolly, M., & Ward, T. (2007). *Morals, rights and practice in the human services: Effective and fair decision-making in health, social care and criminal justice*. London, UK: Jessica Kingsley Publishers.

Cooper, N., & Dumpleton, S. (2013). *Walking the breadline: The scandal of food poverty in 21st century Britain*. Retrieved July 22, 2016, from http://policy-practice.oxfam.org.uk/publications/walking-the-breadline-the-scandal-of-food-poverty-in-21st-century-britain-292978.

Cooper, N., Purcell, S., & Jackson, R. (2014). *Below the breadline: The relentless rise of food poverty in Britain*. Retrieved July 22, 2016, from http://policy-practice.oxfam.org.uk/publications/below-the-breadline-the-relentless-rise-of-food-poverty-in-britain-317730.

Corey, G. (2009). *Theory and practice of counseling and psychotherapy* (8th ed.). Belmont, CA: Thomson, Brooks/Cole.

Coulshed, V., Mullender, A., Jones, D. N., & Thompson, N. (2006). *Management in social work* (3rd ed.). Basingstoke, UK: Palgrave Macmillan.

Coulshed, V., & Orme, J. (1998). *Social work practice: An introduction* (3rd ed.). Basingstoke, UK: Macmillan.

Cournoyer, B. R. (2014). *The social work skills workbook* (7th ed.). Belmont, CA: Brooks/Cole.

Cowan, J. (1998). *On becoming an innovative university teacher: Reflection in action*. Buckingham, UK; Philadelphia, PA: Society for Research into Higher Education & Open University Press.

Cree, V. (2002). The changing nature of social work. In R. Adams, L. Dominelli & M. Payne (Eds.), *Social work: Themes, issues and critical debates* (2nd ed., pp. 20–29). Houndsmills, Basingstoke, UK: Palgrave Macmillan.

Crenshaw, K., & World of Women Festival (WOW). (2016). *On intersectionality.* Retrieved May 28, 2016, from www.youtube.com/watch?v=-DW4HLgYPlA.

Crisp, B. R. (2010). *Spirituality and social work.* Farnham, UK: Ashgate.

Crisp, B. R., Anderson, M. R., Orme, J., & Lister, P. G. (2006). What can we learn about social work assessment from the textbooks? *Journal of Social Work, 6*(3), 337–359. doi: 10.1177/1468017306071180.

D'Cruz, H. (2012). Social work knowledge-in-practice. In A. Schoo, S. Jacobs & H. D'Cruz (Eds.), *Knowledge-in-practice in the caring professions* (pp. 69–92). Farnham, UK: Ashgate.

D'Cruz, H., Gillingham, P., & Melendez, S. (2007). Reflexivity, its meanings and relevance for social work: A critical review of the literature. *British Journal of Social Work, 37*(1), 73–90. doi: 10.1093/bjsw/bcl001.

Dale, O., Smith, R., Norlin, J. M., & Chess, W. A. (2006). *Human behaviour and the social environment: Social systems theory* (5th ed.). Boston, MA; New York, NY; Sydney, NSW: Pearson Education Australia.

Dalrymple, J., & Burke, B. (2006). *Anti-oppressive practice social care and the law.* Retrieved November 14, 2016, from http://ezproxy.ecu.edu.au/login?url=http://site.ebrary.com/lib/ecu/Top?id=10197051.

Das Nair, R., & Butler, C. (2012). *Intersectionality, sexuality, and psychological therapies: Working with lesbian, gay, and bisexual diversity* (Vol. 1). Malden, MA; Chichester, UK: BPS Blackwell.

Davis, K. (2008). Intersectionality as buzzword: A sociology of science perspective on what makes a feminist theory successful. *Feminist Theory, 9*(1), 67–85. doi: 10.1177/1464700108086364.

Davys, A., & Beddoe, L. (2010). *Best practice in professional supervision: A guide for the helping professions.* London, UK; Philadelphia, PA: Jessica Kingsley Publishers.

De Shazer, S., & Berg, I. K. (1997). 'What works?' Remarks on research aspects of solution-focused brief therapy. *Journal of Family Therapy, 19*(2), 121–124. doi: 10.1111/1467-6427.00043.

de Ugarte, L. S., & Martin-Aranaga, I. (2011). Social work and risk society: The need for shared social responsibility. *European Journal of Social Work, 14*(4), 447–462. doi: 10.1080/13691457.2010.500478.

Dean, M. (1998). Administering asceticism: Reworking the ethical life of the unemployed citizen. In M. Dean & B. Hindess (Eds.), *Governing Australia: Studies in contemporary rationalities of government* (pp. 87–107). Cambridge, UK: Cambridge University Press.

Dean, M. (1999). *Governmentality: Power and rule in modern society.* London, UK; Thousand Oaks, CA: SAGE.

Dean, M. (2006). Governmentality and the powers of life and death. In G. Marston & C. McDonald (Eds.), *Analysing social policy: A governmental approach* (pp. 19–48). Cheltenham, UK; Northampton, MA: Edward Elgar.

Deetz, S. (2003). Reclaiming the legacy of the linguistic turn. *Organization, 10*(3), 421–429. doi: 10.1177/13505084030103002.

Dennis, P. (2015). *What is rationality, anyway?* Retrieved February 23, 2015, from www.lse.ac.uk/newsAndMedia/videoAndAudio/channels/publicLecturesAndEvents/player.aspx?id=2812.

Denzin, N. K., & Lincoln, Y. S. (2008). Introduction: The discipline and practice of qualitative research. In N. K. Denzin & Y. S. Lincoln (Eds.), *Collecting and interpreting qualitative materials* (pp. 1–44). Thousand Oaks, CA: SAGE.

Department of Premier Cabinet South Australia. (2008). *Children in state care: Commission of inquiry.* Adelaide: Office of the Commissioner.

Derrida, J. (1966). The decentering event in social thought. In C. Lemert (Ed.), *Social theory: The multicultural and classic readings* (pp. 413–417). Boulder, CO: Westview Press.

Dewey, J. (1910). *How we think.* Retrieved November 14, 2016, from http://ezproxy.ecu .edu.au/login?url=http://search.ebscohost.com/direct.asp?db=pzh&jid=%2220060 3523%22&scope=site.

Dewey, J. (1933). *How we think: A restatement of the relation of reflective thinking to the educative process.* Boston, MA; New York, NY: D. C. Heath and Company.

Dillon, R. S. (2014). *Respect.* Stanford Encyclopedia of Philosophy. Retrieved November 14, 2016, from http://plato.stanford.edu/entries/respect/.

Doel, M., & Shardlow, S. (2005). *Modern social work practice: Teaching and learning in practice settings* (3rd ed.). Aldershot, Hampshire; Burlington, VT: Ashgate.

Dominelli, L. (1998). Anti-oppressive practice in context. In R. Adams, L. Dominelli & M. Payne (Eds.), *Social work: Themes, issues and critical debates* (pp. 3–22). Basingstoke, UK: Macmillan.

Dominelli, L. (2002a). *Anti-oppressive social work theory and practice.* New York, NY: Palgrave Macmillan.

Dominelli, L. (2002b). *Feminist social work theory and practice.* Basingstoke, UK: Palgrave Macmillan.

Dominelli, L. (2004). *Social work: Theory and practice for a changing profession.* Cambridge, UK; Malden, MA: Polity Press; Distributed in the United States by Blackwell Publishers.

Dorsett, P. (2010). The importance of hope in coping with severe acquired disability. *Australian Social Work, 63*(1), 83–102. doi: 10.1080/03124070903464293.

Doshy, P. V., & Wang, J. (2014). Workplace incivility: What do targets say about it? *American Journal of Management, 14*(1/2), 30.

Douglas, M. (1986). *Risk acceptability according to the social sciences.* London, UK: Routledge & Kegan Paul.

Douglas, M. (1994). *Risk and blame: Essays in cultural theory.* London, UK; New York, NY: Routledge.

Dowling, M. (1999). *Social work and poverty: Attitudes and actions.* Aldershot, UK: Ashgate.

Duan, C. (2000). Being empathic: The role of motivation to empathize and the nature of target emotions. *Motivation and Emotion, 24*(1), 29–49. doi: 10.1023/A:1005587525609.

Duan, C., & Hill, C. E. (1996). The current state of empathy research. *Journal of Counseling Psychology, 43*(3), 261–274. doi: 10.1037/0022-0167.43.3.261.

Dunk-West, P. (2013). *How to be a social worker: A critical guide for students.* Basingstoke, UK: Palgrave Macmillan.

Dunlap, K. M. (2011). Functional theory and social work practice. In F. J. Turner (Ed.), *Social work treatment: Interlocking theoretical approaches* (pp. 225–241). New York, NY: Oxford University Press.

Edwards, P. B. (2002). Spiritual themes in social work counselling: Facilitating the search for meaning. *Australian Social Work, 55*(1), 78–87. doi: 10.1080/03124070208411674.

Ekman, E., & Halpern, J. (2015). Professional distress and meaning in health care: Why professional empathy can help. *Social Work in Health Care, 54*(7), 633–650. doi: 10.1080/00981389.2015.1046575.

Ekstedt, M., & Fagerberg, I. (2005). Lived experiences of the time preceding burnout. *Journal of Advanced Nursing, 49*(1), 59–67. doi: 10.1111/j.1365-2648.2004.03264.x.

Ellis, C., & Rawicki, J. (2013). Collaborative witnessing of survival during the Holocaust: An exemplar of relational autoethnography. *Qualitative Inquiry, 19*(5), 366–380. doi: 10.1177/1077800413479562.

Engelberg, E., & Limbach-Reich, A. (2015). The role of empathy in case management: A pilot study. *Social Work Education, 34*(8), 1021–1033. doi: 10.1080/02615479.2015.1087996.

Epstein, L. (1994). The therapeutic idea in contemporary society. In A. S. Chambon & A. Irving (Eds.), *Essays on postmodernism and social work* (pp. 3–18). Ontario, ON: Canadian Scholars Press.

Epstein, L. (1999). The culture of social work. In A. S. Chambon, A. Irving & L. Epstein (Eds.), *Reading Foucault for social work* (pp. 3–26). New York, NY: Columbia University Press.

Ericson-Lidman, E., & Strandberg, G. (2007). Burnout: Co-workers' perceptions of signs preceding workmates' burnout. *Journal of Advanced Nursing, 60*(2), 199–208. doi: 10.1111/j.1365-2648.2007.04399.x.

Esping-Andersen, G., & United Nations Research Institute for Social Development. (1996). *Welfare states in transition: National adaptations in global economies.* London, UK: SAGE Publications in association with the United Nations Research Institute for Social Development.

Estes, B., & Wang, J. (2008). Integrative literature review: Workplace incivility: Impacts on individual and organizational performance. *Human Resource Development Review, 7*(2), 218–240. doi: 10.1177/1534484308315565.

Evans, J. (2008). Dual-processing accounts of reasoning, judgment, and social cognition. *Annual Review of Psychology, 59*(1), 255–278. doi: 10.1146/annurev.psych.59.103006.093629.

Evans, J. (2011). Dual-process theories of reasoning: Contemporary issues and developmental applications. *Developmental Review, 31*(2–3), 86–102. doi: http://dx.doi.org/10.1016/j.dr.2011.07.007.

Evans, J., & Stanovich, K. E. (2013). Dual-process theories of higher cognition: Advancing the debate. *Perspectives on Psychological Science, 8*(3), 223–241. doi: 10.1177/1745691612460685.

Ewald, F. (1991). Insurance and risk. In G. Burchell, C. Gordon & P. Miller (Eds.), *The Foucault effect: Studies in governmentality with two lectures by and an interview with Michel Foucault* (pp. 197–210). Chicago, IL: University of Chicago Press.

Ferguson, I., & Woodward, R. (2009). *Radical social work in practice: Making a difference.* Bristol, UK: Policy Press.

Ferreira, S. B. (2010). Eco-spiritual social work as a precondition for social development. *Ethics and Social Welfare, 4*(1), 3–23. doi: 10.1080/17496531003607891.

Ferris, J., Norman, C., & Sempik, J. (2001). People, land and sustainability: Community gardens and the social dimension of sustainable development. *Social Policy & Administration, 35*(5), 559–568. doi: 10.1111/1467-9515.t01-1-00253.

Flexner, A. (2001). *Is social work a profession? Research on social work practice, 11*(2), 152–165. doi: 10.1177/104973150101100202.

Flyvbjerg, B. (1998). *Rationality and power: Democracy in practice* (S. Sampson, Trans.). Chicago, IL; London, UK: University of Chicago Press.

Flyvbjerg, B. (2001). *Making social science matter: Why social inquiry fails and how it can succeed again.* Cambridge, UK: Cambridge University Press.

Fook, J. (1993). *Radical casework: A theory of practice.* St Leonards, NSW: Allen & Unwin.

Fook, J. (1996). The reflective researcher: Developing a reflective approach to practice. In J. Fook (Ed.), *The reflective researcher: Social workers' theories of practice research* (pp. 1–10). St Leonards, NSW: Allen & Unwin.

Fook, J. (1999). Critical reflectivity in education and practice. In B. Pease & J. Fook (Eds.), *Transforming social work practice: Postmodern critical perspectives* (pp. 195–210). St Leonards, NSW: Allen & Unwin.

Fook, J. (2002a). *Social work: Critical theory and practice.* London, UK: SAGE.

Fook, J. (2002b). Theorizing from practice: Towards an inclusive approach for social work research. *Qualitative Social Work, 1*(1), 79–95. doi: 10.1177/147332500200100106.

Fook, J., & Askeland, G. (2007). Challenges of critical reflection: 'Nothing ventured, nothing gained'. *Social Work Education, 26*(5), 520–533. doi: 10.1080/02615470601118662.

Fook, J., & Askeland, G. A. (2006). The 'critical' in critical reflection. In S. White, J. Fook & F. Gardner (Eds.), *Critical reflection in health and social care* (pp. 40–53). Berkshire, UK: Open University Press.

Fook, J., & Gardner, F. (2007). *Practising critical reflection: A resource handbook.* Maidenhead, UK: Open University Press.

Fook, J., Ryan, M., & Hawkins, L. (1997). Towards a theory of social work expertise. *British Journal of Social Work, 27*(3), 399–417.

Fook, J., Ryan, M., & Hawkins, L. (2000). *Professional expertise: Practice, theory and education for working in uncertainty.* London, UK: Whiting & Birch Ltd.

Foote, C. E., & Frank, A. W. (1999). Foucault and therapy: The disciplining of grief. In A. S. Chambon, A. Irving & L. Epstein (Eds.), *Reading Foucault for social work* (pp. 157–187). New York, NY: Columbia University Press.

Fortune, A. E., & Reid, W. J. (2011). Task-centered social work. In F. J. Turner (Ed.), *Social work treatment: Interlocking theoretical perspectives* (5th ed., pp. 513–532). Oxford, UK: Oxford University Press.

Foucault, M. (1972). *The archaeology of knowledge.* London, UK: Tavistock Publications.

Foucault, M. (1975). *The birth of the clinic: An archaeology of medical perception* (A. M. Sheridan Smith, Trans.). New York, NY: Vintage Books/Random House.

Foucault, M. (1978). *The history of sexuality: An introduction* (Vol. 1). New York, NY: Random House.

Foucault, M. (1980a). The confessions of the flesh. In C. Gordon (Ed.), *Power/knowledge: Selected interviews and other writings, 1972–1977* (pp. 194–228). New York, NY: Pantheon Books.

Foucault, M. (1980b). Two lectures. In C. Gordon (Ed.), *Power/knowledge: Selected interviews and other writings, 1972–1977* (pp. 78–108). New York, NY: Pantheon Books.

Foucault, M. (1988). On power. In L. D. Kritzman (Ed.), *Michel Foucault: Politics, philosophy, culture. Interviews and other writings 1977–1984* (pp. 96–109). New York, NY; London, UK: Routledge.

Foucault, M. (1991). Governmentality. In G. Burchell, C. Gordon & P. Miller (Eds.), *The Foucault effect: Studies in governmentality with two lectures by and an interview with Michel Foucault* (pp. 87–104). Chicago, IL: University of Chicago Press.

Foucault, M. (1995). *Discipline and punish: The birth of the prison* (2nd Vintage Books ed.). New York, NY: Vintage Books.

Foucault, M. (2001). *Madness and civilization: A history of insanity in the age of reason.* London, UK: Routledge.

Foucault, M. (2002). *The order of things: An archaeology of the human sciences.* London, UK: Routledge.

Foucault, M. (2003). *Society must be defended: Lectures at the Collegè de France 1975–1976* (D. Macey, Trans.). London, UK: Allen Lane/Penguin Books.

Foucault, M. (2007). *Security, territory, population: Lectures at the Collegè de France 1977–1978* (G. Burchell, Trans.). Basingstoke, UK; New York, NY: Palgrave Macmillan.

Foucault, M., Miller, P., Burchell, G., & Gordon, C. (1991). *The Foucault effect: Studies in governmentality: With two lectures by and an interview with Michel Foucault.* Chicago, IL: University of Chicago Press.

Foucault, M., & Rabinow, P. (1984). What is enlightenment? In P. Rabinow (Ed.), *The Foucault reader* (pp. 32–50). London, UK: Penguin Books.

Fraley R. C. (2004). *A brief overview of adult attachment theory and research.* Retrieved October 19, 2006, from www.psych.uiuc.edu/~rcfraley/attachment.htm.

Fraser, M. W., Richman, J. M., & Galinsky, M. J. (1999). Risk, protection, and resilience: Toward a conceptual framework for social work practice. *Social Work Research, 23*(3), 131–143.

Fraternali, K. (1998). Sartre's existentialism and social work. *New Global Development, 14*(1), 62. doi: 10.1080/17486839808412604.

Freire, P. (1972). *Pedagogy of the oppressed.* New York, NY: Herder and Herder.

Freire, P. (2004). *Pedagogy of hope* (Revised ed.). London, UK; New York, NY: Continuum.

Gair, S. (2008). Walking a mile in another person's shoes: Contemplating limitations and learning on the road to accurate empathy. *Advances in Social Work Education, 10*(1), 19–29.

Gair, S. (2011). Creating spaces for critical reflection in social work education: Learning from a classroom-based empathy project. *Reflective Practice, 12*(6), 791–802. doi: 10.1080/14623943.2011.601099.

Gair, S. (2012). Feeling their stories: Contemplating empathy, insider/outsider positionings, and enriching qualitative research. *Qualitative Health Research, 22*(1), 134–143. doi: 10.1177/1049732311420580.

Gair, S. (2013). Inducing empathy: Pondering students' (in)ability to empathize with an Aboriginal man's lament and what might be done about it. *Journal of Social Work Education, 49*(1), 136–149. doi: 10.1080/10437797.2013.755399.

Gair, S. (2016). Pondering the colour of empathy: Social work students' reasoning on activism, empathy and racism. *British Journal of Social Work,* 1–9. doi: 10.1093/bjsw/bcw007.

Gale, F., & Dudley, M. (2013). Spirituality in social work. In M. Connolly & L. Harms (Eds.), *Social work: Contexts and practice* (pp. 60–73). South Melbourne, VIC: Oxford University Press.

Gambrill, E. (1997). *Social work practice: A critical thinker's guide.* New York, NY; Oxford, UK: Oxford University Press.

Gardner, F. (2006). *Working with human service organisations: Creating connections for practice.* South Melbourne, VIC: Oxford University Press.

Garfinkel, I., Rainwater, L., & Smeeding, T. (2010). *Wealth and welfare states.* Oxford, UK: Oxford University Press.

Garrity, Z. (2010). Discourse analysis, Foucault and social work research: Identifying some methodological complexities. *Journal of Social Work, 10*(2), 193–210. doi: 10.1177/1468017310363641.

Gerdes, K. E. (2011). Introduction: 21st-century conceptualizations of empathy: Implications for social work practice and research. *Journal of Social Service Research, 37*(3), 226–229. doi: 10.1080/01488376.2011.564024.

Gerdes, K. E., & Segal, E. (2011). Importance of empathy for social work practice: Integrating new science. *Social Work, 56*(2), 141–148.

Gerdes, K. E., Segal, E. A., Jackson, K. F., & Mullins, J. L. (2011). Teaching empathy: A framework rooted in social cognitive neuroscience and social justice. *Journal of Social Work Education, 47*(1), 109–131. doi: 10.5175/JSWE.2011.200900085.

Germain, C. B., & Gitterman, A. (1980). *The life model of social work practice.* New York, NY: Columbia University Press.

Gibbons, J., & Gray, M. (2004). Critical thinking as integral to social work practice. *Journal of Teaching in Social Work, 24*(1–2), 19–38. doi: 10.1300/J067v24n01_02.

Gibson, M. (2015). Intersecting deviance: Social work, difference and the legacy of eugenics. *British Journal of Social Work, 45*(1), 313–330. doi: 10.1093/bjsw/bct131.

Giddens, A. (1990). *The consequences of modernity.* Cambridge, UK: Polity Press in association with Basil Blackwell Oxford UK.

Giddens, A. (1993). *Sociology* (2nd ed.). Oxford, UK: Polity Press.

Gkorezis, P., Kalampouka, P., & Petridou, E. (2013). The mediating role of belongingness in the relationship between workplace incivility and thriving. *International Journal of Employment Studies, 21*(2), 63–78.

Goffman, E. (1991). *Stigma.* New York, NY: Simon & Schuster.

Gordon, C. (1991). Governmental rationality: An introduction. In G. Burchell, C. Gordon & P. Miller (Eds.), *The Foucault effect: Studies in governmentality with two lectures by and an interview with Michel Foucault* (pp. 1–51). Chicago, IL: Chicago University Press.

Gordon, D., Mack, J., Lansley, S., Main, G., Nandy S, Patsios, D., ... PSE team. (2013). *The Impoverishment of the UK: PSE UK first results: Living standards.* Retrieved July 22, 2016, from www.poverty.ac.uk/sites/default/files/attachments/The_Impoverishment_of_the_UK_PSE_UK_first_results_summary_report_March_28.pdf.

Gould, N., & Taylor, I. (1996). *Reflective learning for social work: Research, theory and practice.* Aldershot, Hants, UK: Arena Ashgate.

Grandey, A. A. (2003). When "the show must go on": Surface acting and deep acting as determinants of emotional exhaustion and peer-rated service delivery. *The Academy of Management Journal, 46*(1), 86–96. doi: 10.2307/30040678.

Grant, L. (2014). Hearts and minds: Aspects of empathy and wellbeing in social work students. *Social Work Education, 33*(3), 338–352. doi: 10.1080/02615479.2013.805191.

Grant, L., & Kinman, G. (2011). Enhancing wellbeing in social work students: Building resilience in the next generation. *Social Work Education, 31*(5), 605–621. doi: 10.1080/02615479.2011.590931.

Gray, M., Dean, M., Agllias, K., Howard, A., & Schubert, L. (2015). Perspectives on neoliberalism for human service professionals. *Social Service Review, 89*(2), 368–392. doi: 10.1086/681644.

Gray, M., Joy, E., Plath, D., & Webb, S. A. (2015). What supports and impedes evidence-based practice implementation? A survey of Australian social workers. *British Journal of Social Work, 45*(2), 667–684. doi: 10.1093/bjsw/bct123.

Gray, M., Plath, D., & Webb, S. A. (2009). *Evidence-based social work: A critical stance.* London, UK; New York, NY: Routledge.

Grayling, A. C. (2002). *The reason of things: Living with philosophy.* London, UK: Weidenfeld & Nicolson.

Green, D. (2007). Risk and social work practice. *Australian Social Work, 60*(4), 395–409. doi: 10.1080/03124070701671131.

Greene, R. R. (2007). *Social work practice: A risk and resilience approach.* Australia: Thomson, Brooks/Cole.

Greenslade, L., McAuliffe, D., & Chenoweth, L. (2014). Social workers' experiences of covert workplace activism. *Australian Social Work,* 1–16. doi: 10.1080/0312407X. 2014.940360.

Gregor, C., & Smith, H. (2009). I'm not a performing monkey: Reflections on the emotional experience of developing a collaborative training initiative between services users and lecturer. *Journal of Social Work Practice, 23*(1), 21–34. doi: 10.1080/02650530902723290.

Griffiths, M. (1995). *Feminisms and the self: The web of identity.* New York, NY; London, UK: Routledge.

Griffiths, M. (2005). *A feminist perspective on communities of practice.* Paper presented at the Socio-cultural Theory in Educational Research and Practice, Manchester, UK.

Gustafsson, G., Norberg, A., & Strandberg, G. (2008). Meanings of becoming and being burnout: Phenomenological-hermeneutic interpretation of female healthcare personnel's narratives. *Scandinavian Journal of Caring Sciences, 22*(4), 520–528. doi: 10.1111/j.1471-6712.2007.00559.x.

Gwyther, G., & Possamai-Inesedy, A. (2009). Methodologies a la carte: An examination of emerging qualitative methodologies in social research. *International Journal of Social Research Methodology, 12*(2), 99–115. doi: 10.1080/13645570902727680.

Habermas, J. (1984). *The theory of communicative action.* Boston, MA: Beacon Press.

Habermas, J. (1989). *The structural transformation of the public sphere: An inquiry into a category of bourgeois society.* Cambridge, UK: Polity Press.

Habibis, D., & Walter, M. (2009). *Social inequality in Australia: Discourses, realities and futures.* South Melbourne, VIC: Oxford University Press.

Hacking, I. (1999). *The social construction of what?* Cambridge, MA; London, UK: Harvard University Press.

Hacking, I. (2002). *Historical ontology.* Cambridge, MA: Harvard University Press.

Haggis, T. (2009). What have we been thinking of? A critical overview of 40 years of student learning research in higher education. *Studies in Higher Education, 34*(4), 377–390. doi: 10.1080/03075070902771903.

Haidt, J. (2001). The emotional dog and its rational tail: A social intuitionist approach to moral judgment. *Psychological Review, 108*(4), 814–834. doi: 10.1037/0033-295x.108.4.814.

Hall, G., Boddy, J., Chenoweth, L., & Davie, K. (2012). Mutual benefits: Developing relational service approaches within Centrelink. *Australian Social Work, 65*(1), 87–103. doi: 10.1080/0312407X.2011.594956.

Hamama, L. (2012). Differences between children's social workers and adults' social workers on sense of burnout, work conditions and organisational social support. *British Journal of Social Work, 42*(7), 1333–1353. doi: 10.1093/bjsw/bcr135.

Hames-Garcia, M. R. (2011). *Identity complex: Making the case for multiplicity* (Vol. N - New). Minneapolis, MN: University of Minnesota Press.

Harding, S. G., & Hintikka, M. B. (1983). *Discovering reality: Feminist perspectives on epistemology, metaphysics, methodology, and philosophy of science* (Synthese library v. 161). Retrieved November 14, 2016, from http://ezproxy.ecu.edu.au/login?url=http://site.ebrary.com/lib/ecu/Top?id=10067408.

Harrison, G., & Melville, R. (2010). *Rethinking social work in a global world.* Basingstoke, UK: Palgrave Macmillan.

Hasenfeld, Y. (1992). The nature of human service organizations. In Y. Hasenfeld (Ed.), *Human services as complex organizations* (pp. 3–23). Newbury Park, CA: SAGE.

Hasenfeld, Y., & Abbott, A. D. (1992). *Human services as complex organizations.* Newbury Park, CA: SAGE.

Hay, J. (2012). Considering the spiritual dimension of human life and its relevance to social work education: Social workers', educators' and students' views. *Advances in Social Work and Welfare Education, 14*(1), 52–66.

Healy, K. (2005). *Social work theories in context: Creating frameworks for practice.* Basingstoke, UK: Palgrave Macmillan.

Healy, K. (2014). *Social work theories in context: Creating frameworks for practice* (2nd ed.). Basingstoke, UK; New York, NY: Palgrave Macmillan.

Healy, L. M. (2007). Universalism and cultural relativism in social work ethics. *International Social Work, 50*(1), 11–26. doi: 10.1177/0020872807071479.

Healy, L. M. (2008). Exploring the history of social work as a human rights profession. *International Social Work, 51*(6), 735–748. doi: 10.1177/0020872808095247.

Hekman, S. J. (1999). *The future of differences: Truth and method in feminist theory.* Malden, MA: Polity Press.

Held, V. (1999). Liberalism and the ethics of care. In C. Card (Ed.), *On feminist ethics and politics* (pp. 288–309). Lawrence, Kansas: University Press of Kansas.

Heywood, A. (2000). *Key concepts in politics.* Basingstoke, UK: Palgrave Macmillan.

Hicks, S. (2005). Queer genealogies: Tales of conformity and rebellion amongst Lesbian and Gay foster carers and adopters. *Qualitative Social Work, 4*(3), 293–308. doi: 10.1177/1473325005055597.

Hicks, S. (2015). Social work and gender: An argument for practical accounts. *Qualitative Social Work, 14*(4), 471–487. doi: 10.1177/1473325014558665.

Hickson, H. (2013). *Exploring how social workers learn and use reflection* (PhD dissertation). La Trobe University Bundoora, VIC.

Hodge, D. R. (2003). The challenge of spiritual diversity: Can social work facilitate an inclusive environment? *Families in Society, 84*(3), 348–358. doi: 10.1606/1044-3894.117.

Hodge, D. R., Baughman, L. M., & Cummings, J. A. (2006). Moving toward spiritual competency: Deconstructing religious stereotypes and spiritual prejudices in social work literature. *Journal of Social Service Research, 32*(4), 211–231. doi: 10.1300/J079v32n04_12.

Hofer, B. K. (2002). Personal epistemology as a psychological and educational construct: An introduction. In P. R. Pintrich & B. K. Hofer (Eds.), *Personal epistemology: The psychology of beliefs about knowledge and knowing* (pp. 3–14). Mahwah, NJ: L. Erlbaum Associates.

Holden, M. M. (2012). Using critically reflective practice when implementing ethical and sensitive spiritual frameworks in social work practice. *Reflective Practice, 13*(1), 65–76. doi: 10.1080/14623943.2011.626021.

Hollis, F. (1964). *Casework: A psychosocial therapy.* New York, NY: Random House.

Holloway, M. (2007). Spiritual need and the core business of social work. *The British Journal of Social Work, 37*(2), 265–280. doi: 10.1093/bjsw/bcl014.

Holloway, M., & Moss, B. (2010). *Spirituality and social work.* Basingstoke, UK: Palgrave Macmillan.

Honneth, A. (1992). Integrity and disrespect: Principles of a conception of morality based on the theory of recognition. *Political Theory, 20*(2), 187–201. doi: 10.1177/0090591792020002001.

Hook, D. (2004a). Foucault, disciplinary power and the critical pre-history of psychology. In D. Hook (Ed.), *Critical psychology* (pp. 210–238). Lansdowne: UCT Press.

Hook, D. (2004b). *Governmentality and technologies of subjectivity.* In D. Hook (Ed.), Critical psychology (pp. 239–272). Lansdowne: UCT Press.

hooks, b. (1981). *Ain't I a woman: Black women and feminism.* Boston, MA: South End Press.

hooks, b. (1990). *Yearning: Race, gender, and cultural politics.* Boston, MA: South End Press.

hooks, b. (2003). *Teaching community: A pedagogy of hope.* New York, NY; London, UK: Routledge.

Hopkins, G. (2007). *What have we learned? Child death scandals since 1944.* Retrieved August 24, 2016, from www.communitycare.co.uk/2007/01/10/what-have-we-learned-child-death-scandals-since-1944/.

Hosken, N. (2013). Social work supervision and discrimination [online]. *Advances in Social Work and Welfare Education, 15*(1), 92–104. Retrieved November 15, 2016, from http://search.informit.com.au.ezproxy.ecu.edu.au/documentSummary;dn=479428906488362;res=IELHSS.

Hosken, N., & Goldingay, S. (2016). Making sense of different theoretically informed approaches in doing critical social work. In B. Pease, S. Goldingay, N. Hosken & S. Nipperess (Eds.), *Doing critical social work: Transformative practices for social justice* (pp. 52–70). Crows Nest, NSW: Allen & Unwin.

Houghton, S. (2007). Exploring hope: Its meaning for adults living with depression and for social work practice. *Advances in Mental Health, 6*(3), 186–193. doi: 10.5172/jamh.6.3.186.

Houston, S. (2001). Transcending the fissure in risk theory: Critical realism and child welfare. *Child & Family Social Work, 6*(3), 219–228. doi: 10.1046/j.1365-2206.2001.00205.x.

Howe, D. (1995). *Attachment theory for social work practice.* Basingstoke, UK: Macmillan.

Howe, D. (2009). *A brief introduction to social work theory.* Basingstoke, UK: Palgrave Macmillan.

Howe, D. (2013). Attachment theory. In M. Davies (Ed.), *The Blackwell companion to social work* (pp. 417–419). West Sussex, UK: John Wiley and Sons.

Hudson, J. D. (1997). A model of professional knowledge for social work practice. *Australian Social Work, 50*(3), 35–44. doi: 10.1080/03124079708414096.

Hughes, M., & Wearing, M. (2007). *Organisations and management in social work.* London, UK: SAGE.

Hugman, R. (1991). *Power in the caring professions.* Basingstoke, UK: Macmillan.

Hulko, W. (2009). The time-and context-contingent nature of intersectionality and interlocking oppressions. *Affilia, 24*(1), 44–55. doi: 10.1177/0886109908326814.

Human Rights Watch. (2016). Human rights watch. Retrieved July 22, 2016, from www.hrw.org.

Humphrey, C. (2009). By the light of the Tao. *European Journal of Social Work, 12*(3), 377–390. doi: 10.1080/13691450902930779.

Hunt, J. (2014). Bio-psycho-social-spiritual assessment? Teaching the skill of spiritual assessment. *Social Work and Christianity, 41*(4), 373.

Hyslop, I. (2012). Social work as a practice of freedom. *Journal of Social Work, 12*(4), 404–422. doi: 10.1177/1468017310388362.

Ife, J. (1997). *Rethinking social work: Towards critical practice.* South Melbourne, VIC: Addison Wesley Longman Ltd.

Ife, J. (1999). Postmodernism, critical theory and social work. In B. Pease & J. Fook (Eds.), *Transforming social work practice: Postmodern critical perspectives* (pp. 211–223). St Leonards, NSW: Allen & Unwin.

Ife, J. (2001). *Human rights and social work: Towards rights-based practice.* Oakleigh, VIC: Cambridge University Press.

Ife, J. (2002). *Community development* (2nd ed.). Frenchs Forest, NSW: Longman.

Ife, J. (2008). *Human rights and social work: Towards rights-based practice* (Rev. ed.). Cambridge, UK; Port Melbourne, VIC: Cambridge University Press.

Ife, J. (2012). *Human rights and social work: Towards rights-based practice* (3rd ed.). Port Melbourne, VIC: Cambridge University Press.

Ingram, R. (2013). Exploring emotions within formal and informal forums: Messages from social work practitioners. *British Journal of Social Work, 45*(3), 896–913. doi: 10.1093/bjsw/bct166.

International Federation of Social Workers. (2012). *Statement of ethical principles.* Retrieved June 16, 2016, from http://ifsw.org/policies/statement-of-ethical-principles/.

International Federation of Social Workers. (2014). *Global definition of social work.* Retrieved April 27, 2014, from http://ifsw.org/policies/definition-of-social-work/.

James, R. K., & Gilliland, B. E. (2005). *Crisis intervention strategies* (5th ed.). Australia: Thomson, Brooks/Cole.

Jamrozik, A. (2005). *Social policy in the post-welfare state: Australian society in the 21st century* (2nd ed.). Frenchs Forest, NSW: Pearson Education Australia.

Jessup, H., & Rogerson, S. (1999). Postmodernism and the teaching and practice of interpersonal skills. In B. Pease & J. Fook (Eds.), *Transforming social work practice* (pp. 161–178). St Leonards, NSW: Allen & Unwin.

Johnson, M. M. J. (2011, May 12). *Margaret Archer on reflexivity* [Video File]. Retrieved August 15, 2015, from www.youtube.com/watch?v=bMpJ5wnuB64.

Jones, A., & May, J. (1992). *Working in human service organisations: A critical introduction.* South Melbourne, VIC: Longman Cheshire.

Jones, C. (2001). Voices from the front line: State social workers and New Labour. *British Journal of Social Work, 31*(4), 547–562. doi: 10.1093/bjsw/31.4.547.

Jongerden, J. (2016). Making sense: Research as active engagement. *Kurdish Studies, 4*(1), 94–104.

Jordan, B., & Parton, N. (2004). Social work, the public sphere and civil society. In R. Lovelock, K. Lyons & J. Powell (Eds.), *Reflecting on social work: Discipline and profession* (pp. 20–36). Aldershot, UK: Ashgate.

Jordan, R. (2013). Behaviourism. In M. Davies (Ed.), *The Blackwell companion to social work* (pp. 420–422). Somerset, NJ: John Wiley & Sons.

Kadushin, A. (1985). *Supervision in social work* (2nd ed.). New York, NY: Columbia University Press.

Kant, I., & Meiklejohn, J. M. D. (1934). *Critique of pure reason.* London, UK; New York, NY: J. M. Dent & sons E. P. Dutton & Co.

Kaplan, H. B. (1999). Toward an understanding of resilience: A critical review of definitions and models. In J. L. Johnson (Ed.), *Resilience and development: Positive life adaptations* (pp. 17–83). Hingman, MA: Kluwer Academic Publishers.

Keddell, E. (2011). Reasoning processes in child protection decision-making: Negotiating moral minefields and risky relationships. *British Journal of Social Work, 41*(7), 1251–1270. doi: 10.1093/bjsw/bcr012.

Keinemans, S. (2014). Be sensible: Emotions in social work ethics and education. *British Journal of Social Work, 45*(7), 2176–2191. doi: 10.1093/bjsw/bcu057.

Kemshall, H. (2010). Risk rationalities in contemporary social work policy and practice. *British Journal of Social Work, 40*(4), 1247–1262. doi: 10.1093/bjsw/bcp157.

Kessl, F. (2009). Critical reflexivity, social work, and the emerging European post-welfare states. *European Journal of Social Work, 12*(3), 305–317. doi: 10.1080/13691450902930746.

King, P. M., & Kitchener, K. S. (2004). Reflective judgment: Theory and research on the development of epistemic assumptions through adulthood. *Educational Psychologist, 39*(1), 5–18. doi: 10.1207/s15326985ep3901_2.

King, S. H. (2011). The structure of empathy in social work practice. *Journal of Human Behavior in the Social Environment, 21*(6), 679–695. doi: 10.1080/10911359.2011.583516.

Kirst-Ashman, K. K. (2007). *Introduction to social work and social welfare: Critical thinking perspectives* (2nd ed.). Australia: Thomson, Brooks/Cole.

Kisamore, J. L., Jawahar, I. M., Liguori, E. W., Stone, T. H., & Mharapara, T. L. (2010). Conflict and abusive workplace behaviors. *Career Development International, 15*(6), 583–600. doi: 10.1108/13620431011084420.

Kitchener, K. S. (1986). The reflective judgement model: Characteristics, evidence and measurement. In R. A. Mines & K. S. Kitchener (Eds.), *Adult cognitive development: Methods and models* (pp. 76–91). New York, NY: Praeger Publishers.

Kolb, D. A. (1984). *Experiential learning: Experience as the source of learning and development*. Englewood Cliffs, NJ: Prentice-Hall.

Koopman, C. (2006). Pragmatism as a philosophy of hope: Emerson, James, Dewey, Rorty. *The Journal of Speculative Philosophy, 20*(2), 106–116.

Koopman, C. (2013). *Genealogy as critique: Foucault and the problems of modernity*. Bloomington, IN: Indiana University Press.

Krill, D. (2011). Existential social work. In F. J. Turner (Ed.), *Social work treatment: Interlocking theoretical perspectives* (5th ed., pp. 179–204). Oxford, UK: Oxford University Press.

Krishna, S. (2008). *Globalization and postcolonialism*. Blue Ridge Summit, US: Rowman & Littlefield Publishers.

Laming, L. (2012). *The Victoria Climbie inquiry*. London, UK: Department of Education.

Lamont, J., & Favor, C. (2016). Distributive justice. In E. N. Zalta (Ed.), *The Stanford Encyclopedia of Philosophy*. Stanford, CA: Stanford University. Retrieved November 14, 2016, from http://plato.stanford.edu/entries/justice-distributive/.

Larochelle, C., & Campfens, H. (1992). The structure of poverty: A challenge for the training of social workers in the North and South. *International Social Work, 35*(2), 105–119.

Larrison, T., & Korr, W. S. (2013). Does social work have a signature pedagogy? *Journal of Social Work Education, 49*(2), 194–206. doi: 10.1080/10437797.2013.768102.

Larsen, K. M. (2011). How spiritual are social workers? An exploration of social work practitioners' personal spiritual beliefs, attitudes, and practices. *Journal of Religion & Spirituality in Social Work: Social Thought, 30*(1), 17–33. doi: 10.1080/15426432.2011.542713.

Laschinger, H. K. S., Wong, C. A., Cummings, G. G., & Grau, A. L. (2014). Resonant leadership and workplace empowerment: The value of positive organizational cultures in reducing workplace incivility. *Nursing Economics, 32*(1), 5–15.

Lather, P. (2006). Paradigm proliferation as a good thing to think with: Teaching research in education as a wild profusion. *International Journal of Qualitative Studies in Education, 19*(1), 35–57. doi: 10.1080/09518390500450144.

Lave, J., & Wenger, E. (1991). *Situated learning: Legitimate peripheral participation*. Cambridge, UK: Cambridge University Press.

Leadbetter, D. (2013). Anger management. In M. Davies (Ed.), *The Blackwell companion to social work* (pp. 409–413). West Sussex, UK: John Wiley and Sons.

Leadbetter, M. (2002). Empowerment and advocacy. In R. Adams, L. Dominelli & M. Payne (Eds.), *Social work: Themes, issues and critical debates* (2nd ed., pp. 200–208). Basingstoke, UK: Palgrave Macmillan.

Lee, J. A. B. (1996). The Empowerment approach to social work practice. In F. J. Turner (Ed.), *Social work treatment: Interlocking theoretical perspectives* (4th ed., pp. 192–218). New York, NY: The Free Press.

Lemke, T. (2001). 'The birth of bio-politics': Michel Foucault's lecture at the Collège de France on neoliberal governmentality. *Economy and Society, 2*(May), 190–207.

Leonard, P. (1975). Towards a paradigm for radical practice. In R. Bailey & M. Brake (Eds.), *Radical social work* (pp. 46–61). London, UK: Edward Arnold.

Leonard, P. (1997). *Postmodern welfare: Reconstructing an emancipatory project*. London, UK: SAGE.

Lerner, J., Li, Y., Valdesolo, P., & Kassam, K. S. (2015). Emotion and decision-making. *Annual Review of Psychology, 66*, 799–823. doi: 10.2246/annurev-psych-010213-115043.

Lerner, J. S., & Keltner, D. (2001). Fear, anger, and risk. *Journal of Personality and Social Psychology, 81*(1), 146–159. doi: 10.1037/0022-3514.81.1.146.

Leshner, A. I. (1999). Introduction. In J. L. Johnson (Ed.), *Resilience and development: Positive life adaptations* (pp. 1–3). Hingham, MA: Kluwer Academic Publishers.

Liamputtong, P., Fanany, R., & Verrinder, G. (Eds.). (2012). *Health, illness and well-being: Perspectives and social determinants.* South Melbourne, VIC: Oxford University Press.

Lister, P. G. (2012). *Integrating social work theory and practice: A practical skills guide.* New York, NY: Routledge.

Lister, R. (2003). *Citizenship: Feminist perspectives* (2nd ed.). Basingstoke, UK: Palgrave Macmillan.

Litt, J. S., Soobader, M.-J., Turbin, M. S., Hale, J. W., Buchenau, M., & Marshall, J. A. (2011). The influence of social involvement, neighbourhood aesthetics, and community garden participation on fruit and vegetable consumption. *American Journal of Public Health, 101*(8), 1466–1473. doi: 10.2105/AJPH.2010.300111.

Loewenberg, F. M. (1984). Professional ideology, middle range theories and knowledge building for social work practice. *British Journal of Social Work, 14*(1), 309–322.

London School of Economics and Political Science (LSE), & Ramadan, T. (2016). *Equal rights and equal dignity of human beings.* Retrieved June 21, 2016, from www.youtube.com/watch?v=PjWnWcAZcTA&feature=youtu.be.

Lukes, S. (1974). *Power: A radical view.* London, UK; New York, NY: Macmillan.

Lundy, C. (2004). *Social work and social justice: A structural approach to practice.* Peterborough, ON; Orchard Park, NY: Broadview Press.

Lupton, D. (1999). *Risk.* London, UK; New York, NY: Routledge.

Luthans, F., Avey, J. B., Avolio, B. J., Norman, S. M., & Combs, G. M. (2006). Psychological capital development: Toward a micro-intervention. *Journal of Organizational Behavior, 27*(3), 387–393. doi: 10.1002/job.373.

Luthans, F., Norman, S. M., Avolio, B. J., & Avey, J. B. (2008). The mediating role of psychological capital in the supportive organizational climate: Employee performance relationship. *Journal of Organizational Behavior, 29*(2), 219–238.

Lynch, M. (2000). Against reflexivity as an academic virtue and source of privileged knowledge. *Theory, Culture & Society, 17*(26), 26–54. doi: 10.1177/02632760022051202.

MacInnes, T., Aldridge, H., Bushe, S., Tinson, A., & Born, B. B. (2014). *Monitoring poverty and social exclusion 2014.* Retrieved August 1, 2016, from www.jrf.org.uk/sites/default/files/jrf/migrated/files/MPSE-2014-FULL.pdf.

Mackenzie, C. (2010). Autonomy: Individualistic or social and relational. In G. Marston, J. Moss & J. Quiggin (Eds.), *Risk, welfare and work* (pp. 107–127). Carlton, VIC: Melbourne University Press.

Madigan, S. (2013). Narrative therapy. In M. Davies (Ed.), *The Blackwell companion to social work* (pp. 454–458). Somerset, NJ: John Wiley & Sons.

Marmot, M., & Allen, J. J. (2014). Social determinants of health equity. *American Journal of Public Health, 104*(S4), S517–S519.

Marsh, P. (2013). Task-centred practice. In M. Davies (Ed.), *The Blackwell companion to social work* (pp. 492–495). Somerset, NJ: John Wiley & Sons.

Marsh, P., & Doel, M. (2005). *The task-centred book.* London, UK; New York, NY: Routledge.

Marston, G., & McDonald, C. (Eds.). (2006). *Analysing social policy: A governmental approach*. Cheltenham, UK; Northampton, MA: Edward Elgar.

Marston, G., Moss, J., & Quiggin, J. (2010). Introduction: Shifting risk? In G. Marston, J. Moss & J. Quiggin (Eds.), *Risk, welfare and work* (pp. vii–xvi). Carlton, VIC: Melbourne University Press.

Martin, E. (2003a). Social work, the family and women's equality in post-war Australia. *Women's History Review, 12*(3), 445–468. doi: 10.1080/09612020300200368.

Martin, J. (2003b). Historical development of critical social work practice. In J. Allan, B. Pease & L. Briskman (Eds.), *Critical social work: An introduction to theories and practices* (pp. 17–31). Crows Nest, NSW: Allen & Unwin.

Martin, S. (2004). Reconceptualising social exclusion: A critical response to the neoliberal welfare reform agenda and the underclass thesis. *The Australian Journal of Social Issues, 39*(1), 79–94.

Maslach, C., Schaufeli, W. B., & Leiter, M. P. (2001). Job burnout. *Annual Review of Psychology, 52*, 397–422.

Maslow, A. H. (1943). A theory of human motivation. *Psychological Review, 50*(4), 370–396. doi: 10.1037/h0054346.

Matsuoka, A. K. (2015). Ethnic/racial minority older adults and recovery: Integrating stories of resilience and hope in social work. *British Journal of Social Work, 45*, 135–152. doi: 10.1093/bjsw/bcv120.

Mattsson, T. (2014). Intersectionality as a useful tool: Anti-oppressive social work and critical reflection. *Affilia, 29*(1), 8–17. doi: 10.1177/0886109913510659.

Mautner, T. (Ed.) (1997). *Dictionary of philosophy*. Harmondsmith, Middlesex, UK: Penguin.

McAuliffe, D. (2014). *Interprofessional ethics: Collaboration in the social, health and human services*. Port Melbourne, VIC: Cambridge University Press.

McBeath, G., & Webb, S. (2005). Post-critical social work analytics. In S. Hick, J. Fook & R. Pozzuto (Eds.), *Social work: A critical turn* (pp. 167–186). Toronto: Thompson Educational Publishing.

McCall, L. (2005). The complexity of intersectionality. *Signs, 30*(3), 1771–1800.

McCarter, A. K. (2007). The impact of hopelessness and hope on the social work profession. *Journal of Human Behavior in the Social Environment, 15*(4), 107–123. doi: 10.1300/J137v15n04_07.

McDonald, C. (2006). *Challenging social work: The institutional context of practice*. New York, NY: Palgrave Macmillan.

McDonald, C. (2010). Risk management and the human services: A case study of risk transfer and risk management. In G. Marston, J. Moss & J. Quiggin (Eds.), *Risk, welfare and work* (pp. 212–232). Carlton, VIC: Melbourne University Press.

McDonald, C., & Chenoweth, L. (2009). (Re)shaping social work: An Australian case study. *British Journal of Social Work, 39*(1), 144–160. doi: 10.1093/bjsw/bcm094.

McDonald, C., Craik, C., Hawkins, L., & Williams, J. (2011). *Professional practice in human service organisations*. Crows Nest, NSW: Allen & Unwin.

McGoldrick, M., Gerson, K., & Petry, S. (2008). *Genograms: Assessment and intervention* (3rd ed.). New York, NY; London, UK: W.W. Norton & Company.

McGoldrick, M., & Gerson, R. (1985). *Genograms in family assessment*. New York, NY: W.W. Norton & Company.

McGoldrick, M., Gerson, R., & Shellenberger, S. (1999). *Genograms: Assessment and intervention* (2nd ed.). New York, NY: W.W. Norton.

McLachlan, R., Gilfillan, G., & Gordon, J. (2013). *Deep and persistent disadvantage in Australia*. Productivity Commission Staff Working Paper, Canberra.

McLeod, S. (2007). *Psychodynamic approaches*. Retrieved August 25, 2016, from www. simplypsychology.org/psychodynamic.html.

McMahon, A. (2002). *Redefining the beginnings of social work in Australia*. Paper presented at the Australian Association of Social Work and Welfare Education Conference, Perth, Western Australia.

McNaughton, S. M. (2016). Developing pre-requisites for empathy: Increasing awareness of self, the body and the perspectives of others. *Teaching in Higher Education*, 1–15. doi: 10.1080/13562517.2016.1160218.

Meekosha, H. (2006). What the Hell are you? An intercategorical analysis of race, ethnicity, gender and disability in the Australian body politic. *Scandinavian Journal of Disability Research, 8*(2–3), 161–176. doi: 10.1080/15017410600831309.

Mehrotra, G. (2010). Toward a continuum of intersectionality theorizing for feminist social work scholarship. *Affilia, 25*(4), 417–430. doi: 10.1177/0886109910384190.

Mendes, P. (2009a). Retrenching or renovating the Australian welfare state: The paradox of the Howard government's neoliberalism. *International Journal of Social Welfare, 18*(1), 102–110. doi: 10.1111/j.1468-2397.2008.00569.x.

Mendes, P. (2009b). Tracing the origins of critical social work practice. In J. Allan, L. Briskman & B. Pease (Eds.), *Critical social work: Theories and practices for a just world* (pp. 17–29). Crows Nest, NSW: Allen & Unwin.

Merriam-Webster. (2015). *Isomorphic*. Retrieved June 7, 2016, from www.merriam-webster.com/dictionary/isomorphic.

Mezirow, J. (1990). *Fostering critical reflection in adulthood: A guide to transformative and emancipatory learning*. San Francisco, CA: Jossey-Bass Publishers.

Mezirow, J. (1998). On critical reflection. *Adult Education Quarterly, 48*(3), 185–198. doi: 10.1177/074171369804800305.

Miller, D. B., & Hokenstad, T. (2014). Rolling downhill: Effects of austerity on local government social services in the United States. *Journal of Sociology and Social Welfare, 41*(2), 93–108.

Miller, D. T. (2001). Disrespect and the experience of injustice. *Annual review of psychology, 52*, 527–553.

Milner, J., Myers, S., & O'Byrne, P. (2015). *Assessment in social work* (4th ed.). London, UK: Palgrave Macmillan.

Milner, J., & O'Byrne, P. (2002). *Assessment in social work* (2nd ed.). Basingstoke, UK: Palgrave Macmillan.

Moore, S. E., Bledsoe, L. K., Perry, A. R., & Robinson, M. A. (2011). Social work students and self-care: A model assignment for teaching. *Journal of Social Work Education, 47*(3), 545–553.

Moore, T. (2013). Critical thinking: Seven definitions in search of a concept. *Studies in Higher Education, 38*(4), 506–522.

Moreton-Robinson, A. (2004). Whiteness, epistemology and Indigenous representation. In A. Moreton-Robinson (Ed.), *Whitening race: Essays in social and cultural criticism* (pp. 75–88). Canberra: Aboriginal Studies Press.

Morley, C. (2004). Critical reflection in social work: A response to globalisation? *International Journal of Social Welfare, 13*(4), 297–303. doi: 10.1111/j.1468-2397. 2004.00325.x.

Morley, C. (2008). Teaching critical practice: Resisting structural domination through critical reflection. *Social Work Education, 27*(4), 407–421. doi: 10.1080/02615470701379925.

Morley, C. (2009). Conducting risk assessments. In J. Maidment & R. Egan (Eds.), *Practice skills in social work and social welfare: More than just common sense* (2nd ed., pp. 148–169). Crows Nest, NSW: Allen & Unwin.

Morley, C. (2011). Critical reflection as an educational process: A practice example. *Advances in Social Work and Welfare Education, 13*(1), 7–28.

Morley, C., & Dunstan, J. (2012). Critical reflection: A response to neoliberal challenges to field education? *Social Work Education, 32*(2), 141–156. doi: 10.1080/02615479. 2012.730141.

Morrison, T. (2007). Emotional intelligence, emotion and social work: Context, characteristics, complications and contribution. *British Journal of Social Work, 37*(2), 245–263. doi: 10.1093/bjsw/bcl016.

Morrow, M., Hankivsky, O., & Varcoe, C. (2004). Women and violence: The effects of dismantling the welfare state. *Critical Social Policy, 24*(3), 358–384. doi: 10.1177/0261018304044364.

Moss, B. (2012). *Communication skills in health & social care* (2nd ed.). Los Angeles; London, UK: SAGE.

Moss, D. (2015). The roots and genealogy of humanistic psychology. In K. J. Schneider, J. F. Pierson & J. F. T. Bugental (Eds.), *The handbook of humanistic psychology theory, research, and practice* (2nd ed.). Los Angeles: SAGE.

Moss, J. (2010). Two conceptions of risk. In G. Marston, J. Moss & J. Quiggin (Eds.), *Risk, welfare and work* (pp. 128–142). Carlton, VIC: Melbourne University Press.

Mullaly, B. (2007). *The new structural social work* (3rd ed.). Ontario: Oxford University Press.

Mullaly, R. P. (1997). *Structural social work: Ideology, theory, and practice* (2nd ed.). Toronto; New York, NY: Oxford University Press.

Mullen, E. J. (2004). Outcomes measurement. *Social Work in Mental Health, 2*(2–3), 77–93. doi: 10.1300/J200v02n02_06.

Murphy, J. (2010). Welfare regimes and risk speculations. In G. Marston, J. Moss & J. Quiggan (Eds.), *Risk, welfare and work* (pp. 24–47). Carlton, VIC: Melbourne University Press.

Myers, S. (2000). Empathic listening: Reports on the experience of being heard. *Journal of Humanistic Psychology, 40*(2), 148–173. doi: 10.1177/0022167800402004.

Nakhid, C., Majavu, A., Bowleg, L., Mooney, S., Ryan, I., Mayeda, D., ... Halstead, D. (2015). "Intersectionality revisited: Moving beyond the contours of race, class, gender": Notes on an Intersectionality Symposium. *New Zealand Sociology, 30*(4), 190.

Nathan, J. (2013). Psychodynamic theory: The essential elements. In M. Davies (Ed.), *The Blackwell companion to social work* (pp. 463–465). Somerset, NJ: John Wiley & Sons.

National Association of Social Workers. (2016). *Code of ethics*. Retrieved June 16, 2016, from www.socialworkers.org/pubs/code/code.asp.

Nelson-Becker, H., Nakashima, M., & Canda, E. R. (2006). Spirituality in professional helping interventions. In B. Berkman & S. D'Ambruoso (Eds.), *Handbook of social work in health and aging* (pp. 797–807). Oxford, UK: Oxford University Press.

Nicolson, P., Bayne, R., & Owen, J. (2006). *Applied psychology for social workers* (3rd ed.). Basingstoke, UK; New York, NY: Palgrave Macmillan.

Niedenthal, P. M., & Brauer, M. (2012). Social functionality of human emotion. *Annual Review of Psychology, 63*(1), 259–285. doi: 10.1146/annurev.psych.121208. 131605.

Nipperess, S. (2013). *Human rights: A challenge to critical social work practice and education.* (PhD dissertation), Curtin University Perth.

Noddings, N. (2003). *Caring: A feminine approach to ethics and moral education.* Retrieved November 14, 2016, from http://ezproxy.ecu.edu.au/login?url=http://site.ebrary. com/lib/ecu/Top?id=10745983.

Nolan, D., & Quinn, N. (2012). The context of risk management in mental health social work. *Practice, 24*(3), 175–188. doi: 10.1080/09503153.2012.679257.

Nozick, R. (1974). *Anarchy, state, and utopia.* Oxford, UK; Cambridge, MA: Blackwell Publishers.

Nzira, V., & Williams, P. (2009). *Anti-oppressive practice in health and social care.* London, UK: SAGE.

O'Brien, M. (2013). Social work, poverty and disadvantage. In M. Connolly & L. Harms (Eds.), *Social work: Contexts and practice* (pp. 74–86). South Melbourne, VIC: Oxford University Press.

O'Connor, I., Wilson, J., & Setterlund, D. (2003). *Social work and welfare practice* (4th ed.). Frenchs Forest, NSW: Pearson Education Australia.

O'Connor, I., Wilson, J., Setterlund, D., & Hughes, M. (2008). *Social work and human service practice* (5th ed.). Frenchs Forest, NSW: Pearson Education Australia.

O'Farrell, C. (2005). *Michel Foucault.* London, UK: SAGE.

O'Neill, O. (1986). The public use of reason. *Political Theory, 14*(4), 523–551. doi: 10.2307/191279.

O'Neill, O. (2015). Response to John Tasioulas. In R. Cruft, M. Liao & M. Renzo (Eds.), *Philosophical foundations of human rights.* Oxford Scholarship Online: Oxford University Press.

O'Sullivan, T. (2005). Some theoretical propositions on the nature of practice wisdom. *Journal of Social Work, 5*(2), 221–242. doi: 10.1177/1468017305054977.

Oatley, K. (2009). Communications to self and others: Emotional experience and its skills. *Emotion Review, 1*(3), 206–213. doi: 10.1177/1754073909103588.

Oatley, K. (2010). Two movements in emotions: Communication and reflection. *Emotion Review, 2*(1), 29–35. doi: 10.1177/1754073909345542.

Oksala, J. (2007). *How to read Foucault.* London, UK: Granta Books.

Osmond, J. (2006). Knowledge use in social work practice. *Journal of Social Work, 6*(3), 221–237. doi: 10.1177/1468017306066383.

Owen, D. (1999). Orientation and enlightenment: An essay on critique and genealogy. In S. Ashenden & D. Owen (Eds.), *Foucault contra Habermas* (pp. 21–44). London, UK: SAGE.

Ozanne, E., & Rose, D. J. (2013). *The organisational context of human services practice.* South Yarra, VIC: Palgrave Macmillan.

Parton, N. (2000). Some thoughts on the relationship between theory and practice in and for social work. *British Journal of Social Work, 30*(4), 449–463. doi: 10.1093/bjsw/30.4.449.

Pateman, C. (1988). *The sexual contract.* Cambridge, UK: Polity Press.

Pateman, C., & Gross, E. (1986). *Feminist challenges: Social and political theory.* Sydney, NSW: Allen & Unwin.

Payne, A. (2009). Working poor in Australia: An analysis of poverty among households in which a member is employed. *Family Matters, 81*, 15–24.

Payne, G. (2006). *Social divisions* (2nd ed.). Basingstoke, UK; New York, NY: Palgrave Macmillan.

Payne, M. (2005). *Modern social work theory* (3rd ed.). Basingstoke, UK: Palgrave Macmillan.

Payne, M. (2011). Risk, security and resilience work in social work practice. *Revista de Asistenta Sociala, 10*(1), 7.

Payne, M. (2014). *Modern social work theory* (4th ed.). Basingstoke, UK: Palgrave Macmillan.

Pease, B., & Fook, J. (1999a). Postmodern critical theory and emancipatory social work practice. In B. Pease & J. Fook (Eds.), *Transforming social work practice: Postmodern critical perspectives* (pp. 1–22). St Leonards, NSW: Allen & Unwin.

Pease, B., & Fook, J. (Eds.). (1999b). *Transforming social work practice.* St Leonards, NSW: Allen & Unwin.

Penney, L. M., & Spector, P. E. (2005). Job stress, incivility, and counterproductive work behavior (CWB): The moderating role of negative affectivity. *Journal of Organizational Behavior, 26*(7), 777–796. doi: 10.1002/job.336.

Penny, A. M., Waschbusch, D. A., Klein, R. M., Corkum, P., & Eskes, G. (2009). Developing a measure of sluggish cognitive tempo for children: Content validity, factor structure, and reliability. *Psychological Assessment, 21*(3), 380–389. doi: 10.1037/a0016600.

Pentaraki, M. (2013). 'If we do not cut social spending, we will end up like Greece': Challenging consent to austerity through social work action. *Critical Social Policy, 33*(4), 700–711. doi: 10.1177/0261018313489941.

Perlman, H. H. (1957). *Social casework: A problem-solving process.* Chicago, IL: Chicago University Press.

Perry, W. G. (1970). *Forms of intellectual and ethical development in the college years: A scheme.* Fort Worth: Harcourt Brace Jovanovich College Publishers.

Petersén, A. C., & Olsson, J. I. (2014). Calling evidence-based practice into question: Acknowledging phronetic knowledge in social work. *British Journal of Social Work, 45*(5), 1581–1597. doi: 10.1093/bjsw/bcu020.

Phillips, C. (2014). Spirituality and social work: Introducing a spiritual dimension into social work education and practice. *Aotearoa New Zealand Social Work, 26*(4), 65–77.

Phoenix, A., & Bauer, E. (2012). Challenging gender practices: Intersectional narratives of sibling relations and parent–child engagements in transnational serial migration. *European Journal of Women's Studies, 19*(4), 490–504. doi: 10.1177/1350506812455994.

Pinker, S., & Goldstein, R. N. (2012). *Steven Pinker and Rebecca Newberger Goldstein: The long reach of reason.* Ted Talk Video. Retrieved August 25, 2016, from www.ted.com/talks/steven_pinker_and_rebecca_newberger_goldstein_the_long_reach_of_reason?language=en.

Plath, D. (2006). Evidence-based practice: Current issues and future directions. *Australian Social Work, 59*(1), 56–72. doi: 10.1080/03124070500449788.

Plath, D. (2009). Evidence based practice. In M. Gray & S. A. Webb (Eds.), *Social work theories and methods* (pp. 172–183). Los Angeles, CA: SAGE.

Plath, D. (2014). Implementing evidence-based practice: An organisational perspective. *British Journal of Social Work, 44*(4), 905–923. doi: 10.1093/bjsw/bcs169.

Pope, N. D., & Lee, J. (2015). A picture is worth a thousand words: Exploring the use of genograms in practice. *The New Social Worker, Spring,* 10–12.

Poulin, J. (2000). *Collaborative social work: Strengths-based generalist practice.* Itasca, IL: F.E. Peacock Publishers.

Preston-Shoot, M., Roberts, G., & Vernon, S. (2001). Values in social work law: Strained relations or sustaining relationships? *Journal of Social Welfare and Family Law, 23*(1), 1–22. doi: 10.1080/09649060010012246.

Pruce, J. R. (2015). The practice turn in human rights research. In J. R. Pruce (Ed.), *The social practice of human rights* (pp. 1–20). New York, NY: Palgrave Macmillan.

Rabinow, P., & Rose, N. S. (2003). *Thoughts on the concept of biopower today. Vital politics: Health, medicine and bioeconomics into the twenty first century.* Retrieved March 22, 2007, from www.lse.ac.uk/collections/sociology/pdf/RabinowandRose-BiopowerToday03.pdf.

Ramo, J. (2009). *The age of the unthinkable: Why the new world disorder constantly surprises us and what we can do about it.* New York, NY; Boston, MA; London, UK: Little, Brown and Company.

Rawls, J. (1971). *A theory of justice.* London, UK: Oxford University Press.

Redmond, B. (2004). *Reflection in action: Developing reflective practice in health and social services.* Aldershot, UK: Ashgate.

Regehr, C. (2011). Crisis theory and social work treatment. In F. J. Turner (Ed.), *Social work treatment: Interlocking theoretical approaches* (pp. 134–143). New York, NY: Oxford University Press.

Richardson, L. (2001). Getting personal: Writing-stories. *International Journal of Qualitative Studies in Education, 14*(1), 33–38. doi: 10.1080/09518390010007647.

Rivest, M.-P., & Moreau, N. (2014). Between emancipatory practice and disciplinary interventions: Empowerment and contemporary social normativity. *British Journal of Social Work, 45*(6), 1855–1870. doi: 10.1093/bjsw/bcu017.

Robbins, S. P., Chatterjee, D., & Canda, E. R. (2006). *Contemporary human behaviour theory: A critical perspective.* Boston, MA: Pearson Education Australia.

Robbins, S. P., Chatterjee, P., & Canda, E. R. (2012a). The nature of theories. In S. P. Robbins, P. Chatterjee & E. R. Canda (Eds.), *Contemporary human behaviour theory: A critical perspective for social work* (pp. 1–24). Upper Saddle River, NJ: Allyn & Bacon.

Robbins, S. P., Chatterjee, P., & Canda, E. R. (2012b). Systems theory. In S. P. Robbins, P. Chatterjee & E. R. Canda (Eds.), *Contemporary human behaviour theory: A critical perspective for social work* (pp. 25–58). Upper Saddle River, NJ: Allyn & Bacon.

Robbins, S. P., Chatterjee, P., & Canda, E. R. (2012c). Theories of life span development In S. P. Robbins, P. Chatterjee & E. R. Canda (Eds.), *Contemporary human behaviour theory: A critical perspective* (pp. 201–259). Upper Saddle River, NJ: Allyn & Bacon.

Roberts, S. J., Scherer, L. L., & Bowyer, C. J. (2011). Job stress and incivility: What role does psychological capital play? *Journal of Leadership & Organizational Studies, 18*(4), 449–458.

Robinson, H., & Kaplan, C. (2011). Psychosocial theory and social work treatment. In F. J. Turner (Ed.), *Social work treatment: Interlocking theoretical approaches* (pp. 387–401). Upper Saddle River, NJ: Allyn & Bacon.

Robinson, K. (n. d.). *Social work and human rights conference.* School of Social Policy Sociology and Social Research. University of Kent. Retrieved November 14, 2016, from http://cdn.basw.co.uk/upload/basw_102621-6.pdf.

Roets, G., Rutten, K., Roose, R., Vandekinderen, C., & Soetaert, R. (2015). Constructing the 'child at risk' in social work reports: A way of seeing is a way of not seeing. *Children & Society, 29*(3), 198–208. doi: 10.1111/chso.12115.

Rogers, C. R. (2012). *Client-centered therapy: Its current practice, implications and theory.* UK: Constable. Retrieved November 14, 2016, from www.ecu.eblib.com/patron/FullRecord.aspx?p=895378.

Rogers, K. (2013). Hope springs fraternal: Engendering hope in anti-poverty activism. *Canadian Social Work Review/Revue Canadienne de Service Social, 30*(2), 217–234.

Rohr, E. (2012). Challenging empathy. *Clinical Social Work Journal, 40*(4), 450–456. doi: 10.1007/s10615-011-0339-0.

Rojek, C., Collins, S., & Peacock, G. (1988). *Social work and received ideas.* London, UK: Routledge.

Roscigno, V. J., Hodson, R., & Lopez, S. H. (2009). Workplace incivilities: The role of interest conflicts, social closure and organizational chaos. *Work, Employment & Society, 23*(4), 747–773. doi: 10.1177/0950017009344875.

Rose, N. (1996a). Governing "advanced" liberal democracies. In A. Barry, T. Osbourne & N. Rose (Eds.), *Foucault and political reason: Liberalism, neoliberalism and the rationalities of government* (pp. 37–66). London, UK: UCL Press Ltd.

Rose, N. (1996b). *Inventing our selves: Psychology, power, and personhood.* Cambridge, UK; New York, NY: Cambridge University Press.

Rose, N. (2000). Government and control. *British Journal of Criminology, 40*(2), 321–339. doi: 10.1093/bjc/40.2.321.

Rose, N. (2013). The human sciences in a biological age. *Theory, Culture & Society, 30*(3), 3–34. doi: 10.1177/0263276412456569.

Rose, N., & Miller, P. (1992). Political power beyond the State: Problematics of government. *The British Journal of Sociology, 43*(2), 173–205.

Rowe, S., Baldry, E., & Earles, W. (2015). Decolonising social work research: Learning from critical Indigenous approaches. *Australian Social Work, 68*(3), 296–308.

Rowe, W. (2011). Client-centred theory: The enduring principles for a person-centred approach. In F. J. Turner (Ed.), *Social work treatment: Interlocking theoretical approaches* (pp. 58–76). Upper Saddle River, NJ: Allyn & Bacon.

Ruben, D.-H. (2010). W.B. Gallie and essentially contested concepts. *Philosophical Papers, 39*(2), 257–270. doi: 10.1080/05568641.2010.503465.

Ruch, G. (2000). Self and social work: Towards an integrated model of learning. *Journal of Social Work Practice, 14*(2), 99–112. doi: 10.1080/02650530020020500.

Ruch, G. (2002). From triangle to spiral: Reflective practice in social work education, practice and research. *Social Work Education, 21*(2), 199–216. doi: 10.1080/02615470220126435.

Ruch, G. (2005). Relationship-based practice and reflective practice: Holistic approaches to contemporary child care social work. *Child & Family Social Work, 10*(2), 111–123. doi: 10.1111/j.1365-2206.2005.00359.x.

Ruch, G. (2009). Identifying 'the critical' in a relationship-based model of reflection. *European Journal of Social Work, 12*(3), 349–362. doi: 10.1080/13691450902930761.

Ruch, G. (2010a). The contemporary context of relationship-based practice. In G. Ruch, D. Turney & A. Ward (Eds.), *Relationship-based social work: Getting to the heart of practice* (pp. 13–28). London, UK: Jessica Kingsley Publishers.

Ruch, G. (2010b). Theoretical frameworks informing relationship-based practice. In G. Ruch, D. Turney & A. Ward (Eds.), *Relationship-based social work: Getting to the heart of practice.* (pp. 29–45). London, UK: Jessica Kingsley Publishers.

Ruch, G., Turney, D., & Ward, A. (2010). *Relationship-based social work: Getting to the heart of practice.* London, UK: Jessica Kingsley Publishers.

Rudy, K. (2000). Queer theory and feminism. *Women's Studies, 29*(2), 195–216. doi: 10.1080/00497878.2000.9979308.

Ruffolo, M. C., Perron, B. E., & Voshel, E. H. (2016). *Direct social work practice: Theories and skills for becoming an evidence-based practitioner.* Thousand Oaks, CA: SAGE.

Saddler, S., Tyler, T. G., Maldonado, C., Cleveland, R., & Thompson, L. K. (2011). Connecting dropouts to career pathways. *Reclaiming Children and Youth, 20*(2), 37–39.

Said, E. (1993). *Culture and imperialism.* New York, NY: Vintage Books.

Saleebey, D. (2009). *The strengths perspective in social work practice* (5th ed.). Boston, MA: Allyn & Bacon.

Samson, P. L. (2014). Practice wisdom: The art and science of social work. *Journal of Social Work Practice, 29*(2), 119–131. doi: 10.1080/02650533.2014.922058.

Sánchez-Moreno, E., de La Fuente Roldán, I.-N., Gallardo-Peralta, L. P., & Barrón López de Roda, A. (2015). Burnout, informal social support and psychological distress among social workers. *British Journal of Social Work, 45*(8), 2368–2386. doi: 10.1093/bjsw/bcu084.

Sandhu, S. (2015). *Richest one per cent owns more than half the world's wealth.* Retrieved August 8, 2016, from www.independent.co.uk/news/world/worlds-richest-one-percent-owns-more-than-half-the-worlds-wealth-according-to-report-a6693226.html.

Saunders, P. (2005). *The poverty wars: Reconnecting research with reality.* Sydney, NSW: UNSW Press.

Sayer, A. (2005). Class, moral worth and recognition. *Sociology, 39*(5), 947–963.

Sayer, A. (2011). *Why things matter to people: Social science, values and ethical life.* The Edinburgh Building. Cambridge, UK: Cambridge University Press.

Schatzki, T. R. (2001). Introduction: Practice theory. In T. R. Schatzki, K. K. Cetina & E. Von Savigny (Eds.), *The practice turn in contemporary theory* (pp. 1–14). London, UK: Routledge.

Schatzki, T. R., Cetina, K. K., & Savigny, E. (2001). *The practice turn in contemporary theory.* Retrieved November 14, 2016, from http://ezproxy.ecu.edu.au/login?url=http://site.ebrary.com/lib/ecu/Top?id=10095826.

Schischka, J., Dalziel, P., & Saunders, C. (2008). Applying Sen's capability approach to poverty alleviation programs: Two case studies. *Journal of Human Development, 9*(2), 229–246. doi: 10.1080/14649880802078777.

Schneider, B., Ehrhart, M. G., & Macey, W. H. (2013). Organizational climate and culture. *Annual Review of Psychology, 64*(1), 361–388. doi: 10.1146/annurev-psych-113011-1 43809.

Schofield, T. (2007). Health inequity and its social determinants: A sociological commentary. *Health Sociology Review, 16*(2), 105–114.

Schon, D. A. (1983). *The reflective practitioner: How professionals think in action.* New York, NY: Basic Books.

Schon, D. A. (1987). *Educating the reflective practitioner: Toward a new design for teaching and learning in the professions.* San Francisco, CA: Jossey-Bass.

Schwandt, T. A. (2000). Three epistemological stances for qualitative inquiry. In N. K. Denzin & Y. S. Lincoln (Eds.), *Handbook of qualitative research* (pp. 189–216). Thousand Oaks, CA: SAGE.

Seligman, M. E. P. (1992). *Learned optimism.* Milsons Point, NSW: Random House Australia.

Seligman, M. E. P., & Csikszentmihalyi, M. (2000). Positive psychology: An introduction. *American Psychologist, 55*(1), 5–14. doi: 10.1037/0003-066X.55.1.5.

Shapiro, B. Z. (2003). Social justice and social work with groups: Fragile—handle with care. In N. Sullivan, E. Mesbur, N. Lang, D. Goodman & L. Mitchell (Eds.), *Social work with groups: Social justice through personal, community, and societal change* (pp. 7–24). New York, NY: Haworth Press.

Shaw, I. F. (2015). The archaeology of research practices: A social work case. *Qualitative Inquiry, 21*(1), 36–49. doi: 10.1177/1077800414542691.

Sheppard, M. (1995). Social work, social science and practice wisdom. *British Journal of Social Work, 25*(June), 265–293.

Sheppard, M. (1998). Practice validity, reflexivity and knowledge for social work. *British Journal of Social Work, 28*(5), 763–781.

Sheppard, M., Newstead, S., Di Caccavo, A., & Ryan, K. (2000). Reflexivity and the development of process knowledge in social work: A classification and empirical study. *British Journal of Social Work, 30*(4), 465–488. doi: 10.1093/bjsw/30.4.465.

Shier, M. (2011). Problem solving and social work. In F. J. Turner (Ed.), *Social work treatment: Interlocking theoretical approaches* (pp. 364–373). New York, NY: Oxford University Press.

Shildrick, T., & MacDonald, R. (2013). Poverty talk: How people experiencing poverty deny their poverty and why they blame 'the poor'. *The Sociological Review, 61*(2), 285–303. doi: 10.1111/1467-954X.12018.

Shlonsky, A., & Friend, C. (2007). Double jeopardy: Risk assessment in the context of child maltreatment and domestic violence. *Brief Treatment and Crisis Intervention, 7*(4), 253–274. doi: 10.1093/brief-treatment/mhm016.

Siegrist, J. (2005). Symmetry in social exchange and health. *European Review, 13*(S2), 145–155.

Simpson, J.A. & Weiner, E.S.C. (Eds.) (1980). *The Oxford English dictionary* (2nd edn). Volume VIII. Oxford: Clarendon Press.

Singapore Association of Social Workers. (2004). *Singapore Association of Social Workers Code of Professional Ethics* (p. 3). Singapore: SASW. Retrieved November 14, 2016, from www.sasw.org.sg/public/documents/SASWCodeofEthics2004.pdf.

Singer, P. (1993). *How are we to live? Ethics in an age of self-interest.* Melbourne, VIC: Text Publishing.

Singer, T., & Lamm, C. (2009). The social neuroscience of empathy. *Annals of the New York Academy of Sciences, 1156*(1), 81–96. doi: 10.1111/j.1749-6632.2009.04418.x.

Six, F. (2007). Building interpersonal trust within organizations: A relational signalling perspective. *Journal of Management and Governance, 11*(3), 285–309. doi: 10.1007/s10997-007-9030-9.

Smith, L. M., Andrusyszyn, M. A., & Spence Laschinger, H. K. (2010). Effects of workplace incivility and empowerment on newly-graduated nurses' organizational commitment. *Journal of Nursing Management, 18*(8), 1004–1015. doi: 10.1111/j.1365-2834.2010.01165.x.

Smith, L. T. (1999). *Decolonizing methodologies: Research and indigenous peoples.* London, UK; New York, NY; Dunedin, NZ: Zed Books; University of Otago Press; Distributed in the USA exclusively by St. Martin's Press.

Snyder, C. R. (2002). Hope theory: Rainbows in the mind. *Psychological Inquiry, 13*(4), 249–275.

Solimano, A. (2014). *Economic elites, crises, and democracy: Alternatives beyond neoliberal capitalism.* Retrieved November 14, 2016, from http://ezproxy.ecu.edu.au/login?url=http://dx.doi.org/10.1093/acprof:oso/9780199355983.001.0001.

Solomon, B. B. (1976). *Black empowerment: Social work in oppressed communities.* New York, NY: Columbia University Press.

Sowers, K. M., & Rowe, W. (2007). *Social work practice and social justice: From local to global perspective* (W. Rowe Ed.). Belmont, CA: Thomson Higher Education.

St Vincent de Paul Society. (2015). *"Sick with worry ..." Stories from the front-line of inequality, 2015.* Retrieved May 5, 2016, from www.vinnies.org.au/icms_docs/225819_Sick_with_worry_2015_national_report.pdf.

Stalker, K. (2003). Managing risk and uncertainty in social work: A literature review. *Journal of Social Work, 3*(2), 211–233. doi: 10.1177/14680173030032006.

Stanford, S. (2008). Taking a stand or playing it safe? Resisting the moral conservatism of risk in social work practice. *European Journal of Social Work, 11*(3), 209–220. doi: 10.1080/13691450802075063.

Stanovich, K. E. (2011). *Rationality and the reflective mind.* New York, NY: Oxford University Press.

Stanovich, K. E., & Toplak, M. E. (2012). Defining features versus incidental correlates of Type 1 and Type 2 processing. *Mind & Society, 11*(1), 3–13. doi: 10.1007/s11299-011-0093-6.

Stevens, I., & Hassett, P. (2012). Non-linear perspectives of risk in social care: Using complexity theory and social geography to move the focus from individual pathology to the complex human environment. *European Journal of Social Work, 15*(4), 503–513. doi: 10.1080/13691457.2012.702309.

Stevenson, O., & Parsloe, P. (1993). *Community care and empowerment.* York: Rountree Foundation with Community Care.

Stewart, C., & Koeske, G. (2006). Social work students' attitudes concerning the use of religious and spiritual interventions in social work practice. *Journal of Teaching in Social Work, 26*(1), 31–49. doi: 10.1300/J067v26n01_03.

Stewart, M. (2014). Spiritual assessment: A patient-centered approach to oncology social work practice. *Social Work in Health Care, 53*(1), 59–73. doi: 10.1080/00981389. 2013.834033.

Stolz, M. (2008). *Towards a hermeneutical understanding of the listening process*. Duquesne University, Ann Arbor, MI. UMI Number: 3303030 database.

Stueber, K. R. (2012). Varieties of empathy, neuroscience and the narrativist challenge to the contemporary theory of mind debate. *Emotion Review, 4*(1), 55–63. doi: 10.1177/1754073911421380.

Swedberg, R. (2014). From theory to theorizing. In R. Swedberg (Ed.), *Theorizing in social science: The context of discovery* (pp. 1–28). Stanford, CA: Stanford Social Sciences, an imprint of Stanford University Press.

Tasioulas, J. (2015). On the foundation of human rights. In R. Cruft, M. Liao & M. Renzo (Eds.), *Philosophical foundations of human rights* (pp. 1–44). Oxford Scholarship Online: Oxford University Press. DOI:10.1093/acprof:oso/9780199688623.003.0002. Available at http://www.oxfordscholarship.com/view/10.1093/acprof:oso/9780199688623.001.0001/acprof-9780199688623-chapter-2.

Taylor, B. J. (2010). *Professional decision-making in social work*. Exeter, UK: Learning Matters.

Taylor, B. J. (2012). Models for professional judgement in social work. *European Journal of Social Work, 15*(4), 546–562. doi: 10.1080/13691457.2012.702310.

Taylor, C., & White, S. (2001). Knowledge, truth and reflexivity: The problem of judgement in social work. *Journal of Social Work, 1*(1), 37–59. doi: 10.1177/146801730100100104.

Taylor, C., & White, S. (2006). Knowledge and reasoning in social work: Educating for humane judgement. *British Journal of Social Work, 36*(6), 937–954. doi: 10.1093/bjsw/bch365.

Taylor, I. (1996). Facilitating reflective learning. In N. Gould & I. Taylor (Eds.), *Reflective learning in social work: Research, theory and practice* (pp. 79–95). Aldershot, UK: Ashgate.

Taylor, S. G., Bedeian, A. G., & Kluemper, D. H. (2012). Linking workplace incivility to citizenship performance: The combined effects of affective commitment and conscientiousness. *Journal of Organizational Behavior, 33*(7), 878–893. doi: 10.1002/job.773.

Teater, B. (2013a). Motivational interviewing (MI). In M. Davies (Ed.), *The Blackwell companion to social work* (pp. 452–454). Somerset, NJ: John Wiley & Sons.

Teater, B. (2013b). Solution-focused brief therapy (SFBT). In M. Davies (Ed.), *The Blackwell companion to social work* (pp. 480–483). Somerset, NJ: John Wiley & Sons.

Telle, N.-T., & Pfister, H.-R. (2016). Positive empathy and prosocial behavior: A neglected link. *Emotion Review, 8*(2), 154–163. doi: 10.1177/1754073915586817.

The British Association of Social Workers. (2012). *The code of ethics for social work*. Retrieved May 19, 2015, from http://cdn.basw.co.uk/upload/basw_112315-7.pdf.

The British Library. (n. d.). *The communist manifesto – bourgeoisie and proletariat*. Retrieved August 25, 2016, from www.bl.uk/learning/histcitizen/21cc/utopia/methods1/bourgeoisie1/bourgeoisie.html.

Thompson, N. (1992). *Existentialism and social work*. Aldershot, UK: Avebury.

Thompson, N. (1995). *Theory and practice in health and social welfare*. Buckingham, UK: Open University Press.

Thompson, N. (1998). *Promoting equality: Challenging discrimination and oppression in the human services.* Basingstoke, UK: Macmillan.

Thompson, N. (2006). *Anti-discriminatory practice* (4th ed.). Basingstoke, UK; New York, NY: Palgrave Macmillan.

Thompson, N., Stradling, S., Murphy, M., & O'Neill, P. (1996). Stress and organizational culture. *British Journal of Social Work, 26*(5), 647–665.

Thompson, S., & Thompson, N. (2008). *The critically reflective practitioner.* Basingstoke, UK: Palgrave Macmillan.

Thyer, B. A. (2011). Social learning theory and social work treatment. In F. J. Turner (Ed.), *Social work treatment: Interlocking theoretical approaches* (pp. 437–446). Upper Saddle River, NJ: Allyn & Bacon.

Tonkens, E., & Verplanke, L. (2013). When social security fails to provide emotional security: Single parent households and the contractual welfare state. *Social Policy and Society, 12*(3), 451–460. doi: 10.1017/S1474746413000110.

Toth, M. (2012). *Exploring a relationship between workers' perceptions of leaders and workers' self-efficacy in social services.* (Dissertation/Thesis). Retrieved November 14, 2016, from https://etd.ohiolink.edu/!etd.send_file?accession=bgsu1333397023&dis position=inline.

Treater, B. (2013). Cognitive behavioural therapy (CBT). In M. Davies (Ed.), *The Blackwell companion to social work* (pp. 423–427). Somerset, NJ: John Wiley & Sons.

Trevithick, P. (2011). *Social work skills and knowledge: A practice handbook.* Retrieved November 14, 2016, from http://ECU.eblib.com.au/patron/FullRecord.aspx?p= 915558.

Trotter, C. (2015). *Working with involuntary clients: A guide to practice* (3rd ed.). Crows Nest, NSW: Allen & Unwin.

Tsang, N. M. (2013). Knowledge, professional and practice integration in social work education. *British Journal of Social Work, 44*(6), 401. doi: 10.1093/bjsw/bcs195.

Tully, J. (1989). Wittgenstein and political philosophy: Understanding practices of critical reflection. *Political Theory, 17*(2), 172–204.

Tully, J. (2000). Struggles over recognition and distribution. *Constellations, 7*(4), 469–482. doi: 10.1111/1467-8675.00203.

Tully, J. (2008a). Public philosophy as a critical activity. In J. Tully (Ed.), *Public philosophy in a new key – Volume 1: Democracy and civic freedom* (pp. 1–38). Cambridge, UK: Cambridge University Press.

Tully, J. (2008b). A new field of democracy and freedom. In J. Tully (Ed.), *Public philosophy in a new key - Volume 1: Democracy and civic freedom* (pp. 291–316). Cambridge, UK: Cambridge University Press.

Turbett, C. (2014). *Doing radical social work.* Basingstoke, UK: Palgrave Macmillan.

Turnage, B. F., Hong, Y. J., Stevenson, A. P., & Edwards, B. (2012). Social work students' perceptions of themselves and others: Self-esteem, empathy, and forgiveness. *Journal of Social Service Research, 38*(1), 89–99. doi: 10.1080/01488376.2011.610201.

Turner, B. S. (1997). From governmentality to risk: Some reflections on Foucault's contribution to medical sociology. In A. Petersen & R. Bunton (Eds.), *Foucault health and medicine* (pp. ix–xxi). London, UK; New York, NY: Routledge.

Turner, F. J. (2011). *Social work treatment: Interlocking theoretical approaches* (5th ed.). New York, NY: Oxford University Press.

Turner, J., & Jaco, R. M. (1996). Problem-solving theory and social work treatment. In F. J. Turner (Ed.), *Social work treatment: Interlocking theoretical approaches* (pp. 503–523). New York, NY: The Free Press.

Turner, L. M. (2013). Encouraging professional growth among social work students through literature assignments: Narrative literature's capacity to inspire professional growth and empathy. *British Journal of Social Work, 43*(5), 853–871. doi: 10.1093/bjsw/bcs011.

Twomey, M. (2015). Why worry about autonomy? *Ethics and Social Welfare, 9*(3), 255–268. doi: 10.1080/17496535.2015.1024154.

UNESCO. (2016). *Poverty.* Retrieved May 5, 2016, from www.unesco.org/new/en/social-and-human-sciences/themes/international-migration/glossary/poverty/.

UNICEF. (2016). *Convention on the rights of the child.* Retrieved July 19, 2016, from www.unicef.org/crc/.

United Nations. (1996a). *About the universal declaration of human rights translation project.* Retrieved July 19, 2016, from www.ohchr.org/EN/UDHR/Pages/Introduction.aspx.

United Nations. (1996b). *Declaration on the rights of indigenous peoples.* Retrieved July 19, 2016, from www.ohchr.org/EN/Issues/IPeoples/Pages/Declaration.aspx.

United Nations. (1996c). *Human rights of persons with disabilities.* Retrieved July 19, 2016, from www.ohchr.org/EN/Issues/Disability/Pages/DisabilityIndex.aspx.

United Nations. (2000). *Convention on the elimination of all forms of discrimination against women.* Retrieved July 19, 2016, from www.un.org/womenwatch/daw/cedaw/.

United Nations. (2013). *Inequality matters: Report of the world social situation 2013.* Retrieved August 5, 2016, from www.un.org/esa/socdev/documents/reports/InequalityMatters.pdf.

United Nations. (2016). *United Nations Declaration of Human Rights.* Retrieved July 18, 2016, from www.un.org/en/universal-declaration-human-rights.

Vaillant, G. E. (1977). *Adaptation to life.* Boston, MA: Little Brown.

van de Luitgaarden, G. M. J. (2009). Evidence-based practice in social work: Lessons from judgment and decision-making theory. *British Journal of Social Work, 39*(2), 243–260. doi: 10.1093/bjsw/bcm117.

Van Soest, D. (2012). Confronting our fears and finding hope in difficult times: Social work as a force for social justice. *Journal of Progressive Human Services, 23*(2), 95–109. doi: 10.1080/10428232.2012.666723.

Veninga, J. E. (2015). *Free speech is no excuse for Muslim-baiting.* Retrieved July 19, 2016, from https://theconversation.com/free-speech-is-no-excuse-for-muslim-baiting-47472.

Vokey, D., & Kerr, J. (2011). Intuition and professional wisdom: Can we teach moral discernment? In L. Bondi, D. Carr & C. Clarke (Eds.), *Towards professional wisdom: Practical deliberation in the people professions* (pp. 63–79). Farnham, Surrey, UK: Ashgate.

Walby, S., Armstrong, J., & Strid, S. (2012). Intersectionality: Multiple inequalities in social theory. *Sociology, 46*(2), 224–240. doi: 10.1177/0038038511416164.

Walklate, S., & Mythen, G. (2011). Beyond risk theory: Experiential knowledge and 'knowing otherwise'. *Criminology & Criminal Justice, 11*(2), 99–113. doi: 10.1177/1748895811398456.

Wall, T. F. (2005). *On human nature: An introduction to philosophy.* Belmont, CA: Thomson Wadsworth.

Wallace, J., & Pease, B. (2011). Neoliberalism and Australian social work: Accommodation or resistance? *Journal of Social Work, 11*(2), 132–142. doi: 10.1177/1468017310387318.

Walter, H. (2012). Social cognitive neuroscience of empathy: Concepts, circuits, and genes. *Emotion Review, 4*(1), 9–17. doi: 10.1177/1754073911421379.

Ward, A. (2010). The learning relationship: Learning and development of relationship-based practice. In G. Ruch, D. Turney & A. Ward (Eds.), *Relationship-based social work: Getting to the heart of practice* (pp. 183–198). London, UK: Jessica Kingsley Publishers.

Ward, T., & Connolly, M. (2007). *Morals, rights and practice in the human services: Effective and fair decision-making in health, social care and criminal justice.* London, UK: Jessica Kingsley Publishers.

Warner, D. F., & Brown, T. H. (2011). Understanding how race/ethnicity and gender define age-trajectories of disability: An intersectionality approach. *Social Science & Medicine, 72*(8), 1236–1248. doi: 10.1016/j.socscimed.2011.02.034.

Watabe, Y., Owens, J. S., Evans, S. W., & Brandt, N. E. (2014). The relationship between sluggish cognitive tempo and impairment in children with and without ADHD. *Journal of Abnormal Child Psychology, 42*(1), 105–115. doi: 10.1007/s10802-013-9767-3.

Watts, L. (2015a). An autoethnographic exploration of learning and teaching reflective practice. *Social Work Education, 34*(4), 363–376. doi: 10.1080/02615479.2015.1016903.

Watts, L. (2015b). *Thinking differently about reflective practice in social work education in Australia: A rhapsody* (Doctoral Dissertation), Edith Cowan University, Bunbury. Retrieved November 14, 2016, from http://ro.ecu.edu.au/theses/1758.

Watts, L., & Hodgson, D. (2013). Knowing that and knowing how: Building student confidence through skills assessment. *Advances in Social Work and Welfare Education, 14*(1), 75–88.

Watts, L., & Hodgson, D. (2015). Assessing the needs of carers of people with mental illness: Lessons from a collaborative study of a needs assessment tool. *Practice: Social Work in Action 28*(4), 235–252. doi: 10.1080/09503153.2015.1120279.

Waugh, F. (2011). Risk assessment: Working within a legal framework. In A. O'Hara & R. Pockett (Eds.), *Skills for human service practice: Working with individuals, groups and communities* (2nd ed., pp. 102–120). South Melbourne, VIC: Oxford University Press.

Webb, S. (2001). Some considerations on the validity of evidence-based practice in social work. *British Journal of Social Work, 31*(1), 57–79. doi: 10.1093/bjsw/31.1.57.

Webb, S. A. (2009). Against difference and diversity in social work: The case of human rights. *International Journal of Social Welfare, 18*(3), 307–316. doi: 10.1111/j.1468-2397.2009.00659.x.

Weber, Z., & Giles, R. (2011). Conducting assessment: Some general guidelines. In A. O'Hara & R. Pockett (Eds.), *Skills for human service practice: Working with individuals, groups and communities* (2nd ed., pp. 166–184). South Melbourne, VIC: Oxford University Press.

Weedon, C. (1999). *Feminism, theory, and the politics of difference.* Malden, MA: Blackwell Publishers.

Wendt, S., Schiller, W., Cheers, B., Francis, K., & Lonne, B. (2012). Exploring social workers' personal domains in rural practice. *Journal of Social Work, 12*(2), 194–210. doi: 10.1177/1468017310382323.

Wenzlaff, R. M., & Wegner, D. M. (2000). Thought suppression. *Annual Review of Psychology, 51*(1), 59–91.

White, F. A., Hayes, B. K., & Livesey, D. J. (2013). *Developmental psychology: From infancy to adulthood* (3rd ed.). Frenchs Forest, NSW: Pearson Education Australia.

White, S. (2009). Fabled uncertainty in social work: A coda to Spafford et al. *Journal of Social Work, 9*(2), 222–235. doi: 10.1177/1468017308101824.

White, S., Fook, J., & Gardner, F. (2006). *Critical reflection in health and social care* (pp. xiv, 273 p.). Retrieved November 14, 2016, from http://0-site.ebrary.com.library.ecu.edu.au/lib/ecu/Doc?id=10175268.

White, S., & Stancombe, J. (2003). *Clinical judgement in the health and welfare professions: Extending the evidence base.* Buckingham, UK: Open University Press.

Wiley, N. (2010). Inner speech and agency. In M. S. Archer (Ed.), *Conversations about reflexivity* (pp. 17–38). Abingdon, UK: Routledge.

Wilkins, D. (2015). Balancing risk and protective factors: How do social workers and social work managers analyse referrals that may indicate children are at risk of significant harm. *British Journal of Social Work, 45*(1), 395–411.

Williams, G. (2016). *Kant's account of reason.* The Stanford Encyclopedia of Philosophy. Retrieved November 14, 2016, from http://plato.stanford.edu/entries/kant-reason/.

Wilson, A., & Beresford, P. (2000). 'Anti-oppressive practice': Emancipation or appropriation? *British Journal of Social Work, 30*(5), 553–573. doi: 10.1093bjsw/30.5.553.

Wong, Y.-L. R., & Vinsky, J. (2009). Speaking from the margins: A critical reflection on the 'spiritual-but-not-religious' discourse in social work. *British Journal of Social Work, 39*(7), 1343–1359. doi: 10.1093/bjsw/bcn032.

Woods, M. E., & Hollis, F. (2000). *Casework: A psychosocial therapy* (5th ed.). Boston, MA: McGraw-Hill.

Wronka, J., & Staub-Bernasconi, S. (2012). Human rights. In T. Hokenstad, K. H. Lyons, N. Hall, N. Huegler & M. Pawar (Eds.), *The SAGE handbook of international social work* (pp. 70–84). London, UK: SAGE.

Yanca, S. J., & Johnson, L. C. (2008). *Generalist social work practice with families.* Boston, MA: Pearson Education.

Yelloly, M., & Henkel, M. (Eds.). (1995). *Learning and teaching in social work.* London, UK: Jessica Kingsley Publishers.

Yip, J. A., & Côté, S. (2013). The emotionally intelligent decision maker: Emotion-understanding ability reduces the effect of incidental anxiety on risk taking. *Psychological Science, 24*(1), 48–55. doi: 10.1177/0956797612450031.

Young, I. M. (1990). *Justice and the politics of difference.* Princeton, NJ; Oxford, UK: Princeton University Press.

Young, I. M. (1999). Justice, inclusion and deliberative democracy. In S. Macedo (Ed.), *Deliberative politics: Essays on democracy and disagreement* (pp. 151–158). Oxford, UK: Oxford University Press.

Young, I. M. (2000). *Inclusion and democracy.* Oxford, UK: Oxford University Press.

Young, I. M. (2004). The deliberative model. In C. Forrelly (Ed.), *Contemporary political theory: A reader* (pp. 227–231). London, UK: SAGE.

Youssef-Morgan, C. M., & Luthans, F. (2015). Psychological capital and well-being. *Stress and Health, 31*(3), 180–188. doi: 10.1002/smi.2623.

Zarya, V. (2015). *There is only one country left in the world where women can't vote.* Retrieved August 4, 2016, from http://fortune.com/2015/12/11/one-country-women-vote/.

INDEX